little star™

little star™

by
Andi Watson

book design by
Andi Watson & Keith Wood

edited by
James Lucas Jones

Published by Oni Press, Inc.
Joe Nozemack, publisher
James Lucas Jones, editor in chief
Randal C. Jarrell, managing editor
Maryanne Snell, marketing & sales director
Douglas E. Sherwood, editorial intern

This volume collects Little Star issues 1-6.

ONI PRESS, INC.
1305 SE Martin Luther King Jr. Blvd.
Suite A
Portland, OR 97214
USA

www.onipress.com
www.andiwatson.biz

First edition: April 2006
ISBN 1-932664-38-6

1 3 5 7 9 10 8 6 4 2
PRINTED IN CANADA.

"I SEEM AS NOTHING IN THE MIGHTY WORLD,
AND CANNOT WILL MY WILL, NOR WORK MY WORK."
- TENNYSON

"ALL THE GREATEST BLESSINGS CREATE ANXIETY."
- SENECA

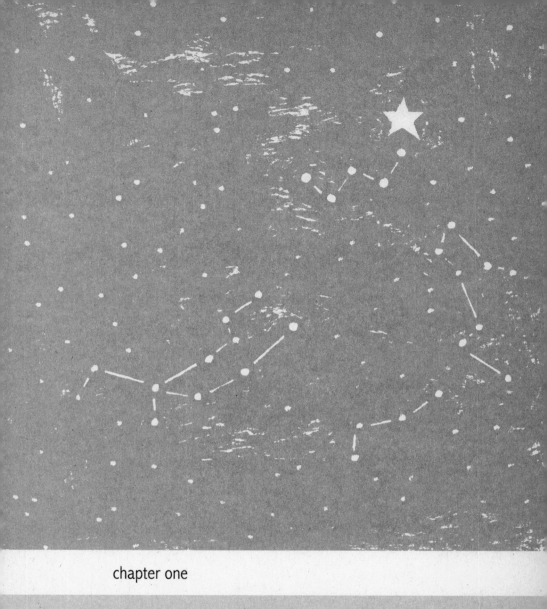

chapter one

I'M FREE RUNNING.

CARTWHEELING AWAY FROM MARS AND INTO JUPITER'S ARMS.

TWICE AROUND THE GAS GIANT, BUILDING MOMENTUM.

THEN FLUNG OUT INTO SPACE LIKE A SLING SHOT.

SATURN A BLUR. TITAN A PINHEAD.

A SCHOOL BOY SNIGGER AT URANUS.

A SHIVER AT NEPTUNE'S MOLTEN ICE.

TOSS A COIN AT PLUTO'S MOON CHARON.

THEN THE LANDMARKS ARE GONE.

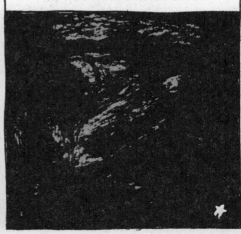

2

I SPIN INTO THE INFINITE VOID OF SPACE.

MUMMY.

MUMMYYY.

I WANT YOU.

FUCK.

I'LL GO.

HUH?

MUMMYYY!

OW!

SHIT.

MUMMYYY.

IT'S NOT LIGHT YET, IS IT, HON? REMEMBER WHAT WE SAID ABOUT...

I WANT MUMMY.

MUMMY'S ASLEEP, DARLIN'.

GO AWAY!

I DON'T WANT YOU.

IT WASN'T SO LONG AGO THAT CASSIE WAS DENYING JACK WILSON HAD A WILLY. APPARENTLY HE WASN'T OLD ENOUGH.

I WANT MUMMY.

WE LIVED IN A GOLDEN AGE OF GENDER NEUTRALITY. THERE WERE MUMMIES, DADDIES, AND BABIES BUT WE WERE ALL, ESSENTIALLY, THE SAME.

MUMMYYY.

NOT ANY MORE.

CASSIE, DADDY CAN SIT ON THE SOFA TOO.

NO. ONLY GIRLS AND YOU NOT A GIRL.

WHEN DID MY DAUGHTER BECOME A FEMINIST EXTREMIST?

MUM-EEE.

DADDY?

DADDY.

YES, SWEETHEART?

YOU CAN PRETEND TO BE MUMMY.

DADDY?

YES, HON?

COME HERE.

FIVE-THIRTY IS TOO EARLY. CHRIST, EVEN TELETUBBIES ISN'T ON YET.

SIT.

WATCH WITH ME BEFORE IT GONE OFF.

...MATERNAL INSTINCT. I WASN'T SO SURE ABOUT THE FATHER.

I DON'T KNOW IF I SHOULD BE PUTTING BOOKS BACK ON THE SHELVES OR PACKING THEM INTO BOXES.

WE'D BEEN WANTING TO MOVE FOR AGES. THIS WAS A NICE HOUSE BACK WHEN IT WAS JUST MEG AND ME, BUT SINCE CASSIE ARRIVED IT'S FELT MORE AND MORE LIKE A RABBIT HUTCH.

TEN TIMES THE RAINS HAVE...

WE'D PUT IN AN OFFER ON THE PERFECT PLACE. A DECENT SIZED GARDEN FOR CASSIE, IN THE CATCHMENT AREA OF A GOOD SCHOOL WHEN SHE DOES EVENTUALLY START, NO LEAKS OR CRACKS OR ANTS OR MICE AND STILL WITHIN DRIVING DISTANCE OF THE NURSERY.

...COME AND GONE.

OUR OFFER WAS ACCEPTED SO WE GOT THE PAPER WORK ROLLING AND ALL THAT. AND WE MAKE A START ON THE BOXES. DECIDE WHAT WE'RE GONNA KEEP AND WHAT WE'RE GONNA THROW, INSTEAD OF LEAVING IT 'TIL THE LAST MINUTE WHERE WE'RE IN A PANIC AND END UP KEEPING EVERYTHING.

A WEEK LATER AND WE'RE MAKING GREAT PROGRESS WITH THE CLEAR OUT WHEN WE GET A CALL OUT OF THE BLUE. SALE'S OFF, BASTARDS HAVE GAZUMPED US.

POP

HON, HOW MANY TIMES HAVE I TOLD YOU?

WAHH

FOR GOD'S SAKE, CASSIE.

I'MMM WET.

YOU HAVE TO REMEMBER TO BREATHE, HON.

I DID.

WHEN YOU SUCK OUT ALL THE AIR IT COLLAPSES.

C'MON, ONE ARM.

GIMME A BIG KISS.

MWAH.

HAVE A LOVELY DAY AT NURSERY AND I'LL SEE YOU BOTH THIS EVENING.

MEG'S A SUPPLY TEACHER. OUR STORY IS WE'VE BEEN MARRIED FOR SEVEN YEARS TOGETHER FOR TWELVE. WE MET AT COLLEGE, LIVED ALL OVER AND THEN EVENTUALLY SETTLED IN STOKE.

GOOD LUCK.

HMM.

MUMMY.

Here we go round the muls bush

little Stars

day nursery

THREE DAYS A WEEK CASSIE COMES HERE. THOSE ARE THE DAYS I GO TO WORK. IT'S A LONG DAY FOR HER, NINE 'TIL FIVE. DO I FEEL GUILTY? SOMETIMES.

IF IT'S SUNNY WE'LL GO TO THE PLAYGROUND.

SEE YA.

SUNNY?

HE HAS A DAUGHTER, DOROTHY, WHO'S A YEAR OLDER THAN CASSIE.

Y'ALL RIGHT, ROB?

CAN'T COMPLAIN, MATE. YOU STILL ON FOR TOMORROW?

DADDY?

SURE, SEE YA.

GIVE US A BELL WHEN YOU'RE READY.

EVER FELT LIKE YOU'RE GOING AROUND IN CIRCLES?

TODAY IT'S PLATES, TOMORROW IT COULD BE FIGURINES OR POTS, MAYBE CUPS OR BOWLS.

THAT'S THE DOWNSIDE OF PART-TIME WORK. I'M HERE TO FILL THE GAPS IN DEMAND.

I USED TO BE A FIGURINE SPECIALIST. PROMENADING LADIES WITH PARASOLS, DOGS, HORSES, THE KIND OF THING YOUR GRAN HAS ON THE SIDEBOARD.

MY GRAN HAD A FEW THAT I'D PAINTED.

SPECIALISTS ARE FULL-TIME. PART-TIMERS HAVE TO BE JACKS-OF-ALL-TRADES. I THOUGHT THE VARIETY OF WORK WOULD KEEP ME INTERESTED.

NAH, YOU NEVER GET SETTLED. YOU'RE JUST GETTING INTO A RHYTHM WITH THE PLATES WHEN THERE'S A JOB LOT OF CUPS THAT NEED DECORATING.

BRIAN'S FULL-TIME.

I'M OFF ON MY FAG BREAK, YOU COMING?

SURE.

WHAT DID YOU WANT TO BE WHEN YOU WERE A KID, SI?

MALE STRIPPER.

NOT YOUR AMBITION NOW, WHEN YOU WERE A KID.

ASTRONAUT.

I WASN'T TOO FUSSED ABOUT THE ASTRONAUT PART, BUT IT WAS THE CLOSEST I COULD GET TO BEING PART OF THE REBEL ALLIANCE.

YOU?

CENTRE FORWARD FOR PORT VALE.

GET Y'SELF DOWN THE GROUND, THEY'LL SNAP YOU UP IN NO TIME.

LISTEN TO YOU.

WHAT THE FUCK DO YOU KNOW ABOUT FOOTY?

ENOUGH TO KNOW ELEVEN DONKEYS WHEN I SEE 'EM.

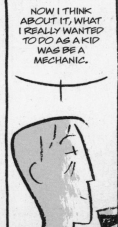

NOW I THINK ABOUT IT, WHAT I REALLY WANTED TO DO AS A KID WAS BE A MECHANIC.

YOU'RE MORE LIKELY TO BE RECRUITED BY ADMIRAL AKBAR.

MECHANICS KNOW HOW TO TAKE THINGS APART AND PUT THEM BACK AGAIN, WHAT EACH PART IS FOR, WHAT IT DOES AND WHERE IT GOES.

YOU DON'T KNOW ANY REAL LIFE MECHANICS, DO YOU?

IT'S A JOB THAT HAS ONE OF TWO OUTCOMES. EITHER THE CAR WORKS OR IT DOESN'T.

NO CONFUSION.

MARY'S AT HER MUMS WITH THE BOYS TONIGHT. Y'WANT TO COME OVER FOR A BEER?

ALL RIGHT, ONCE CASS IS DOWN I'LL POP ROUND. WHAT YOU GOT PLANNED?

I'VE GOT SOMETHING TO SHOW YOU.

OH YEAH?

IT'S BIG.

REALLY BIG.

WELL, AT LEAST I KNOW IT'S NOT YOUR KNOB.

KNOWLEDGE
&
UNDERSTANDING
OF THE WORLD
☆

I'M INVISIBLE, UNSEEN AND UNHEARD.

C'MON, HON, IT'S TIME TO GO HOME NOW.

IN A MINUTE.

JOE, CAREFUL, DARLIN'.

NEED TO PEE.

NOW PLEASE.

I JUST DO THIS.

THIS GO HERE.

CASSIE LOVES NURSERY, SORRY, PRE-SCHOOL. I THINK SHE'D STAY ALL NIGHT IF SHE COULD. I'M GLAD SHE ENJOYS, I SUPPOSE THAT'S GOOD.

MUMMY!

AND THIS HERE. OH!

HELLO, SWEETHEART.

MUMMY.

HAVE YOU HAD A GOOD DAY?

DOESN'T FIT.

LET ME SEE.

DOES IT GO HERE?

THAT'S NOT RIGHT, YOU RUINED IT.

I WILL TELL MY MUMMY ON YOU.

GO AWAY!

COLOURING IN? THAT SOUNDS LOVELY.

LET ME GO. YOU'RE HURTING ME.

SHOULDN'T I FEEL GUILTY FOR PUTTING HER IN NURSERY TOO MUCH AND NOT TOO LITTLE?

WAHHHH

WHAT IS SHE TRYING TO SAY – THE CARE I GIVE AT HOME ISN'T AS GOOD AS THAT PROVIDED BY THE PEOPLE WE PAY?

AREN'T KIDS SUPPOSED TO WANT TO SEE MORE OF THEIR PARENTS, DADS ESPECIALLY? WHAT WITH BRITAIN HAVING THE LONGEST WORK HOURS IN EUROPE.

WAHHHHH

AND YES, I WANT TO PROVE DADS ARE AS GOOD AT THIS AS MUMS.

IT'S DIFFERENT FOR MEN. A SCREAMING CHILD IN YOUR ARMS AND YOU GET THE LOOKS.

SUSPICION OR SYMPATHY? I CAN NEVER TELL.

UNLESS IT'S THE OLD LADIES WHO STOP AND STARE, CLEARLY WEIGHING UP WHETHER OR NOT TO SCREAM FOR THE POLICE.

I WANT MUM-EEE.

AHHHHHHHHH
PAEDOPHILE

IT'S LIKE SOMETHING OUT OF THE BODY SNATCHERS.

NO NO, REALLY, SHE'S MY DAUGHTER Y'SEE, SHE NEEDS A NAP AND...

CAN I HAVE KETCHUP?

YOU'VE GOT PLENTY THERE, HON.

I'VE GOT A LIST OF HOUSES WE SHOULD LOOK AT.

I NOT ASKING YOU, I ASKING MUMMY.

MUMMY, DADDY SAID I CAN'T HAVE...

YOU'VE GOT LOADS THERE, DARLING. FINISH THAT AND YOU CAN HAVE SOME MORE.

I GUESS WE HAVE TO START LOOKING AGAIN.

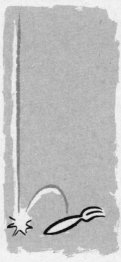

I'LL GET IT.

NO, MUMMY HAS TO GET IT.

GIVE IT TO ME. WE'LL HAVE TO GET A MOVE ON, I GOT A CALL FROM THE ESTATE AGENTS TODAY.

HERE YOU ARE, HON.

WHAT IS IT NOW?

OUR BUYERS ARE GETTING COLD FEET. THEY'RE COMPLAINING THAT WHEN THEY PUT IN AN OFFER ON OUR HOUSE, THE UNDERSTANDING WAS THAT WE HAD A PLACE TO MOVE INTO.

CASSIE, STOP THAT. IF YOU'RE NOT HUNGRY GET DOWN FROM THE TABLE.

IT WAS ACCIDENT.

IT'S NOT LIKE WE WERE ACTING IN BAD FAITH. JEEZUS, IT DOESN'T BENEFIT US ANY. WITH THE MARKET COOLING WE MIGHT LOSE MONEY, NOT GAIN ANY.

MUMMY GET IT.

I'LL GET IT.

THERE'S NO POINT GETTING PISSED OFF AT ME.

I'M NOT I'M—

OW!

YOU ALL RIGHT?

SEEING STARS.

HERE.

I NOT WANT YOU GET IT, I WANT...

OH, CASSIE.

LET'S PUT THE TELLY ON.

ALL HAIL THE CATHODE NANNY. SOOTHER OF TIRED CHILDREN BEFORE BED TIME, DISPENSORS OF STORY AND MORAL GUIDE.

TOUGH DAY?

SHE'S KNACKERED.

WHEN'S SHE GONNA SNAP OUT OF THIS FIVE A.M. CYCLE?

SOON, I HOPE.

...TO BE A CHILDREN'S T.V. CHARACTER. QUESTIONS ARE ASKED AND ANSWERS ALWAYS PROVIDED.

ALL PASTEL SHADES AND HAPPY SONGS. A LIFE OF FOOD AND MUSIC.

IT'S PROBABLY MIND-NUMBING DRIVEL IF YOU DON'T HAVE KIDS. BUT IF YOU DO, IT'S SOOTHING AND REASSURINGLY SIMPLE.

DADDY, FILL THIS UP.

WHAT'S THE MAGIC WORD?

PLEASE.

THIS IS MEDICINE. DRINK IT.

I DON'T REMEMBER AT WHAT POINT WE DECIDED TO HAVE KIDS.

DON'T SPILL ANY.

BACK THEN IT WAS ALL HYPOTHETICAL. WE WERE IGNORANT OF THE BIOLOGICAL AND GENETIC SKELETONS WHICH WE MIGHT BE CARRYING.

DON'T SPILL ANY.

WHEN EXACTLY WAS THE LINE CROSSED? WHAT MADE US THINK THE TIME WAS RIGHT? I DIDN'T HEAR ANY CLOCKS TICKING.

WE JUST DECIDED.

THIS IS BIG BAD FOX, ISN'T IT?

DECIDED TO TAKE THE BIG STEP INTO THE UNKNOWN.

NO, HON, THAT LOOKS LIKE A FROG.

IT'S A FOX ISN'T IT.

YES IT'S A FOX.

LURCHING FROM KNOWING TO NOT KNOWING.

AND THESE ARE THE BEARS...OH!

FROM KNOWING WE WERE PREGNANT TO NOT KNOWING IF IT'LL GO FULL TERM.

FROM KNOWING MORNING SICKNESS MADE MEG PUKE MORNING, NOON AND NIGHT.

WHERE'S THE BEARS GONE?

ENSURING NO ONE ELSE FOUND OUT. EASY FOR ME, NO PUKE, NO BELLY BULGE.

HERE THEY ARE.

AND THE GUILT BEGINS. WE'RE BOTH PREGNANT BUT MEG'S THE ONE THROWING UP ALL HOURS.

OH, THANK YOU.

Panel 1:
I WAS A FATHER BUT NOT A FATHER.

ONE DAY THE BIG BAD FOX CAME TO THE BEAR'S HOUSE.

Panel 2:
I'D LOOK ENVIOUSLY AT OTHER PEOPLE'S KIDS. THEY WERE A REALITY, HAPPY AND HEALTHY.

AND SHE'S GOT BABY BEAR'S PORRIDGE AND...OH.

Panel 3:
WHILE WE WERE PARENTS OF A PROBABILITY. A TWO-THIRDS OF A CHANCE OF GOING FULL TERM.

AND DADDY BEAR'S PORRIDGE WAS TOO HOT?

Panel 4:
ALL WE COULD DO WAS WAIT. WAIT FOR THE CELLS TO DIVIDE AND DIVIDE AGAIN. TAMP DOWN OUR EXCITEMENT AND PREPARE FOR LOSS.

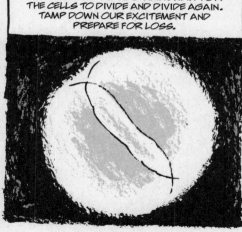

Panel 5:
DADDY'S WAS TOO HOT. MUMMY BEAR'S PORRIDGE WAS TOO COLD.

BABY BEAR'S PORRIDGE WAS RIGHT AND ATE IT ALL UP.

Panel 6:
WE WERE LUCKY.

DADDY BEAR CHAIR IS TOO SOFT.

MUMMY'S TOO HARD.

AND BIG BAD FOX SIT IN BABY BEAR'S CHAIR ...

Panel 7:
NOT THAT ANY OF THE PROFESSIONALS WERE IN ANY DOUBT.

IN ITS CURRENT POSITION I CAN'T SEE THE SPINE. YOU'LL HAVE TO COME BACK FOR ANOTHER LOOK.

WE HAD TO LIVE WITH UNCERTAINTY.

THE BABY'S HEALTHY.

COURSE IT IS.

DON'T THINK ABOUT CATHY LOSING HERS AT EIGHT MONTHS. DON'T THINK ABOUT IT.

JESUS FUCKING CHRIST OUR BABY HAS NO SPINE. WHAT THE HELL WILL WE DO? DON'T PANIC, DON'T PANIC.

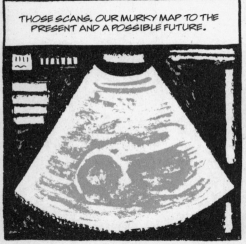

THOSE SCANS. OUR MURKY MAP TO THE PRESENT AND A POSSIBLE FUTURE.

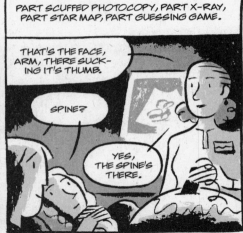

PART SCUFFED PHOTOCOPY, PART X-RAY, PART STAR MAP, PART GUESSING GAME.

THAT'S THE FACE, ARM, THERE SUCK-ING IT'S THUMB.

SPINE?

YES, THE SPINE'S THERE.

THEY WERE RIGHT.

WHO'S GOING TO SING SONGS TONIGHT?

NIGHT NIGHT, SWEETIE.

TWINKLE TWINKLE LITTLE STAR...

WHEN MEG WAS PREGNANT I BECAME MORE AWARE OF MY IGNORANCE THAN EVER.

THE AMOUNT I DON'T KNOW IS ALREADY VAST AND LIKE THE UNIVERSE EVER EXPANDING. WHEN CASSIE ASKS ME QUESTIONS WILL I HAVE ANY ANSWERS?

WHEN SHE WANTS TO KNOW WHY THE SKY IS BLUE AND WHY THE SUN IS HOT WHAT WILL I SAY?

TELL HER TO SHUT UP AND STOP ASKING STUPID QUESTIONS? OR INVITE HER TO RUN ALONG AND FIND OUT ON THE INTERNET?

AS A GROWN UP, AS A FATHER, WASN'T I SUPPOSED TO KNOW STUFF? TO FOSTER A CURIOSITY IN THE WORLD?

MY BIOLOGICAL CONT-RIBUTION DIDN'T FEEL LIKE IT AMOUNTED TO MUCH. ONE SPERM OUT OF A MILLION AND THAT WAS IT?

THE LEAST I COULD DO WAS KNOW A FEW FACTS AND FIGURES TO HELP OUR KID UNDERSTAND THE WORLD BETTER.

I WAS BORN IN THE YEAR OF THE MOON LANDING SO I WENT BACK TO ALL THE STUFF THAT I GREW UP WITH.

IF I'M HONEST I WAS MORE INTERESTED IN DESTROYING STARS THAN LOOKING FOR THEM.

ANYWAY, I NAMED A STAR AFTER CASSIE. ONE OF THOSE, Y'KNOW, INTERNET SITES? YOU GET A MAP AND DIPLOMA AND STUFF.

I KNOW IT'S NOT OFFICIAL BUT I THOUGHT IT'D BE A WAY TO GET CASSIE INTERESTED WHEN SHE'S A BIT OLDER.

SHE'D WANT TO SEARCH FOR HER OWN STAR AND WANT TO KNOW MORE.

THE CONSTELLATIONS, PLANETS, NEBULAE, COMETS AND ASTEROIDS.

IT'S A NICE IDEA BUT THERE'S ONLY ONE THING WRONG WITH IT...I CAN'T FIND HER SODDING STAR.

22

THE MOON'S THERE AND OVER HERE'S NORTH BECAUSE THE OTHER WAY IS THE M6 SOUTH TO BIRMINGHAM. NOT THAT THAT HELPS AT ALL.

I COULD BLAME THE LIGHT POLLUTION OR THAT THE SEEING IN STOKE IS CRAP. BUT NO, THE STARS AREN'T TWINKLING, THE SEEING IS GOOD.

I HAVE THE NIGHT'S STAR MAP BUT I CAN'T SEE ANY CORRELATION BETWEEN WHAT'S ON PAPER AND WHAT'S ACTUALLY UP THERE.

A RANDOM SPRINKLING OF POINTS OF LIGHT IN THE SKY.

I CAN'T MAKE HEAD NOR TAILS OF IT.

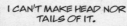

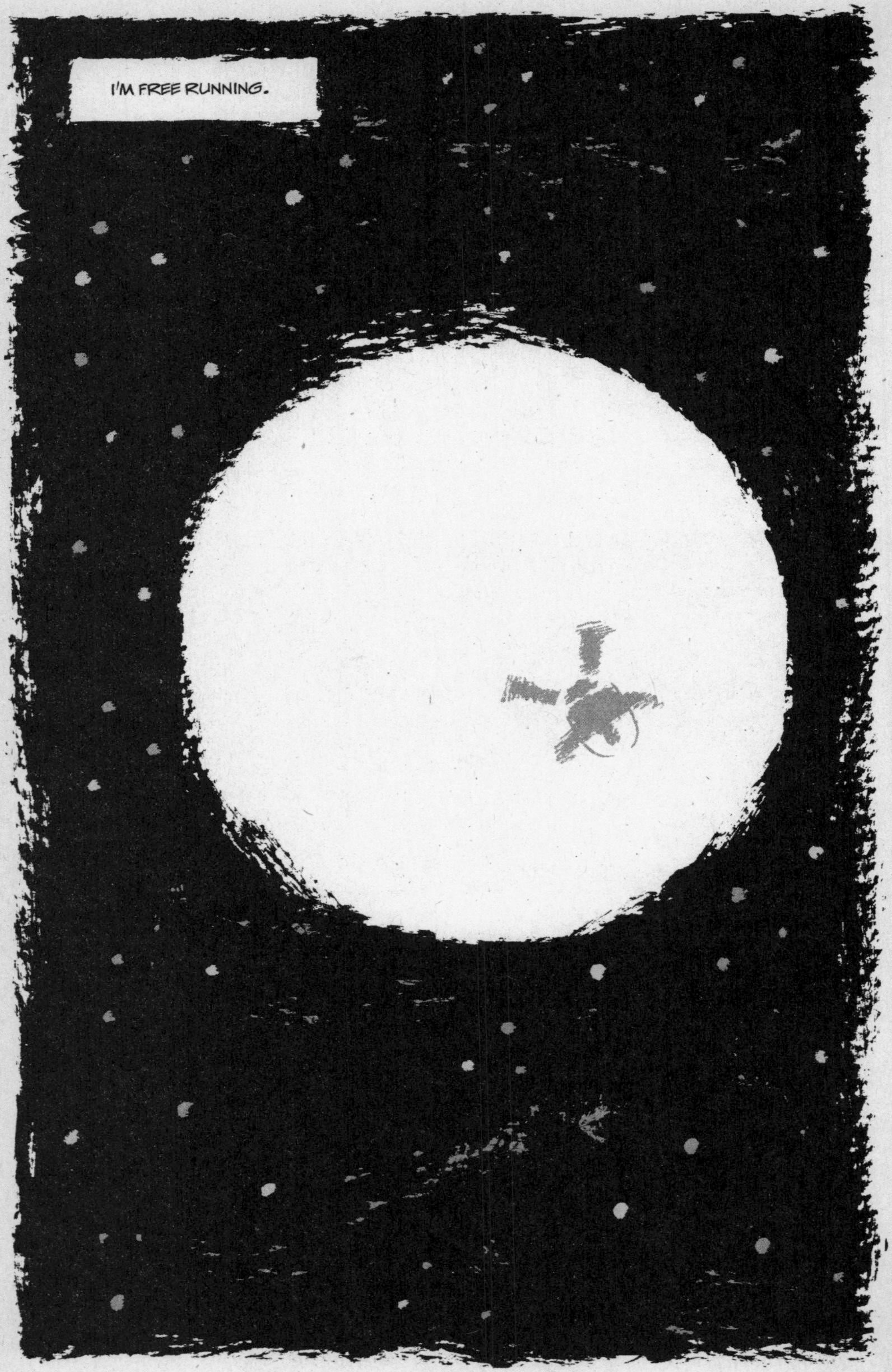
I'M FREE RUNNING.

chapter two

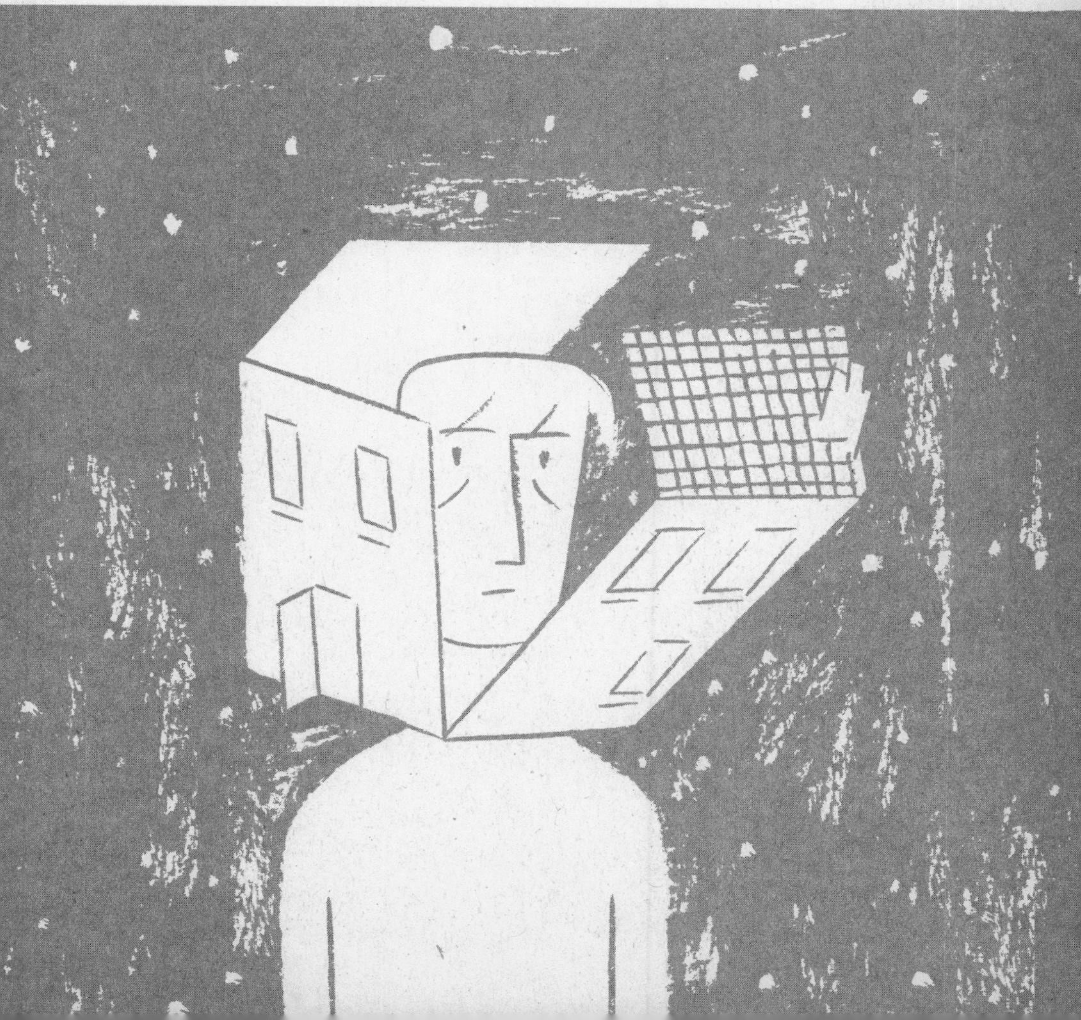

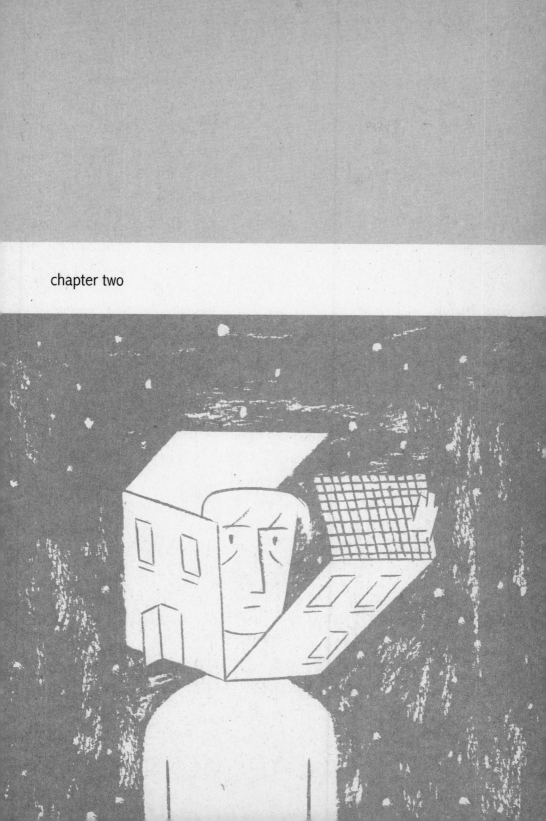

THANKS.

THANKS FOR SHOWING US AROUND.

BYE.

MUMMY.

WHAT DO YOU THINK?

I DON'T KNOW.

WHAT ABOUT YOU?

MUMMY?

MUMMY!

NOTHING'S GOING TO BE PERFECT, IF WE ACCEPT THAT THEN WE CAN MAKE A DECISION.

MUMMY!

SWEETIE, MOMMY'S TRYING TO TALK TO DADDY.

WE HAD THE PERFECT PLACE. COME HERE, HON.

NO, I'M TALK-ING.

I KNOW YOU ARE, SWEET-HEART, I'M LISTENING.

LET'S NOT RAKE OVER THAT AGAIN.

I WANT TO GO HOME.

I KNOW, HON, COME HERE.

I WANT MUMMY.

SHE'S TIRED.

ARE WE GOING HOME NOW?

YES, DARLING, WE'RE GOING HOME NOW.

THE GARDEN'S TOO SMALL.

CAN WE JUST GET HER IN FIRST?

I WANT A JUICE BOX.

DADDY, I WANT A...

I KNOW, HON.

RIGHT THEN, LET ME EXPLAIN IT TO YOU, DARLING.

YOU KNOW WE'RE LOOKING AT HOUSES BECAUSE WE'RE NOT MOVING INTO THE ONE WE THOUGHT WE WERE?

THE ONE WITH THE BIG GARDEN.

IT'S A RIGHT TURN OUT OF HERE.

I THOUGHT IT WAS LEFT?

WE CAME IN LEFT.

NOW WE'VE LOOKED AT FIVE DIFFERENT HOUSES THAT WE CAN AFFORD, WHAT DID YOU THINK OF THIS ONE?

THE GARDEN IS A BIT SMALL BUT THE HOUSE HAS A ROOM FOR YOU, ONE FOR ME AND DADDY, AND ONE FOR GRANDMA AND GRANDAD WHEN THEY COME TO VISIT.

AND ALSO, CASSIE, WE'RE MOVING SO THAT YOU'LL HAVE MORE SPACE TO RUN AROUND OUTSIDE.

IT'S EITHER A BIG GARDEN WITH TWO BEDROOMS OR A SMALLER GARDEN WITH THREE BED-ROOMS. WE CAN'T AFFORD BOTH. NOT FOR A PLACE IN THE CATCHMENT AREA OF A GOOD SCHOOL, A GOOD STATE SCHOOL ANYWAY.

AND IT'S THE A500 NOT THE A34.

YES, I KNOW.

A BIG GARDEN WOULD BE LOVELY, CASSIE'D HAVE SPACE FOR A SLIDE AND...

...AND SO SHE CAN BE OUTSIDE BUT STILL BE SAFE.

SO YOU WANT TO GO WITH TWO BEDROOMS THEN?

WE NEED THREE.

FINALLY, WE'RE IN AGREEMENT.

WHAT ABOUT THE HOUSE WE JUST SAW?

YOU REALLY LIKE IT, DON'T YOU?

IT'S NOT SUPER FANCY BUT IT'S A NICE HOUSE.

IT NEEDS A NEW BATHROOM.

AND REDECORATING, BUT IT'S LIVEABLE WITH, I MEAN, IT MAY NOT BE PRETTY BUT IT ALL WORKS.

YOU'RE NOT CONVINCED, ARE YOU?

I DON'T KNOW.

WE CAN'T DITHER FOR- EVER OR WE'LL LOSE OUR BUYER TOO.

I JUST DON'T SEE THE POINT OF MOVING INTO A PLACE THAT COSTS LESS THAN THE HOUSE WE'RE IN NOW IF IT'S NOT PERFECT.

WE LIKE THE SCHOOL AND THIS WAY WE GIVE OURSELVES A LITTLE FINANCIAL BREATHING ROOM. PUT SOME PENNIES AWAY FOR A RAINY DAY.

FOR WHAT, EXACTLY?

UNFORSEEN CHANGES.

WHAT KIND OF UNFORSEEN CHANGES?

I DON'T KNOW. THAT'S WHY THEY'RE UNFORSEEN.

KIDS DON'T GET TO STRAY OUT OF THEIR PARENTS' SIGHT FOR A SECOND NOWADAYS, NOT LIKE WHEN I WAS A NIPPER. I JUST WANT HER TO BE ABLE TO GET SOME FRESH AIR AND A BIT OF FREEDOM.

THERE'S NO WAY WE CAN AFFORD IT, SIMON. NOT UNLESS I GET OUT OF TEACHING AND YOU GET A DIFFERENT JOB. DO YOU THINK IT'S WORTH SWITCHING JOBS FOR THE SAKE OF A GARDEN?

I DUNNO. I'D THINK ABOUT IT.

I THOUGHT YOU LOVED WORK?

IT'S EMPTY, DAD.

MUMMY, CAN I HAVE A JELLY BABY?

I COULD ALWAYS GO BACK FULL-TIME.

CAN I HAVE...

WHAT'S THE MAGIC WORD, CASSIE?

WOULD YOU REALLY WANT TO DO THAT?

I DON'T KNOW.

PLEASE, PLEASE PLEASE.

IT WOULD HAVE TO BE A DECISION YOU WERE CERTAIN OF.

SHE LOVES PRE-SCHOOL.

SHE DOES LOVE PRE-SCHOOL.

MUMMY, I SAID PLEASE.

I HEARD YOU, HON. HERE YOU GO.

THANKS, MUM.

AFTER PAYING FOR TWO MORE DAYS OF CHILD CARE WE'D STILL BE BETTER OFF. I COULD MAYBE GET SOME OVER-TIME TOO?

SAINSB

IT WOULD MAKE YOU ONE OF THOSE EVENINGS AND WEEKEND DADS YOU WHINGE ABOUT ALL THE TIME. WOULD YOU BE HAPPY WITH THAT?

MUMMY?

YES, DARLING.

I NEED A WEE.

DADDY?

YES, SWEETIE?

HAS MUMMY GOT A BABY IN HER TUMMY?

NOT ANYMORE, SWEETIE.

DADDY, LOOK.

WHAT IS IT, HON?

LOOK DOLLY.

DADDY, LOOK.

LOOK AT DOLLY.

WOW, HAS SHE JUST BEEN BORN? THAT WAS EASY.

OH, SHE'S CRYING.

YOU'D BETTER PUT HER DUMMY IN THEN. HAVE YOU DONE ON THERE YET, HON?

WE'VE GOTTA GET A MOVE ON BECAUSE WE'RE GOING TO SEE ROB AND DOROTHY, REMEMBER?

DADDY?

YES, SWEETIE?

CAN YOU READ MY BABY BOOK?

SORRY, HON, WE'VE GOT TO GO NOW.

BUT I WANT MY BOOOOK.

TELL YOU WHAT, I'LL TELL YOU THE STORY ONCE WE'RE IN THE CAR. HOW ABOUT THAT?

WELL, UM, IT STARTED WHEN I WAS ASLEEP.

YOU'D BEEN IN MUMMY'S TUMMY FOR A LONG TIME AND IT WAS THREE IN THE MORNING. DO YOU REMEMBER SHOUTING OUT LAST NIGHT? WELL ABOUT THAT KIND OF TIME MUMMY WOKE UP WITH INDIGESTION.

THAT MEANS SHE THOUGHT SHE HAD TUMMY ACHE. SHE WENT DOWNSTAIRS AND CALLED THE HOSPITAL AND THEY TOLD HER TO TAKE TWO PARACETAMOL, UM, TO TAKE SOME GROWN UP CALPOL, HAVE A BATH AND THEN CALL BACK WHEN IT REALLY HURT.

AND I WAS STILL ASLEEP BECAUSE I COULD SLEEP A LOT BACK THEN.

AND THEN MUMMY WAS HAVING CONTRACTIONS, WHICH MEANS YOU WANTED TO COME OUT OF HER TUMMY, EVERY TEN MINUTES.

AND SO MUMMY WAITED UNTIL THE BATH WATER WAS COLD AND THEN SHE WENT DOWNSTAIRS FOR SOMETHING TO EAT AND SHE HAD SOME NICE APPLE PANCAKES. AND THEN MUMMY USED SOMETHING CALLED A TENS MACHINE WHICH IS A SPECIAL THING THAT SHE PUT ON HER BELLY TO STOP IT ACHING SO MUCH. AND THAT HELPED UNTIL...

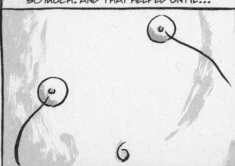

... AT SIX IN THE MORNING MUMMY CALLED THE HOSPITAL TO TELL THEM WE WERE COM...

ROB IS A STAY-AT-HOME-DAD. THAT'S WHAT INTERESTED ME ABOUT HIM. I WONDERED HOW HE DID IT.

SHE BEEN SICK.

B-DUM, B-DUM.

WHAT'LL HAPPEN WHEN DOROTHY STARTS SCHOOL IN SEPTEMBER?

IT'S HALF-DAYS SO SHE'LL STILL NEED ME.

THERE HE GOES, STILL "NEED ME", HE'S SO SURE OF THAT. I'D FEEL GUILTY DROPPING CASSIE OFF ON THE DAYS WHEN SHE'D CRY AND CLING TO MY SLEEVE. THAT'S WHEN I FELT NEEDED. BUT AFTER TEN MINUTES SHE'D CALM DOWN AND FORGET ALL ABOUT ME. I WASN'T ESSENTIAL AFTER ALL.

THE OTHER THING IS... LOUISE IS PREGNANT AGAIN.

THAT'S GREAT NEWS, CONGRAT-ULATIONS.

I'VE SERIOUSLY CONSIDERED GIVING UP WORK. A FEW TIMES IN FACT, THINKING THAT IT WAS ABSOLUTELY THE RIGHT THING TO DO FOR CASSIE.

DADDY, DOLLY'S SICK.

UH, OH. YOU AND DOROTHY'D BEST GIVE HER SOME MEDICINE.

IT SEEMED TO BE THE KEY TO WHAT MADE ROB SO CONTENT. HE HAD ONE ROLE AND AS LONG AS HE FILLED THAT ROLE HE HAD NOTHING ELSE TO WORRY ABOUT.

SO YOU'LL BE DIVING RIGHT BACK INTO THE NAPPIES THEN?

AH, YOU KNOW CHANGING NAPPIES IS THE EASY PART. ANYWAY, I LOVE ALL THAT STUFF, I'M LUCKY I'LL BE THERE TO SEE IT ALL.

THEY GROW UP SO FAST. IF I WAS AT WORK I'D BARELY SEE HER EXCEPT AT WEEK- ENDS.

I WOULDN'T GO BACK NOW, NOT IN A MILLION YEARS. KIDS DO THAT THOUGH, DON'T THEY?

THEY TURN YOUR LIFE AROUND.

IF LOUISE, DOROTHY'S MUM, WASN'T PULLING DOWN A GOOD WAGE IN I.T. AND IF ROB HADN'T BEEN LAID OFF JUST BEFORE THEIR DAUGHTER WAS BORN I DON'T KNOW IF HE'D SEE IT THAT WAY. MAYBE HE WOULD FEEL THE SAME, BUT MY CIRCUMSTANCES ARE DIFFERENT.

CASSIE?

WHAT, DAD?

WHICH DO YOU LIKE BEST, BEING HOME WITH MUM, BEING HOME WITH DAD, OR GOING TO PRE-SCHOOL?

I COULDN'T FIGURE OUT HOW HE ENDURED BEING AT HOME. THE DOMESTIC DRUDGERY I CAN DO, THE CINDERELLA STUFF PUNCTUATED BY THE EXCITEMENT OF THE FIRST STEPS. IT'S THE BOREDOM THAT'D GET ME.

PRE-SCHOOL.

BUT THEN ROB ISN'T THE SHARPEST KNIFE IN THE DRAWER. DON'T GET ME WRONG, HE'S A NICE BLOKE BUT I'M NOT SURE HIS BRAIN IS CRYING OUT FOR STIMULATION. PART OF ME WANTS TO SHAKE HIM UNTIL HE SEES.

I SHOULD BE HAPPY FOR HIM, PROUD EVEN. HE SHOWS IT CAN BE DONE AND DONE WELL.

BUT I DON'T, I FEEL JEALOUS AND RESENTFUL, LIKE HE'S RUBBING HIS CONTENTMENT IN MY FACE.

FASTER.

HOLD ON TIGHT.

FASTER, DAD.

GIMME A SEC.

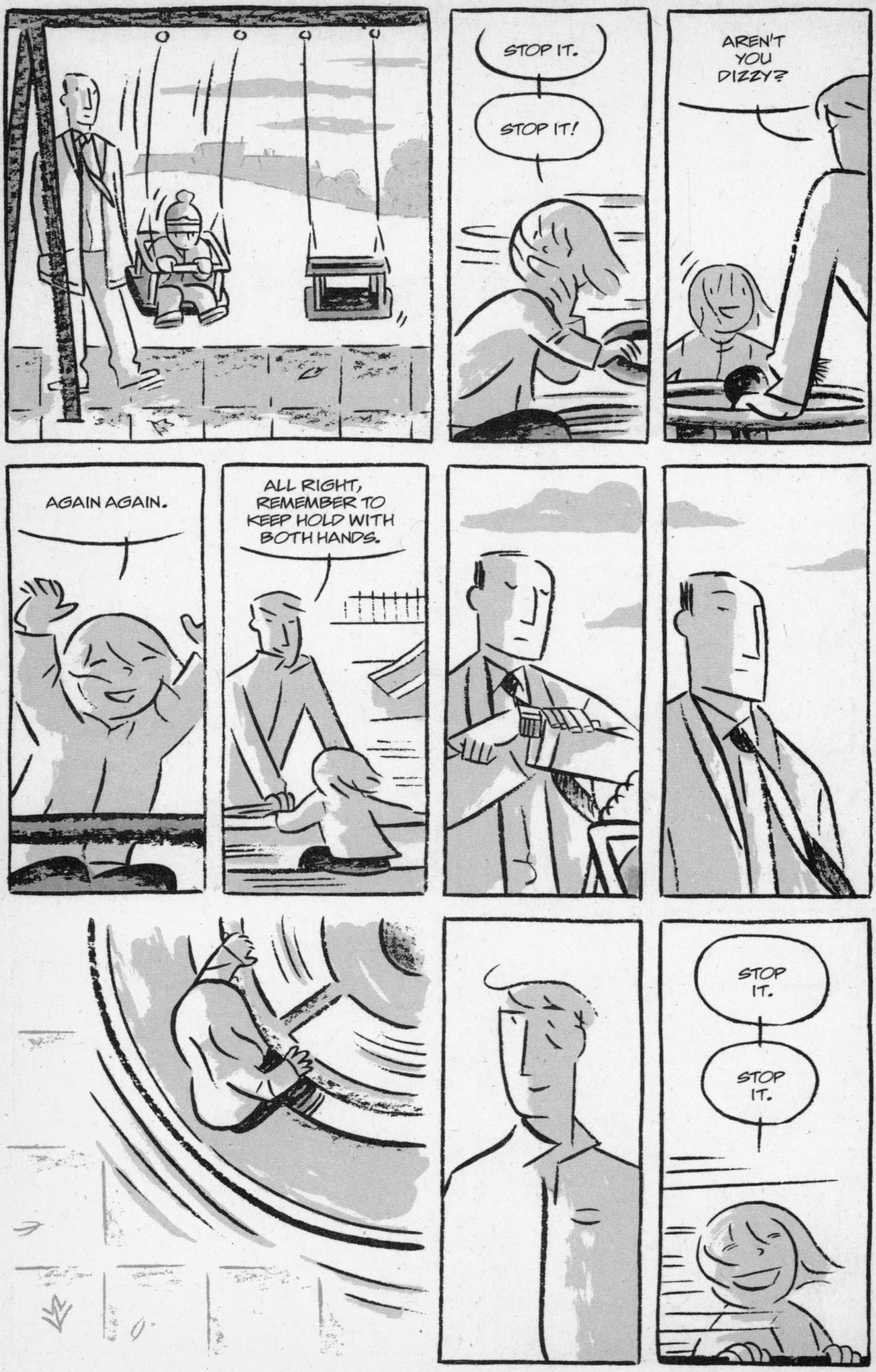
STOP IT.
STOP IT!
AREN'T YOU DIZZY?
AGAIN AGAIN.
ALL RIGHT, REMEMBER TO KEEP HOLD WITH BOTH HANDS.
STOP IT.
STOP IT.

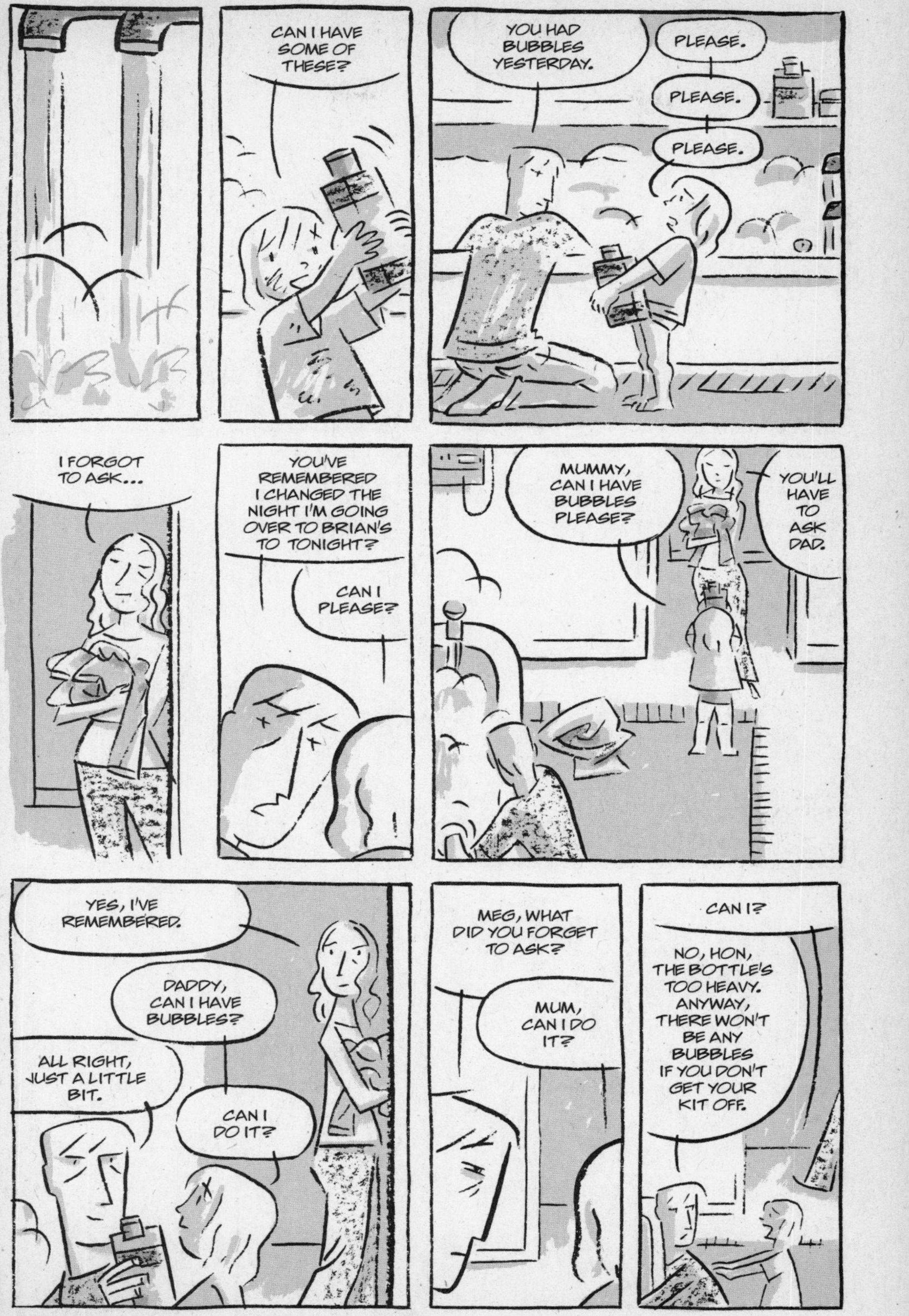
CAN I HAVE SOME OF THESE?
YOU HAD BUBBLES YESTERDAY.
PLEASE.
PLEASE.
PLEASE.
I FORGOT TO ASK...
YOU'VE REMEMBERED I CHANGED THE NIGHT I'M GOING OVER TO BRIAN'S TO TONIGHT?
CAN I PLEASE?
MUMMY, CAN I HAVE BUBBLES PLEASE?
YOU'LL HAVE TO ASK DAD.
YES, I'VE REMEMBERED.
DADDY, CAN I HAVE BUBBLES?
ALL RIGHT, JUST A LITTLE BIT.
CAN I DO IT?
MEG, WHAT DID YOU FORGET TO ASK?
MUM, CAN I DO IT?
CAN I?
NO, HON, THE BOTTLE'S TOO HEAVY. ANYWAY, THERE WON'T BE ANY BUBBLES IF YOU DON'T GET YOUR KIT OFF.

 WHAT?

WHAT WERE YOU ABOUT TO SAY?

 I FORGOT TO ASK IF LORRAINE COLLINGWOOD WAS STILL WORKING AT YOUR PLACE?

 YEAH, SHE'S PART OF THE DESIGN TEAM, WHY?

LET'S GET YOU IN.

 GEMMA TOLD ME SHE WAS SITTING NEXT TO HER AT ST. MARY'S WHILE WAITING FOR HER TWENTY WEEK SCAN.

 LORRAINE'S NOT PREGNANT, IS SHE?

BUBBLES.

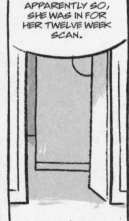 APPARENTLY SO, SHE WAS IN FOR HER TWELVE WEEK SCAN.

 LORRAINE'S THREE MONTHS PREGNANT BUT SHE HASN'T TOLD ANYONE AT WORK. AT LEAST NO-ONE'S MENTIONED IT.

 IT'S ONLY A MATTER OF TIME THOUGH.

 I WONDER IF BRIAN KNOWS?

...YOU'LL LOVE IT. TINA'S COMPLAINING ABOUT THERE NOT BEING ENOUGH SPACE.

BUT I KNOW YOU'LL APPRECIATE IT.

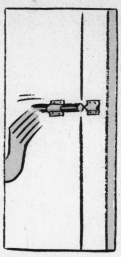

WHAT'S WITH THE LOCK?

IT'S TO KEEP THE NIPPERS OUT.

JESUS, BRI, IF THIS IS SOME KIND OF S&M DUNGEON SET-UP, I DON'T WANNA SEE IT.

THE THOUGHT OF YOU WITH AN ASDA BAG OVER YOUR HEAD AND TINA SLAPPING YOUR NADS WITH A SHAMMY LEATHER DOESN'T DO MUCH FOR ME.

LOOK.

STAR WARS

A STAR DESTRUCTOR? HOW MUCH DID THAT SET YOU BACK?

DESTROYER, SI, DESTROYER.

IT'S EVEN GOT THE LITTLE...

YUP.

41

HOW MUCH?

A FAIR BIT.

COME ON, HOW MUCH?

LESS THAN TWO FIFTY.

TWO HUNDRED AND FIFTY QUID?

BLOODY HELL.

IT'S GOT MORE THAN THREE THOUSAND PIECES.

SO WE SETTLE DOWN TO WATCH THE FILM. NOT THAT I MIND. LATELY ALL I WANT WATCH IS STUFF I'M FAMILIAR WITH.

I'VE SEEN THIS A MILLION TIMES BUT I LIKE THAT I KNOW EXACTLY WHAT HAPPENS NEXT.

I FOLLOW LUKE'S ARC FROM SIMPLE FARM BOY TO THE SAVIOUR OF THE UNIVERSE.

WHY IS IT I FEEL LIKE I'VE BEEN PUSHED OUT OF THE STARRING ROLE IN THE STORY OF MY LIFE? FROM HERO TO SOME RANDOM EXTRA THIRD DOWN ON THE RIGHT.

LORRAINE.

SO YOU THINK YOU'LL HAVE ANY MORE?

I MIGHT GET THE FALCON FOR CHRISTMAS.

I WAS TALKING ABOUT KIDS, NOT LEGO.

YOU'RE JOKING AREN'T YOU?

IS THERE ANY- ONE ELSE AT OUR PLACE WHO IS UP THE DUFF, DO YOU THINK?

HOW THE HELL SHOULD I KNOW? "ALRIGHT MATE, SEE THE MATCH LAST NIGHT, OH AND WHILE I'M ASKING, HAVE YOU GOT YOUR MISSUS UP THE DUFF YET OR ARE YOU STILL FIRING BLANKS?" IT'S NOT SOME- THING YOU ASK, IS IT?

WHY, YOU'VE NOT BEEN SLIPPING IT TO SOME UNFORTUNATE GIRL AT WORK HAVE YOU? WORRIED MEG'LL FIND OUT?

VERY FUNNY.

YOU'VE ALWAYS HAD A THING FOR SUE, YOU SLY DOG.

SHUT UP, BRI.

IT'S IN HERE SOMEWHERE.

GOD KNOWS WHERE AMONGST ALL THIS CRAP.

SHIT!

OLD STAIRGATE, OLD COT.

GOTCHA.

SIMON, WHAT ARE YOU DOING?

NOTHING.

IT DOESN'T SOUND LIKE NOTHING, IT SOUNDS LIKE A BUILDING SITE.

SORRY, DID I WAKE YOU UP?

NEVER MIND, ARE YOU COMING UP?

IN A MINUTE.

I THOUGHT I'D DAZZLED MY WAY INTO THE JOB WITH MY STUNNING PORTFOLIO OF WORK.

LOOKING AT IT NOW, THOUGH, I THINK ALL THEY WANTED WAS SOMEONE WHO KNEW ONE END OF A BRUSH FROM ANOTHER.

SOMEONE WHO DIDN'T KNOW WHAT THEY WERE DOING, SOMEONE WHOM THEY COULD TRAIN UP FROM SCRATCH.

IF I DO PICK UP A PENCIL IT'S USUALLY FOR SOMETHING LIKE A SHOPPING LIST.

BOLLOCKS TO IT, I'M TOO KNACKERED TO THINK.

MUMMY.

MUMMY!

I'LL GO.

NO, I'LL GO. YOU LIE IN.

MUMMY.

47

HOW DO YOU MAKE A PERSON?

YES.

WELL, FIRST YOU NEED A FACE, DON'T YOU?

A CIRCLE.

WELL DONE. ONE EYE.

TWO EYE.

A NOSE?

THAT'S EXCELLENT. NOW, WHAT ELSE DO YOU THINK WE NEED?

WHY?

NOT IN YOUR MOUTH, HON. WHAT ELSE DO WE NEED, HMM?

A BEAR?

A BIG SMILEY MOUTH!

SHE'S NOT SMILING, SHE'S NOT HAPPY.

WHO'S NOT, THE BEAR?

BECAUSE I WEE ON HER.

WHO, ON MUMMY?

YES. SHE SAD.

WELL, NO ONE LIKES TO BE PEED ON, DO THEY?

NO.

THAT'S WONDERFUL, DARLING. SHALL WE PUT IT IN THE GALLERY?

TO DRY.

I WISH I WAS AS INSPIRED.

FROM THIS...

...TO THIS IN TWO YEARS. FROM HOLDING A PEN FOR THE FIRST TIME TO DRAWING PEOPLE AND EMOTIONS. THAT'S ACTUALLY PRETTY AMAZING.

WHAT PROGRESS HAVE I MADE IN TWO YEARS?

NONE.

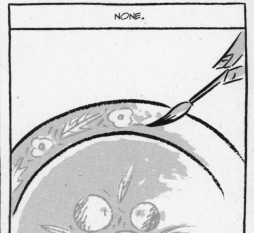

TONIGHT I HAVE TO KNUCKLE DOWN. I CAN'T BE DOING THIS FOR THE REST OF MY LIFE.

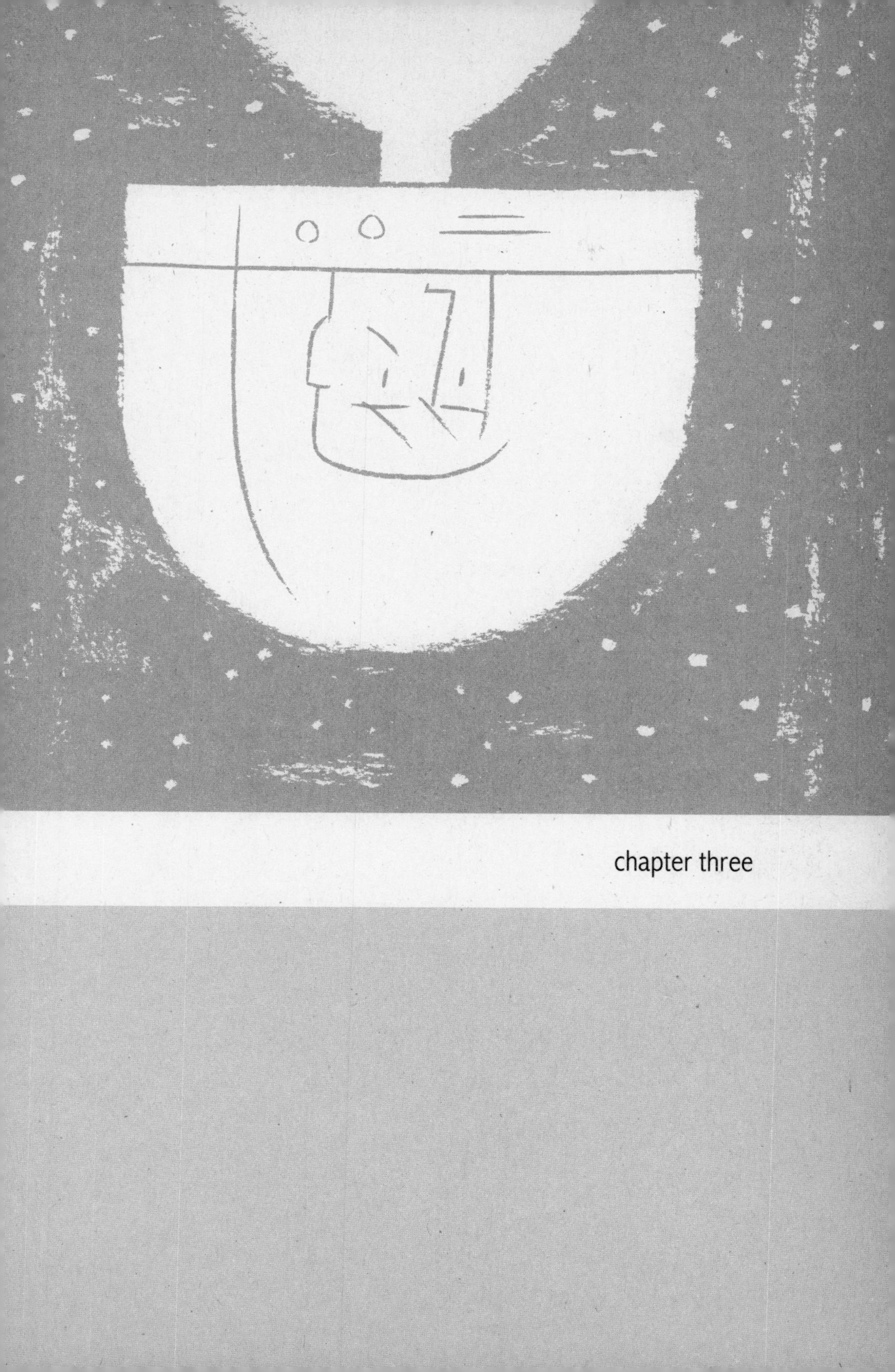

chapter three

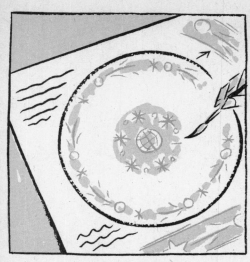

DADDY.

YES, HON.

WHAT ARE YOU DOING?

I'M MAKING PATTERNS.

WHY?

BECAUSE A LADY AT WORK IS GOING TO HAVE A BABY, SO SHE'LL BE LEAVING. SHE MAKES PATTERNS AND I WANT TO DO HER JOB SO I'M MAKING PATTERNS TOO.

WHY?

IT'S LIKE IN THE DVD WHERE THE DADDY CAN'T BE A SUPERHERO ANYMORE. HE HAS TO WORK IN AN OFFICE INSTEAD.

AND IT'S BORING?

THAT'S RIGHT. I DON'T WANT TO WORK IN AN OFFICE ANYMORE. I WANT TO BE A SUPERHERO.

WHY?

BECAUSE IT'S MORE FUN.

WHY?

BECAUSE...

...WHY DON'T YOU HELP ME DRAW SOME PATTERNS TOO?

HOW DO YOU DRAW PATTERNS?

FIRST, LET ME DRAW YOU A CIRCLE.

NOOOOOOO!

WHAT?

YOU'VE RUINED IT.

OKAY, HERE'S ANOTHER PIECE OF PAPER. YOU CAN DRAW YOUR OWN CIRCLE.

EXCELLENT. NOW, CAN YOU MAKE A PATTERN INSIDE IT?

WHAT'S A PATTERN?

IT'S WHERE YOU DRAW ONE SHAPE AND THEN ANOTHER AND ANOTHER.

WHAT SHAPE?

ANY SHAPE, A, UM, TRIANGLE?

I DON'T WANT A TRIANGLE.

HOW ABOUT DIFFERENT COLOURED DOTS?

HERE YOU GO.

THAT'S IT, EXCELLENT, THAT'S A PATTERN.

I NEVER INTENDED TO GO PART-TIME, IT'S JUST SOMETHING THAT HAPPENED.

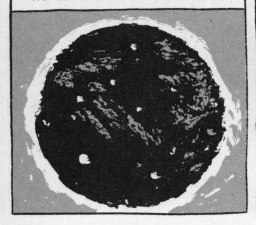

TWO WEEKS AFTER CASSIE WAS BORN, I WAS BACK AT WORK. I WASN'T EVEN A PART-TIME PARENT. I WAS AN OCCASIONAL DAD, STRICTLY NIGHTS AND WEEKENDS.

WE WERE IN THE THICK OF NOT SLEEPING. THOSE NIGHTS OF BEING WOKEN EVERY OTHER HOUR AND ROCKING A BAWLING CASSIE AFTER HER FEED.

THREE QUARTERS OF AN HOUR DOESN'T FEEL LIKE A LONG TIME UNTIL YOU'RE PACING UP AND DOWN TRYING TO ROCK A CRYING BABY TO SLEEP.

Shh Shh

IT'S NOT LIKE MEG HAD ANY REST EITHER. SHE HAD THE REGULAR FEEDS DURING THE NIGHT. I COULDN'T BREAST FEED BUT I COULD ROCK AND SOOTHE.

I WAS GLAD I DIDN'T HAVE THE RESPONSIBIL-ITY AND THE DISCOMFORT OF FEEDING BUT I WAS ALSO JEALOUS. I WASN'T AN ESSENTIAL PART OF THAT BINARY RELATIONSHIP.

WHEN THE BREAST PUMP BECOMES AN OBJECT OF ANXIETY, AND MILK AND AMOUNTS ARE CONFUSED WITH LOVE AND BEING A GOOD MOTHER.

THERE'RE NO WEEKENDS OFF FOR BREAST-FEEDING MOTHERS, DAY AFTER DAY AFTER DAY. DESPITE BEING EXHAUSTED WE'RE A UNIT, WORKING IN UNISON WITHOUT NEEDING WORDS.

IT'S LIKE A PUNCH IN THE GUT SEEING MEG CRY IN PAIN WITH CRACKED NIPPLES. I'M SIMULTANEOUSLY USELESS AND NEEDED.

I GO OFF SICK SO I CAN HELP OUT AT HOME. SOON AFTER I WRANGLE GOING PART-TIME.

WE'RE A BABY-CARING MACHINE. CASSIE IS FED AND CLOTHED AND BATHED, WIPED AND TOWELLED AND LOVED SEAMLESSLY BY US BOTH.

WE TAKE THE PANICKY LATE NIGHT TRIPS TO ACCIDENT AND EMERGENCY, WE KNOW THE TELL TALE SIGNS OF A HIGH TEMP-ERATURE AND TEETHING AND WE CLEAN UP THE PUKE TOGETHER.

57

WHEN MEG GOES BACK TO WORK I BATTLE WITH CASSIE'S START ON THE BOTTLE. I WANTED THAT BINARY RELATIONSHIP AND I GOT IT. IT'S NOT THE WONDERFUL BONDING EXPERIENCE I WAS HOPING FOR.

WE'RE STILL A TEAM BUT WE'RE RUNNING A RELAY.

ONE OF US RUSHES OUT TO WORK AS THE OTHER RUSHES IN.

WE SHARE AN ORBIT, CONSTANTLY FALLING TOWARDS EACH OTHER BUT NEVER TOUCHING.

MUM'S HOME.

HELLO.

MUMMY MUMMY.

HOW IS EVERYONE?

HAD A GOOD DAY AT WORK?

YEAH, I....

LOOK, MUMMY.

CASSIE'S BEEN DRAWING PATTERNS.

I CAN SEE THAT.

IT'S BRILLIANT.

RIGHT, WHO WANTS TO HELP ME MAKE TEA?

ME ME.

I DON'T KNOW WHAT ELSE WE COULD DO. CHUCK IN WORK ALTOGETHER?

HERE YOU GO.

HOW'S THIS SALAD COMING ON?

IT'S LOOKING GOOD.

NOT WORKING ISN'T AN OPTION, FINANCIALLY OR FOR THE SAKE OF OUR SANITY.

WE'LL PLOW ON KNOWING THAT LIFE LOOKS THE SAME OVER ON THE OTHER SIDE BUT WITH A NAGGING SLIVER OF RESENTMENT THAT IT MIGHT BE BETTER OVER THERE.

ARE YOU READY FOR THE DRESSING YET?

NOW BE CAREFUL, DARLIN', REMEMBER THIS IS A CAR PARK.

YAYYYYY.

DID YOU HAVE A GOOD DAY TODAY?

I REALLY LIKE YOUR COLOURING IN, THAT'S LOVELY.

ALICE WASN'T IN TODAY.

AGAIN?

round & round the

COME ON, HON, WE HAVE TO GO TO PRE-SCHOOL NOW. OTHERWISE DADDY WILL HAVE TO TAKE YOU.

DON'T WANT TO.

WHAT'S THE MATTER, SWEETHEART?

ALICE WASN'T IN AGAIN.

BEST FRIEND ALICE?

SHE WASN'T AT PRE-SCHOOL.

SHE MIGHT HAVE STARTED RECEPTION CLASS AT THE INFANTS' ALREADY?

JESSICA'S STILL THERE, YOU PLAY WITH HER, DON'T YOU?

AND JACK WILSON?

COME ON THEN, HON, LET'S GET OUR SHOES ON.

DON'T WANT TO.

REMEMBER, WE'RE LOOKING FOR A PRESENT FOR EMILY.

WHEEEEEEEEE.

I THOUGHT SHE WAS ON HER OWN FOR A MINUTE.

I'M KEEPING AN EYE ON HER.

CASSIE, WAIT FOR ME.

CASSIE?

CASSIE!

TOYS. SHE'LL
BE IN THE
TOYS.

CASSIE?

63

SHIT SHIT SHIT.

CASS...

HI, CASSIE.

DON'T YELL HER NAME, YOU PRAT. WHAT IF SOMEONE HEARS?

SHIT. SHE HAS TO BE AROUND HERE. SHE'S RUN AHEAD A THOUSAND TIMES AND NEVER STRAYED OUT OF MY SIGHT.

OKAY, OKAY, DON'T FREAK OUT. DON'T FUCKING FREAK OUT.

EXCUSE ME, I'VE MANAGED TO LOSE MY DAUGHTER AND I NEED SOME HELP FINDING HER..

WHAT DOES SHE LOOK LIKE?

SHE'S THREE, BLONDE HAIR, WEARING A PINK DRESS WITH STRIPEY TIGHTS.

I'LL INFORM THE CAMERAS ON THE DOORS IN CASE SOMEONE TRIES TO WALK OUT WITH HER.

UNTIL NOW IT HASN'T BEEN REAL BUT NOW I'M FRIGHTENED.

AND PINK AND WHITE TRAINERS.

WHAT WAS SHE WEARING?

ALL I SEE IN MY HEAD IS GRAINY VIDEO FOOTAGE OF MY LITTLE GIRL BEING WALKED OUT OF THE SHOPPING CENTRE WITH THE ANONYMOUS BLUR OF AN ADULT.

PINK DRESS WITH STRIPEY TIGHTS. SHE'S WAIST HIGH. SHE WAS ONLY OUT OF MY SIGHT FOR A SECOND.

I'LL TELL THE STAFF SO THEY CAN LOOK OUT FOR HER.

THEY'RE WATCHING THE DOORS BUT WHAT IF SOMEONE, SOME MAN, SOME SICK BASTARD, DRAGS HER OUT OF A FIRE EXIT OR SOMETHING?

WHAT WAS HE WEARING?

IT'S A GIRL.

I DON'T SEE HER BEING DRAGGED. I SEE HER INNOCENTLY, TRUSTINGLY WALKING ALONG HAND IN HAND.

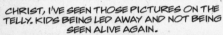

CHRIST, I'VE SEEN THOSE PICTURES ON THE TELLY. KIDS BEING LED AWAY AND NOT BEING SEEN ALIVE AGAIN.

LAST SUMMER IN THE PARK.

DON'T EAT SAND, DARLING.

IT'S YUCKY.

I REMEMBER THINKING, "POOR WOMAN, SHE'S PROBABLY LOST HER KID."

I DIDN'T THINK ANY MORE OF IT.

WHO WOULD LIKE AN ICE CREAM?

ME ME ME.

I THOUGHT YOU MIGHT.

UNTIL I SAW THE NEWS THAT NIGHT. A FIVE YEAR OLD BOY HAD SLIPPED OUT OF HIS MUM'S SIGHT FOR A COUPLE OF SECONDS.

HE'D WALKED AWAY, FALLEN IN THE LAKE AND DROWNED.

I REMEMBER THAT LOOK OF CONFUSION AND PANIC BEHIND THE TEARS.

MY WORLD HAS BEEN TURNED ON ITS' HEAD. I'VE DRIFTED INTO A PLACE WHERE RED-EYED PARENTS, FLANKED BY POLICE OFFICERS, GIVE TV PRESS CONFERENCES.

A WORLD WHERE YOUR CHILD CAN DIE WHILE EVERYONE ELSE CARRIES ON EATING SAND AND LAUGHING.

JUST AS EASILY AS I FELL OUT OF IT I SLIP BACK INTO THE WORLD OF SANDPITS, LAUGHTER AND ICE CREAM.

WHO FOUND HER?

ONE OF THE STAFF. ALL THEY COULD SEE WAS A PAIR OF LITTLE EYES PEEKING OUT FROM BEHIND A CHAIR.

I WAS HIDING.

THANK YOU.

WHERE WERE YOU?

YOU COULDN'T FIND ME.

I WON'T FREAK OUT, CRY OR YELL. I WON'T SCARE HER LIKE SHE SCARED ME.

DON'T DO THAT AGAIN, HON.

CASSIE, LISTEN. DON'T EVER RUN AWAY LIKE THAT AGAIN. I WAS REALLY FRIGHTENED. DO YOU UNDERSTAND?

NO, SHE DOESN'T. WHAT CAN I DO, HAVE HER BE FEARFUL OF EVERY ADULT MALE IN THE WORLD?

WE DON'T PLAY HIDE AND SEEK ANYWHERE BUT AT HOME, OKAY?

WHY?

BECAUSE I DON'T WANT TO LOSE YOU.

ALL'S WELL THAT ENDS WELL.

CASSIE!

HAND.

THANK YOU.

NOW YOU'RE IN TROUBLE.

EH?

YOUR DIRTY SECRET'S OUT.

ARE YOU GONNA TALK BOLLOCKS ALL DAY, OR WHAT?

IT ISN'T SUE WHO YOU'VE GOT UP THE DUFF, IT'S LORRAINE, RIGHT?
LORRAINE?

THE ONE IN DESIGN. SHE CAME IN THIS MORNING TO TAKE ALL HER STUFF HOME. SHE'S OFF WORK WITH HIGH BLOOD PRESSURE, DOCTOR'S ORDERS.

SHIT, SHIT, SHIT.

ARE YOU GOING TO GO FOR HER JOB?

I DON'T SEE HER COMING BACK. HER FELLA'S LOADED.

YOU THINK SO?

IT'LL MEAN MORE MONEY.

I'D RATHER BE DESIGNING THAN DOING THIS.

FULL TIME THOUGH, ISN'T IT, MATE?

YEAH, SO?

OVERTIME, TOO.

I'M OFF ON MY FAG BREAK, YOU COMING?

I ONLY JUST GOT IN.

72

"...HE STILL POPS UP FROM TIME TO TIME."

HUG AND A KISS BEFORE I WASH UP.

WHO DO YOU WANT SONGS FROM TONIGHT, HON?

DADDY.

WELL, THIS IS A SURPRISE.

NIGHT NIGHT, SWEETHEART.

WHAT SONGS WOULD YOU LIKE TONIGHT THEN, HON?

I WANT STORIES.

OKAY, YOU CAN HAVE THREE STORIES. WHAT WOULD YOU LIKE FIRST?

SLEEPING BEAUTY.

ALL RIGHT, ONCE UPON A TIME THERE WAS A KING AND QUEEN AND THEY WISHED THEY COULD HAVE A LITTLE GIRL.

ONE DAY A FROG...

FROG?

YEAH, ER, A FROG SAID THAT THE QUEEN WOULD HAVE A DAUGHTER.

DADDY?

YES, HON.

WHAT'S A FROG?

YOU KNOW WHAT A FROG IS, IT'S LIKE A TOAD.

AND THEN, UM, THE...

THE FROG?

THE KING AND QUEEN HAD A LITTLE GIRL AND THEY WERE SO HAPPY THAT THEY DECIDED TO...

DADDY?

YES, DARLIN'.

I'M THIRSTY.

I TALKED TO THE ESTATE AGENT.

THESE THREE ARE STILL ON THE MARKET BUT THE OTHER TWO HAVE...WHAT'S THIS?

LORRAINE'S GONE OFF SICK EARLY SO NOW EVERYONE KNOWS HER JOB'S UP FOR GRABS. I THOUGHT I'D HAVE AT LEAST A MONTH'S HEAD START.

YOU'RE...IS IT PART TIME?

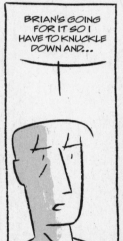
BRIAN'S GOING FOR IT SO I HAVE TO KNUCKLE DOWN AND...

SO YOU'RE APPLYING FOR HER JOB?

WELL, YEAH.

WHEN WERE YOU EVER PLANNING ON TELLING ME? YOU WOULD HAVE GONE FOR THIS JOB WITHOUT DISCUSSING IT WITH ME?

I HADN'T REALLY DECIDED UNTIL...

THERE'S WHAT, A COUPLE OF WEEKS WORK HERE?

I'VE BEEN CONSIDERING IT, YES. IT'S NOT LIKE I'VE JUST GONE AND GOT A JOB IN THE SCOTTISH HIGHLANDS OR ANYTHING.

I CAN'T BELIEVE YOU.

WHAT?

IT'S NOT JUST ABOUT YOU, IT AFFECTS THE WHOLE FAMILY.

SIMON, DON'T YOU THINK IT'S SOMETHING WE HAVE TO TALK ABOUT FIRST?

WELL, OF COURSE, BUT I THOUGHT YOU'D AGREE THAT IT'S A GOOD THING, MORE MONEY AND A WIDER CHOICE OF HOUSES.

IT'S NOT THE HOUSE I'M WORRIED ABOUT.

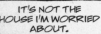

76

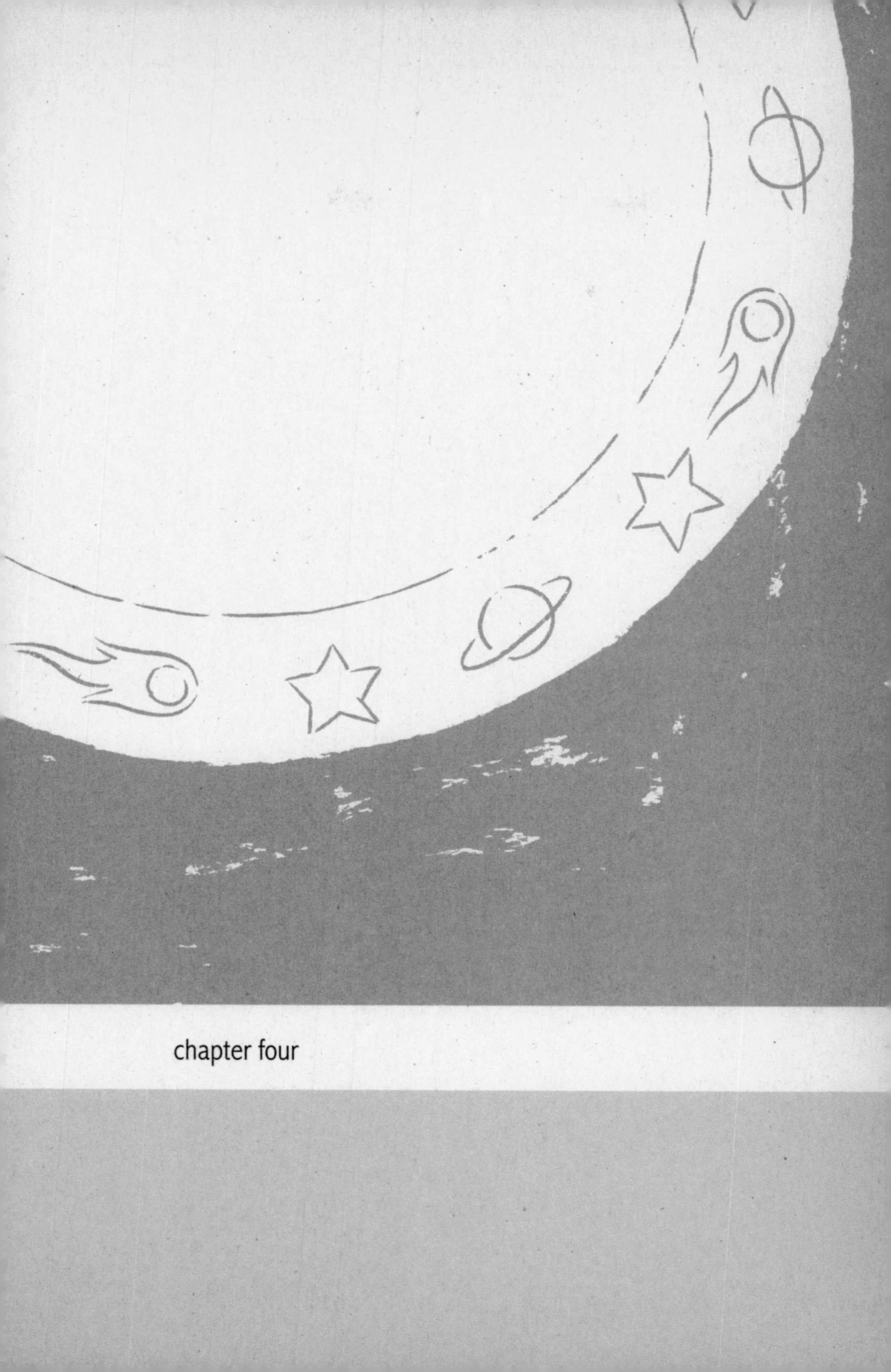

chapter four

WE COULD DISCUSS IT BUT I DON'T SEE THE POINT WHEN YOU'VE ALREADY MADE UP YOUR MIND.

IT WOULD MAKE ME HAPPY IF I GOT THIS JOB. I'D BE CREATING THE DESIGNS RATHER THAN PARROTING SOMEONE ELSE'S. IT WOULD FEEL LIKE I WAS ACTUALLY GETTING SOMEWHERE.

I DON'T WANT YOU TO BE UNHAPPY. I DIDN'T EVEN KNOW YOU WERE UNHAPPY AT WORK, SIMON. HOW AM I SUPPOSED TO KNOW IF YOU DON'T TELL ME ANYTHING?

WHAT, WHAT ARE YOU THINKING?

NOTHING.

THERE'S NOTHING, NOTHING WHAT-SO-EVER WRONG? YOU REALLY BELIEVE THAT?

I WON'T APPLY FOR THE JOB THEN.

WHY NOT?

BECAUSE CLEARLY YOU DON'T WANT ME TO.

OF COURSE I DO, BUT WE HAVE TO CONSIDER WHAT CHANGES WE MIGHT HAVE TO MAKE TO CASSIE'S NURSERY DAYS AND MY WORK SCHEDULE. IF WE DO CHANGE HER DAYS THEN WILL THEY MATCH UP WITH THE TIMES HER FRIENDS ARE IN?

I DON'T SEE HOW WILL IT AFFECT YOUR WORK SCHEDULE.

NEITHER DO I YET. I'M JUST SAYING IT MIGHT.

OKAY.

IT DOESN'T SHOW.

I'M SORRY. OOH, I'M SO SORRY.

DON'T WORRY, HON.

IT'S OKAY, DADDY ISN'T CROSS.

LET'S JUST KEEP AWAY FROM THE BLACKCURRANT JUICE, SHALL WE?

GOT EVERYTHING?

I THINK SO. HAVE YOU GOT CASSIE'S FOLDER?

IT'S ALREADY IN THE CAR.

WISH ME LUCK.

WISH DADDY LUCK.

KISS.

≥ MWAH ≤

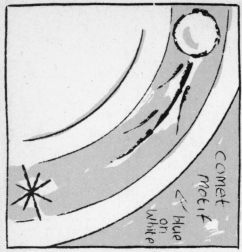

THANKS FOR YOUR TIME, SIMON. YOU'LL HEAR FROM US IN ABOUT A WEEK.

OKAY.

CHEERS THEN.

HOW'D IT GO?

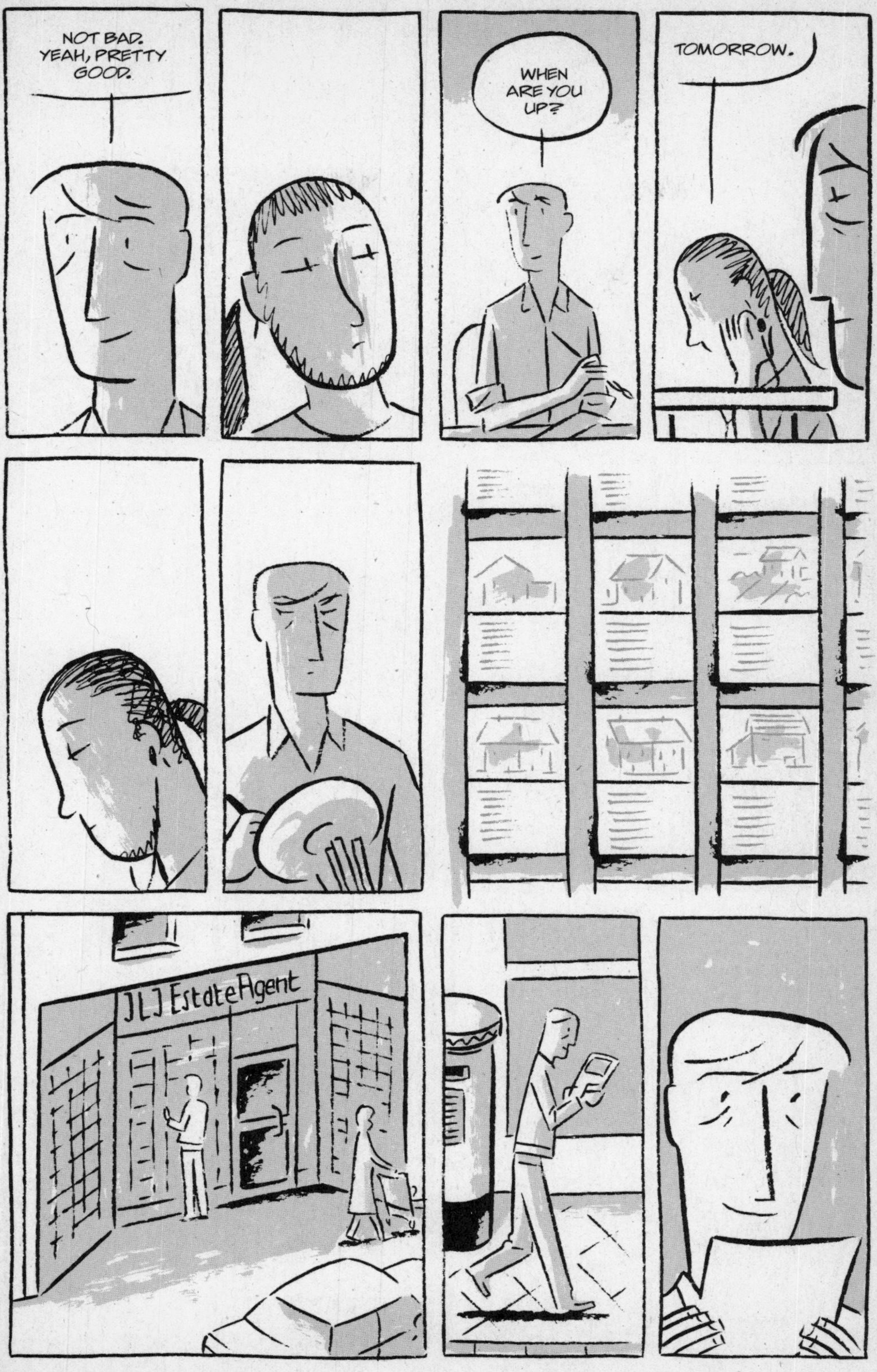
NOT BAD. YEAH, PRETTY GOOD.
WHEN ARE YOU UP?
TOMORROW.
JLJ Estate Agent

IS SHE ASLEEP?

ALMOST.

SO, THE INTERVIEW WENT ALL RIGHT?

YEAH, PRETTY GOOD, AND I FOUND US A HOUSE.

IT'S GOT THE THREE BEDROOMS, NICE GARDEN, AND IS ROUND THE CORNER FROM A GOOD SCHOOL.

IT'S LIKE WE'RE DANCING AROUND A MAYPOLE.

EH?

HOW ARE WE GOING TO PAY FOR IT, SIMON— MAGIC MORE HOURS OUT OF THE DAY?

EVEN IF I DON'T GET THIS JOB WE CAN MANAGE IT AT A STRETCH.

I DON'T WANT TO BE STRETCHED. DON'T YOU FEEL STRETCHED ENOUGH? I'D LIKE LIFE TO BE EASIER, JUST FOR A LITTLE BIT. A BIT LESS WORRY, A BIT LESS STRESS.

YES. I FEEL STRETCHED ENOUGH.

HEAVEN WOULD BE NOT SAYING "NO". NO FIGHTS OVER LEAVING THE HOUSE, NO FIGHTS ABOUT GETTING INTO THE CAR, NO MORE FIGHTS OVER LUNCH OR SAYING "SORRY" OR ANYTHING ELSE.

JUST A STRAY SATELLITE FLOATING THROUGH THE HEAVENS.

YOU ALL SET?

WHAT?

FOR YOUR INTERVIEW, YOU ALL SET?

YEAH,
I'M
READY.

IF I GOT THE
JOB WOULD YOU
WANT TO JOB
SHARE WITH
ME?

YOU'VE GOT THE
JOB?

NO, I'M
JUST
SAYING...

...HYPOTHETICALLY.

WOULD YOU
WANT TO JOB
SHARE?

NAH.

WHAT, NOT
EVEN CONSIDER
IT?

WHAT'D BE THE POINT?
I'D ONLY BE EARNING THE
SAME AS I AM NOW.

BUT IT'D BE FEWER HOURS, NO OVERTIME, YOU'D HAVE THE JOB SATISFACTION AND STILL SPEND MORE TIME WITH THE FAMILY.

I LIKE WORKING, SI.

SO DO I...

YOU EITHER DO THE JOB OR YOU DON'T, MATE.

IF I DO GET THIS JOB IT MEANS I'LL JUMP UP A PAY SCALE AND I'LL BE CHUFFED TO BE ABLE TO AFFORD A NEW KITCHEN. IF I DON'T GET IT, NO HARD FEELINGS.

RIGHT. NO HARD FEELINGS.

WELL, I'D BEST BE OFF TO THIS INTERVIEW.

BEST OF LUCK... MATE.

WE'RE HAPPY TO OFFER YOU THE JOB, SIMON.

TERRI AND I LOVED YOUR DESIGNS. WE THINK YOU'VE GOT AN EYE FOR WHAT WILL APPEAL TO THE GENERAL CONSUMER.

AND WE WERE LOOKING AT YOUR OWN DESIGNS AND THINK THEY'RE QUIRKY ENOUGH TO SELL TO THE YOUNGER SET. WE'LL HAVE TO LOOK INTO THAT.

NO PROMISES, WE'LL GET YOU SETTLED IN FIRST.

THAT'S... THAT'S FANTASTIC. THANK YOU!

NOW WE HAVE TO SCHEDULE IN SOME TRAINING SESSIONS WITH PAT TO GET YOU UP TO SPEED WITH THE SOFTWARE. SHOULDN'T BE A PROBLEM, YOU'LL PICK IT UP IN NO TIME.

BRILLIANT.

THAT'S ALL REALLY. JUDITH WILL SEE YOU ON MONDAY AND GET YOU STARTED RIGHT AWAY.

YEAH, I WANTED TO TALK TO YOU ABOUT THAT... ABOUT JOB SHARING.

NO ONE'S MENTIONED THAT TO ME. IT'S A FULL-TIME POSITION.

I KNOW, BUT WITH LORRAINE COMING BACK...

LORRAINE'S TAKING FULL MATERNITY LEAVE. SHE WON'T BE RETURNING FOR ANOTHER FIFTEEN MONTHS. IN THE MEANTIME I NEED TO GET THE DESIGN TEAM BACK TO FULL STRENGTH.

THE POSITION YOU'RE IN NOW, PART-TIME IS APPROPRIATE. WITH DESIGN WORK YOU CAN'T HAVE ONE PERSON START A PROJECT AND THEN EXPECT SOMEONE ELSE TO FINISH IT OFF, WHERE WOULD BE THE CONSISTENCY? IT'S SIMPLY NOT PRACTICAL.

BUT WITH THE RIGHT PARTNER...?

WE HAVE OTHER APPLICANTS IN HOUSE WHO ARE AVAILABLE FOR FULL-TIME WORK. THAT'S EVEN BEFORE WE OFFER IT UP TO SHORT TERM CONTRACTS FROM OUTSIDE.

I RESPECT YOUR PRINCIPLES, SIMON. FAMILY COMES FIRST.

CAN I THINK IT OVER?

COME SEE ME IN THE MORNING.

I'M AT HOME TOMORROW.

FRIDAY MORNING THEN.

IT'S FULL-TIME OR NOTHING.

CASSIE ENJOYS NURSERY.

SHE USED TO BEFORE ALICE LEFT.

SHE CAN MAKE NEW FRIENDS. IT'S NOT AS THOUGH SHE'S THERE ON HER OWN, IS IT?

WELL DONE, HON. I'M PROUD OF YOU.

NOOOOOO

COME ON, HON.

NO. I DON'T WANT TO DO WHAT YOU WANT ME TO DO.

I'LL CATCH YOU AT THE BOTTOM.

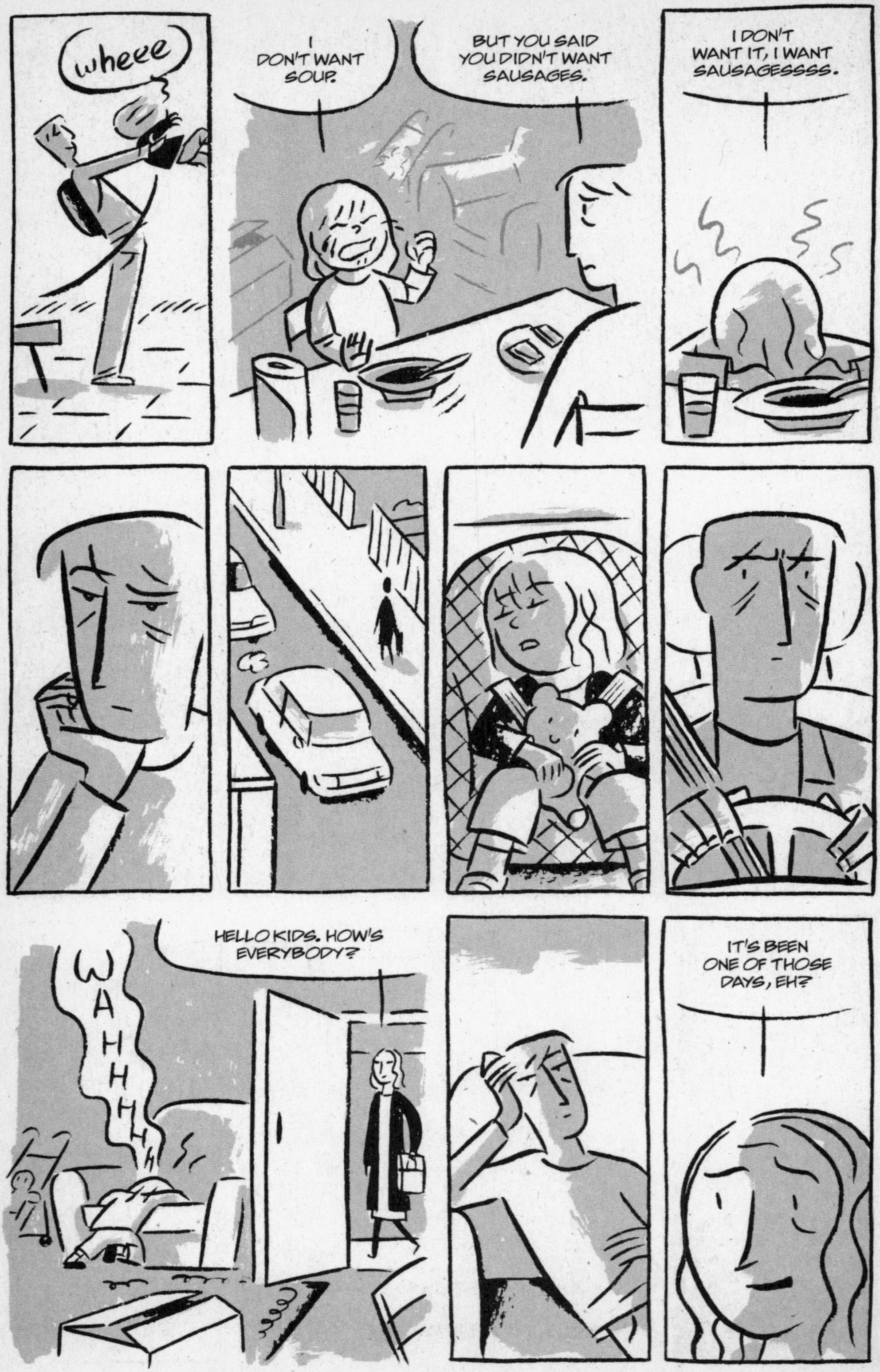
wheee
I DON'T WANT SOUP.
BUT YOU SAID YOU DIDN'T WANT SAUSAGES.
I DON'T WANT IT, I WANT SAUSAGESSSS.
WAHHHHHH
HELLO KIDS. HOW'S EVERYBODY?
IT'S BEEN ONE OF THOSE DAYS, EH?

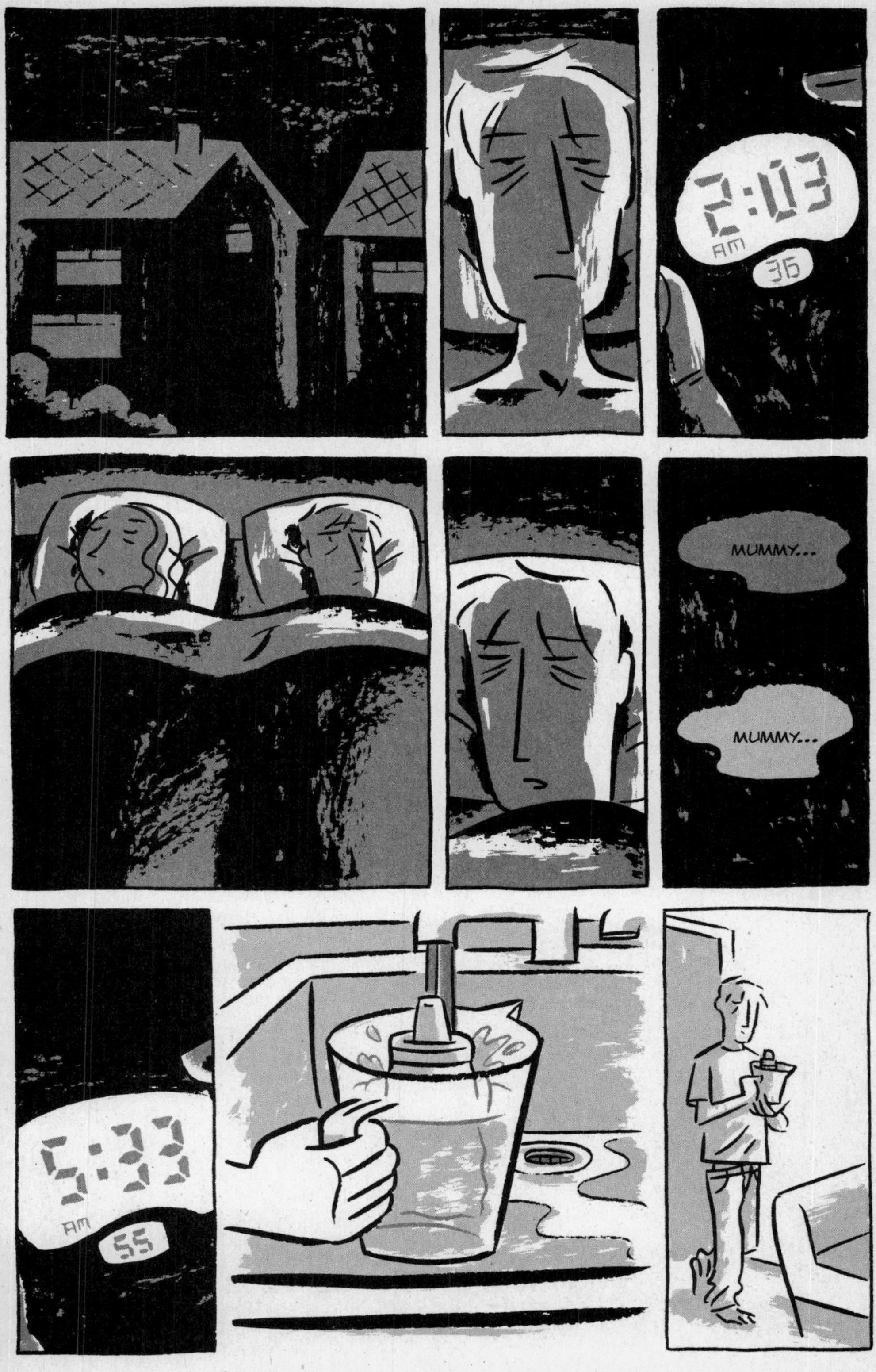
2:03
AM
36
MUMMY...
MUMMY...
5:33
AM
55

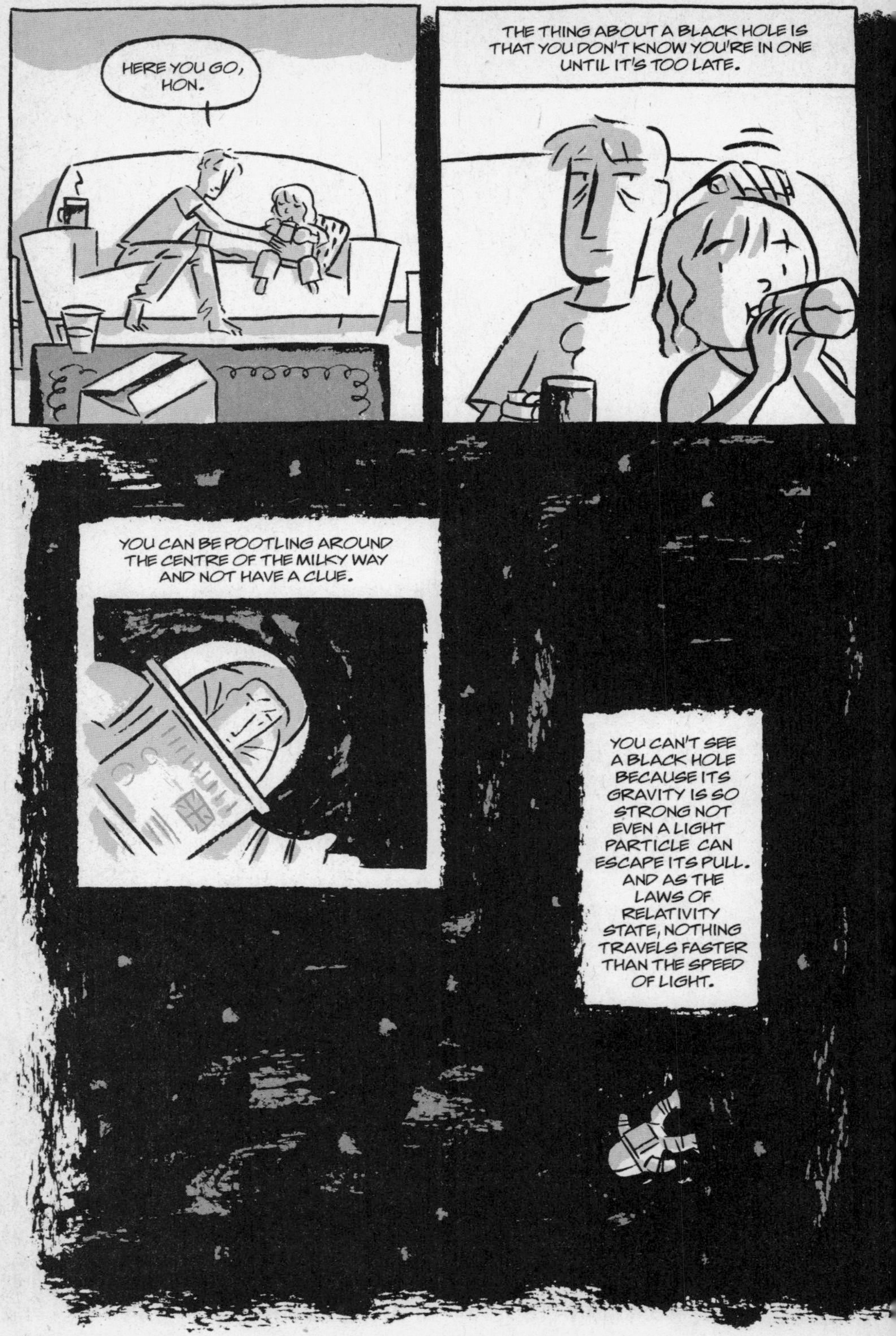
HERE YOU GO, HON.
THE THING ABOUT A BLACK HOLE IS THAT YOU DON'T KNOW YOU'RE IN ONE UNTIL IT'S TOO LATE.
YOU CAN BE POOTLING AROUND THE CENTRE OF THE MILKY WAY AND NOT HAVE A CLUE.
YOU CAN'T SEE A BLACK HOLE BECAUSE ITS GRAVITY IS SO STRONG NOT EVEN A LIGHT PARTICLE CAN ESCAPE ITS PULL. AND AS THE LAWS OF RELATIVITY STATE, NOTHING TRAVELS FASTER THAN THE SPEED OF LIGHT.

YOU'D LOOK OUT AT THE STARS AND MIGHT NOTICE HOW THEY'D BLUESHIFTED. ANYONE LOOKING AT YOU WOULD SEE YOUR GLOW BECOME REDDER AND REDDER UNTIL YOU SLIPPED INTO THE INFRARED SPECTRUM BEYOND THE HUMAN EYE.

BY NOW YOU'D BE IN THE EVENT HORIZON. YOU CAN'T SEE OUT AND NO ONE CAN SEE IN.

THAT'S WHEN YOU REALISE YOU'RE IN A BLACK HOLE. THERE'S NOTHING YOU CAN DO BUT WAIT TO BE PULLED DOWN INTO THE SINGULARITY.

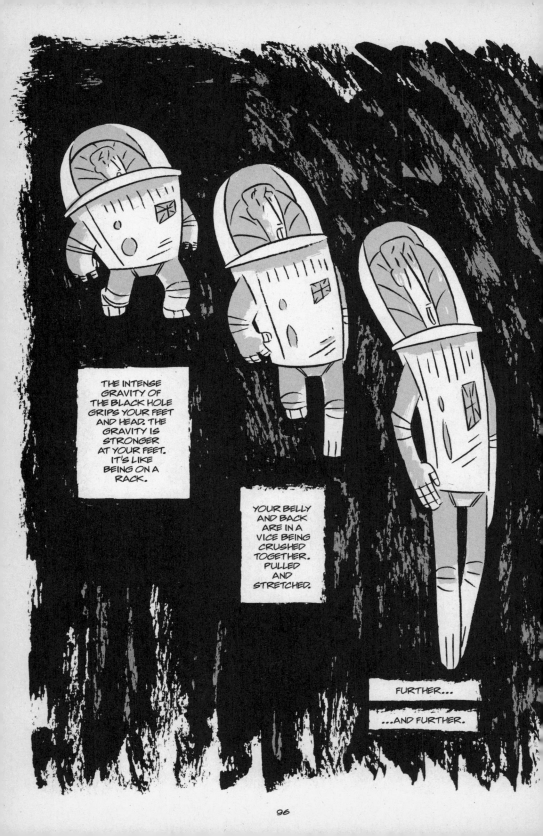

THE INTENSE GRAVITY OF THE BLACK HOLE GRIPS YOUR FEET AND HEAD. THE GRAVITY IS STRONGER AT YOUR FEET. IT'S LIKE BEING ON A RACK.

YOUR BELLY AND BACK ARE IN A VICE BEING CRUSHED TOGETHER. PULLED AND STRETCHED.

FURTHER...

...AND FURTHER.

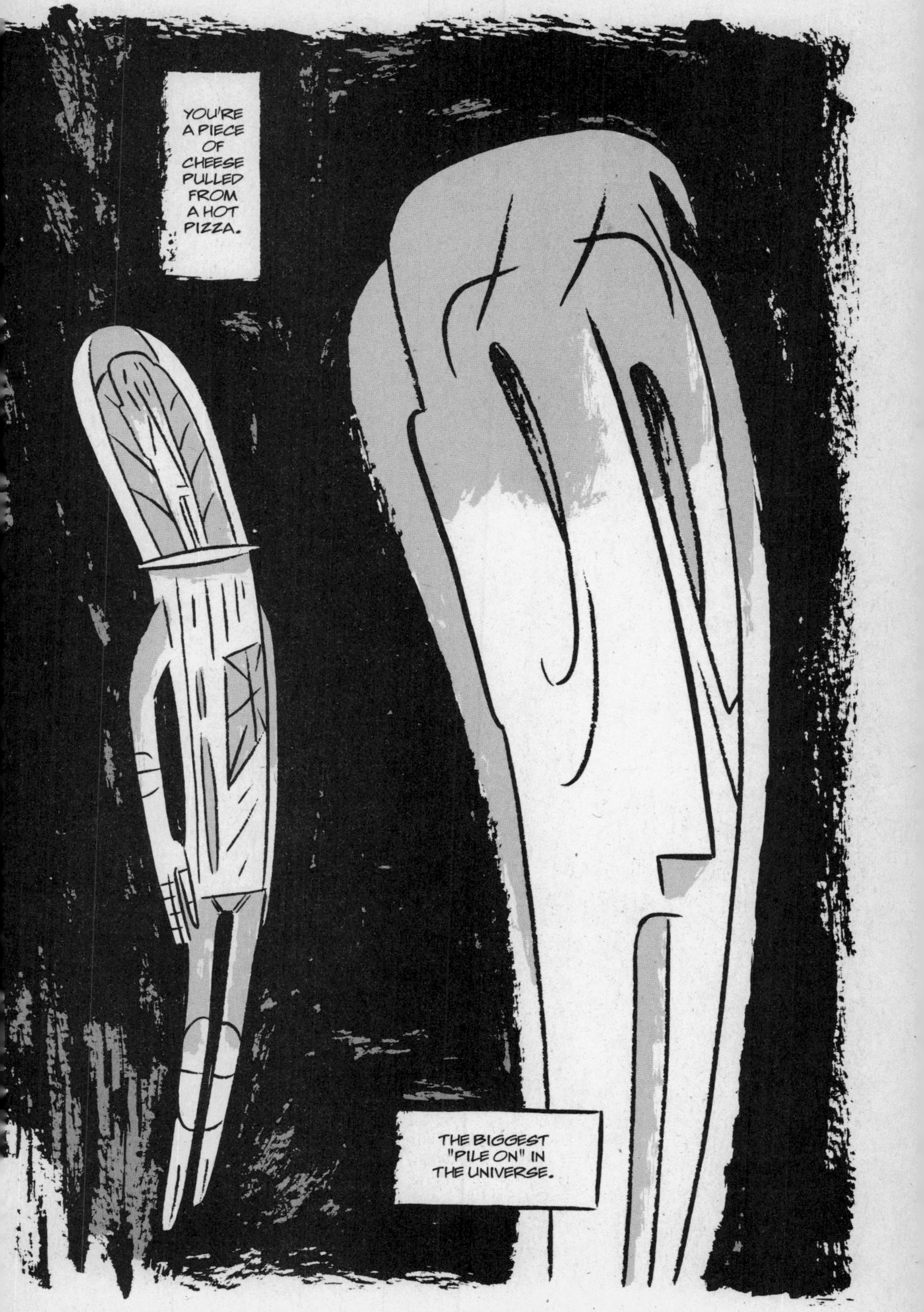
YOU'RE A PIECE OF CHEESE PULLED FROM A HOT PIZZA.
THE BIGGEST "PILE ON" IN THE UNIVERSE.

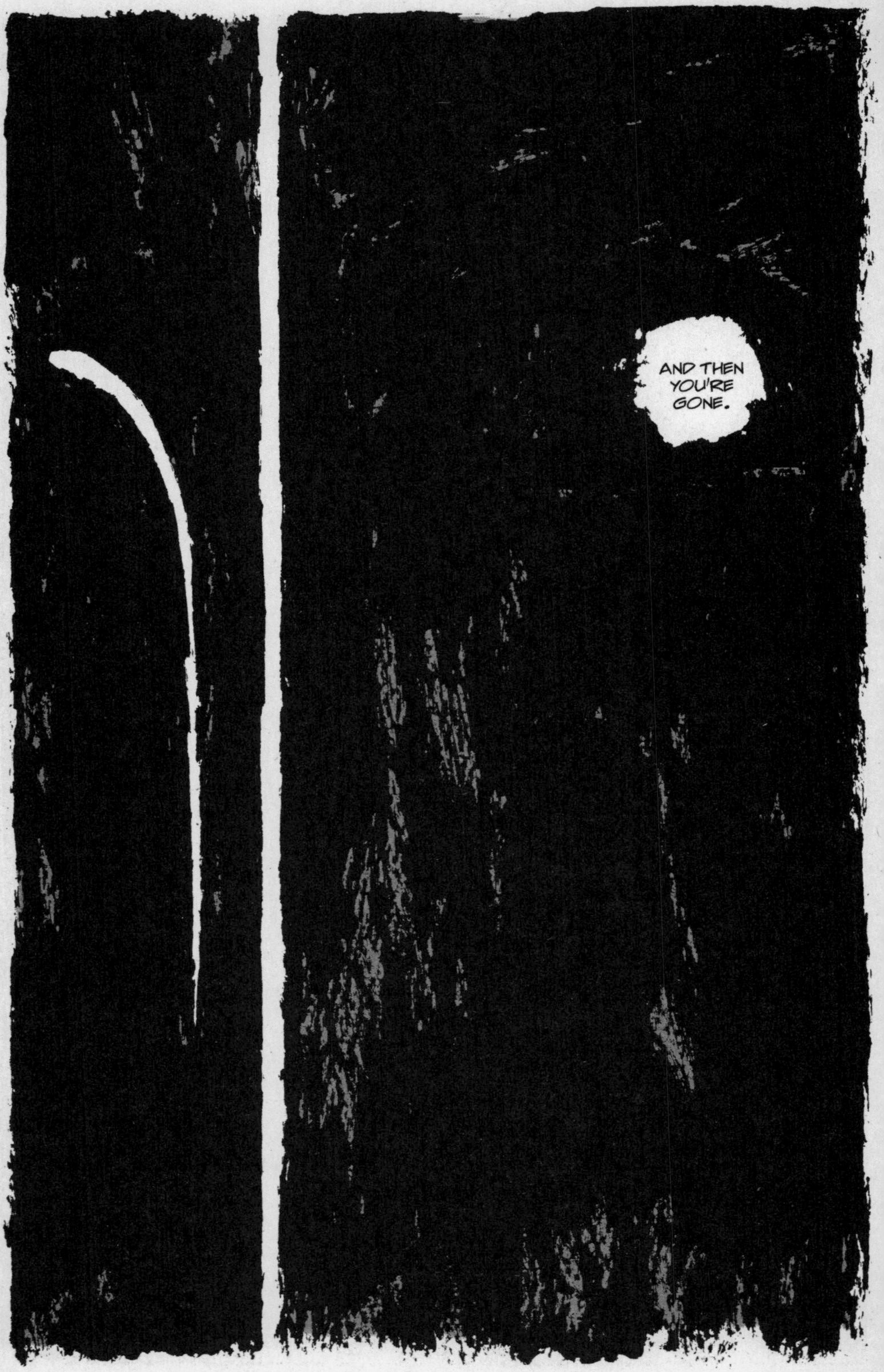
AND THEN YOU'RE GONE.

WHILE TIME STANDS STILL AT WORK, THE REST OF LIFE MOVES ON.

MEG FINDS A HOUSE FOR US. IT'S NOT SO EXPENSIVE. IT'S SMALLER AND NEEDS A FAIR BIT OF WORK

WE STIPULATE IN THE CONTRACT THAT THE OWNER REMOVES ALL OF HIS JUNK.

IT'S FUNNY, USUALLY I'M TAKING STUFF OUT OF A SKIP NOT SHOVING IT IN.

I'LL BE SAD TO SEE IT GO BUT I'M MOVING IN WITH MY GIRLFRIEND. Y'HAVE TO MOVE ON EVENTUALLY, DON'T YOU?

IT'LL LOOK A LOT BIGGER WHEN ALL HIS CRAP IS GONE.

WE FINALLY STOP HALF UNPACKING BOXES AND START FILLING AND TAPING THEM UP.

PRETTY SOON WE'RE MOVING THEM INTO THE NEW HOUSE.

WAVING GOODBYE TO THE OLD PLACE WHERE CASSIE SPENT HER FIRST YEARS.

I DON'T KNOW HOW WE'RE GONNA FIND ROOM FOR EVERYTHING.

YEAH, YOU CAN PUT IT OVER...

...HMM.

WE LIVE OUT OF BOXES FOR A FEW WEEKS WHILE WE GET SORTED.

SO THAT'S WHERE THE TEA BAGS WERE.

It's disconcerting finding that the cutlery drawer is full of batteries and the washing powder is where the pans ought to be.

We're happy but I can't help feeling we've slipped down the property ladder rather than climbed up a rung.

With everything is so scattered that the static routine of work is a comfort.

Before Cassie was born I knew what kind of dad I wanted to be.

I didn't want to be one of those dads who are out the door at breakfast and come home exhausted at tea time.

I wanted to have the energy to play or kick a ball around.

I DON'T TAKE THE JOB.

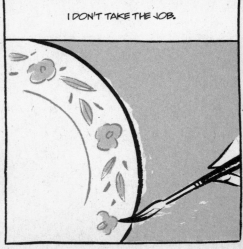

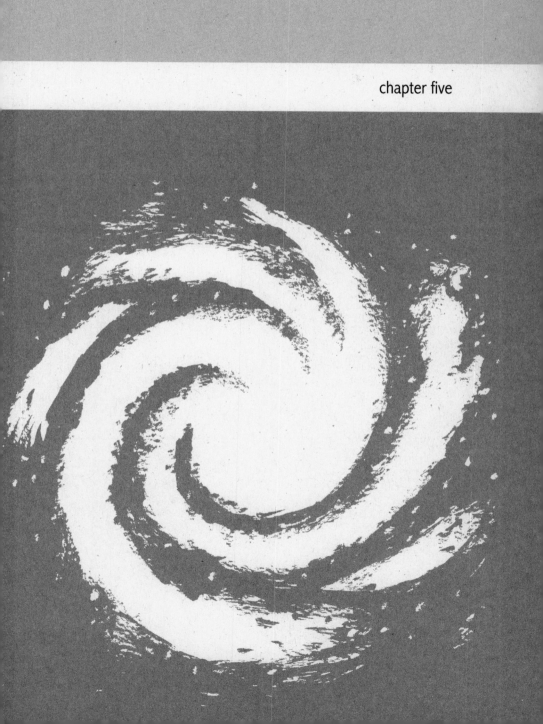

chapter five

IN THE BEGINNING, THE VERY BEGINNING, THE UNIVERSE WAS INFINITELY SMALL AND INFINITELY DENSE.

THAT WAS FIFTEEN BILLION YEARS AGO.

I DON'T KNOW HOW MANY ZEROS THAT IS, TWELVE OR MORE. I GET MY BILLIONS MIXED WITH MY MILLIONS. ANYWAY, IT WAS A LONG TIME AGO.

WHAT EXISTED BEFORE THAT ISN'T KNOWN. THE GENERAL THEORY OF RELATIVITY BREAKS DOWN AT THAT POINT.

ONE MOMENT THERE WAS EVERYTHING CRAMMED INTO ALMOST NOTHING.

THE NEXT MOMENT THERE WAS
EVERYTHING EVERYWHERE AND IT'S
BEEN EXPANDING EVER SINCE.

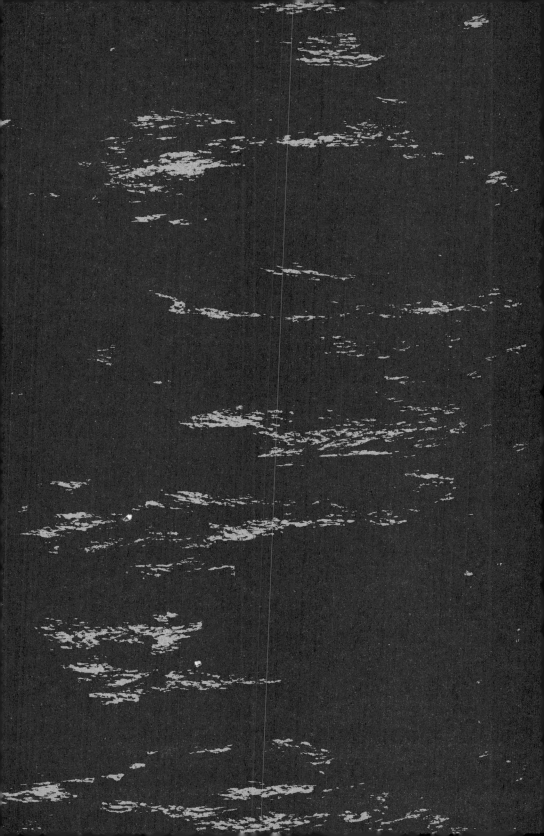

"PLANCK'S TIME" IS THE EARLIEST POINT IN THE LIFE OF THE UNIVERSE THAT WE CAN MEASURE.

IT'S SOMETHING LIKE, POINT FORTY-THREE ZEROS OF A SECOND AFTER THE BIRTH OF THE UNIVERSE.

AT THAT POINT WE KNOW GRAVITY EXISTED. GRAVITY IS ESSENTIAL BECAUSE WITHOUT GRAVITY THERE'S NO LIFE.

WE'D HAD THE BAG PACKED FOR AGES. BOOKS, SNACKS, DOCTOR'S NOTES AND UMPTEEN CHANGES OF CLOTHES. JUST IN CASE OUR BABY CAME EARLY AND WE HAD TO RUSH TO THE HOSPITAL.

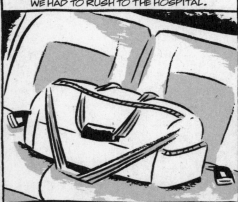

WHAT'D WORRIED US MOST WAS GETTING A PARKING SPACE. WHENEVER WE'D BEEN TO THE HOSPITAL FOR SCANS IT'D BEEN A NIGHTMARE FINDING SOMEWEHRE TO PUT THE CAR.

I'D HAD VISIONS OF ME ENDLESSLY DRIVING AROUND THE CAR PARK FOR HOURS AND BY THE TIME I'D FOUND A SPACE MEG WOULD'VE GIVEN BIRTH AND I'D HAVE MISSED THE WHOLE THING.

BUT THERE WAS NO QUESTION I'D BE THERE.

WHEN WE GOT TO THE HOSPITAL IT WAS SO EARLY IN THE MORNING WE PARKED RIGHT OUTSIDE AND WALKED IN.

PAY & DISPLAY

HOW OFTEN ARE THE CONTRACTIONS?

EVERY SIX MINUTES.

YOU LOOK TOO RELAXED TO BE IN ACTIVE LABOUR.

THEY DIDN'T BELIEVE MEG AS THEY SNAPPED ON THE GLOVES. SHE WAS SO CALM. SHE WAS AMAZING.

WE'LL DO AN INTERNAL EXAM BEFORE WE SEND YOU HOME.

WHILE MEG WAS BEING ZEN I WAS THE ONE LOOPING E.R. BIRTH TRAUMAS THROUGH MY HEAD.

THE CERVIX IS FULLY EFFACED AND FIVE CENTIMETRES DILATED.

I FORGOT THE BEANBAG.

IT DOESN'T MATTER.

I REMEMBER BUYING THAT FROM MOTHER-CARE BACK IN THE EARLY DAYS. IT WAS LIKE BEING DROPPED ONTO AN ALIEN PLANET WHERE EVERTHING IS PLASTIC AND RUBBER.

I DON'T EVEN WANNA KNOW WHAT THIS IS FOR.

IT'S CALLED LABOUR FOR A REASON. LIKE THE WORLD'S STRONGEST MAN CONTEST CROSSED WITH A MARATHON.

THERE'S LOTS OF INTENSE EFFORT, PAIN, DISCOMFORT, SWEAT, AND GRIMACING.

BUT THE RESULT OF THE EFFORT IS A LOT MORE INTERESTING THAN LIFTING A CONCRETE BALL ONTO A HIGH WALL.

MEG PUSHES AND GRUNTS AND STRAINS AS THE MIDWIVES AND I ENCOURAGE HER. TIME DRAGS AND FLIES SIMULTANEOUSLY.

I HOVER ON THE SIDELINES, HOLDING HANDS, OFFERING ADVICE WITH THE GAS AND AIR, AND MOP MEG'S BROW. I WANT TO HELP SO I WON'T FEEL COMPLETELY USELESS AS THE WOMEN GO ABOUT THEIR WORK.

MEG'S HELPED INTO THE MOST COMFORTABLE POSITION, SHE WORKS BETTER ON HER SIDE. WE WATCH AS MEG STRUGGLES TO GIVE BIRTH.

THE MIDWIVES HELP, MAKE NOTES, AND GIVE ADVICE WHILE I STAND THERE WITH A DAMP FLANNEL. THE CONTRACTIONS GRIP MEG'S BODY IN PAUSED SPASMS, WAVES BREAKING FASTER AND DEEPER.

ALL I CAN DO IS WATCH WITH A MIX OF FEAR AND ANTICIPATION AS MUSCLE AND BRUTE FORCE MAKE ONE BODY GIVE BIRTH TO ANOTHER.

MEG WAS INCREDIBLE AS SHE PUSHED THROUGH THE PAIN. SOON I COULD SEE THE CROWN OF THE HEAD AND...

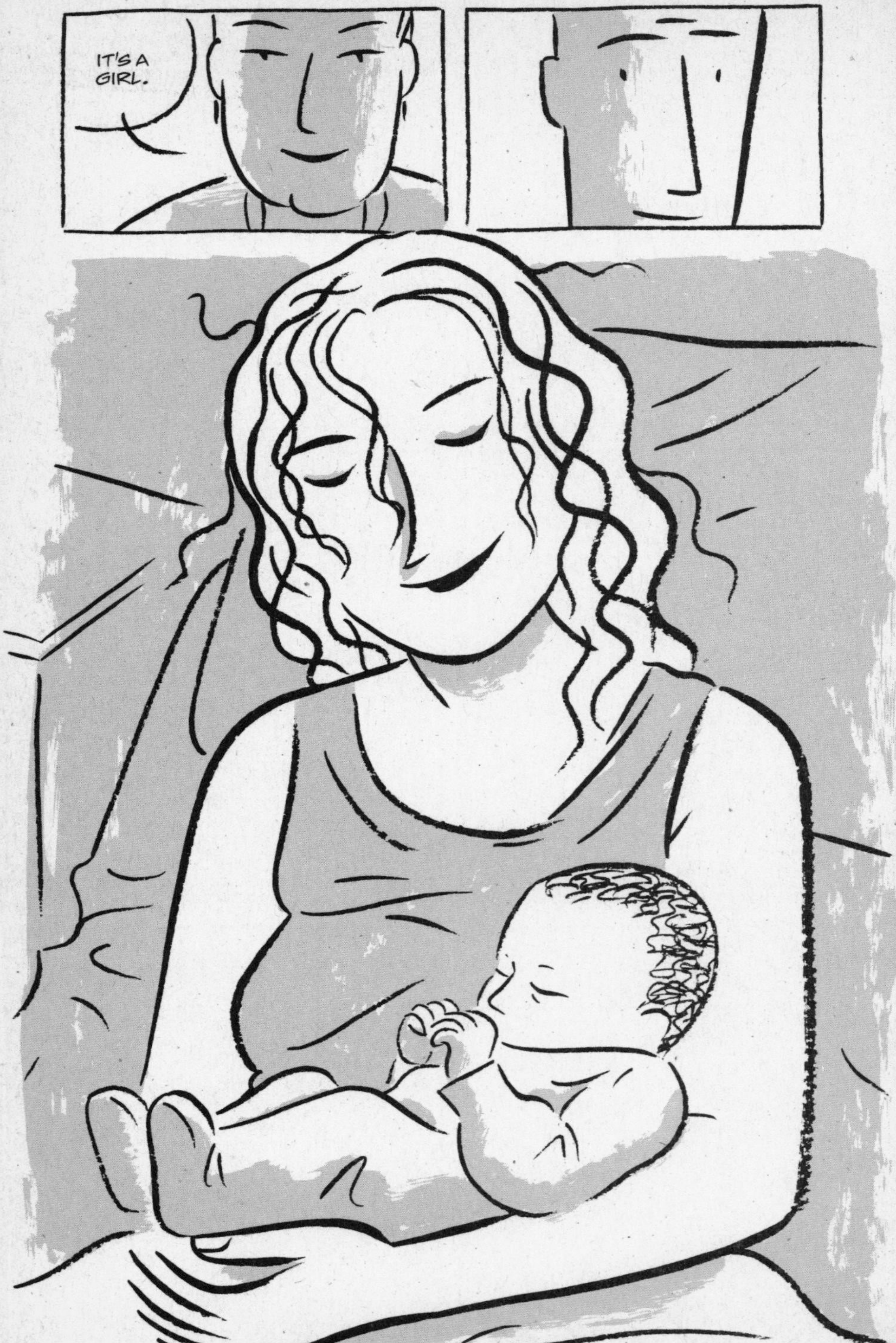
IT'S A GIRL.

A GIRL?

IT'S HARD TO BELIEVE SHE BEGAN FROM HERE.

AND GREW FROM THIS...

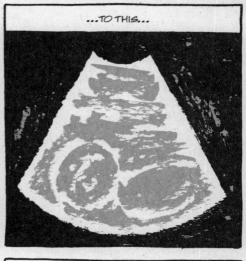

...TO THIS...

...TO THIS. OUR BEAUTIFUL LITTLE BABY.

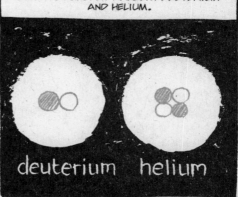

THREE-HUNDRED-THOUSAND YEARS AFTER THE UNIVERSE WAS BORN IT WAS COOL ENOUGH FOR HYDROGEN TO FORM ALONG-SIDE THE ALREADY PRESENT DEUTERIUM AND HELIUM.

deuterium   helium

AFTER ONE BILLION YEARS, MATTER IS COOL AND SLOW ENOUGH TO BE INFLUENCED BY GRAVITY.

GRAVITY DRAWS MATTER TOGETHER AND ROTATES IT.

FROM THIS, THE FIRST GALAXIES ARE FORMED AND WITHIN THEM THE FIRST STARS.

SIT DOWN FIRST, I DON'T WANT YOU DROPPING HER.

I'D CUT THE CORD. THEY GAVE ME A SHARP PAIR OF SECATEURS AND I REALLY HAD TO WORK TO SNIP THROUGH IT. IT WAS LIKE A THICK, BLOODY PIECE OF GARDEN HOSE.

I STARED DOWN AT CASSIE IN AWE. SHE WAS THE MOST DELICATE, BEAUTIFUL THING I'D EVER SEEN. HER TINY FINGERS HELD IN FISTS AND HER EYES NOT YET OPEN. SHE WAS LIKE A FLOWER ABOUT TO UNFURL.

I COULDN'T GET OVER HOW SMALL SHE WAS. HER LITTLE FINGERS WITH THE MINIATURE FLAKING HANGNAILS.

OUR LITTLE GIRL.

AS CASSIE TURNED FROM A ROYAL BLUE TO A RAW, ROSEY PINK I GLANCED OVER AT WHAT WAS HAPPENING WITH MEG.

WE'LL GIVE YOU A LOCAL TO NUMB THE AREA

WITH THE PLACENTA DEALT WITH THE MIDWIFE KNELT DOWN TO SEW UP MEG'S TEAR.

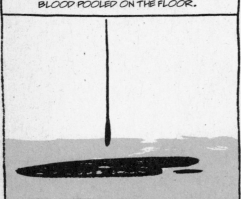

I LOOKED DOWN AT CASSIE AND SMILED, AND LOOKED OVER AT MEG AND WINCED. JOY AND ANXIETY MIXING AS MEG'S BLOOD POOLED ON THE FLOOR.

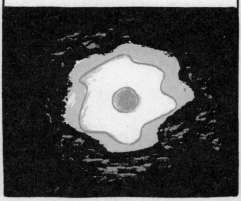

STARS ARE BORN OUT OF THE GAS AND DUST OF A SURROUNDING NEBULA. COSMIC NURSERIES GIVING BIRTH TO NEW SUNS.

GRAVITY DRAWS THE GAS AND DUST TOGETHER. AS THEY ARE PULLED IN, THE ATOMS COLLIDE AND HEAT UP.

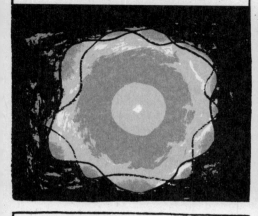

THIS HAPPENS UNTIL THE GAS BECOMES SO HOT THE HYDROGEN ATOMS NO LONGER BOUNCE OFF OF THE HELIUM, THAT'S WHEN THE TWO JOIN TOGETHER.

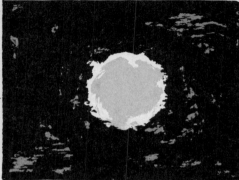

THE CORE OF THE STAR BURNS ITS NUCLEAR FUEL, GAS PRESSURE PUSHING OUT AGAINST GRAVITY PUSHING IN.

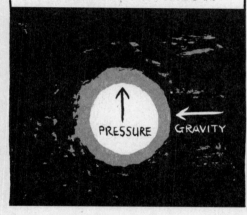

WHEN FUSION STOPS THE TEMPERATURE OF THE CORE FALLS AND THE GAS PRESSURE CAN NO LONGER RESIST THE FORCE OF GRAVITY PUSHING IT BACK IN.

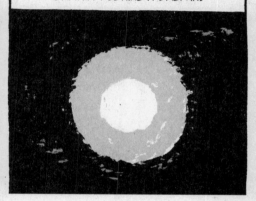

THE ATOMS ARE PUSHED INTO THE CORE MORE TIGHTLY CAUSING THE TEMPERATURE TO RISE AND NUCLEAR FUSION TO KICK OFF AGAIN, REPEATING THE CYCLE.

NUCLEAR FUSION MAKES THE STARS SHINE. ATOM BOMBS KEPT SPINNING BY GRAVITY LIKE BILLION YEAR CATHERINE WHEELS.

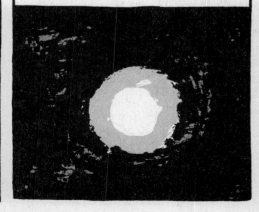

THE BIRTH HAD ONLY TAKEN A COUPLE OF HOURS. FROM THE STORIES WE'D HEARD WE'D EXPECTED A FULL DAY OF EXHAUSTING LABOUR FOLLOWED BY DRAMATIC BLOOD LOSS AND AN EMERGENCY C-SECTION.

WE SPENT HOURS SITTING AND GRINNING STUPIDLY AT EACH OTHER WHILE HOLDING CASSIE. WE WERE PROUD BEYOND BELIEF THAT WE'D CREATED THIS LITTLE PERSON. WE WERE THE LUCKIEST AND CLEVEREST COUPLE IN THE WORLD.

WE COULDN'T KEEP OUR EYES OFF HER. WE WERE ELATED AND GLOWING IN THOSE PRECIOUS FEW HOURS OF UNQUALIFIED JOY BEFORE THE WORRIES ABOUT BREAST FEEDING AND EXPRESSING MILK BEGAN.

EVEN THE FIRST POO WAS AN OBJECT OF WONDER, LIKE A THICK GREEN DOLLOP OF MASHED CABBAGE. NOW WE'D USE THE WORD POO INSTEAD OF SHIT. WE WERE PARENTS AND PARENTS TALK POO WITH DOCTORS.

WE'D KEEP THE LITTLE ANKLE LABELS THE HOSPITAL PUT ON CASSIE FOR POSTERITY, STICKING THEM IN A BOOK ALONGSIDE THE TAPE THEY USED TO MEASURE HER WHEN SHE WAS BORN.

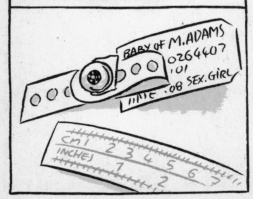

AND THEN AT EIGHT O'CLOCK IN THE EVENING ALL THE DADS WERE TURFED OUT OF THE STIFLING HOT MATERNITY WARD AND SENT HOME WITHOUT THEIR PARTNERS AND NEWBORN CHILDREN.

NIGHTY NIGHT, HON. I'LL SEE YOU IN THE MORNING.

MUMMY, CAN YOU SING ME ANOTHER SONG? PLEASE, OH PLEASE.

SORRY, DARLING, I HAVE A BIG PILE OF MARKING TO DO. IT'S TIME FOR SLEEP NOW.

CAN I GET YOU A CUPPA, HON?

PLEASE.

HAS SHE GONE DOWN OKAY?

IT'S A BIT QUIET.

DADDY!

I SPOKE TOO SOON.

ARE YOU IN YOUR BED YET, HON?

NO.

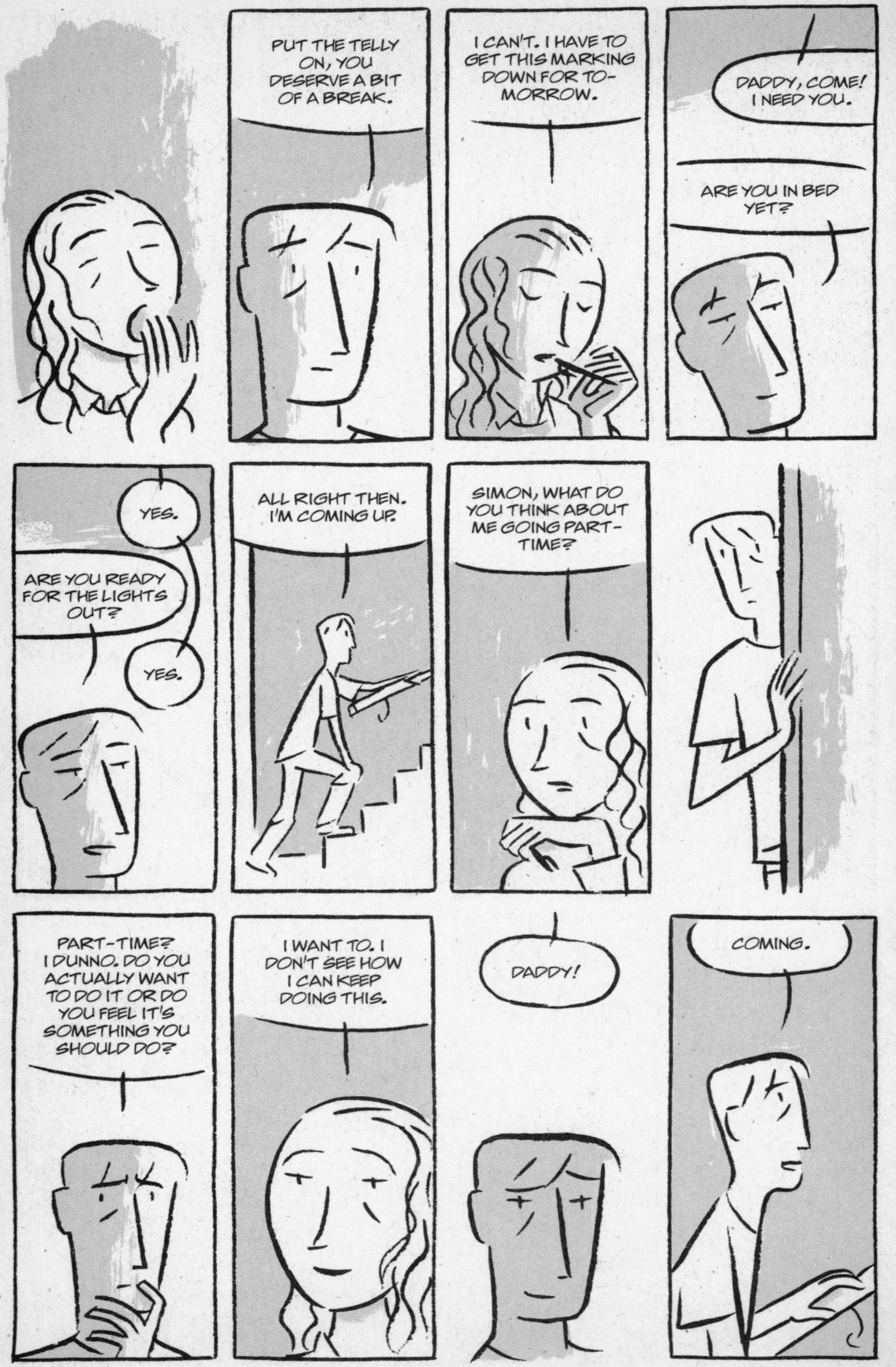
PUT THE TELLY ON, YOU DESERVE A BIT OF A BREAK.
I CAN'T. I HAVE TO GET THIS MARKING DOWN FOR TO-MORROW.
DADDY, COME! I NEED YOU.
ARE YOU IN BED YET?
YES.
ARE YOU READY FOR THE LIGHTS OUT?
YES.
ALL RIGHT THEN. I'M COMING UP.
SIMON, WHAT DO YOU THINK ABOUT ME GOING PART-TIME?
PART-TIME? I DUNNO. DO YOU ACTUALLY WANT TO DO IT OR DO YOU FEEL IT'S SOMETHING YOU SHOULD DO?
I WANT TO. I DON'T SEE HOW I CAN KEEP DOING THIS.
DADDY!
COMING.

DADDY, CAN YOU TELL ME A STORY?

WHICH STORY WOULD YOU LIKE?

CAN YOU TELL ME A STORY ABOUT MY BABY?

YOUR BABY? YOU MEAN WHEN YOU WERE BORN?

OKAY. ONCE UPON A TIME I WAS ASLEEP IN THE MIDDLE OF THE NIGHT AND...

...MUMMY WOKE UP WITH A TUMMY ACHE AND IT WAS YOU WANTING TO COME OUT.

SO HOW'S IT GOIN?

GOOD. I'M GETTING TO KNOW THE ROPES WITH THE SOFTWARE AND ALL THAT.

YEAH?

YEAH. HOW ABOUT YOU, HOW'S IT DOWN ON THE FLOOR?

SAME AS ALWAYS, REALLY. NOTHING EXCITING.

I GOT THE FALCON BY THE WAY.

YOU'VE FINALLY PUT THE STAR DESTROYER TOGETHER?

NOT YET. YOU SHOULD COME ROUND AND GIVE ME A HAND PUTTING IT TOGETHER.

YEAH.

WELL, I'D BEST GET BACK TO IT. SEE YA.

ME TOO. I'LL SEE YA.

little Stars

clari nursery

DADDY!

HAVE YOU HAD A NICE DAY TODAY? I CAN SEE YOU'VE BEEN PAINTING.

DADDY, HAVE YOU GOT A JUICE BOX?

A FLOWER.

A FLOWER, CAN I SEE?

WOW, HONEY, THAT'S BEAUTIFUL. WE'LL HAVE TO PUT THAT UP IN THE GALLERY WON'T WE?

IT'S A FLOWER FOR MUMMY.

FOUR-AND-A-HALF BILLION YEARS AGO THE EARTH WAS BORN, MOULDED FROM THE GAS AND DUST OF DEAD STARS.

BOUND AND SPUN BY GRAVITY, THE EARTH SITS IN THE GOLDILOCKS ZONE. TOO NEAR THE SUN AND WATER WOULD EVAPORATE, TOO FAR AND IT WOULD FREEZE.

TOO HOT

TOO COLD

THE SURFACE OF THE PLANET IS BOMBARDED BY METEORS AND ASTEROIDS UNTIL JUST UNDER FOUR MILLION YEARS AGO.

AN ATMOSPHERE OF METHANE, HYDROGEN, AMMONIA, NITROGEN, CARBON MONOXDE, AND DIOXIDE IS COOKED BY LIGHTNING WHILE THE SURFACE IS MARKED BY CONSTANT VOLCANISM.

ADD WATER TO THESE BASIC ELEMENTS AND YOU HAVE THE "NICE WARM POND," THE HOT SOUP, FROM WHICH LIFE MIGHT POSSIBLY BEGIN.

CARBON IS THE KEY ATOM IN THE PROCESS OF LIFE. IT'S HALF-FILLED STRUCTURE MEANS IT'S EAGER TO JOIN WITH OTHER ELEMENTS TO FORM MORE COMPLEX MOLECULES.

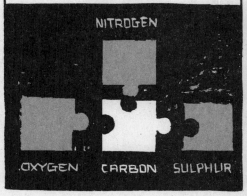

NITROGEN

OXYGEN   CARBON   SULPHUR

AFTER THE BOMBARDMENT PERIOD ENDS THE FIRST FOSSILS APPEAR, ROUGHLY THREE-AND-A-HALF-BILLION YEARS AGO. LIFE IS THOUGHT TO HAVE EVOLVED EVEN EARLIER THAN THAT.

JUST HALF A BILLION YEARS AFTER THE EARTH IS HOSTILE TO LIFE IT BEGINS. GIVEN HALF A CHANCE IT SEEMS LIFE WILL GRASP THE OPPORTUNITY, STARTING FROM A CELL WALL AND THE ABILITY TO SELF REPLICATE.

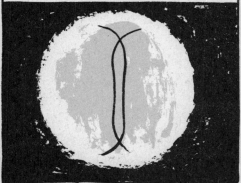

TAKE THAT CELL AND INTRODUCE IT TO DARWINIAN EVOLUTION. FAST FORWARD A COUPLE OF BILLION YEARS.

AND WE GET HERE, DOWN TO EARTH.

AND WHEN I LOOK UP THERE?

IF I TOOK A METEOR AND BROKE IT DOWN INTO IT'S COMPONENT PARTS, WHAT WOULD I FIND?

AMINO ACIDS AND A FEW OF THE BASES THAT ARE IN DNA. THE BASIC STUFF OF LIFE ON EARTH.

DADDY, LOOK, A CASTLE.

FROM DOWN HERE IT'S HUGE BEYOND COMPREHENSION. THE FURTHEST VISIBLE OBJECT IN THE UNIVERSE IS EIGHTEEN BILLION LIGHT YEARS AWAY.

I'LL BE THE PRINCESS AND YOU BE THE PRINCE. NO. YOU BE THE EVIL QUEEN.

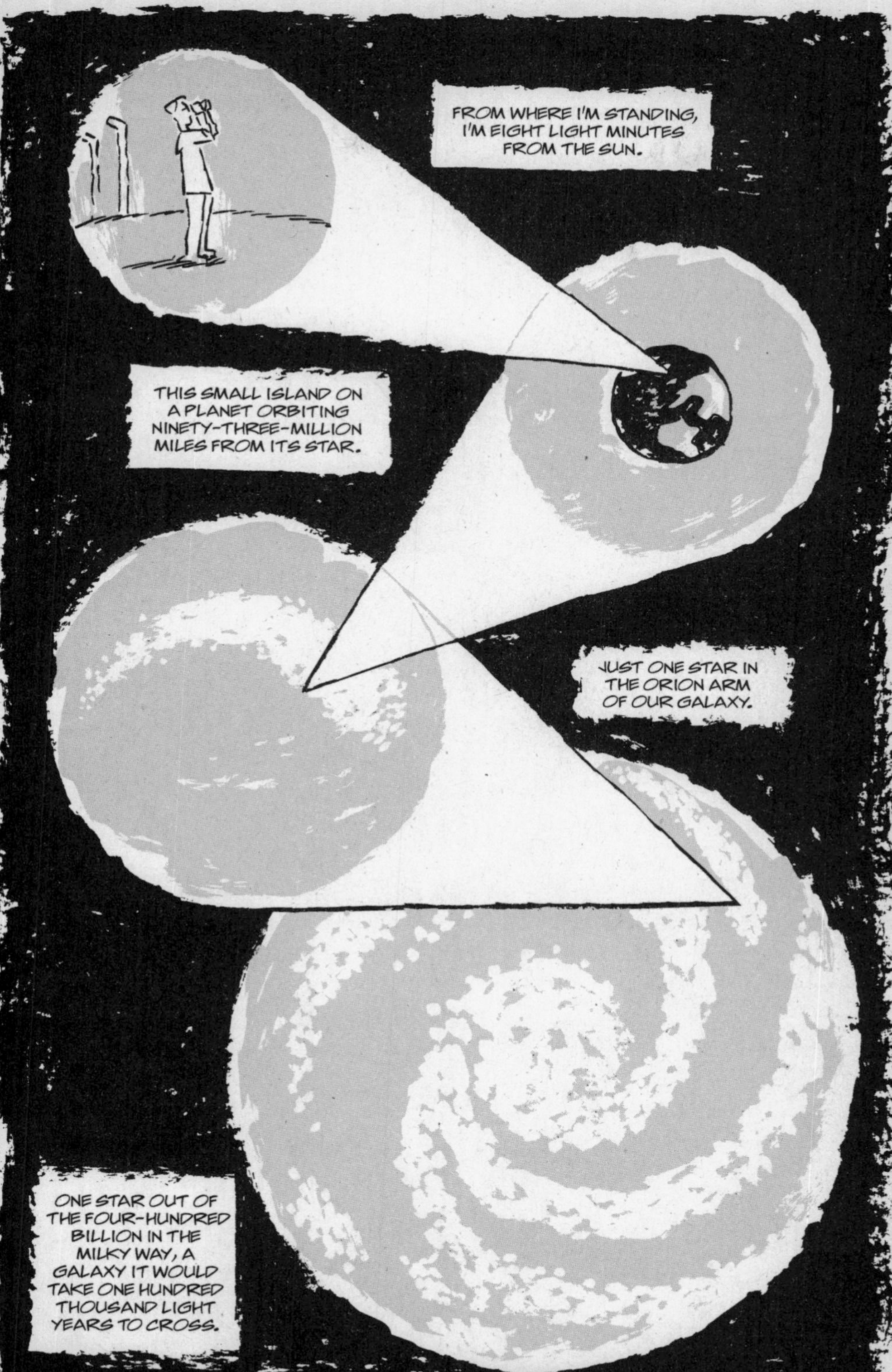

FROM WHERE I'M STANDING, I'M EIGHT LIGHT MINUTES FROM THE SUN.
THIS SMALL ISLAND ON A PLANET ORBITING NINETY-THREE-MILLION MILES FROM ITS STAR.
JUST ONE STAR IN THE ORION ARM OF OUR GALAXY.
ONE STAR OUT OF THE FOUR-HUNDRED BILLION IN THE MILKY WAY, A GALAXY IT WOULD TAKE ONE HUNDRED THOUSAND LIGHT YEARS TO CROSS.

THE MILKY WAY IS ONE POINT OF LIGHT IN A UNIVERSE OF BILLIONS.
AND WE'RE ALL MADE OF THE SAME BASIC ELEMENTS. THE STUFF UP THERE, ME, MEG, AND CASSIE.
WE'RE ALL WORDS MADE OF THE SAME NINETY-TWO LETTER ALPHABET.

chapter six

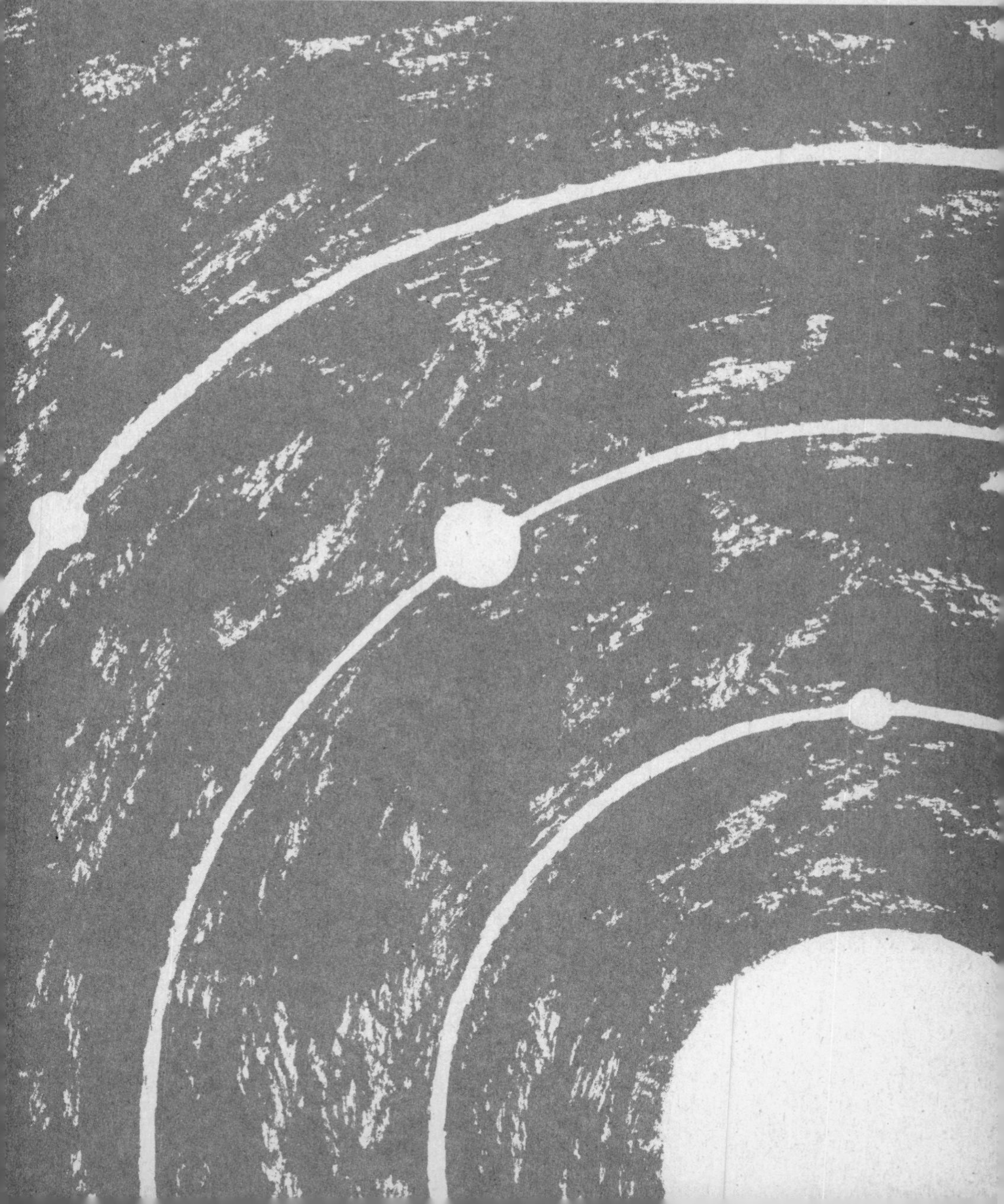

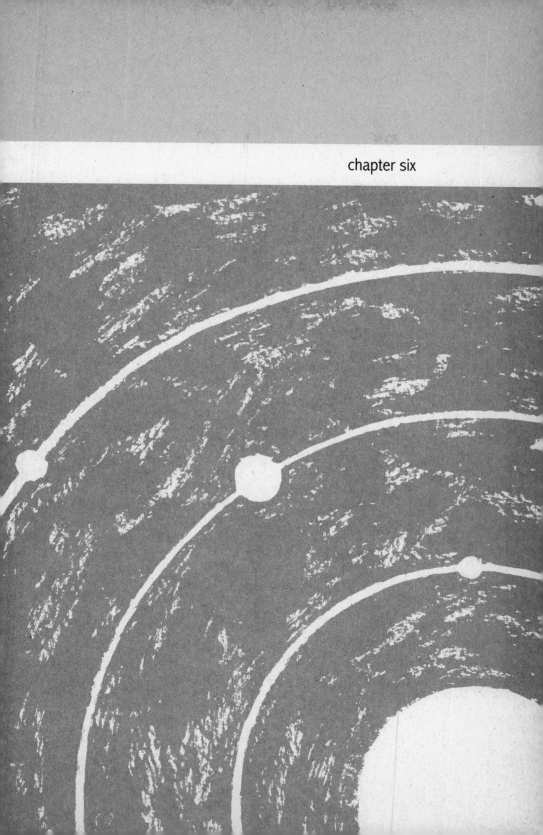

...THE END. WHAT A LOVELY STORY.

NOW, WHO DO YOU WANT TO TELL YOU STORIES, MUMMY OR DADDY?

MUMMY.

ALRIGHT THEN, HON, GIVE ME A HUG AND A KISS.

NO. I WANT DADDY.

≒ MWAH ≒

THE SEEING FROM OUR NEW BACK GARDEN IS LESS THAN PERFECT.

I STRUGGLE TO THE TOP OF OLD HILL WHERE IT'S FREEZING BUT THE SEEING IS BETTER.

SOMEWHERE DOWN THERE IS OUR HOUSE. OVER THERE SOMEWHERE IS JODRELL BANK AND AT THE TOP OF THAT HILL IS MOW COP.

THE MONUMENT IS JOHN WEDGWOOD'S TOMB. 1760-1839 A.D. LOCAL COLLIERY OWNER.

IT USED TO BE A LOT BIGGER BUT BLEW DOWN IN A STORM WHEN I WAS A KID.

IN ITS PRIME, BEFORE THE SEVENTIES, IT WAS WAY UP THERE.

AFTER THE STORM NO ONE BOTHERED TO PUT IT BACK TOGETHER AGAIN.

THEY JUST PUT THE TOP BACK ON THE PLINTH AND LEFT IT AT THAT.

A QUARTER OF WHAT IT USED TO BE.

THERE'S ALSO THIS OTHER THING. A TRIG POINT.

A BIG CONCRETE PILLAR USED AS A REFERENCE POINT TO MAP BRITAIN. THE ORDNANCE SURVEY MAPS ARE BASED ON TRIG POINT MEASUREMENTS.

USING THEIR COORDINATES YOU CAN FIND OUT PRECISELY WHERE YOU'RE STANDING WITHIN THE NATIONAL GRID.

"S2676 CONDITION GOOD. WAYPOINT TP 1357. N 53 DEGRESS, W 002 DEGREES. AN AVERAGE RATING OF 5 OUT OF 10."

I AM HERE.

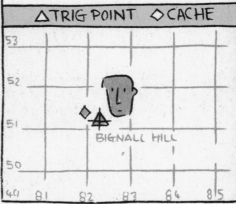

A CACHE IS A REFERENCE TO GEOCACHING. BASICALLY IT'S TREASURE HUNTING FOR GPS AND MAP NERDS.

THE ONE STASHED NEAR THE MONUMENT IS DOWNHILL TO THE WEST. IT'D BE AN AWFUL LOT EASIER TO FIND IF I COULD READ A MAP.

THIS IS ONLY A TWO OUT OF FIVE STAR DIFFICULTY. I END UP RUMMAGING AROUND IN THE DARK FOR AGES.

GOT YA!

TREASURE.

THE ETTIQUTTE IS TO TAKE ONE ITEM AND REPLACE IT WITH ANOTHER. SIGN IN THE LOG BOOK AND TAKE A PICTURE OF YOURSELF.

NO, I'LL COME BACK AND DO IT ANOTHER TIME.

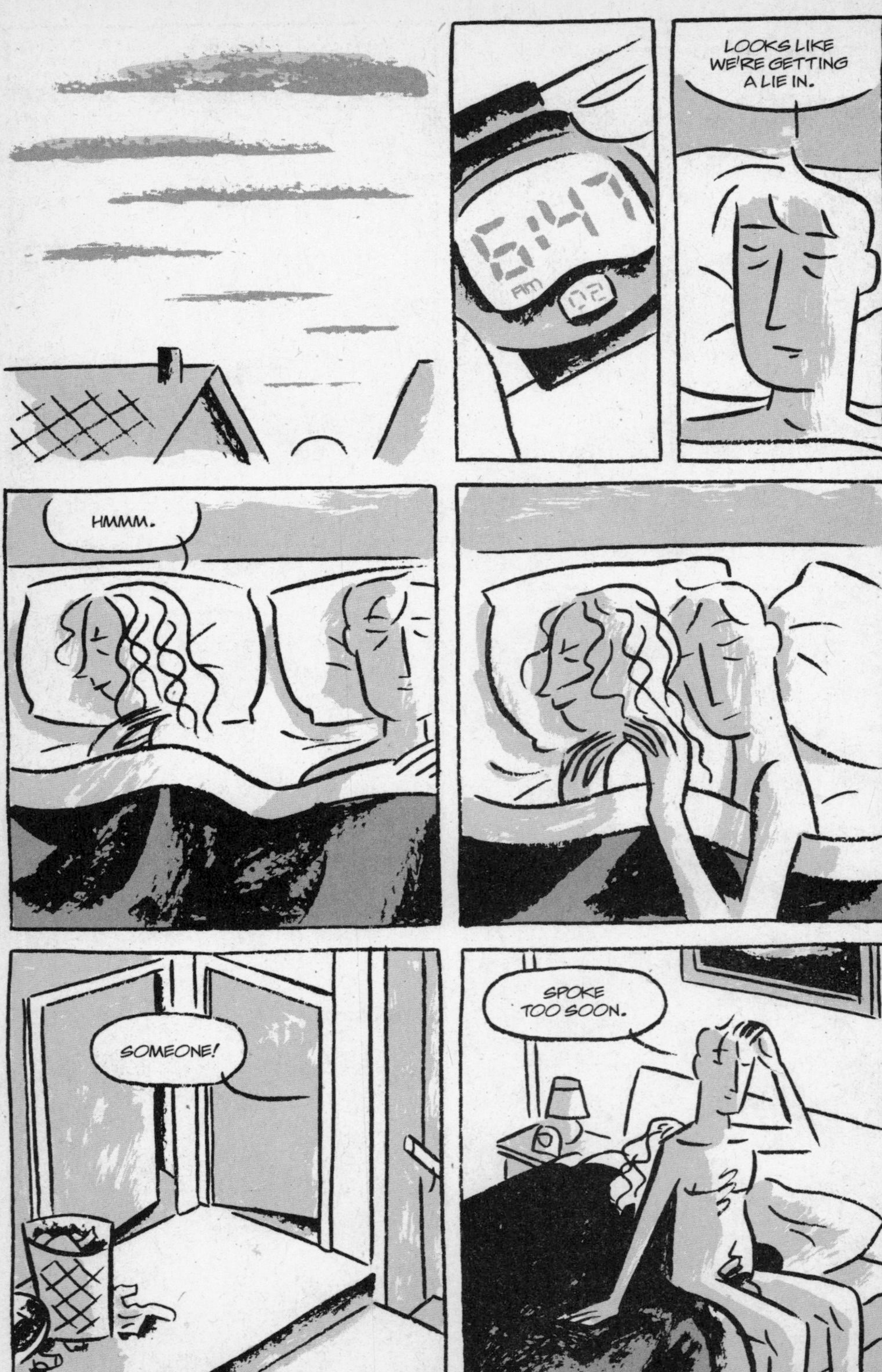
6:47
AM
02
LOOKS LIKE WE'RE GETTING A LIE IN.
HMMM.
SOMEONE!
SPOKE TOO SOON.

IT STARTED WITH A SHADOW ON THE LUNG. A BLACK HOLE IN THE X-RAY.

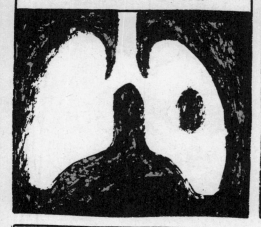

A HEALTHY CELL DOUBLES ITSELF FIFTY OR SIXTY TIMES AND THEN STOPS. CANCER CELLS ARE IMMORTAL, THEY CAN'T STOP REPRODUCING.

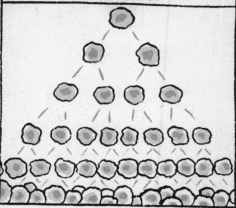

THE DIAGNOSIS WAS TERMINAL, "FORMING AN END". THE BLACK CIRCLE AT THE END OF THE VERY LAST SENTENCE.

I STAYED UP WITH GRANDAD IN THE SPARE ROOM. MUM AND DAD WERE EXHAUSTED, THEY HADN'T HAD A PROPER NIGHTS SLEEP FOR MONTHS. HIS DYING IS FRIGHTENINGLY QUICK AND PAINFULLY SLOW.

BY NOW THE LUNG TISSUE WAS SO DAMAGED THAT NOT ENOUGH AIR WAS GETTING TO HIS BRAIN. EVERY BREATH WAS A RAGGED STRUGGLE.

SUSAN.

SUSAN.

IT WASN'T OKAY. THERE WAS NOTHING I COULD DO BUT SIT. WHEN THE DOCTOR HAD BEEN CALLED AGAIN ALL HE COULD SUGGEST WAS AN ASPIRIN.

COME HERE.

SUSAN.

IT'S OKAY, GRANDAD, IT'S OKAY.

AN ASPIRIN? EVEN OUR GALLOWS HUMOUR FAILED US AT THAT. IT WAS ABSURD AND TRAGIC AND MUNDANE AND HEARTBREAKING ALL AT THE SAME TIME.

SUSAN. COME HERE.

HE WASN'T REALLY WITH US ANYMORE, HE WAS LIVING IN MEMORY CALLING MY MUM'S NAME OVER AND OVER.

IT'S OKAY, GRANDAD. IT'S OKAY.

HE WASN'T CALLING HER IN THE PRESENT BUT IN HIS MEMORY. I HOPED IT WAS A GOOD MEMORY...

COME HERE.

SUSAN.

...BECAUSE IT WAS HIS LAST.

SUSAN.

COME HERE.

CASSIE, COME HERE.

IT'S HALF SEVEN IN THE MORNING ON A WET AUTUMN WEEKEND IN BLACKPOOL.

WHAT?

WE'VE COME TO SEE THE LIGHTS.

LOOK. A STAR FISH.

WHERE?

OOOH.

AMAZING, ISN'T IT?

I'LL FEED IT.

WELL, OKAY, BUT I DON'T THINK IT'LL EAT ANYTHING.

HE'S HUNGRY.

HE'S DEAD.

DADDY, GO OVER THERE AND SCARE OFF THAT BIT WHEN IT COMES.

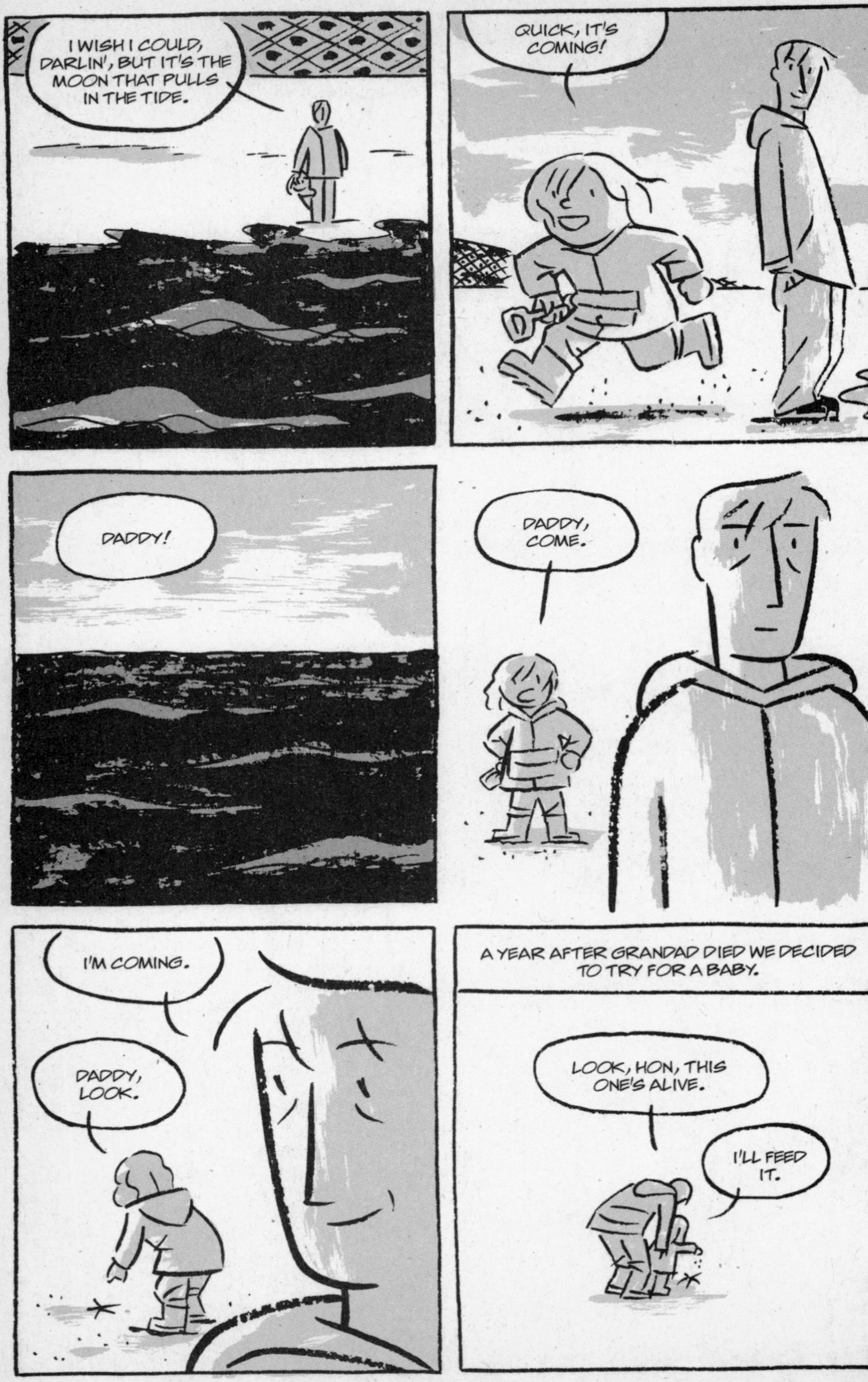

I WISH I COULD, DARLIN', BUT IT'S THE MOON THAT PULLS IN THE TIDE.
QUICK, IT'S COMING!
DADDY!
DADDY, COME.
I'M COMING.
DADDY, LOOK.
A YEAR AFTER GRANDAD DIED WE DECIDED TO TRY FOR A BABY.
LOOK, HON, THIS ONE'S ALIVE.
I'LL FEED IT.

MEG'S CUT BACK ON HER HOURS AND SEEMS TO BE A BIT LESS STRESSED.

WE'RE STILL RELAYING BUT THE CHANGE-OVERS ARE LESS FRANTIC AND MORE RELAXED.

TODAY IS CASSIES FIRST DAY AT SCHOOL.

SHE LOOKS SO GROWN UP IN HER UNIFORM IT'S TERRIFYING.

IT'S HARD TO BELIEVE THE BABY DAYS ARE ALREADY GONE.

I KNOW HOW TO BOTTLE FEED A BABY, CHANGE A NAPPY AND RECOGNISE THE SYMPTOMS OF A TEMPERATURE.

I CAN PREDICT AN APPROACHING TANTRUM AND KNOW FROM EXPERIENCE THAT THOSE LITTLE TEETHING BISCUITS ARE RUBBISH.

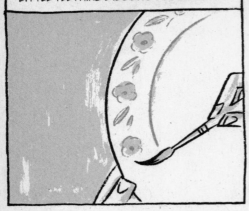

I CAN RISK ASSES A ROOM FOR SHARP CORNERS, BREAKABLES AND EXPOSED PLUG HOLES IN THREE SECONDS FLAT.

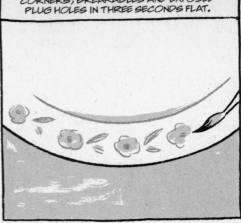

SKILLS THAT ARE ALREADY OBSOLETE, CONSIGNED TO THE PAST.

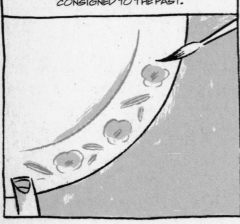

WE'RE PUSHED FORWARD BY THE ARROW OF TIME, CONSTANTLY BUMBLING OUR WAY INTO NEW TERRITORY.

JUST AS WE GET TO GRIPS WITH ONE SET OF PROBLEMS NEW ONES POP UP OUT OF NOWHERE.

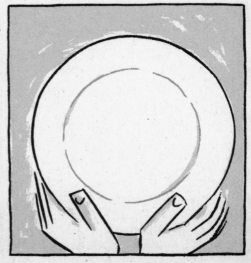

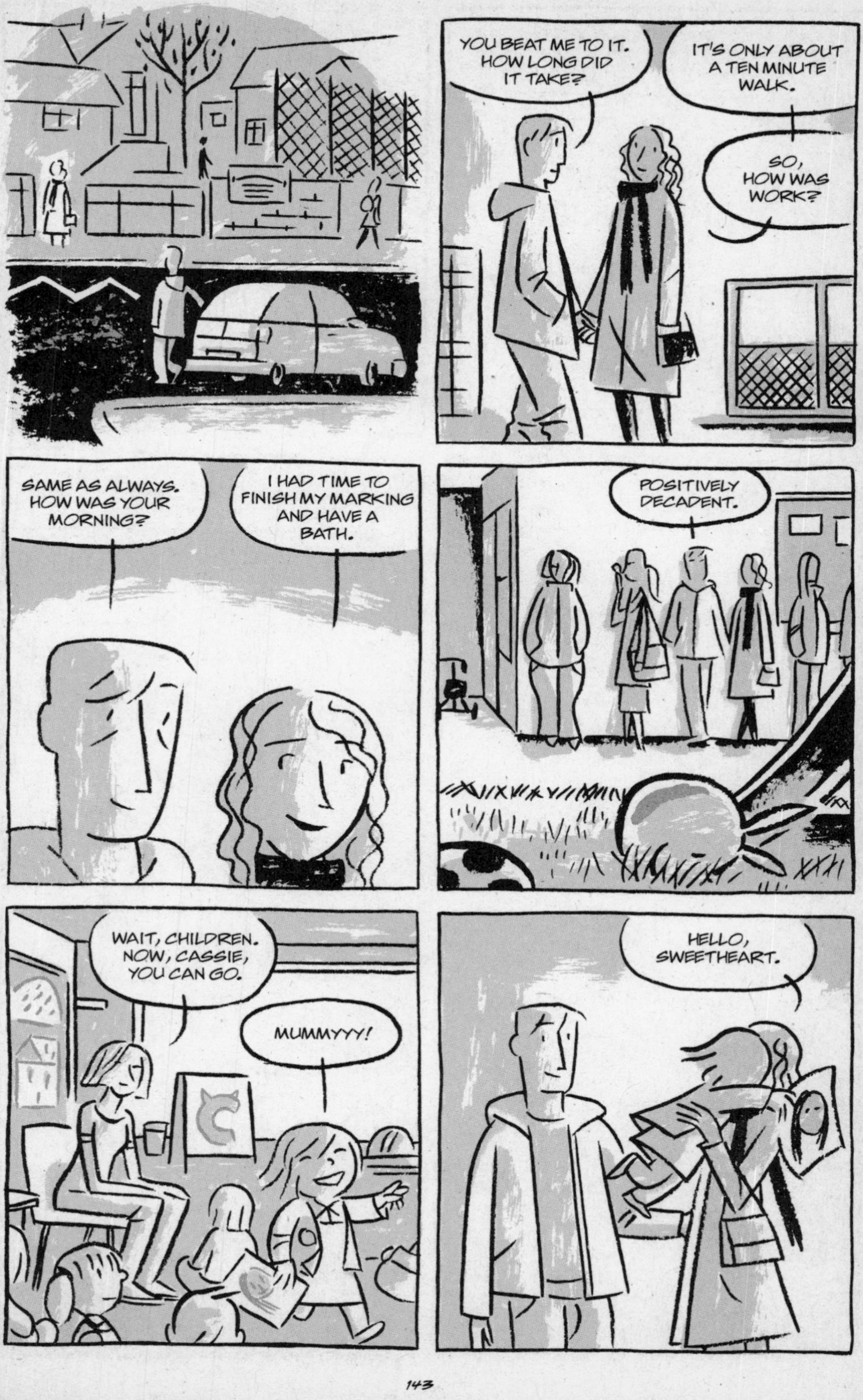
YOU BEAT ME TO IT. HOW LONG DID IT TAKE?
IT'S ONLY ABOUT A TEN MINUTE WALK.
SO, HOW WAS WORK?
SAME AS ALWAYS. HOW WAS YOUR MORNING?
I HAD TIME TO FINISH MY MARKING AND HAVE A BATH.
POSITIVELY DECADENT.
WAIT, CHILDREN. NOW, CASSIE, YOU CAN GO.
MUMMYYY!
HELLO, SWEETHEART.

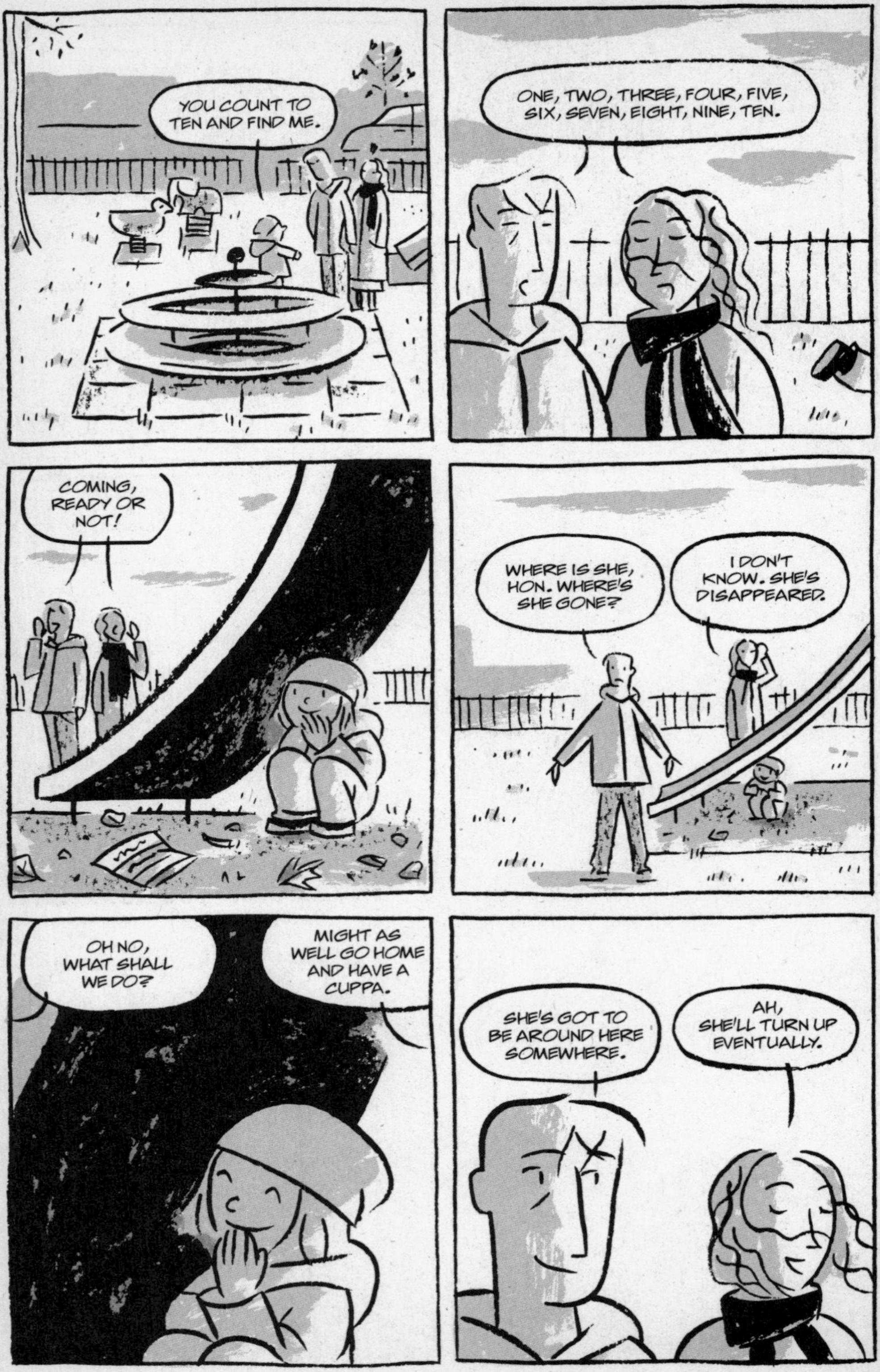
YOU COUNT TO TEN AND FIND ME.
ONE, TWO, THREE, FOUR, FIVE, SIX, SEVEN, EIGHT, NINE, TEN.
COMING, READY OR NOT!
WHERE IS SHE, HON. WHERE'S SHE GONE?
I DON'T KNOW. SHE'S DISAPPEARED.
OH NO, WHAT SHALL WE DO?
MIGHT AS WELL GO HOME AND HAVE A CUPPA.
SHE'S GOT TO BE AROUND HERE SOMEWHERE.
AH, SHE'LL TURN UP EVENTUALLY.

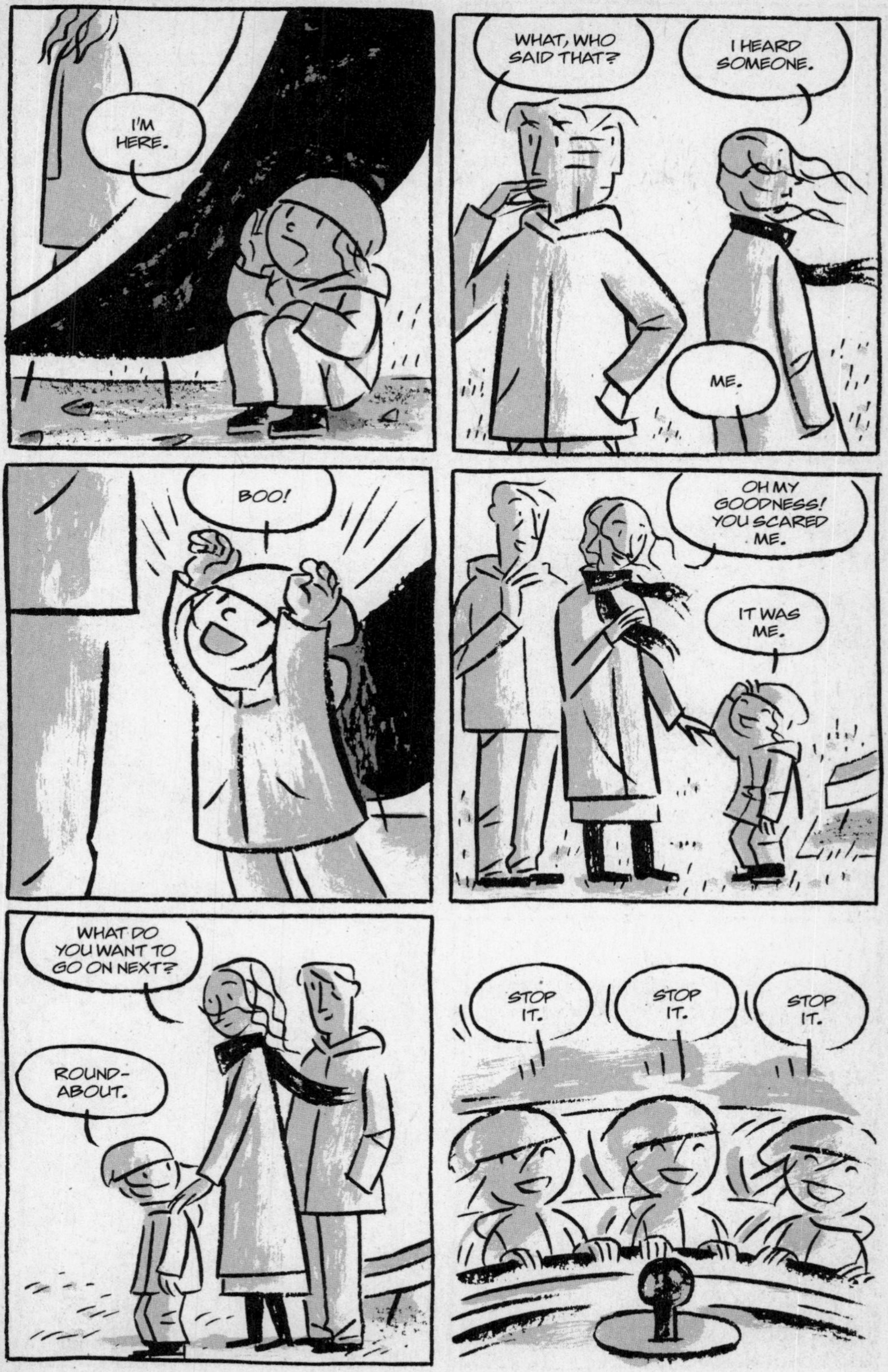
I'M HERE.
WHAT, WHO SAID THAT?
I HEARD SOMEONE.
ME.
BOO!
OH MY GOODNESS! YOU SCARED ME.
IT WAS ME.
WHAT DO YOU WANT TO GO ON NEXT?
ROUND-ABOUT.
STOP IT.
STOP IT.
STOP IT.

WE'RE FOREVER PLAYING CATCH UP.

CONSTANTLY LEARNING ON THE JOB.

CLINGING TO THE COAT TAILS OF OUR LITTLE GIRL.

OUR BABY WHO'S GROWING AWAY FROM US AT SEVEN MILES A SECOND.

WHEN PEOPLE ASK "WHAT IS IT LIKE TO BE A DAD" I USUALLY SHRUG AND TELL THEM IT'S GOOD.

IT'S A MEANINGLESS ANSWER BUT IT GETS ME OUT OF TRYING TO DESCRIBE WHAT IT REALLY MEANS TO ME.

I'M NOT A BETTER PERSON BECAUSE I'M A FATHER. I'M NOT SUDDENLY FULL OF WISDOM AND INNER CONTENTMENT.

IN FACT I'M LEFT PONDERING MORE UNANSWERED QUESTIONS THAN EVER.

DADDY.

IF ANYTHING FATHERHOOD HAS MADE ME MORE OF A PERSON.

COMING, HON.

I'M HAPPIER THAN I'VE EVER BEEN, AND SADDER.

I'M MORE AWARE OF THE MOMENT AND MORE ANXIOUS FOR THE FUTURE. I'M ANGRIER AND MORE CONTENT.

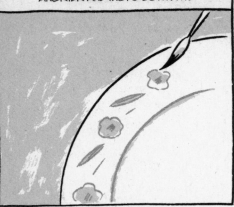

I'M MORE PATIENT AND MORE FRUSTRATED, MUCH MORE MENTALLY STIMULATED AND A LOT MORE BORED.

IT'S A VERY LONG SHOPPING LIST OF CONTRADICTORY EMOTIONS OFTEN EXPERIENCED SIMULATNEOUSLY.

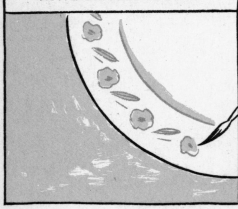

I'M A PRINCE AND STEPMOTHER, KING AND STEPSISTER, HORSEY AND FAIRY GOD-MOTHER.

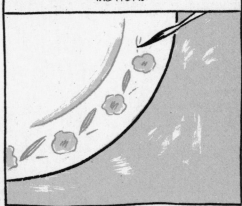

I'M A SLOB AND CHAUFFEUR, TEACHER AND PUPIL, NURSE AND SERGEANT MAJOR.

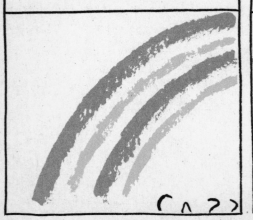

DISPENSER OF HUGS, SYMPATHY, ULTIMATUMS, AND, MORAL GUIDANCE. THE MANNERS POLICE AND THE HYGIENIST.

I'M A CHEMIST AND CASH DISPENSER.

DANCER AND TICKLER. MONSTER.

BUM WIPER AND BATHER.
GRUMP AND STORYTELLER.

TYRANT, PUSHOVER, BUILDER, AND
CLEANING LADY.

HUSBAND AND SON.

DAD.

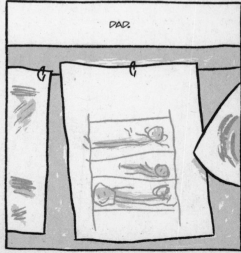

149

AND WHEN WE GET TO THE TOP WE NEED TO GO WEST.

WHERE'S WEST?

I THINK IT'S DOWN THERE SOMEWHERE.

HAVE YOU TWO FOUND ANY TREASURE YET?

NO, DADDY.

WELL LOOK OVER HERE. WHAT'S THIS?

IS IT THE TREASURE?

LOOK, MUMMY, TREASURE.

NOW WE NEED TO TAKE A PICTURE WITH THE CAMERA.

AND SO WE JOIN THE LIST OF THOSE WHO CAME BEFORE US. WINNIE BEE, DOVEY, AND DOMINO.

SUBWAY, DAVIES AND THE BOYS, TROGGY AND JEAN, MISTY, BEADY AND TREV.

HOOTY, QUAVER, LIBBY L AND JUNE C.

IS EVERYONE READY?

SAY CHEESE.

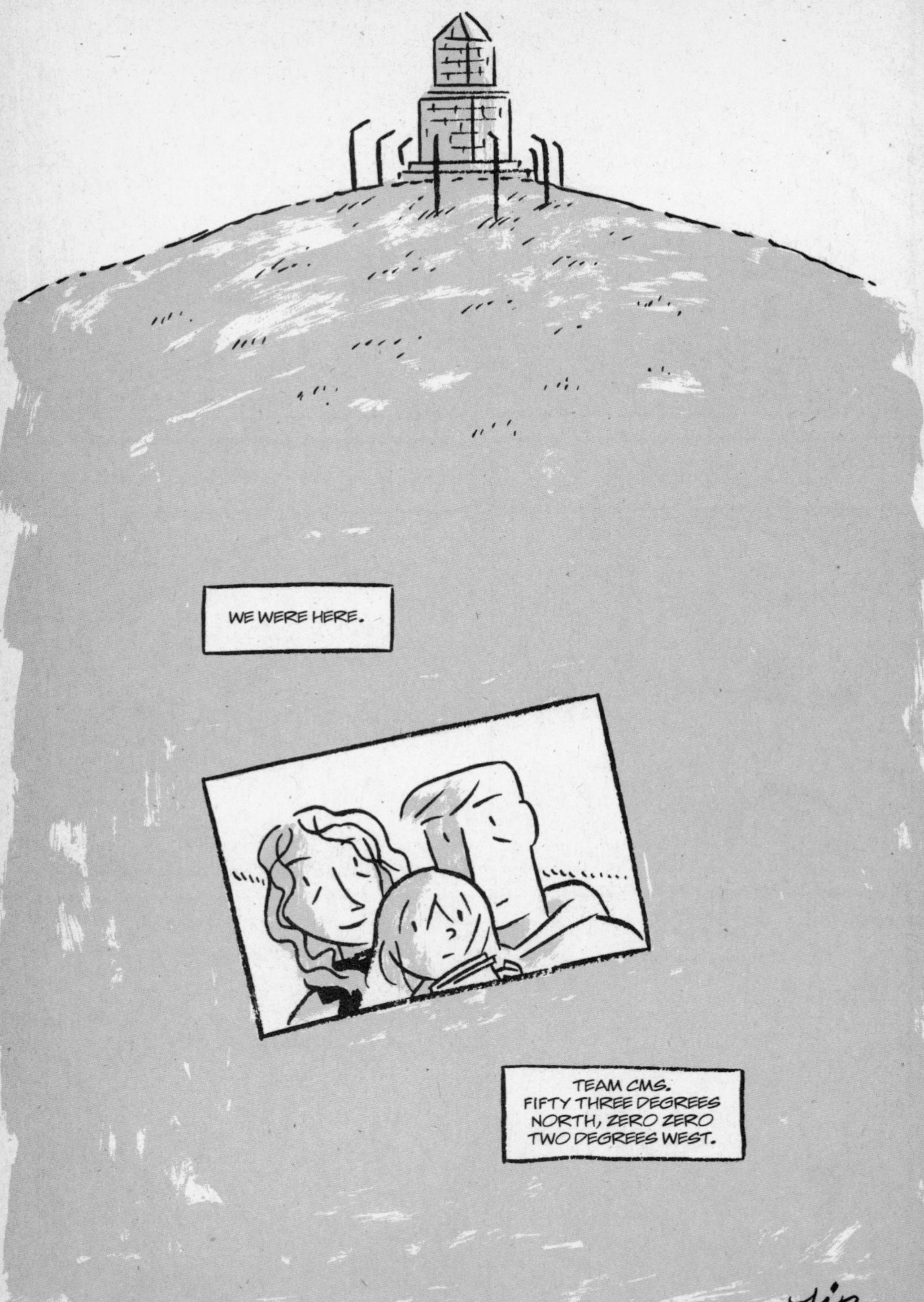
WE WERE HERE.
TEAM CMS.
FIFTY THREE DEGREES
NORTH, ZERO ZERO
TWO DEGREES WEST.
Jin

extras

little star

little Star

little star

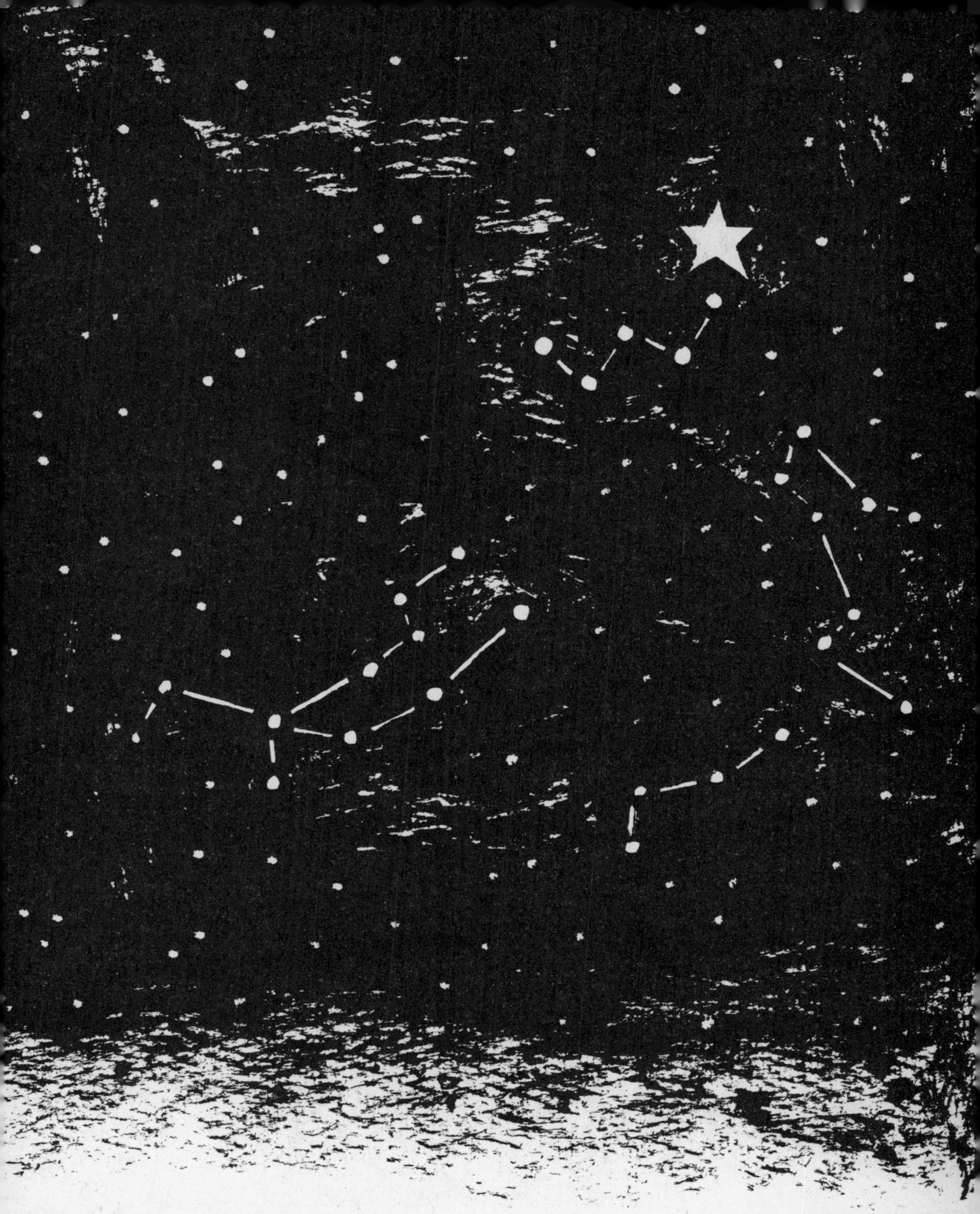

little star

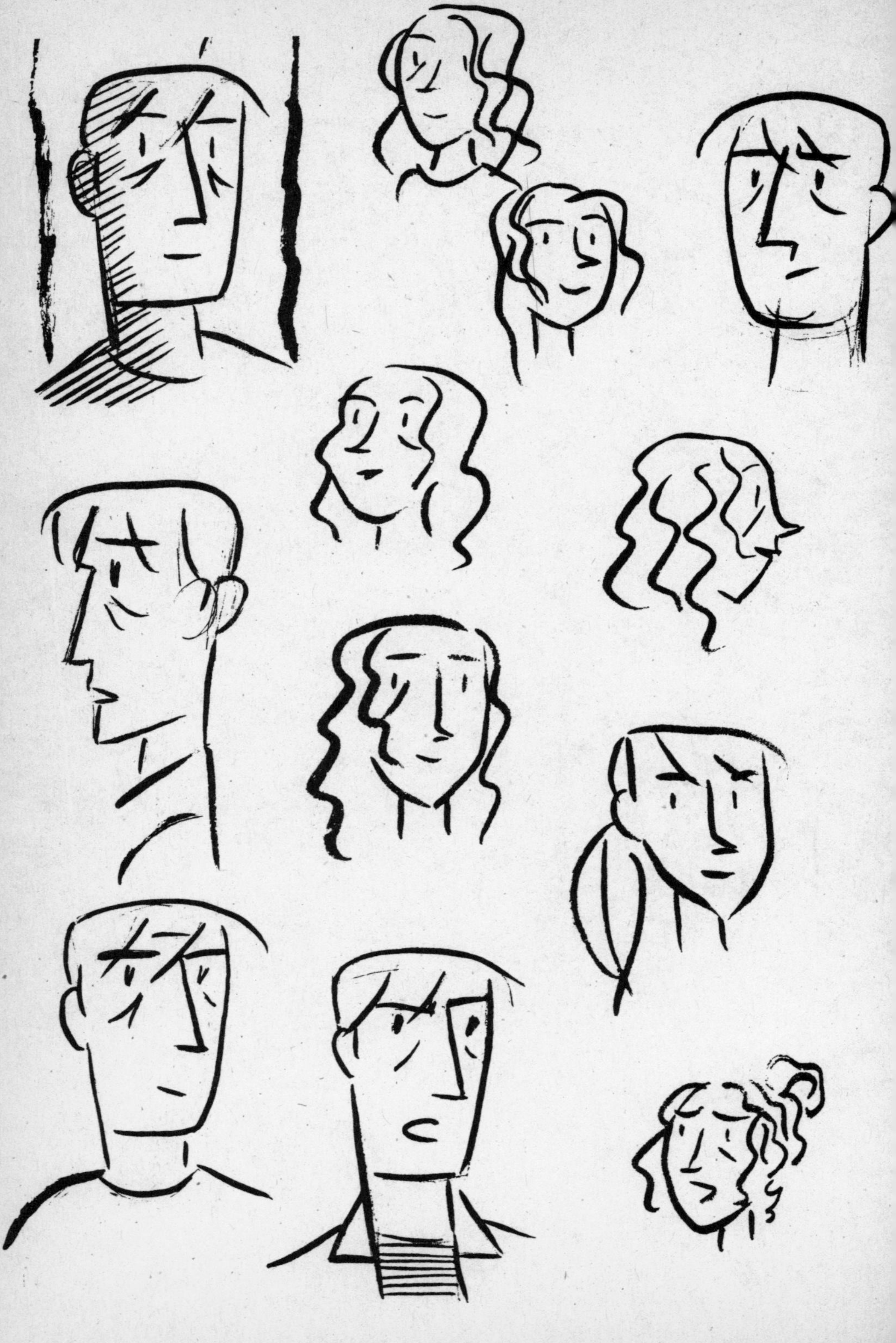

10/04

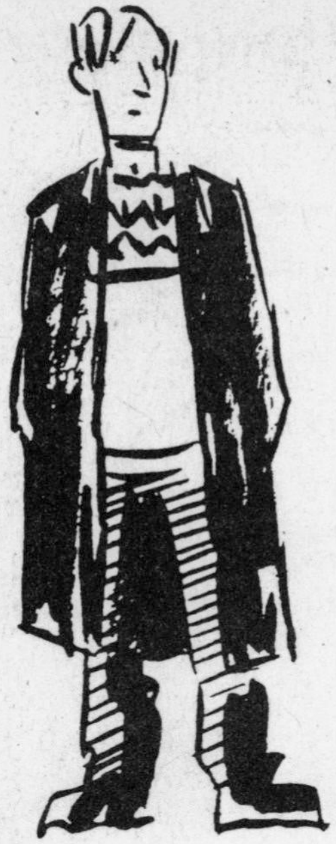

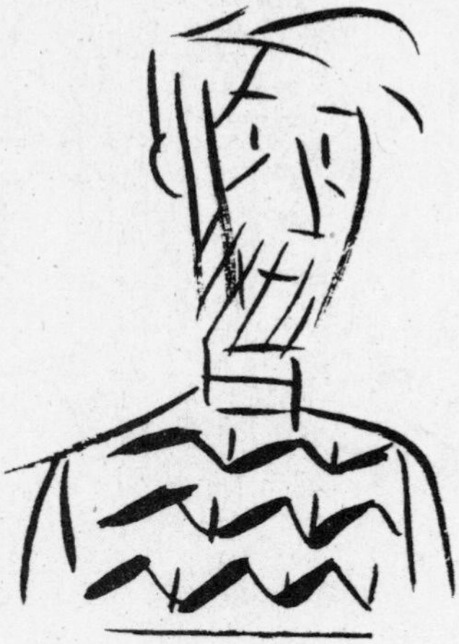

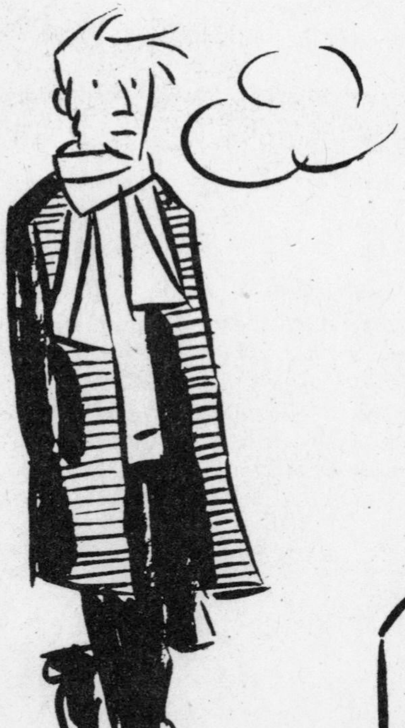

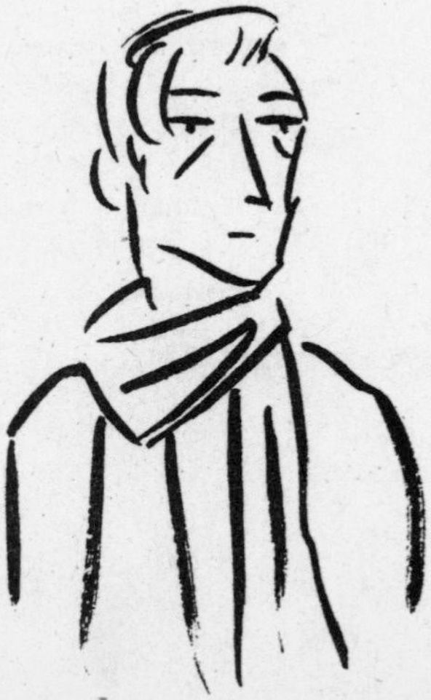

Andi Watson is the creator of *Skeleton Key, Geisha, Dumped, Slow News Day, and Love Fights*. He's also scripted various licensed comics, including *Buffy the Vampire Slayer*, and done work for the big superhero publishers, Marvel and DC. In 2000, the collected version of *Geisha* was nominated for an Eisner Award, and the following year his comic book *Breakfast After Noon* was nominated as Best Limited Series. He is currently writing *Paris* for artist Simon Gane and Slave Labor Graphics and developing future comics projects from his home in rural England, where he lives with his lovely wife and even lovelier daughter.

Other books from Andi Watson & Oni Press...

BREAKFAST AFTER NOON
208 pages, black-and-white interiors
$19.95 US
ISBN: 1-929998-14-7

THE COMPLETE GEISHA™
152 pages, black-and-white interiors
$15.95 US
ISBN: 1-929998-51-1

DUMPED™
56 pages, black-and-white interiors
$5.95 US
ISBN: 1-929998-41-4

LOVE FIGHTS™ vol. 1
168 pages, black-and-white interiors
$14.95 US
ISBN: 1-929998-87-2

LOVE FIGHTS™ vol. 2
168 pages, black-and-white interiors
$14.95 US
ISBN: 1-929998-98-2

CUT MY HAIR™
by Jamie S. Rich
w/Chynna Clugston-Major, Scott Morse, Andi Watson, &
Judd Winick
236 pages, black-and-white text with illustrations
$15.95 US
ISBN: 0-9700387-0-4

HOPELESS SAVAGES, vol. 2: GROUND ZERO™
By Jen Van Meter & Bryan O'Malley
w/ Chynna Clugston-Major, Christine Norrie, & Andi
Watson
128 pages, black-and-white interiors
$11.95 US
ISBN: 1-929998-52-X

The Aid Chain
Coercion and Commitment in Development NGOs

Praise for *The Aid Chain*

'...a scholarly and readable guide...this work will be a classic.'
Tony Benn

'This disturbing and dramatically important book has been crying out to be written. It is a stark revelation of uncomfortable realities from which we often try to hide...
Anyone working in an aid organisation who is serious about achieving the MDGs has to read this book, and to act on its lessons.'
Robert Chambers, Institute of Development Studies, UK

'...a very important resource that will influence all the relevant actors to reflect upon the issues and questions discussed.'
Algresia Akwi Ogojo

'...honest case studies and a reflexive analysis... This is a must-read for everyone interested in civil society, gender and aid-related development and for anyone curious about the paradox of persistent poverty in "aidland".'
Prof. Barbara Harriss-White, Director of Queen Elizabeth House, University of Oxford's International Development Department

'...timely and well researched.'
Kumi Naidoo, CIVICUS: World Alliance for Citizen Participation, South Africa

The Aid Chain
Coercion and Commitment in Development NGOs

Tina Wallace
with
Lisa Bornstein and Jennifer Chapman

PRACTICAL ACTION
Publishing

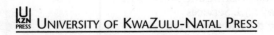 UNIVERSITY OF KWAZULU-NATAL PRESS

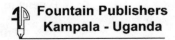
Fountain Publishers
Kampala - Uganda

Intermediate Technology Publications Ltd
trading as Practical Action Publishing
Schumacher Centre for Technology and Development
Bourton on Dunsmore, Rugby,
Warwickshire CV23 9QZ, UK
www.practicalactionpublishing.org

© Intermediate Technology Publications Ltd, 2006

This edition published in 2007

ISBN 978 1 85339 626 7

Published in South Africa, Namibia, Botswana, Lesotho, and Swaziland by
University of KwaZulu-Natal Press, Private Bag X01, Scottsville 3209,
South Africa
www.ukznpress.co.za
ISBN 978 1 86914 118 9

Published in Uganda, Kenya, Tanzania and Rwanda by Fountain Publishers,
PO Box 488, Kampala, Uganda
www.fountainpublishers.co.ug
ISBN 978 9970 02 671 5

A catalogue record for this book is available from the British Library.

The contributors have asserted their rights under the Copyright Designs and
Patents Act 1988 to be identified as authors of their respective contributions.

Since 1974, Practical Action Publishing has published and disseminated
books and information in support of international development work
throughout the world. Practical Action Publishing (formerly ITDG
Publishing) is a trading name of Intermediate Technology Publications Ltd
(Company Reg. No. 1159018), the wholly owned publishing company of
Intermediate Technology Development Group Ltd (working name Practical
Action). Practical Action Publishing trades only in support of its parent
charity objectives and any profits are covenanted back to Practical Action
(Charity Reg. No. 247257, Group VAT Registration No. 880 9924 76).

Index preparation: Indexing Specialists (UK) Ltd
Typeset in Trade Gothic and Stone Serif
by S.J.I. Services
Printed by Replika Press

Contents

Preface   ix
Acknowledgements   xi
Figure, tables and boxes   xiv
About the authors   xv
Acronyms   xvii

1   **Introduction**   1
    Coercion and compliance   4
    Commitment   5
    The research   7
    The research methodology   9
    Structure of the book   17

2. **The changing context for the work of development NGOs**   19
    Introduction   19
    The new funding mechanisms   21
    The challenges of the new aid architecture   23
    Contrasting definitions of development: what is the project?   26
    Concluding comment   28

3. **The management of development**   31
    Introduction   31
    NGOs and the packaging of aid   32
    The language and practice of rational management   34
    Given the flaws, why has this approach dominated?   37
    Those with power can promote the approaches they prefer   38
    The hold of logframe analysis   39
    Participatory planning and human development   40
    The conceptual basis of participatory planning within donor frameworks 43
    Other approaches to planning and implementation exist   44
    The missing elements   45
    Concluding comment   47

4. **The major UK donors and the flow of aid through the NGO sector**   49
    Introduction   49
    The donor context: funding flows 2000–3   51
    DFID   52

Who can access this funding?   53
Changing grant models and conditions   56
Local funding   60
Contracts   60
The European Union   61
Medium-sized UK donors: Community Fund and Comic Relief   63
Small UK donors: trusts and foundations   68
UK NGOs as aid recipients   69

5. **The NGO context in Uganda and South Africa**   **73**
    Uganda   73
    NGOs in Uganda   76
    South Africa   82
    Development challenges in South Africa   84
    Conclusion   89

6. **Normative conditions: rational management of the aid chain**   **91**
    Project cycle management tools in the UK   92
    Some different trends   94
    Project cycle management tools in South Africa   95
    Project cycle management in Uganda   100
    Comparative perspectives on the benefits of the logframe   104
    Conclusion   106

7. **The ties that bind**   **109**
    Questioning the status quo as heresy   109
    The ties that bind   111
    Donor contracts deepening the trends   120
    Loosening the ties   122
    Conclusion   128

8. **Relationships: partnerships, power and participation**   **129**
    Introduction   129
    The experiences of a faith-based organization in relating to
    European donors   130
    Donors encouraging alliances and networking: relationships in practice 133
    Trying to build different, sustainable relations with local NGOs   140
    Conclusion   144

9. **Chains of influence in South Africa**   **147**
    South African NGOs as partners: from negotiation to vulnerability   148
    NGOs and gender mainstreaming: power, tools and meanings   150
    Beyond negotiation: training and organizational development
    NGOs in South Africa   155
    Conclusions   157

10. **Listening to the past and building a new future** **161**

Other research supports our findings, which are relevant globally 161

The key findings concerning the policies and procedures of the aid chain 161

The questions raised by these findings 168

But isn't this all very depressing? 173

Alternative ways of working 176

Appendix **179**

Organisations interviewed for the mid-level survey of
NGO-donor relations in South Africa and Uganda
(see Figure 1.2 in chapter 1) that were not in the original
aid chain sample established in the UK (see Table 1.1 in chapter 1). 179

References **181**

Websites 189

Index **191**

Preface

This book is about the way in which non-governmental organizations have been influenced by their close links with governments and business, upon which they are increasingly dependent for funds to sustain their work.

The subject is of fundamental importance to the campaign to end world poverty and for that reason merits attention, despite the complexity of some of the issues involved.

It is a very well-researched book documenting in detail the way in which ideas of management and accounting that are taken for granted in the western world have come to be imposed on the work of NGOs whose strength has always lain in the independence that characterizes voluntary organizations.

This independence has given NGOs a capacity to work effectively with local organizations in the developing world, many of which are themselves voluntary, working within the culture and traditions that they know and to that extent free from the cult of modern management, tied to free market thinking which, in the west, we now take for granted, however much we may dislike it.

Neo-liberalism, despite its claim to be serving the consumer is, in practice, a top-down power system that dictates policies from above, whereas developing countries see their role as part of a bottom-up system that identifies the problems locally and needs resources to meet those needs.

In short, this book clarifies the basic conflict of interest that divides the desire for democracy and democratic planning from the demands for compliance with the diktats laid down by the IMF, WTO, World Bank and multi-national corporations, none of which have any electoral legitimacy.

In that sense we can see a parallel with the pressures put upon elected governments all over the world to obey rules imposed on them by the same international forces that set strict limits to their own freedom to act in accordance with their mandate from their own people and which influence – and to some extent control – the policy adopted by the EU and the British Government.

The only exception to this rigid pattern of world government is now to be found in Latin America, where rapid strides towards development are planned and are taking place entirely free of these ideological restraints.

Perhaps the most dramatic example is to be found in Cuba where, despite the rigid trade embargo imposed by the United States, health and literacy standards are higher than are to be found in the USA and its rate of economic growth now outpaces that of its powerful northern neighbour. The move to the left in Venezuela, Brazil, Bolivia, Peru and Chile offers an alternative strategy for development that should be taken seriously and studied with great care. For their strategy is entirely free from the neo-liberal restraints that dominate in the west and have now penetrated the NGOs.

Tina Wallace and the international research team have produced a scholarly and readable guide to all these issues and this work will be a classic for those who draw more inspiration from the ideas of the World Social Forum than they do from the Global elite who paraded themselves at Gleneagles.

For we all face the same choice: are we to accept the dictates of capital or insist upon democracy as the basis on which our societies and economies are to be built?

Tony Benn
February 2006

Acknowledgements

This book is the product of a great deal of work by a wide range of people, and thanks are due to all those who gave their time and energy to working on this research project in different ways: some collected case material on organizations they knew and understood well, some wrote from their experience to contribute to our understanding, some worked on the project from the design through to completion, while others came in and out as time allowed and kept us going with their insights and humour. Thanks also to all the staff of donor agencies and NGOs who gave us their time and thoughts, which we have tried our best to capture faithfully here.

The Economic and Social Research Department of DFID (ESCOR) was the primary funder of the research; sadly this department is now defunct. We received a responsive grant, given to fund the ideas generated by the research leaders in South Africa, Uganda and the UK. With the closing of ESCOR such funding is now no longer available from DFID, which has moved into large research bids designed and put out to tender by DFID itself. We mourn the passing of responsive and relatively small research funding from DFID for innovative and sometimes controversial research, although the budget was always too small for the scale of the task we undertook.

The Nuffield Foundation, which supported us in many ways throughout and hosted the final feedback workshop in UK, also funded the research. In addition they gave funding towards ensuring the book was written and that it will be widely disseminated in Africa, especially Uganda and South Africa. ActionAid in Uganda, under the leadership of Meenu Vadera, offered a great deal of support to the research in Uganda, and IDRC contributed funding towards the South African research. To all our funders we give many thanks, especially those who accompanied us throughout. We need to remind our readers, of course, that the views expressed in the book are not endorsed by these funders but are ours alone.

The research was supported by an active advisory group, which tried its best to keep us focused and introduced us to many critical concepts and ideas. They were John Hailey, then of Oxford Brookes University, Maggie Baxter, director of Womankind, Sarah Crowther and David Harding, both freelance researchers and consultants at that time. Warm thanks are given to all of them for their support throughout the ups and downs of this project. The research was originally based at Oxford Brookes Business School and was completed under the auspices of the Business School at the Open University.

The team leader and principal author of the South African report was Lisa Bornstein, who contributed to the writing of the final book, especially the Introduction, Chapter 3 and the key sections on South Africa in Chapters 5 and 9. Her colleagues in South Africa, especially Terry Smith in the early days, and later Isaivani Hyman of the School for Development Studies and Annsilla Nyar of the Centre for Civil Society at University of KwaZulu-Natal, were core research staff and greatly contributed to the research, thinking and the writing of the SA report; their hard work in the field, insights and feedback on South Africa and UK findings were invaluable. The studies of individual NGOs conducted by Lisa's students Vicci Tallis and Shelly Dill provided important in-depth views on the dynamics under study, with additional research from Catherine Ogunmefun and Dan Setsile. From the NGO sector, Carol-Ann Foulis of Olive and Allan Kaplan of CDRA made significant additions to the research in SA. Our real thanks are extended to these individuals for the ways in which they strengthened the research. Thanks are also extended to Mike Morris, Vishnu Padayachee and Kanagie Naidoo of the School of Development Studies, who gave crucial support and friendship that made the South African research possible.

Many were also actively involved in the Uganda research, and wrote individual chapters for the final Uganda report; many of the cases presented in this book are based on their original studies. Those who initiated the work were Patrick Mulindwa of the Makerere Institute of Social Research, with the support of the director. He worked with Crispin Kintu of the Centre for Basic Research and researchers from MISR in the early stages. Pressure of time led to a change of leadership during the research process, with Tina Wallace becoming the lead person. Much of the later research was carried out by CDRN and ActionAid Uganda, which contributed a great deal to the research. Thanks are especially due to John de Coninck and Rosemary Adong of CDRN, Kampala, and Meenu Vadera of ActionAid Uganda. Others who contributed from CDRN were A. Kasingye, A. Nanfuka, S. Basemera and B. Mboizi. Research was also drawn from the work of a PhD student, Mary Ssonko Nabacwa, and Martin Kaleeba who had recently completed a Master's degree on related issues, both of AAU. Rashid Sesay from Sierra Leone helped Martin Kaleeba with some of the data analysis, Juliet Kiguli undertook some case studies, and Rajiv Khandawal provided support, insights and a case study that was central to the Uganda report. Thanks are due to all of them and given unreservedly.

It is unfortunate, but a reflection of the reality of the lack of funding available for writing books, that most of these people were not able to give the unpaid time required to actually write the final product, this book. But their contributions remain a bedrock of the work.

Doing research across countries and continents over a long time on a limited budget is not easy and this research encountered many challenges. The support and consistent work of Jennifer Chapman, the other half of the UK research team, was critical in enabling the work to come to fruition, especially during the long and at times lonely journey from the completion of the country reports to the finishing of the final book. The overall lead authorship is Tina Wallace's only in so far as she spent the hours, days and weeks taking all the ideas, material, studies and contributions and writing them into the finished product. In this she had essential support from Jenny Chapman and Lisa Bornstein, although both had many other work obligations to meet during that time.

Really the work belongs to all of those who were involved, those asking the questions and those answering them, in the UK, South Africa and Uganda. Huge thanks are due to all and we hope that you feel we have done justice to the many, complex and difficult issues raised by this wide-ranging research, and that in future others will be able to take on some of these ideas and deepen our understanding and ability to work better in development in the future.

Figures, tables and boxes

Figures

Figure 1.1   Mapping aid chain and flows   13
Figure 1.2   The research design   14
Figure 4.1   The size of donors relative to UK NGO sector   52
Figure 4.2   Relative growth in development funding, research and humanitarian aid, DFID   54
Figure 4.3   DFID funding to UK NGOs by size, including emergencies but not research   55
Figure 4.4   Mechanisms of UK NGO funding (DFID 2003/4)   59
Figure 4.5   EU NGO cofinancing budget line (commitments)   63
Figure 4.6   Trends in funding to NGOs by medium-sized donors   64
Figure 4.7   Trends in funding to NGOs by: small donors   68
Figure 5.1   Country of origin of NGOs working in Uganda   78
Figure 5.2   Geographical spread of NGOs in Uganda   79
Figure 10.1   The broken aid chain   166
Figure 10.2   The project management cycle in reality   167

Tables

Table 1.1   UK NGOs interviewed for the research   15
Table 3.1   Changing development priorities and aid instruments for UK donors and NGOs   32
Table 4.1   DFID support for civil society, including NGOs and research institutes (£ million)   54
Table 4.2   The top five UK NGOs receiving most DFID funds   55
Table 4.3   The JFS, the PPAs and CSCF compared   57
Table 7.1   Broad concerns about reporting, monitoring and evaluation   112
Table 8.1   Summary of expectations from the partnership   141

Boxes

Box 7.1   The UPPAP programme in Uganda   127
Box 9.1   Common platforms and different views of gender and gender mainstreaming (excerpts from Tallis [2005: 104–6])   153
Box 9.2   Allan Kaplan on NGOs and donor relationships at CDRA   158

About the authors

Lisa Bornstein is currently an assistant professor in the School of Urban Planning at McGill University in Montreal, Canada. Trained in urban and development planning at the University of California, Berkeley, she worked as a consultant, facilitator and trainer in project planning and management in Mozambique and South Africa, where she was based from 1993 to 2003. As a senior lecturer in Development Studies at the University of Natal, she has researched and written about NGO–donor-state relations in southern Africa, conflict dynamics in postwar Mozambique and the effects of institutional change on patterns of poverty. From her new home in Montreal, she continues to research planning dynamics in southern Africa. New initiatives include work on planning, institutional change and community dynamics in the cities of Quebec, Honduras and Nicaragua.

Jennifer Chapman is a consultant and a researcher with over 20 years' experience working in the development sector with a whole range of organizations. She was a key researcher in the UK and with the EU for this book. She recently left the Impact Assessment Unit of ActionAid International where among other things she coordinated an action research initiative with country programmes and partners in Brazil, Ghana, Nepal and Uganda on planning, learning and assessing advocacy work. The resulting manual, 'Critical webs of power and change' (edited with Antonella Mancini) accompanied by a CD Rom has recently been published by ActionAid International. She is now working as a freelance consultant with particular interest in deepening and supporting learning processes in north–south relationships, partnership and advocacy, including looking at issues of power and gender.

Tina Wallace has been a researcher, university teacher, NGO worker and more recently a consultant in Africa and the UK for over 30 years. Her focus has been wide-ranging and includes education, water and refugees, as well as organizational issues around strategic thinking, learning, monitoring and evaluation. All her work is undertaken from a gender perspective. The research idea behind this book started when she was employed by a large UK NGO and continued when she became a teacher/researcher in development studies first at the University of Birmingham, then at Oxford Brookes and most recently as an Honorary Senior Research Fellow at the Open University. She was the overall research team leader for the project. She is currently also a research associate at

International Gender Studies, Queen Elizabeth House, Oxford University and has published widely; her publications include *To Ride the Storm* (on the Bristol race riots in UK) (Heinemann), *Changing Perceptions* (Oxfam), *New Roles and Relevance* (Kumarian Press) and *Gender, Water and Development* (Berg).

Acronyms

ACORD – Agency for Cooperation and Research in Development
ALPS – Accountability, Learning and Planning System [Action Aid International]
ANC – African National Congress
ARVs – Anti-retrovirals
BOAG – British Overseas Aid Group
CAFOD – Catholic Agency for Overseas Development
CBO – community-based organization
CDRA – Community Development Resource Association [South Africa]
CDRN – Community Development Resource Network [Uganda]
CEDAW – Convention on the Elimination of All Forms of Discrimination against Women
CIDA – Canadian International Development Agency
CIVAW – Coalition Against Violence Against Women
COPAW – Coalition of Politics and Women
CORE – Cooperative for Research and Education
CSCF – Civil Society Challenge Fund [DFID]
CSO – civil society organization
CSU – Civil Society Unit
DFID – Department for International Development
DRB Coalition – Domestic Relations Bill Coalition [Uganda]
EC – European Commission
EU – European Union
GOPP – Goal Oriented Project Planning
HDI – Human Development Indicators
HIPC – Highly Indebted Poor Countries
IGAs – income generating activities
IDASA – Institute for Democracy in South Africa
IMF – International Monetary Fund
INGO – International NGO
JFS – Joint Funding Scheme [DFID]
KHP – Kapa Housing Project [South Africa]
LFA – logframe analysis
M&E – Monitoring and evaluation
MDGs – Millennium Development Goals
MO – Member organization
MOU – Memorandum of Understanding

NEPAD – New Partnership for Africa's Development
NGO – Non-Governmental Organization
NRM – National Resistance Movement [Uganda]
ODA – official development assistance
PEAP – Poverty Eradication Action Plan
PGRF – Poverty Reduction and Growth Facility
PLWHAs – People Living with HIV/AIDs
PPA – Programme Partnership Agreement [DFID]
PRA – Participatory Rural Appraisal
PRSPs – Poverty Reduction Strategy Plans
SA – South Africa
SALGA – South African Local Grantmakers Association
SA NGO – South African NGO
SANGOCO – The South African National NGO Coalition
SNGO – Southern NGO
SWAPS – Sector Wide Approaches
TAC – Treatment Action Campaign
UK – United Kingdom
UK NGO – UK-based NGO
ULA – Uganda Land Alliance
UN – United Nations
UNGO – Ugandan NGO
UPPAP – Uganda Participatory Poverty Assessment Project
US – United States
USAID – United States Agency for International Development
ZOPP – Ziel Orientierte Projekt Planung (Objectives Oriented Project Planning)

CHAPTER 1
Introduction

The global poverty agenda, long promoted by non-governmental organizations (NGOs), was formally endorsed by the World Bank in 2000, marking a major shift in official approaches to aid. This new international focus has led to calls to greatly increase aid, drop the debt and change the terms of trade that keep poor countries excluded from benefiting from the global economy. Finding effective ways to reduce poverty concerns governments and NGOs, and there is at times a growing convergence of thinking around the causes and solutions to poverty among donors, governments and NGOs worldwide. Expectations run high that further increases in aid will be forthcoming and that the targets set to focus all aid efforts, the Millennium Development Goals (MDGs) will be met, albeit later than anticipated. Strategies for achieving these goals include addressing poverty directly and tackling factors such as good governance, corruption, the role of the state and civil society, and identifying drivers of growth and change that will enable positive change to be sustained.

Although figures on aid flows are contested, aid from the UK and the European Union is certainly increasing, and both are promising much more aid, especially for Africa. The volume of aid to Africa is already high, though erratic and overshadowed by the lack of direct foreign investment and debt (UNCTAD, 2000: Lockwood, 2005). Significant and increasing proportions of aid go directly to governments through direct budget support; money from donors and public-giving flows to NGOs in the countries of the north and south. Yet the problems of poverty continue to grow, and for many of the world's people, especially in Africa, poverty, hunger and economic insecurity persist and even increase. Aid is not fulfilling its promise and donors, practitioners and academics talk about the crisis of aid and the apparent failure of aid to enable many countries in Africa to progress. The need to show demonstrable and positive outcomes from aid is now critical for both donors and NGOs; assumptions of the role and performance of NGOs are being examined to see if they hold true and whether NGOs can achieve their ambitious aims (Lewis, 2003b).

Donors and NGOs have responded to questions about the legitimacy and effectiveness of aid in a number of ways. Donors have introduced new mechanisms and conditions for aid going directly to states, including the concept of selectivity, which allows them to work only with states that have adopted good pro-poor policies, defined according to their criteria. The mechanisms of aid to African states are changing, from projects to programmes, sector and even budget support, tightly tied to national poverty plans that have to be agreed by donors. Direct budget support is accompanied by heavy technical support and conditions, especially around governance and accountability. For funding going via NGOs, donors have heightened their control through new conditions, tighter selectivity and growing demands for accountability, these last encoded in specific management procedures and practices. The increase in conditionality, selectivity and paperwork, especially for accountability, is widespread among donors, with most adopting similar measures and policies. Northern NGOs, in their turn, adopt and promote the new aid approaches – from needs to rights, from projects to programmes, from service delivery to advocacy – and implement them through largely standardized management procedures.

[BUT NGOS ARE NOT DOING BUDGET SUPPORT!]

Yet many observers, including some NGO commentators, fear that part of the problem and challenge of aid lies precisely in this increasing reliance on the management models, and the ideology that underpins them, that dominate aid disbursement. They are seen as 'depoliticising development' (Ferguson, 1990), treating intensely political choices as technical and managerial ones, and imposing control and regulation through external solutions to local problems. Some critics argue that these rational, managerial models privilege the scientific and rational while devaluing essential knowledge, analysis and action at the local level; they reinforce existing relations of power and so place achieving the broad aims of poverty reduction and development at risk (Mawdsley et al., 2002; Long and Long, 1992; Mosse, 2005).

The increasingly bureaucratic management of aid, which seeks to control, count and account tightly for both finances and complex processes of social change, is underpinned by a set of beliefs about how to achieve change, which are drawn less from experience and the analysis of success or failure in practice, and more from the shifting ideologies of those designing the development project:

> For many working in development, getting theory right is the key to addressing the failures and disappointments of development...better theory, new paradigms and alternative frameworks are constantly needed (Mosse, 2005: 1).

Debates continue about which theory or framework will hold the key to success and enable aid to be most effective. The tensions between very different aid paradigms are referred to in this book; however, our key concern is to explore an area that has largely been neglected until recently, namely whether the existing aid processes widely used by NGOs are effective in tackling poverty and exclusion. We believe that the way aid is disbursed (the procedures and conditions of aid) affects the implementation of NGO policies on the ground and shapes the way they work, that is, their development practice.

We begin with the observation that aid too often follows routes and is accompanied by practices that mirror and reinforce the structural inequalities that it is there to challenge. Foreign aid, including aid that passes through international (usually northern-based) NGOs to contribute to development activities conducted by NGOs based in the south, often comes with conditions, stated or not, that limit its positive impacts. Answering the question of how much aid to whom must, in our view, be accompanied by greater attention to the mechanisms of aid and their effects on the organizations and individuals involved in the aid project. It is also important to understand what drives the constantly changing aid agenda and associated procedures, to see how far they are rooted in learning from practice and how far they are driven by the changing ideologies and perceptions of those with power. Attention must be paid to the theory and paradigms that underpin current aid practices. Yet research on NGOs rarely engages seriously with the relationship between theory, policy and practice:

> Despite the enormous energy devoted to generating the right policy models, strangely little attention is given to the relationship between these models and the practices and events that they are expected to generate (Mosse, 2005: 1).

In an era when impact is all, the disregard for the impact of changing aid processes is interesting. However, studies are starting to appear, with increasingly sophisticated theoretical, empirical and ethnographic approaches to studying NGO practice and the way in which aid shapes it (Lewis, 2003b; Brehm, 2001; Mawdsley et al., 2002). These studies are critical in a field where much previous research has been normative and carried out by people closely involved in the NGO sector.

The research on which this book is based fits well alongside this growing literature. We explicitly attempt to understand the impact of the globally dominant aid procedures on development work, using empirical data. Our research explores how aid policy and procedures, and the values and analysis they carry within them, originating from donors and NGOs in the north – specifically in this book from the UK – shape the work of those receiving aid funding. It explores how far recipients can change the terms and conditions of that funding, and the nature of the interactions along the aid chain (Simbi and Thom, 2000) that help to explain how effectively aid is being used on the ground.

The research focuses only on NGOs that are part of the international aid chain, which receive some or all of their funding from institutional donors – governments, the EU, the UN, the World Bank and other multilaterals – to promote development in Africa. The data used are primarily drawn from donors and NGOs based in the UK, Uganda and South Africa (SA), but the findings apply widely and the trends uncovered occur in many other aid chains in the global arena. In focusing only on NGOs incorporated into international aid chains *LOOK AT* (Martens, forthcoming 2006), the research does not look at voluntary and not-*NGOs IN* for-profit organizations that raise all their funds locally, i.e., from members or *INT'L AID* supporters. Their motivation, values, behaviour, focus, accountability *CHAIN* mechanisms and the roots of their legitimacy may be very different. Our focus is on NGOs deeply involved with global aid funding, as recipients, as donors and also often as lobbyists for change. These NGOs (in the north and south) are part of the global aid chain, which deeply influences the way they conceptualize, implement and account for development work. In understanding the way these influences work we employ two concepts to guide the analysis: coercion and commitment.

Coercion and compliance

The first concept, coercion, is a dynamic often touched on in discussions of development. Since donors, and increasingly international NGOs (INGOs), have control over funds, many say that this inevitably means they call the shots. Compliance with, or consent to, the terms and regulations of a grant are seen as an inevitable outcome of the aid chain. The concept of coercion, while it can include force, is also used to communicate the way dominant and accepted norms lead to compliant behaviour. A framework of norms can exist that shape behaviour and ways of working, that are rarely questioned or challenged; indeed many would see them as the right and best way to approach development because they are so universally accepted and used (Martens, forthcoming, 2006).

This compliance may happen in a context where a contrasting discourse, which professes to promote local ownership and the participation of southern partners, is also in play: a participatory approach implies that there is room for negotiating conditions and moderating the unequal financial power of different parties to a grant. These competing frames of reference, meeting the international conditions of aid and opening up space for a more responsive and locally owned way of working, suggest a need to investigate empirically how compliance and coercion work in practice, how far NGOs feel obliged or coerced by the existing funding norms and how far they feel able to change these and challenge accepted international development practices.

Within a single aid chain and set of funding conditions, coercion and consent may play out in multiple ways. Relationships and conditions may be experienced as compatible at one level, where unequal power may not be a major issue, but become coercive and restricting at another level in the chain where relationships of power are much more unequal. For example, donor conditions that can be willingly accepted at senior management level in UK, where incorporation into the aid chain is seen as mutually beneficial, can become heavy demands or impositions when they are passed down to field staff and partners. Individuals at distinct points in the aid chain, and different agencies that have uneven status and access within the aid chain, do not experience the conditions uniformly: while some find considerable room for manoeuvre and negotiation others find little, often depending on the existing relations of power.

Power is often mentioned but rarely analysed in NGO relationships (Chambers, 2004), yet the funders define the rules and regulations to which NGOs must adhere. INGOs, in turn, have the power of funding but also of global knowledge networks and superior communication channels that make them feared competitors of local NGOs; their power is often used to set the terms and conditions of funding and accountability for their partners. Power privileges some voices to be heard and others ignored; it underlies international aid behaviour along the aid chain. Organizations and the individuals in them can sometimes fall back on insidious forms of power, based on past histories of colonialism, racism and gender inequalities, to shape behaviour and sap confidence. The use and misuse of power can undermine the ability of the less powerful to challenge the status quo (Gaventa, 1980; Chapman et al., 2005). Often their responses are limited to full compliance or passive resistance and there is evidence of covert subversion in reaction to the coercive nature of the prevailing agenda. Resistance shows that NGOs are not simply clones of the aid industry and they can take independent action in opposition to the dominant development paradigms. The relationships of unequal power, generating compliance and resistance, are found all along the aid chain and exist between local NGOs and their communities as well as between donors and INGOs.

This broad concept of coercion allows us to explore a wide range of issues around how the norms of development work are set, how power is negotiated at different levels, and how far different strategies and responses support or undermine development work in practice. It is interesting that while NGOs advocate widely on many issues concerning the dominant development paradigms coming from the World Bank and others, there is little overt protest at the terms and conditions of donor aid to the NGO sector; this is an area where NGOs seem reluctant to challenge the major players. └> ACCEPTANCE OF FUNDING PLAYING FIELD AND ITS TERMS

Commitment

The second concept is commitment, which brings the analysis to a more subjective level. NGO work rests on a sense of individual and organizational commitment to change and the mission of the organization. Without commitment, often manifest in long hours of unpaid or unremunerated work in difficult conditions, much development would never take place. Volunteers remain an important source of labour – and goodwill – for many NGOs, and donations, again rooted in a sense of individual commitment, trust and faith, are crucial to many organizations.

Commitment, however, goes beyond good intentions and includes working to achieve change in a professional and accountable manner, guided by values or a vision of positive change. It is the reason for doing the work that goes beyond day-to-day monetary or status rewards, or even organizational survival. In development NGOs this commitment is often founded on beliefs in justice, equality, inclusion and participation, and the rights of marginalized people to have voice and access resources.

In reflecting on commitment, issues of agency and trust become important. The concept of commitment implies a wide range of responses is possible based on the agency of the individual or the organization. Strong interpersonal relations of trust can be built that go beyond the requirements of modern aid systems (Kaplan, 2000; Mawdsley et al., 2002). New ways of working can be developed to ensure that development workers listen and respond to the needs and voices of those most affected by poverty or HIV/AIDS, for example (Cornwall and Welbourn, 2002). NGO actors can and do exert influence through advocacy and policy-level lobbying and by deciding how to act differently in any given situation. Agency is a concept with many meanings, but for our purposes this definition is useful:

> agency refers not to intentions people have in doing things but to their capacity of doing things in the first place…agency concerns events of which an individual is the perpetrator, in the sense that the individual could, at any phase in a given sequence…act differently. (Giddens, 1984, quoted in Seckinelgin, 2006)

Actions may be based on commitment to the values and mission of the NGO, individual staff motivations and relationships, or analysis that takes account of the needs of local government or other civil-society actors. Commitment also refers to the positive relationships that can be created between individuals and organizations in the aid chain, which extend beyond the temporal and contractual limits of funding agreements. Forging relationships – between northern and southern NGOs, or NGOs and community groups – characterized by trust and mutual learning requires a commitment to the other and to a vision of development that opens up new opportunities and ways of behaving (Kaplan, 2002; Harding, 2004 , Said, 2003).

Personal relationships of commitment can be complex. Actors may feel commitment towards their immediate work colleagues and the organization as it strives to work towards its mission in a hostile environment, as well as commitment to the wider purpose and vision of the work. If these feelings are not balanced by good development understanding and practice there is a danger that organizational imperatives – such as cultivating good relationships with donors or propagating a brand – can overshadow the need for building good and different relationships with partners, and in turn with the poor and their representatives. It is usually more comfortable to equate one's commitment to the organization's mission with organizational survival rather than with being 'passionate about the poor' (Chambers, 2004).

Some writers are trying to articulate this broader sense of commitment or professional practice through the idea that as a development practitioner one should have a commitment to something other – and greater – than the organization one works in. Su Soal (2002) of the Community Development Resource Association (CDRA), Cape Town, claims, like some others, that this is the only real defence against the debilitating cynicism found in much of the sector:

> In the development sector, we work in one of the most cynical environments on earth. In this context, it is hard to imagine taking practice seriously. Yet those of us who pursue human and holistic development, amongst all of the other purposes of development, must take it seriously. It is all we have to set

us apart from grand-scale structural engineering that has scant regard for human dignity and the good of the planet, irrespective of its rhetoric. (Soal, 2002: 4–5)

She affirms the need to develop a commitment to professional practice so that what is brought to each situation goes well beyond a set of delivered services:

> To work with professionalism is not simply to deliver a service that is reliable in its predictability and consistency of standards. The development sector is teeming with people who can provide respectable, even reputable, services: trainers who have their workshop 'packages' that get sold all over the world; consultants who ply their methods and ready solutions; NGOs that make their reputation developing something original – then peddle it endlessly, with little regard for need or context.

> Professionality goes beyond this, generating in its adherents the abilities to face each situation they confront, anew, to recognise these and to formulate from a confident inner capacity, responses and interventions that best suit that situation at that time. (Soal, 2002: 6)

This links very closely with the work of MacIntyre who, like Soal, believes that practices are 'never just a set of technical skills' but should extend and expand the practitioner. Individual behaviour and practice need to be contrasted with the role of institutions, which by their very nature are concerned with 'acquiring money and other material goods; they are structured in terms of power and status, and they distribute money, power and status as rewards' (MacIntyre, 2002: 194). The ideals and creativity of individual practice are 'always vulnerable to the acquisitiveness of the institutions, in which the cooperative care for the common goods of the practice is always vulnerable to the competitiveness of the institution' (MacIntyre, 2002: 194), and the only way to uphold them and so combat the often corrupting power of institutions is for practitioners to promote the virtues of justice, courage and truthfulness.

The research

The initial purpose of the research was to explore empirically where NGOs were seeking and finding their funding, what conditions were attached to that funding and how those conditions were shaping the ways in which these NGOs worked with their donors, staff and partners on the ground. While a set of increasingly standardized approaches and conditions attach to funding from institutional and other donors in Europe, the US and the UK, little research has been done to understand whether and how these actively encourage good development practice. There is insufficient evidence to show whether they promote the achievement of the goals of development, or whether they are in fact part of the problem that causes disappointing end results (Wallace, Crowther and Shepherd, 1997). Over time these simple questions led us to explore a wide range of issues concerning development, including partnership and participation, the nature of relationships within and between organizations, sustainability, ownership, legitimacy, learning and accountability, and the role of aid to the state and relations between state, donor and NGO. The canvas became very broad, but the core issues remained and serve to structure and shape the book.

The first phase of the research was undertaken in the UK. It explored the growing adoption of certain management techniques by UK NGOs, and the resulting book by Wallace, Crowther and Shepherd, *Standardising Development* (1997) documented the growing number of policies and procedures introduced for project management, largely in response to changing donor and trustee demands. From relatively minimal procedures and light measures, NGOs were shifting to a more tightly structured and bureaucratic set of systems. There was a growing convergence with the techniques used to manage development aid from the UK and, more troubling, a disjuncture in the language used. The language of accountability to donors – project planning, indicators and impact assessment – was paralleled by the language of participation for building strong local civil society, ownership and sustainability. Yet they seemed not to fit well together conceptually or in practice. A second phase of the research was consequently developed to explore what the impact of these changes were on the work of southern NGOs supported financially and in other ways by UK NGOs. An international team of researchers, working alongside Ugandan and SA academics and NGO staff, conducted this research in three countries, the UK, SA and Uganda: the research that took place in the UK now spans almost 10 years, providing a good picture of changes over time. The findings of each country are written up separately (Wallace and Chapman, 2004b; Bornstein et al., 2005; Wallace, 2004b).

This book presents the second phase of the research, analysing the changing aid requirements of donors and UK NGOs and their impact down the aid chain to Uganda and SA. While it was clear that certain practices – such as logframes, indicators, targets, measurable outcomes, the need for detailed paper-based reporting for accountability – had become widespread, there was little work being done to understand their impact on both relationships and practice in southern NGOs (Mawdsley et al., 2002 and Brehm, 2001 were two noticeable exceptions). We were interested to see how these procedures, founded on concepts of controlled change and rational management, meshed with the commitment to participation, locally driven solutions and ownership, and how these different approaches were negotiated within organizations and how well people were able to work with them in practice. We wanted to explore the ability of organizations and individuals at different points in the aid chain to negotiate their ways of working in relation to project financing, project scope, timelines, deliverables and assessment and see how far they were able to work with the procedural requirements as well as associated conditions, such as paying attention to the environment, gender equality, HIV/AIDS, rights, participation and advocacy. The nature of the relationships that these procedures encouraged and how these shaped the development work actually being undertaken became core interests.

We know aid procedures and their associated relationships are rooted in the wider context. Therefore, it was important to try to understand the role of national contexts – historical and political – to see how far new aid practices have similar effects in different places, or whether responses and modes of implementation are context-specific. The role of the state and donor–state relations in shaping NGO responses were recognized, although these were not the central focus of the research.

Two contrasting countries in Africa were chosen for these comparative purposes, each with their own history of development and different civil societies. Uganda and SA have undergone rapid development and positive change in the past 10 years, although the nature of change differs in the two countries. Changing domestic politics and heavy international financial support contributed to the strong economic growth seen in Uganda, although the democratic transition has seen some reverses and conflict continues to affect the country. While growth has led to poverty reduction for some, deepening poverty is the reality of 20 per cent of the population, and the relationship between growth and poverty reduction, and even the poverty figures, are highly contested (Wallace, Caputo and Herbert,1999). In SA, international financial inputs have been less critical to political and economic outcomes, and SA has an economy that is not aid-dependent; indeed economic growth has been fuelled in part by the expansion of SA capital across the continent. The political transition to democracy continues, without major civil strife, although the huge inequalities characteristic of the apartheid period continue. Development assistance in the form of project grants boomed in the 1990s as part of the global effort to reverse racial inequalities, bolster economic performance and assure political stability.

UGANDA vs, SOUTH AFRICA

The research methodology

Researching NGOs is difficult. They are not transparent organizations, and almost always request that discussions on tensions and issues concerning their funding and relationships with donors, partners and states are held behind closed doors (Wallace, Crowther and Shepherd, 1997). Although many NGO staff debate the inherent contradictions and difficulties with trying to meet donors' requirements while also meeting the needs of participation and local empowerment, they rarely do so in public. The majority of NGOs in all three countries requested complete confidentiality from this research.

In this context getting access to people and documents and having sufficient interaction to understand the terrain and language of NGOs usually requires inside knowledge and connections. Several of the researchers have worked in NGOs and continue to work with them as trainers, consultants, mentors and evaluators. This enabled unusual access, but also meant that it was sometimes hard for the teams to stand back from the day-to-day interactions to analyse what they were observing. Some researchers were more academically based, and while this sometimes hampered access it enabled them to bring a more critical eye to discussions.

It proved important to pay attention to the composition of the research teams in SA and Uganda, where race, ethnicity, class, gender, place of residence and education are key social issues – and sources of inequality. These can affect both access and the quality of information collected. The researchers in SA, for example, included South Africans of Indian descent, several non-South Africans (black and white) and several white South Africans (male and female). The way in which respondents interacted with a white male South African was different from their relations with a foreign researcher or a young woman. Repeated visits, sometimes by different people, contacts in different settings and discussions with multiple individuals in an organization helped to overcome some of these challenges. In Uganda the team was drawn from academic, practitioner and research/training backgrounds and all but two team members were Ugandan, albeit from different ethnic groups. All were urban-based and only the team leader lived outside Uganda. Originally the plan was for a wholly Ugandan team but time pressures, staff turnover and the complexity of the research meant that external support became critical. All the Ugandan findings were fed back and refined in the light of three feedback workshops over three years.

Working with donors is sometimes difficult because of their lack of time and the very diverse ways they keep their financial and other data on funding NGOs. The experience of the researchers working with the Department for International Development (DFID) (UK) on this project changed significantly over time. The research moved from a collaborative venture with high interest and involvement of one or two DFID staff and open access for collaboration in the mid-1990s to one run by an administrator in 2000. While the first assessment was done by DFID staff, subsequently assessment was outsourced and the comments received from professional external assessors could not be negotiated. Reporting requirements increased greatly, and became codified in set formats; there were no discussions of the implications of the research for DFID, as there had been previously.

This experience paralleled changes UK NGOs have experienced in their relations with DFID, as the government cuts transaction costs. It contrasted strongly with the interaction and support given by staff from the other funder, the Nuffield Foundation, which remained deeply interested and supportive, concerned to ensure the research was relevant and of good quality. They hosted the final feedback session in the UK. Relations with other donors were based largely on personal relationships, which ensured good access and open discussions, many of which cannot be included in this book, however, because of shortage of space.

The research encountered many of the difficulties that NGOs experience when working at a distance, in partnerships where access to resources and time are unequal, and where the power did remain, in spite of our best efforts, with the signatories to the contracts for delivery. Many issues of past historical

[handwritten margin note: CHANGE OVER TIME IN DFID'S ATTITUDE TOWARD RESEARCH]

relationships and patterns of behaviour, north and south, were encountered, including for example staff overcommitment because of the need to ensure financial solvency in cash-strapped universities and NGOs, a lack of resources for reading, different motivations for being involved and patterns of consultancy rather than research that are all too evident in universities of the south. Efforts were made on all sides to address the inequalities in rewards for time invested and access to knowledge resources especially, but they could not be wished away. The field teams changed in composition over time partly because of these issues, although everyone involved contributed important ideas towards the research project. The final writing was done by a few but drew heavily on the work of all, and credit must be widely shared.

The research questions

The research was driven by a number of clear questions.

1. What are the current patterns of donor-giving to UK NGOs, and how are these changing over time?
2. How far do conditions and requirements concerning funding from donors (institutional, bilateral, NGOs) influence and direct the work of NGOs?
3. What is driving the adoption of the current managerial approaches to development?
4. Do NGOs have room for manoeuvre in negotiating these requirements? What role does the external environment play in enabling NGOs to find more or less room for manoeuvre?
5. How do the policies and procedures of UK NGOs affect their relationships with southern counterparts? What kinds of relationships are being built?
6. What implications do increasingly tight donor contexts have for southern institutions and their:
   - relations to communities;
   - ability to promote participation, empowerment and local ownership;
   - autonomy and ability to become strong independent civil-society organizations;
   - ability to ensure that local knowledge and cross-cultural issues are central to development?

Several definitions are important at the outset.

- The term '*donors*' is used interchangeably with the term *funders*, referring to all organizations that provide official or private development assistance. We did not address corporate sources of development funding, and the scope of the research largely excluded non-UK funders.
- *Back donors* refers to institutional sources of funding, whether government (e.g. DFID, national lotteries) or private (e.g. Comic Relief, trusts and foundations).
- *UK NGOs* refers to international NGOs based in the UK whether or not they have field headquarters or offices based in the south; they were the main focus of the research in the north.

- *INGOs* include UK NGOs, but the term goes wider to include UK NGOs which have moved their headquarters to Africa, and other European/US NGOs. All INGOs raise their money from donors globally, work in several countries of the south, and have access to the sources of influence, knowledge and capital in the north.
- *SA NGOs* or *Ugandan NGOs* refer to all NGOs based in those countries, and run locally by national staff or volunteers. Although not all are formally incorporated, our focus was on registered indigenous NGOs primarily engaged in development, whether national or local in scope. They are referred to generically as *southern NGOs* (SNGOs).
- *Conditions* or *conditionalities* refer to requirements that funding recipients must adhere to in pre-finance, project, or post-project phases, regardless of whether they are relevant or stated explicitly or not.
- The *aid chain, stream* or *flow* refers to the series of organizations and actors involved in the process of moving funds from their initial institutional source to be spent on behalf of the targeted beneficiaries in the recipient area, and the associated processes of accounting to donors for the use of these funds.

A diagram of a simple aid chain is provided in Figure 1.1. Typically, proposals come up the aid chain to donors, funding and funding conditions go down the chain and later, reports come back up. Most aid chains are far more complex than the one depicted here, for example with money flowing from donors to a UK NGO to their field office, then perhaps to an umbrella organization before going into a local NGO. Often multiple donors are involved and they can come into the aid chain at different points, sometimes funding from Europe and sometimes funding within Africa directly. Figure 1.1 highlights key characteristics of the aid chain.

The research process in each country

In each country, research followed three directions (see Figure 1.2):
- broad research to understand the context within which NGOs are working;
- medium-depth (or mid-level) research with NGOs in each country around management and development practices;
- Deep research with a limited number of NGOs to follow the links from donors and UK NGOs through to work on the ground in the country concerned.

The research began by profiling country-specific elements that would inform our comparative study: the central development challenges, key actors, their resources and their constraints for each country. This was done using literature and the knowledge of the local researchers, who also undertook interviews concerning these contextual issues. The broad research also encompassed a scan of the literature on civil society, grant-making and development NGOs in the three countries, and interviews with key individuals located in aid agencies, mainly from the UK but also including the EU, USAID, GTZ and the Canadian

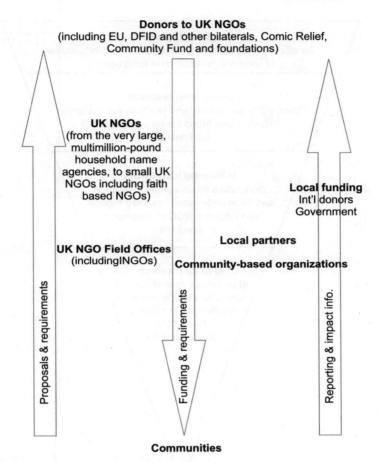

Figure 1.1 Mapping aid chain and flows
Aid and information flows around this complex aid chain follow many different paths, each with their own conditions and requirements. However, it is broadly correct to say that there are three main flows:
- project/programme proposals and requests UP the aid chain;
- funding and funding requirements DOWN the aid chain;
- reporting and information on impact UP the aid chain.

International Development Agency (CIDA). Exploratory visits were made to a range of well-informed NGOs in Uganda and SA (usually large national NGOs, training and umbrella organizations) to get an overview of the issues for NGOs in each country. Researchers also attended development forums, NGO meetings, and conferences on civil society in each country.

The mid-level research in Uganda and SA focused on understanding the range of development management practices employed by NGOs, the reasons for their use and any positive or negative implications associated with their adoption. As part of this we also interviewed NGOs providing training and

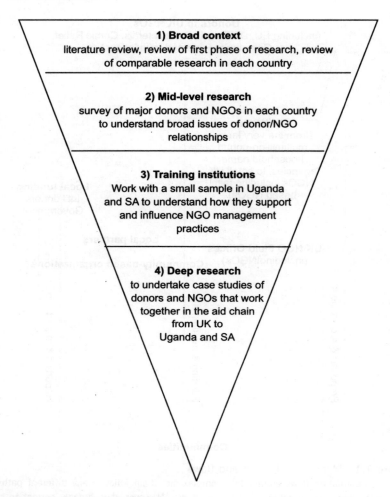

Figure 1.2 The research design

organizational development (OD) support to other NGOs. Our hypothesis was that trainers and OD practitioners would have insights on the changes and challenges facing the NGO sector and that the orientations of such organizations could affect the range and choice of practices NGOs employed. We asked several such practitioners to prepare material for the research project reflecting on their individual experiences.

In UK repeat interviews were undertaken with most, but not all, of the NGOs who participated in the original research written up in Wallace, Crowther and Shepherd, 1997). NGOs that were excluded were those that had ceased to get official funding, and those working on specializations not usually defined as development, for example in micro-finance and with plants or animals. A few new NGOs were included on the basis of their niche (e.g., gender) or to increase the number of small NGOs. The full list of UK NGOs interviewed for this phase and which provided the sample on which aid chains were to be followed to Africa is presented in Table 1.1. Because we were looking for organizations that work in both SA and Uganda there was an overall bias in the research to focusing on the larger UK NGOs; however, in the field these organizations worked with a wide range of smaller NGOs.

In SA 15 donors and NGOs, which were not part of the aid chain sample, in addition to some NGOs that were (see Table 1.1), were interviewed for this overview work. They were mainly large training and delivery organizations familiar with the current aid agendas. In Uganda 16 additional NGOs outside

Table 1.1 UK NGOs interviewed for the research

| | | Projects or field office in: | |
		South Africa	Uganda
Small INGOs	AFFORD,	No	No
(Global expenditure	Childhope	No	No
per year < £2	Transform Africa	No	Yes
million)	Womankind	Yes	No
Medium INGOs	Amref	Yes	Yes
(£2 million–5 million)	BOND (Umbrella for UK NGOs)	Yes	No
	Farm Africa	Yes	Yes
	Population Concern	No	No
	SOS Sahel		
Large INGOs →	ACORD	No	Yes
(£5 million–20 million)	Help Age International	Yes	No
	Plan International	No	No
	Practical Action	No	No
→	Save the Children Fund (SCF)	Yes	Yes
	Wateraid	No	Yes
Very large INGOs →	ActionAid	No	Yes
(> £20 million)	CAFOD	Yes	No
→	CARE (not in UK)	Yes	Yes
	Christian Aid	No	Yes
→	Oxfam	Yes	Yes
	VSO	Yes	No
→	World Vision	Yes	No
Institutional donors	Baring	Charles	DFID, EU
	Comic Relief	Stewart Mott	
	Community Fund	Foundation	
	DFID	DFID	
	Diana Fund	EU	
	EU		
	Nuffield		

the aid chain sample NGOs were interviewed, along with some who were part of the original sample; these additional NGOs were all based in Kampala; they were large umbrella organizations, training organizations, and lobbying and service delivery organizations, again well versed in current development methodologies and often able to speak on behalf of a large membership or client base. The aim was to gather a good understanding of the issues for NGOs in each country (a list of the additional NGOs interviewed is presented in Appendix 1; of course none of them is identified individually in the data presentation in the book so as to ensure the confidentiality of their views).

The in-depth research entailed work with organizations linked in the aid chain. A number of the UK NGOs mentioned in Table 1.1 were selected for follow-up in SA and Uganda. Neither these, nor their partners, are listed individually because of the request for anonymity; however, in each country four or five agencies were selected and interviews undertaken. The research teams tried to meet a range of people occupying different roles: directors, board members, managers, line staff, fieldworkers and, to a limited extent, beneficiaries. In some cases, the interviews began with senior staff who had an understanding of the issues facing their organizations; in other cases the researchers had worked long-term with the NGO and knew a wide range of staff and partners. Some of the case studies were done as part of Master's or PhD studies and were much more detailed than others. Some interviews were done with groups of staff rather than individuals; some developed into more detailed case studies; others were written by key staff reflecting on their own experiences of being part of a complex aid chain and the compromises and challenges involved. The research involved examining many facets of the organizations, finance, management, planning, implementation, monitoring and reporting, as well as less clearly charted areas of relationships, multiple accountabilities and political activism. Throughout the research, we relied on published reports, policy documents, NGOs own public and grey material, as well as interviews with NGO staff (focus group and individual), interviews with other key informants, surveys and visits to projects.

The organizations that were the focus of the case study work ranged between very large and medium-sized international NGOs with their headquarters in the UK (although some relocated to Africa during the research), and from small local to large SA and Ugandan NGOs with national coverage. The case study NGOs were drawn from organizations that had funding relations with some of the listed UK NGOs and represented a wide range of experiences and perspectives, with varying visions, missions, values and goals. Some were membership and or network organizations representing the interests of their members or special groups, while others were either international or local NGOs involved in different development programmes. It is unfortunate that the confidentiality requirement prevents us listing the NGO partners involved in the research in each country; this inevitably makes the presentation of the data muddy and opens the research up to accusations of lack of transparency. Ultimately, readers have to trust that the overall sampling was valid and allowed the researchers to hear the voices of a wide range of actors, as representative as possible in one study of the complex array of donors and NGOs that make up the development sector in each country.

The research in its concept phase was expected to follow funding beyond local NGOs and community-based organizations (CBOs) into communities, to see how aid was being used in practice. Unfortunately this proved difficult in all but a few cases. The problems were many, including a lack of time and funding for in-depth fieldwork in rural areas. Researchers did not have easy, or indeed any, access to vehicles and drivers, or money for staying away from home, and the research budget was too tight to cover these costs. Although the researchers based outside Africa were able to give some of their time without charge, this is a luxury research staff in Africa cannot afford. Research funding did not cover all the costs of the research, and only a fraction of the costs of writing. One casualty was the loss of the in-depth fieldwork that was originally planned; the second was the loss of the wider research team in writing the book.

LACK OF RESEARCH RESOURCES

Structure of the book

The book is organized into 10 chapters. The first chapters present the background to the study and the concepts of change underlying current development approaches. These discussions are followed by an analysis of donor aid flows and the packaging of aid to NGOs: who can access it and under what conditions. The planning and management tools built into the funding relationships are then described and analysed, leading into discussions of the impact of these tools on the relationships and practice of development, based on the presentation of in-depth case studies from Uganda and SA.

The research started with a tight focus on policies and procedures for the giving and accounting of aid money. But the parameters grew as the research progressed and it became clear that the way aid is handled directly affects the nature of the relationships built around aid-giving. Perhaps inevitably, over time, the focus became increasingly tied to understanding the way policies and procedures shape relationships in the aid chain and the extent to which these relationships resemble any kind of partnership. It became essential to understand who holds power in each situation and how that power is used and negotiated. We found that too often the relationships forged around aid-funding were characterized by poor communication, lack of trust and fear of censure, but the field research did reveal important exceptions where relationships proved more constructive for all parties involved.

Within this overall framework critical issues that are rarely openly discussed emerged. Although issues of gender in the development process are debated, gender issues in the aid chain and how these shape relationships are often glossed over. Issues of race and ethnicity are rarely acknowledged yet underlie many of the interactions, decisions and actions taken by agencies and individuals. They have not been easy to surface in this research, but are highlighted wherever the issues seemed to be underlying events, decisions and actions.

This is not a book calling for the end of aid. We recognize that the vast majority of people involved in the development and aid industries are motivated by a sincere and heartfelt concern to address poverty, inequality and injustice. We also recognize that their commitment is usually matched by effort. While good intentions are not enough, we also operate from a belief, backed by some positive examples from the field, that aid can work. The problems, for us, are that too much effort is being expended on activities peripheral – if not contrary – to processes of human and organizational development and much of that poorly expended effort appears to arise in direct response to the ways in which development is planned and managed, and where power lies.

This introductory chapter sets out key concepts and concerns, along with the methodology and the structure of the book. Chapter 2 explores the changing context for development, highlighting emerging development ideologies and practices. Chapter 3 explores the different languages of development and whether they can work well together, as many claim, or whether results-based management is fundamentally at odds with a development process that is locally rooted and driven. The next two chapters present the changing terrain for development in each of the three countries under study, our first level of analysis. In Chapter 4, we map the changing donor landscape, comparing this with baseline information from 1995, and analysing the impact of these ongoing changes on UK NGOs. In Chapter 5, a profile of both the Ugandan and SA NGO landscape is provided, together with information about key development challenges facing each country. In Chapter 6, the key elements of the dominant paradigm, project cycle management, and how they are experienced in each country are presented and discussed, and Chapter 7 addresses these management practices, the ways they are understood and adopted, and their effects, bringing together information from in-depth case study work in the three countries. Chapter 8 draws on different cases in Uganda, more in-depth, to show how the different paradigms and organizational cultures – our two languages – work together in practice. Chapter 9 uses case material to explore the room for manoeuvre available to NGOs there as they negotiate their funding and conditions with a wide range of donors, and highlights similarities and differences from Uganda. Chapter 10 pulls together the conclusions drawn from the data about the way the aid chain works, how much it coerces and shapes NGOs, how far it enables commitment and individual agency to flourish, and whether current aid mechanisms do enable or inhibit NGOs to meet their stated and long-held aims for poverty reduction and the empowerment of the poor.

CHAPTER 2
The changing context for the work of development NGOs

Introduction

The global development context has changed significantly since the research started in 1995, though it is less clear whether development practice on the ground or conditions for the poor have changed commensurately. There is, perhaps, a growing gulf between the ambitious international debates, concepts and approaches to development and the reality of the work being undertaken to address the deepening poverty of many.

The broad ideological paradigms and priorities within the neoliberal agenda have shifted as new solutions to old problems are sought. In the mid-1990s the Bretton Woods institutions saw development as economic growth and attempted to prime its engines through liberalization and privatization, moving money away from supporting governments into the private sector. Markets were seen as the key to promoting economic development and governments were increasingly relegated to a minor role. Issues of growing inequalities and the redistribution of wealth were largely ignored. Concern about the overblown nature of the state in many countries, and perhaps particularly in sub-Saharan Africa, meant it was defined as a stumbling block to the economic reforms defined as necessary to achieve development. The trend was for privatizing aid; this led to a rise in funding for NGOs.

STRUCTURAL ADJUSTMENT & EMPHASIS ON MARKETS

Within this broad global agenda NGOs were seen as both critical service providers and the crucible for innovative development work, especially economic development for the poor. NGOs were recipients of aid money for basic service delivery, replacing the government as prime players in reaching the poor with essential services or expected to fill gaps left by market failure. Many donors felt that NGOs understood the local context better than governments or official donor agencies, and were better placed to reach the very poorest. They were perceived to be working at the grassroots level using more participatory approaches. This approach to development led to a massive rise in the number and size of NGOs in the north and south, and enabled NGOs to gain an international voice and often a place at the table of powerful decision-makers. NGOs were also expected to experiment and provide successful models of working with the poor that other donors, markets or governments could then replicate. They had a clear political role and were expected to promote the political pluralism that was seen as necessary for developing new liberal democracies.

Since then the growing realities of poverty round the world and the voices of NGOs, civil-society movements and other critics in international debates have led to a refocusing of the Bretton Woods institutions on the problems of poverty: how to meet the needs of the poor in the neoliberal agenda and increasingly globalized economies? The reality of economic growth alongside growing poverty and the marginalization of some countries in the new global economic paradigm resulted in the 2000 World Bank development report on poverty: issues such as safety nets and redistribution of wealth returned to the agenda and economic growth, trickle-down and markets were no longer the only approaches to the reduction of poverty.

The focus of the development project has changed dramatically with the chief drivers of pro-poor change now defined as enabling governments (possibly modelled on the successful East Asian states of Taiwan and Korea) rather than only markets and NGOs, though these still have important roles to play. Governments, NGOs and the private sector are all now charged with working together to meet the MDGs. These have eight defined and measurable targets that are time-bound: the broad goals of halving poverty, greatly increasing access to clean water and primary education and addressing gender inequalities are to be achieved by 2015, although anxiety is growing that most of these will not be met in sub-Saharan Africa until at least 2050. Within this paradigm, African governments are expected to create the appropriate frameworks for economic growth, collaboration, decentralization, and responsive policy and planning that are sensitive to the needs of the poor. The dominant belief is that aid given to governments without appropriate policies and delivery structures achieves little. In this scenario civil society has a new role to play in poverty reduction: promoting good pro-poor policies by fostering the direct involvement of poor people in policy development. It is also expected to hold governments to account for their actions and the use of aid, especially when it is disbursed in the form of general budget support, which donors have no real way of monitoring. In addition NGOs are expected to play a role on both the international and national stage, undertaking advocacy work on behalf of the poor to ensure that their needs remain high on the aid agenda and that policies are developed that explicitly meet those needs (Bornstein and Munro, 2003).

Many issues of concern from the NGO agenda of the 1990s have now been taken up and incorporated into the language and approaches of the World Bank, DFID, EU and other major donors. The link between poverty and debt has been acknowledged and partially addressed through limited debt relief. There are now several countries meeting the Highly Indebted Poor Countries (HIPC) criteria and new frameworks have been developed for dispersing the financial aid that is available from debt cancellation to address an explicit poverty agenda. Other perspectives that are now common in debates on aid, drawn largely from NGO agendas, include the focus on participation and empowerment, the concern with building local organizations and promoting local civil society, gender, the importance of advocacy and the fledgling rights agenda. However, in adopting these concepts and mainstreaming them the radical and transformative agenda implicit in their original formation has largely been lost; the concepts are depoliticized and seen more as technical approaches to development, rather than approaches that challenge the way aid is understood and delivered. The way that the World Bank has adopted and reinterpreted the concept of empowerment is a case in point (Chapman et al., 2005).

The new funding mechanisms

Effective government is now seen as essential to pro-poor development, especially in relation to the promotion of democracy, the participation of local people in policy and planning, and providing an enabling framework for economic growth and the delivery of essential services. The IMF and World Bank have shifted their major funding frameworks, which together set the overall aid context that many bilateral and multilateral donors, including the EU and DFID, support, from tight economic structural adjustment conditionalities and mechanisms, to fewer detailed conditions but increased selectivity of the countries to focus aid on, choosing those that have adopted good pro-poor policies. These are identified through the use of Comprehensive Development Frameworks and more recently Poverty Reduction Strategy Plans (PRSPs). The former focuses primarily on financial issues and the latter overtly include policies and procedures for issues as wide as democracy, governance, participation and the role of civil society in setting government policies. They reach deep into the social, economic, political and cultural heart of countries receiving aid. Governments that adopt good policies for poverty (i.e. policies that match those set by the major international institutions) receive increased international aid; countries where governments resist the international agenda, including political and social conditionality as well as economic structural adjustment requirements, theoretically do not get access to it. However, while the concept of greater selectivity and the need to work with states that have clear pro-poor policies are widely discussed, the evidence suggests that in fact donors continue to support states that are poor performers and have not met the conditions of their aid (Lockwood, 2005). The growth of conditionality to change the behaviour of so-called failing states and the reliance on selecting more so-called good-policy states to support with less conditional aid does not yet seem to be working well in practice.

The mechanisms for funding within countries have also changed significantly. The World Bank, DFID and many other donors have progressively moved away from individual project funding for work in education, health or transport for example, to Sector Wide Approaches (SWAPs); this work was pioneered in sub-Saharan Africa. Here donors contribute to a pool of funding for a sector on the basis of a sector strategy plan; this plan has to be agreed with the donors who often actively participate in developing it through their staff or funding consultancies. The most recent shift takes this one step further; most major international donors, including DFID but excluding the US and Japan, now provide direct budget support to governments in countries with appropriate pro-poor policies clearly expressed in the PRSPs.

Governments, in collaboration with civil society, are expected to develop the PRSP framework. The strategies have to encapsulate the new principles for development, namely that economic growth is a necessary condition but is not sufficient for addressing poverty; pro-poor policies must include redistribution mechanisms, such as provision of services directly to the poor, and the involvement of key stakeholders across the country. PRSPs must be developed in ways that ensure they are comprehensive, promote ownership by the country, are based on broad participation and take a long-term approach. PRSPs are expected to achieve concrete results.

The move towards budget support through the PRSP process has been accompanied by a trend to promote decentralization to bring the planning and control of sectoral services closer to the people. Devolution of budgets from national to subnational levels of government is intended to move the decisions for allocating that budget closer to the people, reduce the power of central government and make services more responsive to local needs. NGOs are allocated major roles in the new scenarios. They are to develop and promote the voice of civil society in the planning and policy processes, they are to enable the poor to participate in planning, and they are to monitor the effectiveness and transparency of budget allocation and use, questioning the government when services are not reaching the poor. NGOs north and south are seen as critical actors: 'The UK seeks to achieve this [empowerment at the grassroots] by reinforcing the capacity of northern NGOs to work with southern NGOs to strengthen civil society, both by enhancing the quantity and quality of information available to poor people and by promoting their voice in local decision-making processes.' (Development Assistance Committee of EU, 1999)

The drivers of the new aid mechanisms

The logic driving the changes in the new funding mechanisms and the focus on accountability is multiple. The ideological shift in the World Bank and the broad donor community is only one factor. A second has been a growing disillusion with the results and effectiveness of projects and the lack of sustainability built into ways of working that often set up parallel structures that are not viable beyond the end of the project. A third relates to the fact that the transaction costs of working via projects have been very high, requiring many staff and myriad complex systems; donors are deeply concerned about cutting these costs as treasuries demand increased accountability for aid budgets. In DFID as aid budgets rise transaction costs have to fall, stripping out staff and often expertise, and resulting in a huge rise in the outsourcing of key donor functions to private consultancies. The desire to disburse large sums of money without extensive staff inputs means that direct budget support, large contracts and mega-projects are increasingly seen as the way forward. Fourth, there was evidence that while aid was leading to limited growth in some countries (Lockwood, 2005), poverty was not necessarily diminishing accordingly, so new structures and mechanisms for ensuring poverty reduction were needed.

The evidence to support some of these shifts is lacking and their validity seems questionable; a recent paper by Killick (2004) suggests that, again, development changes are driven more by politics and ideology than by learning from experience and analysis of what happens on the ground. He particularly highlights the push for decentralization and the focus on budget support as being poorly rooted in research and analysis. These changes are primarily fuelled by changing foreign policy positions, along with the outputs of think-tanks and certain key individuals, often funded by the same donors that fund NGOs; evidence-based research does not noticeably shape analysis. This suggests to him that they are likely to fail – as other policy approaches before them – to meet the great hopes pinned on them in relation to achieving the MDGs.

It is interesting to note that the decentralization model also rests on unproved beliefs about the effectiveness of local government and the role of civil society in Africa. Much research, as well as the existing realities in Africa, suggests that local government and civil society are arenas where power can be abused as easily as at a national level. For example, Maina's research in Kenya showed that the most distrusted institutions were in fact provincial administration and local councils, with no respondents having high confidence in these institutions and 93 per cent having no or low confidence in them. They fared even worse than political parties in the survey (Maina, 1998).

Similarly the concept and role of civil society in Africa are often problematic, and poorly analysed and understood (Van Rooy, 1998). Yet donors rely on and expect civil society to play a definitive role in providing accountability mechanisms for governments through, for example, budget tracking and publicizing the misuse of donor funds, despite evidence that in many countries the state curtails the arena for such work and that the larger conflicts in political society are reproduced in civil society. Maina claims that the Kenyan state actively fragments and dissipates the energies of those that question it at all levels. He questions: 'the carnival air surrounding much of the recent discussion of civil society as the midwife of democracy. It argues that the complexities of associational life in Africa are less elegant and seamier than much of the literature cares to admit' (Maina, 1998: 134).

The challenges of the new aid architecture

These changes in thinking and practice bring new challenges for the major institutional donors. The first is finding convincing ways to justify the approach of selecting some countries to be supported via direct budget support on the basis of their domestic policies (Bornstein and Munro, 2003). Donors have developed a range of criteria for those they wish to partner and these are priority countries, but some commentators, not least UNCTAD (2000), have questioned the wisdom and equity of working in this way. They argue that the amount of aid given is so small in relation to need that using selection criteria based on good policies will be relatively meaningless because insufficient money is given to enable governments to deliver on them. Indeed, they argue that the current fluctuating aid funding flows tied to donor conditionalities actually disable governments from taking responsibility for their own policies and delivery. They go further and point out that addressing unreliable and fluctuating aid flows would be a better way to give real support to governments. Sachs (2005) has recently reversed his position on aid and has joined the calls for massive aid increases, which would go some way towards addressing the concerns of many economists about the unreliable and sometimes meagre flows of aid.

Other commentators, such as Development Initiatives, highlight the fact that conditionality does not actually work. In addition, it implies a lack of confidence that donors and recipients share goals and intentions and so cannot lead to the building of strong partnerships or relationships, something that donors now see as essential for effective aid (Pomerantz, 2004). Others argue that this tie between donors and southern government policies reduces the accountability of governments to their own people, and this is an issue donors find hard to refute. There is a common fear, expressed in the media in many African countries, that as long as governments seek out and secure donor funding tied to certain policies, they can remain in power. This was debated heatedly in the Ugandan press during the 2002–3 elections, when many argued that Museveni was able to ignore the needs of Ugandans because of his financial support from the international donor community.

This selection approach also raises problems for donors, because it ties them closely to key recipient governments that may subsequently do things they do not endorse. This dilemma was highlighted in Uganda when Museveni, while heavily supported by donors, displeased them by refusing multiparty democracy for many years and continuing Uganda's involvement in the Congo war. In addition, rumours of corruption in Uganda grew. Divergences from donor policy cause real dilemmas, which donors often have to overlook or address through quiet diplomatic lobbying. They can then stand accused of double standards, where for example a country not selected for budget support because of corruption (such as Kenya under Moi) appears no more corrupt in many ways than one that is selected for support (such as Uganda).

Another major challenge is how best to ensure financial control and accountability. Donors are handing over money to governments to spend according to agreed policies tied to the PRSP, but how can this be tracked? Tracking studies done by the World Bank show a high degree of seepage as money passes through government ministries to new decentralized systems (School of Public Policy, 2000), and finding ways to monitor and counteract this seems elusive. Donors have tried two different approaches: the first is to put their own staff and supervisors into key posts, to help develop and then monitor policy implementation. The ministries of finance in many countries in Africa now have many donor staff working in them in different roles. A second approach is to expect local civil society to become the watchdogs and monitors of government probity and spending. Local-level organizations are now expected to be involved in developing good monitoring frameworks for spending through the PRSP.

Thus the responsibility for the accountability of donor funds is being shifted from the donors themselves to government departments and civil society. This requires a huge change of role for civil society, including many local NGOs, which were until recently seen primarily by donors as service providers for the poor. Playing this role may be complicated by a parallel expectation that now NGOs must access funding for their work directly from national or local governments and work within local and national delivery plans. NGOs are thus to be both watchdogs of government and also dependent on funding from them for their work (Lister, 2004).

Critiques of key elements of the new architecture

These are relatively new frameworks and approaches. However, concerns have been raised already about PRSPs and the way they have been developed. Many observers argue that their content is largely dictated by the World Bank and that there has been limited room for challenging or questioning IMF and World Bank economic paradigms. The time allocated for their development has often been too limited to allow real participation, yet issues of who has been represented, and who has not, are critical (Richmond, 2003).

The World Bank talks of PRSPs putting governments in the driving seat. However, some governments describe themselves instead as chauffeurs: for example, the Uganda High Commissioner used this analogy in a speech he gave at the Africa Centre in 2002. Lack of representation is apparent. For example, gender inequalities play a key role in keeping many women and girls in poverty and this is overtly recognized in all policy documents, where gender mainstreaming is defined as essential for poverty reduction, yet gender analysis is sadly lacking in most PRSPs, except in relation to girls' access to education (Whitehead, 2003).

There is also growing criticism that donors do not pay adequate attention to global issues. The PRSPs focus on poverty, as do the donors, but it is a national framework, looking only at the internal workings of a country, its government and institutions. It does not allow for the analysis of the international trends that cause or contribute to poverty, but many argue that these – especially restrictive trade agreements and the often low prices paid for primary commodities – are critically important in shaping the entire development agenda. These are the subjects of major campaigns by such organizations as Oxfam, ActionAid and the World Development Movement. Many argue that unfair and unequal trade is more critical to the continuation of poverty than aid flows; the Fair Trade movement highlights this continually. Trade was central to the Make Poverty History campaign in 2005 and was accepted as critical by the G8 in that year, yet few changes were proposed to lessen the bias against poor countries in the global trade system. The lack of focus on the global structures

that reproduce deep inequalities between countries and regions make PRSPs a
flalwed mechanism.   ⌈THIS IS IMF SO HARDLY ⌉

Behind the PRSPs stands the Poverty Reduction and Growth Facility (PRGF),
which is actually the core aid disbursement mechanism. There are many
problems with the PRGF approach and critics argue that this economic approach
can never enable countries to meet their commitments on poverty; it is described
by some as a continuation of past IMF and World Bank neoliberal, structural
adjustment economic policies (Nyamugasira and Rowden, 2002; Matthews,
2003).

Contrasting definitions of development: what is the project?

In order to understand the implications for NGOs of these enormous shifts in
aid mechanisms it is important to try and unpick the contested notion of
development itself. Concepts and ideologies of development and how to promote
positive change for poor people vary widely. In the past these have shifted from
modernization, to theories of underdevelopment, to the neoliberal model of
promoting capitalist development globally, based on economic development as
the driver of change. Strategies based on leftist ideologies suffered a collapse at
the end of the cold war, leading some to reject development as a process altogether
and to advocate for social movements as the key to real change for poor people
(Parfitt, 2002). These more theoretical issues are often absent from the current
development debates. Yet it is essential to grasp what development is, or could
be, in order to guide NGOs in deciding what funding and conditions to accept
or reject, and how best to work to achieve benefits for the poor.

When many NGOs started their work in development during the 1960s and
1970s there were essentially two dominant paradigms of development. One
was rooted in capitalism and promoted an understanding of history as progress,
based on five stages of development culminating in economic development
mirroring the most economically advanced nations (Rostow, 1953). The thinking
is pervasive 50 years on. The other was based on an analysis of how the rich
world was recreating the inequalities of the colonial past through active
engagement with the processes of extraction and underdevelopment in poorer
countries, which was a Marxian analysis of history (Rodney, 1973).

Since the fall of the Soviet block, which provided Africa with an alternative
ideology, analysis and funding, development has increasingly been defined in
the neoliberal economic terms described above. At the current time the global
agenda is clearly dominated by the belief in economic development and growth,
with a growing recognition of the need for policies to ensure trickle-down,
which was in the past assumed. There are few alternatives to this model at
present, although there are post-modern and post-colonial thinkers who reject
the whole concept of historical progress and the notion of the slow improvement
of humanity. They see the global development project as one shaped in the
image of the world powers, which ignores the diversity and complexity of
other histories and other criteria for achieving and assessing well-being, the

public good and equality. This writing is to be found in feminist literature, environmental analyses, reflections on race and racism and much post-colonial writing coming out of Africa, Asia and Latin America. Many of these thinkers reject all forms of the modern development project, which they see as necessarily intrusive, dominating, carrying northern models and ideas into other cultures and contexts in ways that are disempowering and which fail to bring about positive change. These thinkers include Sachs (1992), Esteva (1992) and Escobar (1995). They feel that: 'development has been harmful and that consequently it should be consigned to the dustbin of history in order to make way for the new strategies of emancipation' (Parfitt, 2002: 5).

A few of these commentators see the main hope for the poor lying in new social movements, outside the influence and dominance of organizations and agencies working to development agendas set by the economic institutions of the powerful capitalist industrialized countries. These social movements include a wide range of forms, including reactionary as well as progressive ones. Some are violent, though most are based on peaceful approaches to fundamental change.

Recent debates about the model are also to be heard around the NEPAD (New Partnership for Africa's Development) initiative. People ask whether it is just more of the same economically, dominated and orchestrated by the north, or whether it does offer hope of a different political approach, shifting some decision-making power and control to Africa, even though it is firmly rooted in neoliberal economics (Parfitt, 2002; Petras and Veltmeyer, 2001; Hirsh, 2003).

The context provides a difficult and challenging terrain for NGOs. In the past they were often the alternative voice, challenging the relevance and value of neoliberal approaches in meeting the needs of the poor. In recent times the hegemony of the Washington consensus brooks little opposition despite its lack of success in reducing poverty: within the IMF, dissent is discouraged, and people who raise questions about whether the approach is actually working are actively silenced. For example in reflecting on his tenure as Chief Economist at the World Bank, Stiglitz observed:
   CABOUT THE IMF!

Alternative opinions were not sought. Open, frank discussion was discouraged – there was no room for it. Ideology guided policy prescriptions and countries were expected to follow IMF guidelines without debate (Stiglitz, 2002: xiv).

Although many NGOs continue to have misgivings about the nature of globalization and the spread of IMF and World Bank economic paradigms around the world, they often find themselves distanced from the new social movements – though they come together at the World Social Forum annually – and find few alternative models on which to draw. Many NGOs now see their job as working within the economic and social model of development while trying to limit its excesses, through focusing on economic growth with a human face, demanding better trade rules and calling for debt relief in favour of the poorest countries or increased aid. They also work to raise public awareness of global inequalities.

Others do not question the larger paradigm, but rather focus on projects that they can see might benefit poor people in the countries where they work, such as providing service delivery for poor people who are being overlooked. Some NGOs provide support to those for whom the conditions of survival have been so eroded, through conflict or environmental degradation, that they require welfare support; the number of NGOs working in humanitarian and emergency aid, and global funding for it, has risen significantly in recent years.

However, there are a few NGOs which do openly grapple with the larger questions raised by the wider context and where NGOs should sit within the current economic paradigm. The Bretton Woods project, an NGO project, actively engages with the IMF and the World Bank on issues of ideology, policy and practice (Wallace, 2004). A minority of NGOs in the south and some academics and NGOs in the north do fundamentally question the economic model and its ability to ever be inclusive or address the multiple needs of the poor in Africa. Some NGOs have picked up on the idea of social movements as the drivers of positive change and have actively committed themselves to working to support movements of poor people demanding and addressing the need for major change, for example ActionAid International and the Agency for Cooperation and Research in Development (ACORD). These recognize that to work in solidarity with social movements requires very different ways of working and have, as a first step, relocated their headquarters in Africa. To date they experience many dilemmas in operating within this new paradigm while maintaining their work as formal development agencies.

NGOs, especially those based in the north, are increasingly being challenged to identify where they sit in the aid business and what their role and ideology actually are. Lister and Lewis were asked by different UK NGOs to look forward to identify northern NGO roles and strengths in 10 years time (Lister 2004; Lewis 2003b). One issue they both honed in on was how northern NGOs are viewed by southern NGOs, many of which are becoming especially hostile to northern NGOs, which are often seen as part of the problem rather than part of the solution, mainly because of their close relationships – in receiving funding and consulting with – the levers of global power. They challenged UK NGOs to rethink their role; to redefine their understanding of development and change their relationships with donors and their southern partners; and they highlighted real problems concerning their reception in the south.

Concluding comment

NGOs are operating in an environment in which they are asked, and expected, to deliver in fundamental ways on the improvement of conditions for the world's poor. At the same time, as this chapter suggests, the broader model of development is flawed and obstacles to improvements are constituted at the international as well as national (and subnational) level. The issues presented in this chapter are critical in helping to situate NGOs within the wider global context and identifying the concepts and approaches to development that they implicitly support.

The book goes on to explore empirically how far NGOs are working within these paradigms to challenge and change them or whether they are implementing these approaches and acting as carriers of these ideologies and ways of working deep into the countries where they work. However, before moving to the presentation of the data, some of the core languages of development and their theoretical underpinnings are explored in more depth in the following chapter.

central site mechanisms and approaches to [illegible] that they [illegible] support.

The next chapter sets out to explore empirically how the NGOs [illegible] in challenging and [illegible] more [illegible] implementing [illegible] into the communities where they work. However, [illegible] meaning [illegible] representation of the data [illegible] following chapter.

CHAPTER 3
The management of development

Introduction

The understanding of development and how to promote it changes constantly among development thinkers and practitioners. Some thinking and analysis are informed by contributions and thinking from the south; more often they are driven by changing ideology and theories of how best to manage development and address the mistakes of the past generated in the north. This chapter explores how NGOs in the UK have responded to the changing context, where broad ideological lines have shifted, belief in the development project has foundered, new mechanisms of funding, selectivity and poverty-related packaging have emerged, and NGOs have found, or been given, new roles. The focus is on the language of development and associated ways of working. As the analysis and language of development have changed, so too have the conditions of funding and the way development is undertaken.

There are two distinct languages, one of rational management, the other broadly focused around participation, which coexist in development discourses. These are founded on different understandings of how development occurs (concepts of change), who directs it (concepts of agency) and where accountability lies (concepts of control). The first emphasizes planning for predictable outcomes, management designed to achieve planned results, with strict lines of accountability; the other focuses on finding ways to engage with people very different to oneself in order to promote participation and ownership, and draws on an understanding of change as contingent and locally driven. NGOs and their funders use participatory and management techniques and methodologies, often without recognizing or reconciling their very different conceptual and ideological foundations; this poses problems for development practitioners, as later chapters will illustrate.

While the packaging of aid by institutional donors and INGOs draws heavily on these different languages, the mechanisms of rational management have [*RATIONAC MANAGEMENT*] been systematized, institutionalized and embedded in aid bureaucracies. Our concern, confirmed by the research, was that this heavy reliance on one managerial model would overshadow and possibly undermine a commitment to participatory approaches to development. In understanding how one language has come to dominate through standardized procedures and systems of accountability, it is important to recognize where power lies and how it is currently used in north–south funding aid chains, something often acknowledged but rarely analysed (Chambers, 2004, Mosse, 2005).

NGOs and the packaging of aid

The broad, changing ideologies presented in Chapter 2 guide much contemporary financing of development work. Funding patterns and practices change in line with political priorities, global strategies and current theories of how development can be best effected, as seen in Table 3.1 below.

Past critiques of why development fails highlight problems in both approaches (rational and participatory): poor planning, weak ownership by local stakeholders, lack of beneficiary participation, corruption and the weak capacity of individuals, organizations, and institutions (Cernea, 1991). These still cause problems in contemporary grant-making. The push to improve planning and control is reflected in the shift away from varied and loose project formats to the

Table 3.1   Changing development priorities and aid instruments for UK donors and NGOs

Time period	Donor focus	Donor instruments	NGO focus	NGO instruments
1970s	Basic needs Household surveys Support to governments (concern about corruption)	Projects, especially infrastructure Integrated rural development projects Technical experts	Solidarity between NGOs north & south. Focus on voluntary spirit & voluntary donations	Very varied project application forms, individually developed within each NGO. Many NGOs have no centralized uniform documents or policies
1980s	Effective projects, donor-controlled Appropriate macro-economic policies Structural adjustment (later with a human face) mandatory for many countries	Logframes Technical cooperation Overseas training Social investment funds Structural Adjustment Programmes upholding IMF requirements for liberalization Projects continue to dominate aid disbursement	Reducing role of expatriates, employing national staff NGOs as pilots & catalysts Identifying good practice: gender, environment, poverty focus, participation & PRA Concern with appropriate images of the south Development education in north Growing use of official aid	Some NGOs start to adopt logframes, most still use own frameworks Many NGOs have few organizational policies & uniform procedures; larger ones start to introduce policies on project management & gender Some NGOs focus on evaluation

Table 3.1 (Contd)

Time period	Donor focus	Donor instruments	NGO focus	NGO instruments
1990s	Projects to focus on the poor, address gender & be environmentally sensitive Democracy, good governance, sound economic policies & national government ownership of poverty agendas End to poverty	Participatory rural appraisal, stakeholder analysis, process projects within LFA. More direct funding of NGOs, less technical cooperation, more consultancies Sector-wide approaches (SWAPs), HIPC initiatives (debt rebates to the poor) Different approaches to getting good reports from NGOs (always a problem)	Focus on capacity-building for southern NGOs Scaling up successful service delivery projects Sustainability Advocacy work in the north Gender mainstreaming Moving from projects to programmes Massive increase in donor funding	Sharp rise in use of logframes as key project management tool Adoption of strategic planning as main organizational tool Concerns with accountability; rise in reporting Significant growth of M&E Beginning to assess impact of advocacy work
2000s	Reduction of corruption Transparent & accountable governments Decentralization of governments & donors Sound macroeconomics & pro-poor growth Ending poverty through MDGs Getting voices of the poor into policies Making globalization work for people	National programmes & frameworks: PRSPs & PRGFs, comprehensive development frameworks Targets & MDGs Funding to government — budget support. Influencing as important as resource transfers Harmonization between donors Decline of projects Contracts	Increase in advocacy & lobbying work Focus on rights Shift toward 'learning organizations Global strategies Growing reliance on donor funding Anxiety about decline of DFID funding as it shifts to direct support to governments	Focus on learning organizations Almost universal use of LFA, strategic planning, reporting systems, impact assessment & use of development indicators, from project to global level Focus on MDGs, impact, efficiency, & effectiveness Rise in evaluation & concerns with cost-effectiveness

Source: Eyben, 2002.

almost universal use of logical frameworks (logframes), the proliferation of project cycle assessment procedures and guidelines, and indicator-based reporting systems designed to show cost-effectiveness and impact. Participation and a sense of local ownership (at government or community level) are now promoted as essential to achieving relevant and lasting change. There has been a burgeoning of participatory techniques (PLA notes, 1988 onwards; Welbourn, 1995; Braden, 2004) and the methodologies of participation are innovative, many and varied; however, they are not codified beyond agency manuals.

Aid is not disbursed using participatory mechanisms but on the basis of logframes. The need for planning and control outweighs the push for participation at the bureaucratic level. While participation usually features as an essential part of the logframe it is only one component in the system of planning, implementation, monitoring and reporting.

The language and practice of rational management   *THE LOGFRAME*

The logframe is the most well-known tool for aid disbursement, used by almost all donors and NGOs in the UK, Europe and US; it is the basic project document that includes project goals, plans, timetables for implementation, required inputs and expected outcomes with associated measurements (indicators), and an analysis or listing of external factors and internal assumptions that may be a risk to the achievement of the goals. It aims to tighten the links between objectives, inputs and activities in order to achieve predicted outputs and longer-term outcomes. Proponents of the logical framework note that, by summarizing the essential elements of a complex programme in a simple format, information can be easily shared and reviewed by donors, implementers and other stakeholders. It is often described as a neutral management tool, a way of systematizing volumes of information and a good way to handle complexity manageably. The logframe has undergone rapid diffusion since the 1990s (Wallace, Crowther and Shepherd, 1997) and most UK funders and NGOs now rely on this way of documenting development work. It has spread from its original use in project planning into programme and sector work, framing strategic relationships (partnership agreements with DFID are based on a logframe) and even global-level work. For instance, donor direct budget support to national governments (a multimillion-pound programme) is conceptualized in a logframe (Lawson and Booth, 2004).

Logframes are increasingly presented as a series of causal arrows, from the goal to the final outcomes, taking the reader from the overall purpose to the expected changes in an unbroken line. The risks that could derail the process are captured beside each step of the process, but are often superficial and rarely revisited. Reporting, based on monitoring and evaluation procedures, is done against the predicted changes and indicators laid out in the logframe; a great deal of time in NGOs is spent identifying methodologies to generate relevant indicators. Yet especially at the global and strategic levels these are hard to delineate.

The management of controlled and predictable change also underlies the development of the MDGs, where the assumption is that increased aid for specific sectors can, if well managed and not misused (the fear of corruption is a major concern), produce the expected reductions in poverty. This approach to development identifies key targets for reducing poverty and indicators for measuring success. The approach was heavily promoted globally by DFID, among others, once the critical importance of securing universal buy-in became apparent and donor-driven development targets became global goals. Almost all countries signed up to these, in spite of the abundant evidence of the failure of targets in other sectors in the UK, for example education and health. The global failure to meet the MDGs is now an issue, especially in sub-Saharan Africa where almost no goals are on target. However, rather than re-evaluating the appropriateness of a target-focused approach, governments and NGOs continue to push for increased funding and corruption control to ensure they will be met (Lockwood, 2005). National Poverty Reduction Strategy Plans (PRSPs), the tool on which debt relief and direct budget support rely, are also based on clear poverty plans leading to measurable change. PRSPs ostensibly promote participation in the planning stage, though this has occurred with variable success and only within a wider framework of what international agencies agree are the right ways to tackle poverty (Whitehead, 2003; Richmond, 2003).

The conceptual basis of rational planning and management

It is curious that in the same period as the rise of many 'post-' concepts – post-modernism, post-Fordism, post-colonialism – and concomitant demands that the global powerful should hear other voices, that development practice should be dominated by techniques rooted in technocratic, mechanistic and positivist thinking. It is surprising that given the wide range of planning and management approaches available, a model has been chosen that others, such as some in the corporate sector, have dropped (Hailey, 2003).

Planning literature is replete with examples of the flaws of positivist top-down, rational-comprehensive planning. Such planning presumes that change can be controlled and directed, that a 'good' plan done in the public interest – or according to a commonly defined collective objective – can be carried out, leading to the desired change. It presumes that planners and other technical experts have the specialized knowledge to plan well; and thus planning is seen as a technical exercise. The multiple weaknesses of such approaches were identified long ago (Altshuler, 1965; Schön, 1983), based on procedural, epistemological and moral concerns. Some writers focused on the impossibility of ever capturing complex realities in a single immutable plan; limited information and ill-defined complex causal relationships meant that planning was likely to be incremental, satisficing and rationally bounded (Lindblom, 1959). Differing public understandings of issues and their different interests regarding resolutions further contributed to 'wicked problems', ones that were messy and unlikely to be resolved on the basis of any technical analysis of a best way forward (Webber and Rittel, 1973). The public or community interest was left largely unexamined, with the experts drawing up plans for intervention based on their analysis of a public good; differences of class, race and gender were 'not considered relevant' (Sandercock, 1998: 88). In reality plans and programmes often fed into prevailing imbalances of power and assumed rather than built consensus. However, although the limitations of such approaches are very well known, the model remains highly influential.

The rational management techniques employed in contemporary development practice are not as ambitious as some of the worst rational-comprehensive planning approaches, yet there are many similarities. The planning and management tools mimic much of the rational engineering approach; the logical framework is a blueprint approach (Howes, 1992: 393) reflecting a positivist worldview in which development is characterized by linear causality; progress is a question of achieving the specified steps. Change at individual and organizational levels is presumed to be measurable, a simple comparison between achievements and predefined milestones. The analysis of the external environment requires boiling complex realities down into a set of risks and assumptions that could affect the links between one action and its desired outcomes. Yet in development much activity is process-oriented, and outcomes are the product of multiple forces, open-ended and hard to attribute to well-designed inputs (Bornstein, 2003; Cracknell, 2000; Gasper, 2000).

Even if multiple causes are acknowledged, the logframe rests on what Brinkerhoff calls a 'convergent model of assessment', wherein the focus is on the intended effect (Brinkerhoff and Tuthill, 1987). Left out is careful consideration, or measurement, of unintended and secondary effects. The tight structure with its predetermined goals makes it difficult to incorporate or adjust for deviation (Fowler and Biekart, 1996). It presumes a level of autonomy from wider social and political forces that is known to be illusive if not impossible. Moreover, it underestimates the importance of social interactions and perceptions – such as friendship, trust, embarrassment and prestige (Uphoff, 1996) – that may be crucial to processes of change: 'The linear view of change, prompted by the logframe, where processes feed into each other in an orderly hierarchical manner is perhaps a Western construct, and is certainly one imposed by agencies from above, bearing little relation to the "reality" of development work' (Earle 2003: 2).

The approach to expertise is also problematic. Despite donor or NGO instructions to the contrary, often the logical framework is constructed or finalized by a few individuals, staff or consultants, sitting in an office, working with a vague mandate from local people and a clear set of strategic objectives from potential donors. They may know that they are not constructing the best possible plan, but they are putting together one that is plausible on the basis of their own knowledge. This also raises questions about the legitimacy of the resulting plans and documents, for both beneficiaries and staff.

Given the flaws, why has this approach dominated?

The use of rational planning in development does not take place in isolation; it is deeply embedded in current UK political and managerial approaches to change. There are strong similarities between the reliance on controlling and managing work to achieve fixed targets in development and these approaches in the UK. Alisdair MacIntyre, a moral philosopher, argues that it is a modern bureaucratic managerial illusion that people or organizations have the ability to control and shape events yet this belief drives the new public management. While there is some predictability and logic in the world enabling us to plan and engage in long-term projects, 'the pervasive unpredictability in human life also renders all our plans and projects permanently vulnerable and fragile' (MacIntyre, 2002: 103). He challenges the concepts of managerial expertise and effectiveness, which create an 'illusion of social control', but belie the complexity of the unpredictable and the limits of social control in reality, although he recognizes that the notions of planning and control are beguiling.

[Margin note: CRITIQUE OF PLANNING]

Other critics, who highlight the potentially destructive nature of this approach, also acknowledge its attraction for those in power; targets and the audit are paramount even when they undermine treasured goals:

> the demands and expectations of central and local government – with their strict performance criteria, emphasis on quantitative outputs and formal participatory structures, such as local strategic partnerships – all act against community projects achieving their aim…as this report shows, a heavy audit culture often breeds an atmosphere of distrust and risk aversion, which encourages uniformity in programme design and inhibits the distinctive contribution that CBOs [community-based organizations] make (Demos, 2003).

While they advocate focusing on 'extending and developing people based systems that emphasize ongoing, face-to-face contact between partners and rest on horizontal or mutual forms of accountability' (Demos, 2003) and locally determined outcomes, this is not the norm. Seddon (2005) also demonstrates how widely the UK government has adopted command and control principles across the board, in his view damaging public services and demoralizing workers. This demoralization, and even cynicism, is reported by those in local government, services and businesses, where workers try to grapple with inappropriate and often irrelevant centrally set targets in contexts unrelated to those described on paper. He urges the dismantling of this approach, while recognizing that even challenging it now is seen as suspect.

The rational approach to change denies the limits of control, and bureaucracies assume ever greater degrees of power and dominance in an attempt to manage unpredictability. When things go wrong, the belief in the centrality of the tools for achieving targets leads to efforts to invent new and better tools and an insistence on even tighter bureaucratic controls in the mistaken assumption that the right managerial approach will control complexity and solve problems. Questions are rarely raised about the approaches, a point made strongly in relation to the World Bank, which is said to consistently blame poor policy implementation as the cause of failure in Africa rather than examining the validity of the policies themselves (Stiglitz, 2002).

Those with power can promote the approaches they prefer

This approach to managing development is promoted by those who hold the power in the aid chain, the institutional donors and many of the trustees of UK NGOs and independent donor organizations. It is not possible to ignore the dynamics of 'he who calls the piper plays the tune' that are so evident in the development aid chain, although there is a reluctance among donors and UK NGOs to get to grips with the issue of their power over funding and funding conditionalities. Some literature emphasizes the power of funders over recipients, showing the inequality that is rooted in the direction of aid flows (Fowler, 2000a; Sogge, 2002), while noting that relationships of power and influence are not solely one-sided (Hulme and Edwards,1997; Fowler, 2000a) and individuals have the power to refuse to comply with agreements, or to bend rules and adopt unruly practices (Fraser, 1989).

The power of the donors is often mentioned, yet it is rarely central to the analysis of how development works and little attention is paid to the ways in which people negotiate the use of new practices and funding conditions, with a few important exceptions (Chapman et al., 2005; ActionAid, 2001). Inequalities are acknowledged, then brushed aside or hidden through the use of language: the terms 'partner' and 'partnership' replace the concepts of donor-recipient or subcontractor. While donors and NGOs in the UK universally use these terms, many so-called partners in Africa feel more like supplicants or dependents. For many this language of partnership denies the relationships of power, but in reality these are strong and defined by some as the new colonialism. References to Fanon were heard in discussions, especially in Uganda, where many said aid relationships echoed their colonial past: those with the power and control talk of cooperation and shared aims while those at the receiving end dissemble, fall in line and play their part convincingly. Some commit to their recipient roles with enthusiasm because there are many financial and status gains to be made by participating in the international aid process, and ideas from outside Africa are believed by some to be superior and more professional (Fanon, 1991). In SA, power sometimes played out along racial lines, with white educated NGO leaders able to negotiate the terms and conditions of aid with donors, who were similar in outlook and profile. However, many NGO leaders in Uganda and SA felt unable to take such a proactive stance and were relatively disempowered as 'the other' in the relationship (Said, 2003).

The reality of donor power and the urgent need of local NGOs to access scarce funding means that most people at every level have an interest in buying into the dominant paradigm of how to manage development in 'aidland'. Apthorpe (2003) captured well the current ahistorical and apolitical, universal approaches to planning and accounting for aid in contexts of poverty that are hugely diverse. While this standardization makes little sense in a differentiated world, the way power and funding work together mean, he argued, that it is in everyone's interests to subscribe to the accepted way of doing development work. Attention to politics and power would require challenging the norms, and development practitioners would have to broaden their repertoire of skills and approaches. The reality is that 'development management is inherently political and (requires)...the diagnosis of political context and organisational politics [is] more than techniques' (Staudt, quoted in Lewis, 2001: 19) but the tools attempt to ignore that, iron out complexity and create a sense that universally applied approaches can bring the solutions needed if everyone works to the dominant agenda.

The hold of logframe analysis

The 'specification and inspection regime' (Seddon, 2005) is what holds the managerial approach firmly in place. The audit culture is predicated on the need for control and accountability, and a fear of people cheating; it fits easily with global concerns about corruption and the misuse of funds in both government and NGOs in the south (Simbi and Thom, 2000). The use of rational planning tools presumes a world in which people can design and manage development processes to produce certain results and accountability can be tightly tied to reporting on plans. Unpredictability, complexity and incremental or non-linear change need not be addressed seriously, if at all, at the reporting stage, where the focus is on demonstrating the expected impact to ensure future respect, influence and funding.

The tensions between accountability to donors and accountability to beneficiaries are well known (Paton, 2003) and organizations need to find ways to satisfy both if they are to survive, in theory at least. So while large companies have to report to shareholders, they also have to meet the needs of their customers; sometimes what is good for shareholders is not good for customers. However, because they feel their survival ultimately lies in being passionate about their customers, they know the importance of communication with them in order to flourish. For development agencies there is a recognized need to be closely in touch and accountable to donors, beneficiaries and partners; the same tensions apply and what may be best for the donors sometimes may not work well for the beneficiaries. However, in this case only one side has real power, the donors, and reporting against the logframe shifts accountability firmly away from beneficiaries and partners (and even host governments) towards the donors. While there is much talk of downward accountability, there is little evidence of this in practice, and as one development worker put it in the UK, 'You don't see NGOs being passionate about the poor and wanting to meet their needs in the way (a large supermarket) does with their customers.' Indeed, workshops and conversations in NGOs in the UK are now far more likely to focus on how to secure new funders, extra funding and meet the demands of new funding streams than they are to be on how to listen to the poor or examining what the poor need from us; there is an urgent need for NGOs to start using as a yardstick whether their work is what a poor person wants from them (Chambers, 2004).

O'Neill highlights the way the accountability function ties public-sector life tightly to external control: 'Central planning may have failed in the former Soviet Union but it is alive and well in Britain today. The new accountability culture aims at ever more perfect administrative control of institutional and professional life' (O'Neill, 2002: Lecture 3).

This approach, according to O'Neill, risks replacing trust and judgement, 'distorting the proper aims of professional practice and indeed...damaging professional pride and integrity'. Efforts to achieve better performance and results often actually threaten the quality of work, by inhibiting people from using their skills in innovative ways and hedging them about with bureaucratic controls. The pressure for counting and accounting is so strong that trust, flexibility, and the ability to adapt and change are often undermined.

Demonstrating impact has become a watchword in development: the purpose is both to account for the use of funds and highlight achievements. Perhaps partly because of the paucity of internal learning and lack of knowledge about what has been achieved long term by UK NGOs the pressure is now on to prove their added value. In turn, DFID is now tied to a public service agreement with the Treasury and has to demonstrate the value of its work to the UK parliament and by extension the taxpayer. This resulted in the first DFID Development Effectiveness Review (2002), which, while unable to reach firm conclusions, did initiate discussions about the need for DFID to become more accountable for its work; this knocks on to those organizations DFID funds. Questions about the use and relevance of EU funding have also been asked and led to a consultancy by COTA (2004) to explore how to assess impact. The Community Fund started questioning the impact of their funding under a new chair of the board in 2002, and since then it has been searching for ways to ensure their funding has demonstrable impact, which some call the Coca-Cola effect. In 2004 Comic Relief trustees asked management consultants to look at how to increase the impact and effectiveness of its funding: their major concerns were identifying tangible outcomes on the ground and learning how to back success. Within individual UK NGOs trustees ask chief executives to explain and justify the use of their income in terms of positive impact on the lives of those with whom they work and also on the profile of the NGO.

Participatory planning and human development

Management literature suggests there are multiple management approaches to working cross-culturally, over distance, and in contexts of uncertainty and threat (Hailey, 2003; Lewis, 2001). There are approaches that stress the need to focus on actors rather than systems, to promote bottom-up approaches rather than top-down methodologies. The list of analysts calling for alternative development focused on people, local knowledge and participation includes Escobar (1995), Long and Long (1992) and Chambers (1997). The shared elements in these different approaches to planning are attention to: power relations in the planning process and within communities; the role and authority of the development practitioner vis-à-vis other actors with other types of knowledge and authority; the importance of communication for decision-making; and the justice and legitimacy of actions. One practitioner organization, CDRA in SA, for example proposes a radically different understanding of how to manage change, talking of the need for deep skills to work with change that is in fact difficult to control, count and measure. It warns of the dangers of approaches that reduce complex concepts to measurables:

> The dominant, competitive, market driven global paradigm dictates that power is used to the advantage of those who have the advantage. The view of practitioners closer to the periphery is that those at the centre are about to take ownership, and thus control, of what is most important to them. There is a deep fear that in order to effectively measure it, empowerment will be reduced to the level of becoming the next development deliverable or handout, provided by the more powerful through capacity building workshops, training programmes and participatory projects (Taylor, 2002: 1).

Amartya Sen and others argue that a rich mix of organizational cultures is essential for democracy and deep-rooted development to flourish. The importance of diversity was recognized in a speech by the UK Chancellor:

> So, I believe, with you, that the great strength of voluntary action – and why we should value your independence – is your capacity for the individual and unique rather than the impersonal and standardised approach…(you)…are far better positioned than ever a government official could be, both to see a problem and to define effective action. It is about being there…and governments should have the humility to recognise that voluntary organisations can provide solutions that governments cannot offer (Brown, 2004).

Yet current approaches promote a move away from 'letting a thousand flowers bloom', once seen as a major strength of the non-government sector, towards very uniform global approaches. Logframes, indicators and reporting guidelines are found everywhere and often referred to in English because the terms are untranslatable locally (Mawdsley et al., 2002). This seriously risks undermining the variety and diversity critical to building strong civil societies.

Many NGOs pride themselves on their support for local participation and their commitment to enabling local beneficiaries to identify development problems, plan interventions and carry out implementation. Most NGOs recognize that a failure to include participation and 'put people first…seriously undercuts the effectiveness of projects that attempt to induce and accelerate development' (Cernea, 1991: 8). Information on local needs and conditions, buy-in by elites, officials or other community actors, and local monitoring are among the obvious advantages of including participatory elements in a project.

Of course there are flaws that have to be guarded against, including the possibilities of participants feeling exploited and co-opted, increased levels of external surveillance and control (Scott, 1998), domination by local elites and the exclusion of marginalized people (Mosse, n.d.), and the many divisions and complexities of 'communities that make them hard to work with as entities' (Gujit and Shah, 1998). The many challenges of tackling exclusion on the basis of gender, disability, HIV/AIDS and minority status are the subject of workshops and several books. Nonetheless, if practised sensitively, participation is expected to improve the likelihood that projects are relevant to people and ensure that enough local support is generated to make implementation feasible. Increased stakeholder involvement can minimize the misappropriation of funds and maximize the possibility of the project continuing beyond the end of external funding.

In addition to these pragmatic considerations, participation is also viewed as an end in itself, an integral – if not the central – part of any development process. Chambers and Korten are well-known proponents; however, there are many well-known contributors to the contemporary practice of making participation and empowerment the central development project (Freire, 1972). Rahnema summarizes the ethics and legitimacy underlying this approach: 'Participation is justified because it expresses not only the will of the majority of the people, but also it is the only way for them to ensure that the important moral, humanitarian, social, cultural and economic objectives of a more humane and effective development can be peacefully attained' (1992: 120).

Such a participatory focus is, by definition, highly contingent, sometimes slow and often unpredictable. Improvements in social conditions, services and skills are core activities around which human development can flourish, but must be accommodated to fit locally defined priorities, timeframes and constraints. Allowing space for local knowledge is essential; people often have intimate knowledge of their own conditions, sociopolitical dynamics, customs, beliefs and attitudes that will directly affect the way development processes proceed or unravel. This knowledge is now tapped through a wide range of participatory methodologies that include visual, oral, dramatic and written traditions.

Many donors the world over also accept the significance of participation in improving aspects of project development and acknowledge that, in spite of ambiguities and challenges, local contributions and inputs are essential and must appear in project plans. Local beneficiaries, and sometimes local government and civil-society representatives, must be consulted at various points in the project cycle, from identification to evaluation. Beneficiaries must often supplement the project by contributing time and labour, typically 10–25 per cent of the value of the grant. Most donors want to know what proportion of project staff and community participants are women or, less systematically, are from historically disadvantaged groups. Other donors have more elaborate approaches, outlining, for example, the use of specific participatory methodologies.

There are numerous challenges associated with donors' introduction of participatory approaches. While official recognition of the role of local actors in development is important, such donor approaches can systematize and often depoliticize the push for participation (Ferguson, 1990; White, 1996), which all too easily becomes a technical exercise. Moreover, the 'empiricist predilection' of participatory methods can result in 'insufficient attention…to legitimacy and justice', and a 'tendency to get bogged down in methods and techniques without stopping adequately to consider initial assumptions of broader issues (e.g. about the purpose of the techniques)' (Kapoor, 2002: 102).

The conceptual basis of participatory planning within donor frameworks

Concepts of change underlying participatory approaches are difficult to tease out, in part because the literature is vast, with little consensus on what constitutes participation or how it is to be promoted (Long, 2001). From the well-known ladder of participation (Uphoff, 1986) to Cornwall's work on gender and participation (2000), researchers have established that the language of participation can encompass everything from tokenism to empowerment. As applied in development practice in Africa, the approaches range from the modest inclusion of potential beneficiaries in consultations and contributions in kind to those that build on local knowledge and place empowerment at the centre.

Change in the empowerment approach is defined as contingent and unpredictable; true development is seen as constructed locally, incrementally and with the consent of those whom it most affects. Change rests upon individuals comprehending their local and personal experiences in new ways that allow them to develop the capabilities to act and shape their own future; change also rests on transformations at other levels, from the individual and household to the structural (Friere, 1996; Fanon, 1991), though the latter is not always incorporated. As a consequence, change is political in profound ways, and at multiple levels, from the individual's own sense of self to his or her relationship to society and wider political and socio-economic processes. Moreover, much change is unanticipated and outside defined project boundaries; causality is multiple and difficult to discern or assign.

In contrast, more instrumental approaches to participation appear to take a view of change that is relatively easily contained within the overall management approach based on controlled, linear change, with clear and politically unproblematic roles for local people and agents of change, and often externally set indicators for success. The quality of change is understood to be improved through the involvement of local people in largely externally documented projects and programmes, but their participation does not fundamentally question or overturn the assumptions or understanding of change contained within them.

Other approaches to planning and implementation exist

Given the flaws of rational planning, and the problems with making participation work effectively in bureaucratic structures, there is much interest in developing ways to improve planning and implementation. The most significant innovation is strategic planning, which has become almost universal in the UK NGO sector in the last 10 years, and is increasingly used as a basis for focusing and raising the organizational profile and fundraising in the UK. It has also become a requirement for southern partners who often receive capacity-building support to introduce strategic planning. Many observers believe that strategic planning is replacing project and programme planning, although it is interesting to note that this has not changed the use of the key method of documenting the plan in the development armoury, and donors and UK NGOs often – and increasingly – formulate strategic plans within a logframe.

Mintzberg (1998) explains the wide range of different approaches covered by the term 'strategic planning', and Harding defines some of the core approaches in terms of tight and loose strategic planning (Harding, 2002). Tight strategic planning, he argues, comes out of the rational management of change stable, and draws on management by objectives/results frameworks. It provides a clear and detailed plan of future work with timed activities, clear objectives, outputs and outcomes. It is detailed, comprehensive and falls squarely into the command and control way of working. This kind of strategic planning fits well with the logframe way of working, and is indeed the dominant style of strategic planning currently found in NGOs. In theory, accountability rests primarily with the organization and those charged with its strategic management, though there are other types of accountability (towards the various external stakeholders) that come into play, especially when funding agreements with donors are based on strategic plans as is increasingly the case for block funding.

The opportunity to do things differently is offered by a looser approach to strategic planning, but evidence of process approaches to strategic planning is scarce. In looser forms of strategic planning Harding shows that the concept of change is one of contingency and choice, of managing risks and adapting to change, and continuously reassessing, resituating the organization and redefining actions in line with the strategies, principles and missions established. These elements are defined not by a set of experts but rather through a deep process of engagement with staff and other stakeholders, and perhaps even other informed individuals. The aim is to ensure clear and shared values and a broad agreed sense of direction and purpose. There are boundaries of what will and will not be acceptable, which everyone involved develops and owns through discussion and analysis. To work well this kind of strategic planning requires robust feedback loops to ensure that information – internally and externally generated – is fed back to inform what is to be done next, and highlights what works well and what needs adjusting. It requires a learning culture and openness to flexibility, an ability to change on the basis of experience. It tries to work with the needs and requirements of senior management as well as the needs of staff and partners far away, to find ways to meet very diverse needs within the organization and attend to accountabilities to all stakeholders; this is of course very tricky and some NGOs who have tried top-down/bottom-up planning have found it problematic (Wallace and Burdon, 1993). It is more common now, where consultation and the involvement of stakeholders do take place, for senior managers to make the final decisions about strategic priorities.

The missing elements

To close the chapter we want to detail some elements missing in both the rational and participatory approaches that proved significant in helping us to understand aspects of relationships along the aid chain and how well work was being done. Among the neglected elements were: attention to learning and reflection; willingness to address the emotional and subjective components of development; recognition of cross-cultural and interpersonal dynamics; and attention to power, politics and history.

Reflective practitioners and emergent change

Practitioners (north and the south) are questioning how far rational approaches to development, based on linear understandings of cause and effect, are appropriate. Many see the barriers to change embedded in social and political relations. They highlight the need for reflective practitioners, highly attuned to local realities, working as facilitators and supporters, accepting and learning from failure, thinking about and analysing the work in very different sets of conceptual frameworks (Harding, 2004; Kaplan, 2002; Welbourn, 1999). These approaches focus on the development practitioner as a professional and potential agent of change, engaged in ongoing conversations about possibilities and practices rather than driving towards defined ends.

Rondanelli (1993), Senge (1990) and Schein (1999), among others, have written about the need for open-ended, flexible and responsive approaches to unpredictability and change. Schön (1983: 39) called for reflective practitioners who think about how they frame and set problems (and solutions) and the limits of their professional knowledge. Yet these approaches, while often cited, do not appear to be shaping the way most development bureaucracies and individuals undertake development work. Instead, the tight focus on outputs has pressured staff in development organizations to act, achieve and count, a pressure that Harrison (1995) well describes as one that overwhelms efforts to understand, analyse and learn.

Subjectivity and interpersonal relationships

The way in which linear managerial approaches to change tend to eclipse participatory ones has resulted in a widespread neglect of the personal and interpersonal dimensions of development. In a powerful chapter on participation in planning, entitled 'Not leaving your pain at the door', the planning theorist J. Forester (1999) writes about how the resolution of fundamental differences between people – whether over past injustices, development priorities or allocation of future projects – requires a willingness to work with people's anger, pain and passions. In a similar vein, Sandercock (1998) calls for a 'therapeutic planning' approach that encourages planners and practitioners to read the emotions in a community meeting, and demands that they do their homework on the history and politics of the local area, with particular attention to marginalized and diverse groups. Freirian community development practitioners, working out of New Mexico, start with the individual and their subjective understandings as a basis for collaborative and participatory work together.

Chambers goes further, and like Kaplan puts the development worker and the organization firmly into the development equation; it is not simply about changing them but also understanding and changing ourselves; something echoed in SA by Pieterse and Meintjies (2004). The problems of development are not only out there; many are entrenched in current attitudes and approaches to aid and development. To redress what he calls 'this bizarre omission' of the role of individuals and agencies in what happens in development Chambers advocates the concept of 'responsible well-being' to put the personal dimension back into development. This demands we examine who we are, what we do, how we understand reality, even though for practitioners 'it can disturb profoundly to reflect on what one does and does not do. It embarrasses to be confronted by poverty and suffering compared to one's own condition' (Chambers, 2004: 12).

In this literature, there is also increasing attention to the ways in which information is conveyed. Greater attention to narratives, stories and metaphors is emerging in diverse studies, from African conflicts over resources (Bornstein and Fungalane, 2000) to organizational theory (Schön, 1983). Participative video and drama are seen as key ways to listen more openly to the voices of others (Braden, 2004). In our study of NGO management practices, questions of subjective understanding and interpretations were found to be critical, as was the tendency to ignore the significant role played by donors and NGOs themselves in creating the conditions that enabled or prevented success.

Cross-cultural dynamics and communication

The work of cross-cultural researchers, Hofstede (1984), Quinn (1988) and others, was explored in preparation for this research and led us to expect the tensions and power imbalances found between the UK and Africa. They also stressed the fact that the imposition of systems and tools by the most powerful player is not unusual, and that those with power often have little recognition that other frames of reference are also relevant. Quinn's attention to cultural variations in the ways people deal with paradox and incongruities was particularly useful in guiding how we interacted with people and collected information. Marsden (2003) explored some of the key concepts in development from a cross-cultural viewpoint, and showed how far many dominant and received truths about other cultures, their problems and needs, are from those peoples' reality and ways of thinking about the world.

The issues of who defines the concepts and in what language are critical, and there are many simplistic assumptions about how to transfer concepts from one culture to another. Clearly for those able to manipulate English, this provides a key to working with external players, especially from the UK and the US, yet it is a blanket beneath which issues such as who has power, cultural analysis and understanding, class, education level, gender and race remain well hidden. While gender has at least been discussed and tackled by some agencies, the development world still tends to ignore or even deny issues of cultural imperialism, hegemony and race; yet these clearly shape relationships and interactions (Crewe and Harrison, 1998; Goudge, 2003). The researchers were pushed to reread Fanon and revisit concepts such as the colonization of the mind to understand some of the resentment and anger they experienced during the research. Discussions by African leaders and thinkers have explored the problems facing the continent, highlighting the long-term plunder of ideas and confidence in Africa by colonization and ongoing globalization (Teveodjre, 2002). In the foreword Amartya Sen wrote:

> The story of the undermining of African strength and self-confidence is a complex one, in which external intrusion was often supplemented by internal divisions and conflicts. [This] report emphasizes the need for unity and cooperation, in addition to the importance of resisting subjugation and cultivating constructive capability (Sen in Teveodjre, 2002: 19).

The research acknowledges writers who have questioned the cultural assumptions embedded in written, linear and logical tools and have shown that these can act to prevent proper communication with people from oral and non-linear cultures whose concepts of change and development are very different (Braden, 2004). However, overall ethnographies of NGOs are scarce and the impact of external cultural concepts and behavioural norms on local organizations has, to date, been poorly researched; how these affect local NGOs' ability to perform is as yet poorly understood. This research could not undertake this detailed organizational work, but some of these concepts were important in helping to understand the emotions and experiences expressed during the research in Uganda and SA.

Concluding comment

There is little doubt that the dominant discourse and associated procedures of development aid currently are rooted in a paradigm of controlled, predictable change, that can be managed according to clear rules and accounted for in standard documents. If policies are followed properly the benefits, it is believed, will follow; if the work fails to deliver the problems are usually deemed to lie in a lack of capacity or willingness to implement the policies and procedures professionally. The answer then lies in capacity-building rather than a re-examination of the assumptions behind these approaches. These norms are strong and, as we will see, are largely accepted by development agencies.

The focus on the measurable is strong and yet this can fit uneasily with a commitment to being responsive and empowering while undertaking work that is long-term and intended to tackle some of the world's most intransigent problems. Participative and responsive approaches are fitted into logframes as and when possible, but they rarely challenge too deeply or overturn the strategies, programmes or projects funded – and often designed – by external donors and INGOs. There are many alternative, innovative ideas and methodologies being tried on the ground, but they usually have to coexist alongside the current management systems.

These rational, linear systems, based on external cultural norms, appear at a theoretical level to do little to counteract the erosion of confidence and self-determination that many feel is part of the problem of development in Africa, where solutions to poverty must be found:

> The African continent experiences, more dramatically than any other region in the world, the negative effects of unadjusted development strategies conceived by their leaders or imposed by the great powers. In spite of its human resources, natural wealth and the laudable efforts of many governments and peoples of the continent, the African economies have not realized significant growth levels, they have not been able to achieve a degree of autonomous growth and indigenous development...[but we are reminded that] African women and men are well versed in their own problems and that penetrating reflection on our own condition will permit us to find solutions to the ongoing problems of our continent (Teveodjre 2002: 22, 25).

The rest of the book explores, using empirical evidence, how well current methodologies enable NGOs at all levels to address the problems of development facing civil society in Africa. While combining compliance with prevailing management norms and participative approaches appears relatively unproblematic to many, the questions remain to be answered about how easy it is for NGOs to combine their commitment to responsive and empowering approaches with the prevailing conditions for accessing aid.

CHAPTER 4

The major UK donors and the flow of aid through the NGO sector

Introduction

Understanding relations between donors and NGOs in the north and south requires clarity on financial flows and the conditions that attach to them, a surprisingly difficult undertaking. Of course, relationships do not revolve only around funds, and in the UK negotiations, consultations and advocacy also provide important arenas for exchange. Communications between donors and NGOs take diverse forms and the factors that shape who is involved and how range from personal relations, persistence and communication skills to the perceived status and legitimacy of the NGOs and their approaches to advocacy work.

Tracing these relationships is difficult for several reasons. First, reliable and comparable financial data for the period under study are hard to find, and sometimes contested. For example, while some said that UK overseas development assistance to civil society was falling (Lewis, 2003b), DFID said it was rising. Aid flows through NGOs are not well documented or transparent (Sogge, 2002). Financial data are not adjusted in real terms; often categories of spending, financial years or ways of presenting the accounts change between years. Clarifying who receives which kind of funding, on what terms and conditions, and which UK NGOs are experiencing rising or declining funding from donors, proved tricky. The additional challenge is that accurate data on donor funding are hard to compile and match with experience, leaving much room for disagreement about trends and patterns.

Second, UK NGOs have a wide range of different interactions with donors. In the 1980s some NGOs, such as Christian Aid, did not take any donor funding on principle, preferring independence from government without compromise, while others, such as Oxfam, put a ceiling of 10 per cent on all income from institutional donors. Since then most UK NGOs have dramatically changed their position on official donor funding, with Oxfam receiving 50 per cent of its programme funding from institutional donors by 2003. Most large NGOs in the UK now employ fundraisers to access as much official donor funding as possible. Many small and medium-sized UK NGOs are highly dependent on donor funding, and some were established in response to the rise in DFID funds for civil society available during the 1990s.

These shifts affect the relationships between donors and NGOs. At one end of the spectrum some only receive funding, at the other end some large or specialist NGOs, in addition to receiving substantial government financial support, are included on government delegations to UN meetings and work alongside donors developing standards, especially for humanitarian aid. A few NGOs have intense contact with policy issues and these 'representative' NGOs have become incorporated into official aid activities to speak for the whole sector (Martens, 2006). For these NGOs contact has greatly increased in recent years, and donors certainly have been influenced, since the language of NGOs is now reflected in development debates and policies, although concepts may be watered down or adapted as they are taken up and mainstreamed by donors (Wendoh and Wallace, 2005; Chapman et al., 2005).

Third, the donor scene is changing extremely fast. The landscape is very different from 10 years ago, with new donors and funding streams, the loss of old ones, less personal interaction around grant-making, changed funding conditions and very different development priorities. The situation has continued to change since the research ended, with more shifts in the models and mechanisms of grant-making, changing criteria for accessing grants, outsourcing for grant appraisal and management, and new ways of accounting for grant use. Many changes have been driven by the need to keep operating costs low (often referred to as the transaction costs of delivering aid) and a growing concern with identifying the results of development aid. There is now an overt desire to demonstrate the positive impact of the financial investments to the Treasury, trustees and chief executives. There are real anxieties about whether aid money is used appropriately and how to prevent corruption. Fourth, the flows of aid have fluctuated. Funding can stop completely when a donor develops a new aid paradigm or restructures to meet newly refined aims. The lack of predictable funding flows certainly affected some NGOs heavily, especially those most reliant on donor funding. The stop-start nature of funding makes analysing trends difficult, and also changes the way NGOs and donors interrelate.

In analysing financial aid and conditions, it is essential to recognize that the relationships between donors and NGOs are influenced by a range of factors, including the personalities and cultural, educational and gender backgrounds and experiences of staff involved, the existence or not of shared values and perspectives, and where legitimacy is felt to lie. The movement of personnel between NGOs and donors, rare in the 1980s but now increasingly common, at times blurs the line between the ideology and focus of NGOs and donors. Agendas are increasingly similar as the language of development becomes universal, and the current political climate encourages development to be approached as a shared endeavour between the public and private sectors and civil society.

The financial relationship, however, remains pivotal. Through the control of funds donors have the power to shape thinking and behaviour. This chapter presents the donor context for UK NGOs, from 2000 to early 2004, focusing on funding flows, changing grant models and the shifting conditions attached to that aid. It draws on history to provide a comparative perspective where this is illuminating, and discusses briefly some of the NGO responses to the donor context. We attempt to enter this contested arena through focusing on the funding policies and practices of the main UK donors and NGOs' experiences of working with them.

One important caveat should be noted. The book looks only at funds that originate from institutional sources, whether public or private. Importantly, there is no discussion of public giving to NGOs, although this constitutes a major resource especially for the large NGOs in the UK. For example, Oxfam raised £76 million from donations, £66.2 million from shops and also from the public, and £40.3 million from government and other public funders in 2004. ActionAid raised £48.5 million from committed giving in UK in 2003 and £9.6 million from other donations; their income from official donors was £15.2 million. However, funds raised from the public remain the responsibility of the NGOs themselves, which chooses, within the norms of public auditing, what information to share with its donating public. Feedback and publicity is designed for building the legitimacy and credibility of the NGOs as well as further fundraising, and they have greater leeway in the use of and reporting on publicly raised funds than they do for institutional funding.

Despite this leeway, NGOs with large flows of untied public giving do not behave all that differently from those receiving donor funding tied to clear conditions. They increasingly use similar procedures for planning and accounting for aid as those who are highly donor-dependent. The standard-ization appears to be based on a reliance on significant institutional funds and the need to maintain good relations with donors for advocacy purposes. Also many agencies have selected trustees from business whose dominant concerns are to ensure the efficient and effective use of funds, clear results and strong lines of reporting to trustees (Wallace, Crowther and Shepherd, 1997). Indeed, some run along corporate lines: 'Spurred by a growing number of global conflicts, increased outsourcing of aid work by Western governments and the boom in private philanthropy, nongovernmental organizations...have become big business' (Foroohar, 2005).

Estimates for UK NGO total income in 1998 varied between £428 million and £1.1 billion, with a plausible figure of £937 million (Development Initiatives, 2000). With figures varying by over 100 per cent, it is difficult to make confident statements. DFID estimated that total UK NGO income in 1998/9 was £428 million, 57 per cent from voluntary income and 43 per cent from DFID funding, although they appear to exclude funding from independent donors and the EU altogether from these figures.

The donor context: funding flows 1997–2003

Donor funding is a significant or sole source of funding for most UK NGOs. The major donors include DFID and the EU, two large independent funders, Comic Relief and the Community Fund (now the Big Lottery Fund), and a large number of trusts and foundations including Nuffield, Baring and the Princess Diana

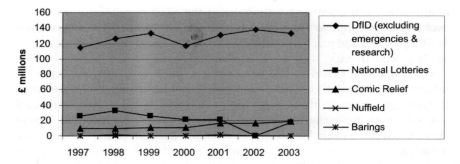

Note: The Nuffield and Baring lines are identical.

Figure 4.1 The size of donors relative to UK NGO sector

Fund. The donors and their relative sizes are shown in Figure 4.1, although the EU cannot be included because it was not possible to separate out their figures for UK NGOs.

The broad data indicate an increase in overall donor funding since 2000, albeit with some years of stagnation (Reality of Aid Report, 2002). Data collected by Johns Hopkins University, 2005, provides a timely reminder about global funding for NGOs and their significance in the wider aid community:

> The first global estimate of just how big [the NGO sector is]...studied 37 nations and found total operating expenditures in 2002 of $1.6 trillion. To put these figures in context, the authors point out that if nonprofits were a country, they would have the fifth largest economy in the world...these increasingly visible players on the global political scene have become a multibillion-dollar industry (*New Statesman*, 5 September 2005).

However, while aid flows remain strong, if unpredictable, the distribution of aid is becoming highly differentiated. This results in the growth of a few, large NGOs. Some are huge (Lindenberg and Bryant, 2002), and some are successful niche NGOs, while smaller and medium-sized NGOs often struggle and a few go to the wall.

DFID

The International Development Act (2002), following two white papers focusing aid on to poverty in 1997 and 2000, legally required DFID to work on poverty reduction through sustainable development. DFID signed its first public service agreement with the Treasury (2003/6), tying their performance closely to achieving the MDGs. They have renewed their commitment to increase official aid to ensure the MDGs are reached: poverty reduction spending was £2,754 million in 2002/3 and £2,829 million in 2003/4, and £3,777 million in 2004/5 and £5,323 million by 2008 (DFID, 2003). How much of this funding does and will go through NGOs is hard to assess accurately because of the multiple and changing funding streams. Compared with other OECD countries the UK NGO sector receives significantly less government funding than their counterparts in Europe.

Data on DFID expenditure to UK NGOs for 1996/2003 were collected from a number of sources, but were difficult to triangulate. The way data are categorized changes over time, as do the grant systems. Eventually the research team used figures supplied in 2005 by the Civil Society Unit at DFID, although these did not always match data published in official sources. Although these 2005 figures diverged a little from those collated by us from raw data accessed from the Civil Society Unit (CSU) in 2001/2, they broadly supported our original findings. The collection of spending data has recently greatly improved, although tracking funding to UK NGOs from DFID's many funding mechanisms remains difficult. Aggregated figures for UK-based DFID funding are obtainable, but these do not reveal the growing differentiation that is undoubtedly taking place in the sector.

While overall aid funding is rising, the size of government funding to UK NGOs is less clear. The different ways of analysing and presenting the figures can create difficulties. We were told:

> I feel the overall total figure is the only valid indicator of support for UK civil society organizations. The boundary between the other funding lines is so blurred that it is not valid to use them separately. There were many pieces of work funded under the JFS in 1996, which could well have been funded under the research line in 2000 or the humanitarian line in 2000. Then the 'other funding' line includes a range of different funding schemes (personal communication, CSU, October 2005).

While the figures supplied by CSU show that aid to UK NGOs has risen when funding for emergencies and research are included, if they are excluded (to show funding for NGO development work) the figures show a drop between 1999 and 2000, followed by a steady rise, as shown in Figure 4.2.

The overall total is not useful to people wanting to trace funding for development work via NGOs. Although the overall figure has almost doubled (see Table 4.1), a statistic often quoted by DFID, the amount available for development NGOs has grown slowly and looks even more modest when we remember that the figures are not adjusted for inflation. [who could have converted...]

The paucity of detailed data and the difficulty of extracting trends for particular purposes go a long way towards explaining why different groups make different claims about what the trends are. While DFID and some research institutes are lauding large increases in aid to civil society, NGOs find this is not borne out in their experience of trying to raise funds for development work. The final column in Table 4.1 explains their experience.

Who can access this funding?

In the past the proportion of official funding spent through different UK NGOs varied dramatically. For example, in 1994/5 the Joint Funding Scheme (JFS),

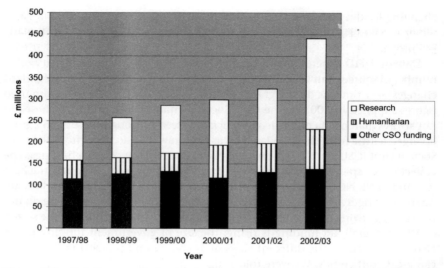

Figure 4.2 Relative growth in development funding, research and humanitarian aid, DFID

Table 4.1 DFID support for civil society, including NGOs and research institutes (£ million)[1]

[handwritten: DOES THIS COVER PROJECTS ??]

	CSCF[1]	PPAs[2]	Humanitarian	Research[3]	Other funding[4]	Total funding	Total funding available for development work via NGOs
1997/8	16.75	47.39	43.66	88.90	50.07	246.77	114.21
1998/9	16.47	46.13.4	38.10	93.84	63.64	258.18	126.25
1999/00	15.84	46.28	42.12	111.18	70.96	286.38	133.08
2000/1	10.57	50.93	76.89	104.75	56.08	299.21	117.58
2001/2	14.52	53.65	68.66	126.14	62.52	325.49	130.69
2002/3	13.01	57.23	93.82	209.63	67.59	441.33	137.87

[1] This column covers funding through the Civil Society Challenge Fund and the Joint Funding Scheme.

[2] This column covers Joint Funding Scheme Block Grants and the Programme Partnership Agreements.

[3] Research funding goes mainly in large grants to research centres at Universities and as such is not of interest to this study.

[4] This column covers country office funding as well as other central funding schemes like the Small Enterprise Fund. Some research funding and humanitarian funding has been included in this category in some years and not others. To make the figures more comparable, these have been moved accordingly.

the main conduit of aid from the government to NGOs, disbursed over £34 *1994/95* million, with approximately 45 per cent of this going to the five block grant agencies (Oxfam, Save the Children, VSO, Christian Aid, CAFOD), essentially as general budget support with loose systems of accountability. Between £18 million and £19 million was available for proposals from all other NGOs, and there were many, because DFID had increased funding from 1983 to 1993/4 by almost 400 per cent (to £68.7 million for all NGOs), which led to a proliferation of new agencies. Competition for this funding was strong.

DFID funding has continued to favour the five large agencies that have collectively received more than half the total funds going to NGOs between 1997/8 and 2002/3, with one exception (see Table 4.2).

Funding to medium-sized NGOs (annual turnover of between £3 million and £5 million) remained fairly static up to 1999/2000 and dropped dramatically – by over a third – between 1999/2000 and 2000/1. The success of small NGOs in fundraising from DFID dropped by almost a quarter between 1999/2000 and

Table 4.2   The top five UK NGOs receiving most DFID funds

NGO	% DFID funds to NGOs going to this NGO (excluding research but including emergencies)					
	1997/8	1998/9	1999/2000	2000/1	2001/2	2002/3
British Red Cross Society	14.8	13.8	13.1	16.5	18.5	24.3
VSO	12.8	13.4	12.9	12.3	12.0	10.5
CARE	7.8	9.2	9.0	11.2	11.9	11.2
Save the Children Fund	11.4	7.4	9.8	8.8	7.5	8.3
Oxfam	6.6	6.1	5.8	7.5	4.8	4.2
Total	**53.5**	**49.9**	**50.6**	**56.2**	**54.7**	**58.6**

BIG FIVE GETTING > 50%

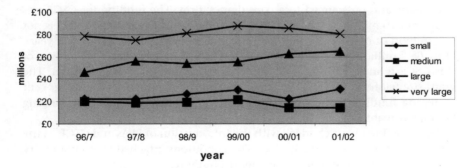

Figure 4.3   DFID funding to UK NGOs by size, including emergencies but not research

2000/1, though it picked up in 2001/2; this happened despite DFID's promise that their new civil-society procedures would not result in funding gaps for any agency (Bond, 2001). DFID graphs on its website show a different picture, with an unbroken upward trend, but they have omitted the years 1997/2001. They also show only central funding for NGOs, not the growing funds that are being accessed through other sources.

Changing grant models and conditions

In 1999, DFID set up an extensive consultation with UK civil society concerning its roles, funding and relations with government. Following that consultation and contributions from the minister for international development new grant systems were established. The JFS was abolished and two new mechanisms were introduced: Programme Partnership Agreements (PPAs) and the Civil Society Challenge Fund (CSCF).

The aim of PPAs was to maximize collaboration with selected UK NGOs that DFID identified as key development players, by providing substantial programme funding to them to enable them to realize their potential and make significant strategic contributions to DFID's aims. Initially these agreements were for block grant agencies, but the intention was to quickly expand the number of NGOs with close ties to DFID. Initially large NGOs were invited to apply; later some smaller specialist NGOs were also asked to apply. Later a tender system was established, with a two-tier application process; a statement of interest followed by a full proposal. Since the process has become more open many NGOs apply in every round. There were 15 NGOs with PPAs in 2003/4 receiving over £59 million (VSO received £24.46 million of this), a big increase from the block grants nine years earlier totalling £16 million (excluding VSO, which received around £20 million). In 2005, 23 NGOs were chosen to submit full proposals, although only four or five PPAs will succeed.

A two-stage application process was also introduced for the CSCF, which focused on funding projects that met DFID's development priorities. The appraisal process was moved away from DFID and their resource centre, Edinburgh University, and outsourced to a consultancy firm. The funding for CSCF was steady at £10 million a year from 2000 to the financial year 2003/4 (this is not £10 million of new money but includes all disbursements to NGOs that year). Only £8.7 million was disbursed in 2003/4: 15 NGOs received £3.7 million of this CSCF money, with another 119 sharing £5 million between them. The grant size fell from £500,000 to £250,000 and the requirement for 50 per cent matching funding was changed in April 2003, when 100 per cent funding became available.

Funding flows have changed with the introduction of PPAs and CSCF, as the bulk of funding goes through PPAs. The conditions attached to each are very different from those attached to earlier JFS funding.

The table shows significant increases in all conditions, most markedly around responsive funding through the CSCF. NGOs have to be able to demonstrate

Table 4.3 The JFS, the PPAs and CSCF compared

Terms and conditions	JFS including block grants	PPA CORE SUPPORT	CSCF SUPPORT INNOVATIVE WORK
Eligibility; what NGOs have to show	5 block grant agencies got funding year on year; all other registered NGOs could apply for JFS funding if they were working on sustainable development issues	1. Congruence between the organization's mission and objectives and DFID's strategic objectives 2. At least 5 years' relevant track record 3. Experience of working in a range of developing and/or transition countries 4. Demonstrated capability to link grassroots work with wider policy/ influencing/ advocacy 5. History of substantial DFID funding over the previous 3 years	1. Work in DFID priority countries, in sectors DFID wants to focus on 2. Incorporating approaches DFID wants to promote 3. Focus on advocacy and rights, promoting local civil society and ensuring government accountability 4. Innovation and lesson learning/dissemination are critical 5. Funding not available for basic service delivery only 6. Funding unavailable for project second phases
How to apply	Direct application to JFS, logframes encouraged but not essential	Expressions of interest in response to tenders, full proposal from those selected showing how their strategy fits DFID's strategy Logframes and outcome indicators essential Last 3 years and renewal appears to be almost automatic	Two-stage process: expressions of interest followed, if selected, by full proposal. Selection depends on meeting above criteria Logframes and outcome indicators essential
Conditions	Could work outside UK government priority countries; programme was responsive to NGO agendas, but with increasing concern about need for	Conditions have to be met before applying A focus on innovation, NGO work supports that of DFID, advocacy, learning and dissemination are all important PPAs to be evaluated after 3 years. Aims and objectives are framed in global/strategic	Projects must show that they: 1. help poor people have more effective control over decisions which affect their lives, locally, nationally and internationally 2. help people understand the causes of their poverty 3. help people understand their rights and entitlements

Table 4.3 (Contd)

Terms and conditions	JFS including block grants	PPA	CSCF
	professionalism, from planning to evaluation	terms, though money increasingly allocated for specific activities with expected outcomes. Agencies invest heavily in developing global indicators to try to undertake this kind of evaluation, though few had taken place at time of the research, and these were seen as less than rigorous by NGOs	4. provide poor people with information and knowledge (the most important resource transfer for poor people) 5. understand development as leverage and not development as delivery; must be able to link work on the ground to policy change 6. engage explicitly in capacity-building 7. have clear achievable objectives contributing to MDGs 8. must be implemented by partner organization with established links with the NNGO applying 9. illustrate that the UK partner is providing more than the transfer of funds 10. explain how achievement will be assessed – methodology must be participatory and include views of partners and beneficiaries to show how the work links to effective rights-based work and capacity building
Who assesses	Projects sent to Social Development Advisers; then to in-house staff, later contracted out to Edinburgh University	NGOs work with PPA staff to reach agreements; at start this could take up to 18 months. Process became more streamlined and more prescriptive over time	External consultancy assessments, sent to DFID for final approval Feedback obtained from DFID departments and country offices
Account-ability	Evaluation guidelines, BOND established in part to generate	Outcome indicators are integral to the PPA, and are evaluated externally at	Outcome and impact indicators integral to proposals. External evaluations required at end

Table 4.3 (Contd)

Terms and conditions	JFS including block grants	PPA	CSCF
	good NGO practice on project cycle management. Major concerns about poor reporting/ accountability for block grants	end of agreement period. Evaluations of PPAs now available on the DFID website	

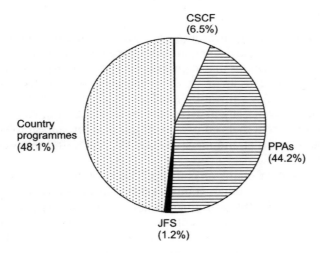

Figure 4.4 Mechanisms of UK NGO funding (DFID 2003/4)

that they are working at multiple levels on a range of issues including rights, awareness and policy change; only innovative service delivery will be supported, and more recently service delivery in difficult contexts will be considered. The PPAs take time to negotiate and agree, and over time the frameworks have become more prescriptive about the use of funds. Recently NGOs were asked to do risk assessments against the expected outcomes of their PPAs to enable DFID to understand the likelihood of the predicted outcomes being achieved. DFID's concern is that strategic grants should deliver demonstrable, measurable change in the chief areas of poverty reduction, thus enabling DFID to meet the MDGs. However, the problems of assessing aid effectiveness and finding global measurements of change are well known to DFID, as evidenced in the draft 'Development effectiveness review' (DFID 2002), which highlighted weaknesses in definitions, available information and methodologies that prevented good assessment of DFID effectiveness. In spite of this, DFID continues to demand that NGOs demonstrate impact, although NGOs are far smaller players and often work in the most challenging areas.

The rise in CSCF conditions has had a profound effect on some medium-sized and small NGOs, who have found it hard to meet the myriad criteria, including those working in services and in contexts where asserting rights is almost impossible. One small NGO, enquiring why its proposal had been refused, was told it had not addressed the issue of poor people's rights; however, no one explained how or from whom people living in conflict and without a government could do this. Another was refused funding because its participatory approaches were not deemed to be an adequate way of ensuring poor people obtained their rights.

Local funding

DFID has been decentralizing for several years and country offices now have a large degree of autonomy. Some in Africa have established direct funding for civil-society organizations that align with the DFID country assistance strategy. Different funding strategies for NGOs are found in each country; this approach has been perceived as a threat by some UK NGOs. While the larger ones can position themselves locally to access this funding (often in competition with their local partners in that country, an ethical issue few appear to be grappling with seriously), smaller and medium-sized UK NGOs find themselves largely excluded from it.

CSU is currently working on collating how much funding goes to local and international NGOs through country offices, including DFID contributions that are spent via multilateral programmes. The broad figures available show that these are important sources of funding for civil society; the figures have risen from £49.9 million in 2000 to £64.3 million in 2003/4, indicating that some UK NGOs are adept at sourcing funds in Africa.

Contracts

Contracts form a growing source of DFID funding for UK NGOs. DFID, like many other bilateral donors, uses contractors to do work essential for fulfilling its country strategies. Contracts are put out to tender and NGOs compete with private contractors, consultants, governments, universities and independent think-tanks; sometimes they submit joint bids. UK NGOs also now have to bid alongside (and sometimes in cooperation with) southern NGOs for contract funding. The money is channelled through the agency that DFID finds the most competitive, with no inbuilt preferences for funding UK NGOs.

Only large NGOs with sufficient resources to develop bids are in a position to compete for these contracts, which are often worth between £15 million and £20 million over three to five years. Even the largest NGOs find it hard at times to successfully compete with professional consulting agencies and firms, and often struggle at the implementation phase because the contracts are vast compared with the scale of much traditional NGO funding. The funding figures for contracts are included under the country programme figures, although it remains unclear how much NGOs increase their official funding through contracts and what overall percentage of funding to UK NGOs is paid through formal contracts.

The European Union

The European Commission (EC) is the next largest donor and supports NGOs through contracting and particular budget lines. Contracts are included in the figures for sectoral aid and cannot be accounted for separately; consequently it is hard to get an accurate figure of total EC aid to NGOs. This research has therefore focused on the main budget lines for NGOs: 'Co-financing operations with EU NGOs' (21 02 03 exB7-6000) and 'Support for decentralised co-operation in the developing countries' (21 02 13 exB7-6002 or B7-6430).

The co-financing scheme started in 1976 and goes mainly to Africa, Asia and Latin America: European based NGOs can apply on behalf of partners. It was set up in response to the longstanding commitment and support of the European public for NGO work to improve the living conditions of the poor (Cox and Chapman, 1999). In 1979 a component was added for raising European public awareness. In 1997 it was agreed by the Council of Ministers that NGO co-financing should aim at poverty reduction as well as enhancing the target group's quality of life and development capacities.

In the past the Commission saw NGOs as vehicles for targeting the poorest and most marginalized, who tend to be neglected by official policies or have difficulties accessing bilateral aid. Development was understood to be best served using diverse approaches, innovation and experimentation, and NGOs were encouraged to work out their own programmes and projects for addressing poverty (Loquai, 1998). NGOs were also seen as playing a vital role in encouraging participatory development and the creation of a democratic base at grassroots level. Current changes challenge this approach: there is a growing trend to 'contract' NGOs to provide services for Commission designed projects and programmes; many NGOs fear they will become 'sub-contracting agencies' for mainstream development aid (Loquai, 1998).

However, the NGO cofinancing line remains rooted in the principles of NGO autonomy, the right of initiative and the recognition of the pluralism of the EU NGO community (see Europa website). EC aid to NGOs through this line has increased steadily and is expected to be around €174 million in 2004 (Europa website). As a rule 90 per cent is allocated to the co-financing of activities in developing counties and 10 per cent to the co-financing of development awareness activities in Europe. This scheme underwent a crisis and between November 1999 and June 2000 no new applications were accepted. It was subsequently reshaped, echoing many of the criteria developed by DFID. From

June 2000 new applications could only be submitted under an annual call for proposals published by the Commission, and applications must fit its political priorities and targets.

The new system was driven by a number of factors including the need to: reduce the number of projects handled to about 500 to cut the backlog of grants waiting for decisions; ensure funds were fully committed, something that had been difficult in the past; and reduce the project appraisal process to six months from an average of 13 months. It was also intended to introduce greater transparency and accountability by standardizing and harmonizing appraisal criteria and ensuring they fully conform to the requirements set out in the Commission's grant management rules. One implication of this was that Commission staff should no longer hold discussions with NGOs about their project applications.

The first call for proposals allocated €60 million from the 2000 euro cofinancing budget of €200 million; in 2003 175 contracts were agreed from 1,054 requests and 16 block grants were given out of 91 requests (Europa website). Applications heavily outweigh supply, but many NGOs that received EU funding in the past, through the NGO budget line, no longer access it. The reasons they fail include increased competition, the complexity of the bids, new contract conditions including bank guarantees for large grants, lack of staff time and capacity, and because their work no longer falls within the designated themes. The new funding regime appears to favour large agencies able to meet the bidding and contract requirements and with the staff capacity to respond quickly to new themes.

Discussions with European NGOs revealed that the selection system allows no dialogue, so project applications take a lot of preparation. They face only a small chance of selection due to strong competition, so NGOs tend to only submit projects they know will score well. Self-censoring of innovative work and risk avoidance are high, especially because the scoring system is done against a written checklist rather than allowing for the use of judgement and experience in evaluating the proposals.

The other main budget line is for decentralized cooperation in the developing countries; data on this are hard to find. Decentralized cooperation emerged in the 1980s to enable the EC to contribute outside the conventional external aid framework of government aid. Funds were channelled directly to NGOs and organizations outside the formal governmental apparatus and local public authorities. The budget for 1999/2001 was €18 million; it was then extended to December 2003 and in April 2004 extended for a further three years. The money was administered under calls for proposals from 2002. Agencies were asked to submit proposals to access this funding in 2002, but only 13 out of 492 were selected to access funding from the €6 million budget.

Decentralized cooperation activities are designed to promote a more participatory approach to development, responsive to the needs and initiatives of the population in the developing countries. It is intended to help diversify and strengthen civil society and grassroots democracy, and mobilize

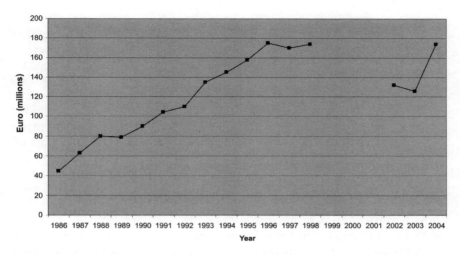

Figure 4.5   EU NGO cofinancing budget line (commitments)
Source: ODI database prepared for Cox and Chapman (1999) and Europa website.
Figures for 2004 indicative only.

decentralized agents in the EU and the developing countries in pursuit of these objectives (Cox and Chapman, 1999). A 2003 evaluation of the budget line stressed the importance of defining its specific purpose (to distinguish it from the NGO co-financing line), which is to provide support for civic projects, that is, any project wholly focused on civil society. Projects should increase the operating capability of that group so that it becomes increasingly competent and able to act as interlocutor with the local decision-making authorities (Europa website).

SA is a special case for the EC because it was not part of the Lomé agreement until 1997. With the advent of democracy, the EU's approach changed from supporting anti-apartheid work to a more usual channelling of aid through government. However, the original civil-society channel was maintained, with the full agreement of the government, and 25 per cent of the annual EU aid budget was to be administered through NGO partners. The European Programme for Reconstruction and Development in South Africa has largely focused on education (33%), governance and civil society (21%) (Cox and Chapman, 1999).

Medium-sized UK donors: Community Fund and Comic Relief

There are two other important sources of significant funding for UK development NGOs, the national lotteries (later the Community Fund, and in 2005 the Big Lottery Fund) and Comic Relief, a charity set up in 1990s to be an innovative fundraiser and funder of development work. These two sources of revenue have provided UK NGOs with sources of funding and have been a lifeline for many small and medium-sized NGOs. In 2001 the Community Fund provided these

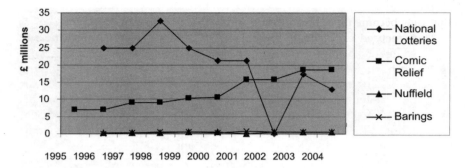

Figure 4.6 Trends in funding to NGOs by medium-sized donors

NGOs with £17 million (just over half that spent at its peak in 1998, which was £32.6 million) and Comic Relief spent £13 million. The Community Fund's international programme came under scrutiny in 2002 and there was a total hiatus in funding for 18 months; when funding resumed in 2003 only £11 million was allocated.

The average size of Community Fund grants rose over time, resulting in fewer organizations receiving funding: 73 in 2000 compared with 158 in 1998. Comic Relief's funding has risen steadily over time, and the size of their average grant has fluctuated, between £197,000 in 2001/3, to £254,312 in 2003/5, with only a small shift towards larger grants. In 1999/2001 55 per cent of their funding went to very small agencies of under £1 million a year turnover, with 18 per cent going to large agencies with over £5 million annual income. There was a significant shift in 2003/5, with Comic Relief giving 68 per cent of its income to small agencies (50 per cent of these had less than £100,000 income a year) and only 13 per cent to agencies with over £5 million a year turnover.

Community Fund

The Community Fund, relying on fluctuating lottery income, is susceptible to government trends. For many years its international grants department had to convince the board that public money spent on the lottery should be spent outside UK; funding allocations reflect both variations in lottery income and uncertainty among some board members about the importance of funding international work. The media have kept an eagle eye on lottery funding and periodically campaigns against the use of funds overseas have erupted.

The Community Fund was initially very consultative, working with the NGO sector to identify needs. They wanted to be innovative and encouraged NGOs to present their projects in their own ways, but they did not find that NGOs used imaginative or alternative ways of designing and managing projects and most automatically used logframes. The staff team held regular consultation meetings around the country each year to consult NGOs, and they built up a rapport and understanding of the UK NGO sector, although NGOs observed that they became more bureaucratic and less flexible over time.

They focused on strategic themes which changed a little over time and included in 2003: education, health, natural resources and human rights, with cross-cutting themes of gender and diversity, participation, influencing opinion, capacity-building and alliance/collaboration and networking. They had a formal assessment system, based on a long questionnaire, administered by external assessors. Gradually, and in the light of their experience of working with NGOs, they increased their demands and tightened the application form (in contrast with their desire for innovation); by 2004 the application form had expanded to almost 50 pages. The assessment process required NGOs to show wide coverage, impact and effectiveness, an ability to link service delivery and policy work, to show that their work gives good value for money and takes in to consideration current development issues.

The form was also designed to try to explore as far as possible the financial health and management of the UK organization and the southern partner, and the purpose and expected outcomes of the proposed project. The challenge for all funders based in the UK funding development through distant partners has always been how to assess the quality and nature of the relationships between the UK NGO and their partners, and the quality of the work on the ground. Often a range of questions and requirements have grown up as proxy ways to try to understand on paper complex questions of the legitimacy, representation and effectiveness of NGOs working thousands of miles away and their involvement in generating the project on the table. The application process was complicated and demanding, especially for smaller NGOs and those less experienced in writing and form-filling in English. Many of the evolving criteria and conditions were in fact similar to those required by DFID under the CSCF programme.

A cumulative score was then assigned to each application. Grants were ranked by score and taken for checking to grants officers and then to a professional external advisory panel that discussed which of the best scoring grants should be recommended and taken to the board for funding. A huge number of grants were processed annually, seen in one day by the committee. That work is now done by the board following their decision to take more responsibility for grants, and the professional advisory committee was disbanded.

The process of application and assessment was detailed. The Community Fund employed a large team of assessors and perhaps inevitably there was a bias to rely heavily on the quantitative issues that can be checked and easily scored – such as evidence of clear policies, procedures and systems – rather than more difficult qualitative issues. They did, however, grapple with how to score relationships, capacities and performance, and continually refined their systems. The challenges of allocating resources on the basis of a written questionnaire, assessed by a constantly changing team of assessors, were well understood by the grants team which worked hard at training, monitoring and supporting assessors, and at continuing to build their understanding of development.

The approach was frequently reviewed, and new guidelines and a narrower set of themes were published in July 2002. These changes were made in response to diminishing funds, and also because the new board wanted to find ways to identify real impact from the use of Community Fund money. This desire for demonstrable change remains a challenge for funders who are not operational but are financing a chain of organizations to work in complex and diverse contexts. It led the Community Fund to adopt more stringent evaluation and tracking processes and higher reporting requirements over time.

In 2004–5 the Community Fund merged with the New Opportunities Fund and became part of the Big Lottery Fund. The structures, purpose and functioning of the international work have changed drastically, and although funding has been agreed for 2005 and beyond at a level of £20 million a year, £10 million of this will be for Big Lottery Fund defined strategic programmes or projects and only £10 million for responsive grants. The international grants team will be disbanded, the headquarters moved to Birmingham and assessments and grant management for future grant funding will probably be outsourced to consultants.

Comic Relief

The BBC and a range of media stars help with a big fundraising week every two years to support Comic Relief; the money is spent in the UK and Africa, with Africa taking the largest part. Comic Relief has been largely protected from media criticism because of their involvement and funding has steadily increased over the years as each Red Nose Day raises more income from the viewing public. They have a unique relationship with TV and use the media heavily in fundraising and for public awareness, though as in all agencies the tensions between these two aims often cause difficulties.

Comic Relief has always tried to keep an open conduit between themselves and those they fund, though as their funding increased and staff came under more work pressure, they too set up a system of external assessors to work on project assessment with NGOs that were asked to submit full applications. An external team of assessors was appointed and trained during the research period, although Comic Relief relied on a smaller team of long-term assessment staff, people with whom it had built a good relationship over time. These assessors, as for the Community Fund, were often drawn from a pool of people versed in DFID assessment and reporting requirements, and who easily took a logframe approach to assessment and how projects should be evaluated. However, there was room for diversity of thinking and presentation, and flexibility in the assessment process, and Comic Relief worked to ensure that assessors were working in open ways. They also sought out and funded African diaspora NGOs, with £3.5 million going to such organizations in 1999/2001 and £5 million in 2001/3.

Comic Relief worked hard to ensure that their assessment processes did not mirror too closely the increasingly tight funding procedures of the EU and DFID, although like them they had increasing concerns about UK NGOs' performance, including their apparent weak ability to demonstrate impact. In order to try to promote more learning, in addition to face-to-face assessment meetings they had occasional meetings with UK NGOs concerning their key themes, and each grants officer built up a relationship with two or three NGOs to promote sharing and discussion. Over time trustees in Comic Relief, as in the Community Fund, became more focused on how to generate major change using their funds strategically, and how they could know what change their funding had promoted. They were concerned with issues of what Comic Relief was learning from all this grant-making, with what was working well and what was not.

Comic Relief has grappled with complex, hard to measure issues such as the assessment of and support for risk-taking, understanding the strengths and weaknesses of relations with southern partners, and how to improve these relationships. It has also looked at how to enable organizational strengthening, improve development work and ensure that the work is responsive to local people in the context of written project plans. Comic Relief has worked with five themes for several years (people affected by conflict, towns and cities, women and girls, pastoralists and the disabled) and the only major changes have been to add two new themes, HIV/AID and an innovations grant which was withdrawn after two years. Like the Community Fund, Comic Relief found a lack of innovative thinking and approaches coming from the NGO sector for funding. Some experiments, for example partnership funding, were tried during this period, but failed to produce the expected results.

Their guidelines have remained fairly constant, though there has been a growing concern with reporting (as in the Community Fund) because the quality and timing of reports are often poor. The biannual review of the grants process, achievements and problems, led to adjustments and improvements without any seismic changes during the research period. However, as with all the funders, the numbers of project applications have been high and staff time has been inevitably focused on assessment; far less time has been put into evaluation and learning. Although Comic Relief has prided itself on good, open working relations with NGOs, over time the workload, lack of staff time, individual relationships and their own concerns about aspects of NGO work have affected some of their interactions. Some NGOs have expressed concerns about Comic Relief becoming bureaucratic, distant and hard to talk to, and staff turnover in some areas has made building good relationships difficult.

Since the research ended Comic Relief has, like the Community Fund, undergone major changes. Trustees invited in management consultants to help them to address key concerns of how to work as one coherent organization, how to involve trustees in decision-making and grant-giving, and how to learn from experience. This agency, inexperienced in hands-on development work, provides management expertise to large NGOs in the UK, and uses a set of management concepts and analyses drawn from business experience in the US and UK. A number of changes resulted from their advice, including the disbanding of the advisory committees for grant-giving (as in the Community

Fund), the move to strategic as well as responsive grant-making, and a policy of cutting transaction costs and giving fewer larger grants to release staff time for learning. They, like the trustees, were concerned to promote the Comic Relief brand and wanted it to show what it was achieving with funding and what changes it was making to poverty, especially in Africa.

Both these donors are following wider trends to cut transaction costs; find ways to do high-impact strategic grant-making; and to show what changes they have brought to poor people, even though they work through other agencies and have no operational role themselves.

Small UK donors: trusts and foundations

The money available from foundations and small donor trust funds, often more flexible and more prepared to take risks, has been declining because of the slowdown of economic growth and declining stockmarket values. For example, the Princess Diana Fund ceased work during much of the research period, though it is giving grants again now, and Baring saw a decline in the funds available for grant-making in the mid-1990s.

Some have revised their strategic focus and changed their funding from a range of small scattergun projects to four or five large grants given under more coherent and directive guidelines, expecting that larger grants will increase impact and coherence rather than peppering a lot of agencies with smaller grants (e.g. Baring and Nuffield). This has affected some small and medium-sized NGOs.

The two sample foundations are some of the largest UK trusts funding development. Baring and Nuffield have refocused their grant-giving to concentrate on specific issues, Baring on the problems facing displaced people, associated with forced migration of all kinds, and Nuffield on building strong north–south partnerships to develop specific expertise in key areas of development such as health and education. To ensure that the fewer, larger

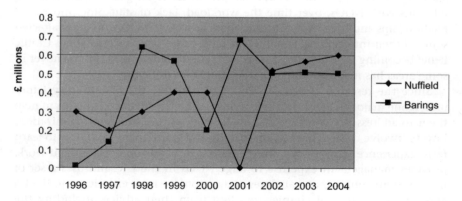

Figure 4.7 Trends in funding to NGOs by: small donors

grants are well selected and can achieve what the foundations hope from them, their selection processes include two stages. A shortlisting process follows the submission of short summaries, written following clear guidelines. Shortlisted NGOs are then invited for interviews, conducted by some trustees and two external advisers at Baring, and an advisory group working with one trustee at Nuffield. They then make recommendations to the full board.

Both foundations invite the UK organization to bring a partner to the meeting, for which money is provided. They find this direct personal interaction with the applicants, especially from the south, critical; it often changes their understanding and perception of the project or the organization, and it is revealing about the nature and quality of the relationship between the UK organization and the partner. Time is taken especially to probe the relationship with southern partners, and how involved local people have been in generating the project, issues that are extremely difficult to assess solely from paper applications.

Both trusts are keen to learn from their grant-giving, and Nuffield has employed a long-term consultant to undertake reviews of all their grants, building on her experience and knowledge of Nuffield and the partners as she goes. Feedback is shared at occasional meetings with the advisory group. Baring requires external evaluations to be undertaken and has started a series of forums with the NGOs they fund to hear what learning is emerging and how this can be used for future work. The NGOs find this interaction stimulating and a good opportunity for reflection on the challenges they face, their achievements and how to progress their work in future. There is an intimacy in these relationships, which allows problems as well as successes to be discussed; the funders see themselves as supporting and encouraging success while openly learning from experience – good and bad.

The foundations and trusts remain a critical resource for NGOs, especially the smaller ones and those trying to take risks and innovate.

UK NGOs as aid recipients

Donor changes affect UK NGOs differently: the largest have been able to tap into the new PPAs, bid for contracts and access strategic funding from donors, and have grown significantly. They are also able to access humanitarian aid, which in some years greatly increases their income. The smaller ones have been hit by the overall trend among donors to giving fewer, larger grants; they have also found it hard to meet the increasingly complex and multifaceted requirements of aid and have fewer staff available to put in the time needed for working on contract bids.

Looking back to phase 1 of the research, a number of other trends emerge, partly at least in direct response to wider funding changes. UK NGOs which did not have field offices in Africa have been establishing them, partly to access the new locally available funds, but also for capacity-building and advocacy purposes. Three have relocated to Africa; two of these are committed to working closer to those they serve, aiming to provide close support to social movements of the poor in Africa tackling poverty; one also agreed that financing was another reason for the move. The third, a medium-sized NGO, found the squeeze on operating costs in UK too hard to resist and – as the parameters of donor funding changed and this NGO was deemed to no longer fit strategic priorities, they were forced to close in the UK. It has now evolved – with the help of one independent sympathetic donor – into an agency based in Africa, with a fundraising and advocacy arm in the UK.

Many other small and medium-sized NGOs in the UK have felt the pinch because of the increasing lack of funding available for UK operating costs from institutional donors, and this period has been marked by a constant search for new grants to ensure their survival, and the relocation of some functions to the south. All but a few smaller donors have shaved their funding for core costs, so raising funds for UK staff is increasingly hard without access to public giving. One trust that does offer substantial core funding was surprised that few NGOs took advantage of this budget line, surmising that the reason for this might be that NGOs are now unused to budgeting their core costs openly. While many are committed to working more extensively in the south, decisions are not always being taken for programme reasons but rather because of funding realities.

The larger agencies, while growing, were also feeling under pressure to constantly increase their fundraising to sustain their work and expansion globally. One response to the constant quest for funding has been to require country field offices to fundraise locally: most large UK NGOs no longer fully fund their field offices as before, but expect each country director to fundraise in-country, securing grants and contracts from donors located there. They need to access the full range of funding available globally and fundraising departments have grown; most large NGOs have significant numbers of specialist staff working to secure institutional funding around the world. New alliances have been forged to raise profile and encourage funding opportunities. Fundraising has become much more professional, significant and diverse in the largest agencies since the research began, and fundraisers who understand the language of donors increasingly submit proposals and bids because their expertise in meeting donors' requirements increases the chances of success.

Perhaps inevitably, as donors' demands have risen so NGOs claim they can meet these in order to access the funding. This 'promise inflation', as Comic Relief describes it, is evident in many proposals; NGOs certainly feel pressured to claim they can meet all the diverse and complex funding requirements, otherwise they fear they will lose out on grants or contracts. At times almost regardless of the problems and realities on the ground they make claims that they may not be able to meet. The smaller NGOs felt this tension between the realities of what their partners can do and the funding criteria and demands strongly, because the same people apply for the funding and support the work on the ground. In larger agencies these tensions are played out between different departments, with hostilities and lack of a shared understanding often in evidence between marketing and fundraising departments and those working on programmes with field offices and partners.

Fundraising, how to raise funds, what donors want, how best to attract their interest were dominant concerns in all the UK NGOs interviewed. There has been, at the same time, a noticeable rise in advocacy and lobbying work; influencing has risen rapidly up the NGO agenda in the past few years. This work has been different from, but related to, the fundraising agenda and each agency has been concerned to mark out a clear territory and ensure that their name is associated with their lobbying work in order to ensure a good public profile. This focus on promoting a brand contrasted with the work of 10–15 years ago when NGOs saw themselves more as accompaniers, working in solidarity promoting those they worked with. The evidence from the field during the research was that at times the advocacy agenda and the need to ensure good publicity cut across international NGOs promoting their partners in favour of ensuring their logo and name were on the publicity platforms and materials.

The picture is complex and at times confusing, as UK NGOs react differently to the changing funding climate depending on where they are based, their mission, their vision and commitment, and their size. As service delivery has become unfashionable, so some health and education NGOs have suffered; as the concerns to meet the MDGs rise they may come back into fashion. Some niche NGOs have found new ways to promote their work and increase their funding through advocacy work as well as taking contracts and working closely with others towards the MDGs; others find they have fallen out of fashion and their approaches are no longer valued. In-depth field-based work, long-term gender work and responsive projects are among some approaches that have suffered during this period. Most NGOs now undertake advocacy work, most because they want to and have the capacity, but some because it has become a requirement for accessing funds. The pressures to fit the new funding agendas were felt widely, but experienced in very different ways.

Whatever their views and commitments, all the UK NGOs interviewed had adopted the dominant donor procedures and approaches to managing development in order to access donor funds. The diversity of policies and procedures, seen in the mid-1990s, especially in smaller and faith-based organizations, was diminishing; some retained an interesting range of participatory and learning methodologies, but these had to coexist alongside the project cycle management paradigm.

The NGO sector was changing in many ways, with the flourishing of the larger players and the increasing struggle or decline of many smaller ones. These changes have been taking place largely in response to donor shifts, and all donors have shifted in similar ways. Yet this has been happening without any articulated analysis, or indeed hard evidence, about what kind of NGOs deliver best on the ground; changes have been made by donors without clear evidence about how valid the new approaches are and without coordination between them. The donors appeared not to recognize their critical role in shaping the UK NGO sector and have not coordinated, discussed or set up systems to analyse their impact on the sector. NGOs have found themselves reacting to the many changes – though some also try and influence donor thinking – and working hard to meet the next round of demands more skilfully than their rivals, while trying to stay true to their purpose and deliver effective development. Some agonized more about the possible conflicts between their mission and mandate and the way they have to raise funds than others; some appeared comfortable with current funding norms and compliance was unproblematic for them. Competition, always evident, was inevitable in the funding climate of declining funds for some and increased rewards for others; it was all pervasive during the research, and seemed to effectively cut across the many proposals to increase cooperation and joint working that have yet to bear real fruit among development NGOs.

CHAPTER 5
The NGO context in Uganda and South Africa

In the previous chapter the aid flows available to UK NGOs were outlined, along with some of the key responses observable in the NGO sector. UK NGOs, in turn, fund NGOs in Uganda and SA, along with bilateral and multilateral donors who provide some direct funding for civil society in each country. Analysing the volume of aid flows to civil society in each country proved too difficult because the available data were incredibly patchy and unreliable (Sogge, 2002); this information is critical but remains to be collected. However, the research did track and analyse the impact of the changing priorities and conditions of donors, including UK NGOs as donors, on the work of a range of local NGOs. By choosing two very distinct countries with contrasting histories and relationships to the global aid system, the research explored how far responses and reactions to changing donors' ideas and procedures differed, and where there were common trends.

Clearly, civil society in Uganda and SA are distinct: Uganda is highly aid-dependent and local NGOs emerged largely in response to the provision of external funds, while aid accounts for only 2 per cent of the SA budget and many SA NGOs came out of the different historical traditions of struggle against apartheid and the provision of social welfare for the poor. The different political and economic contexts shape the nature and role of civil society in addressing poverty in each country today. They also have implications for the way NGO leadership relates to donors, their level of knowledge about the development industry and their confidence to challenge conditionality. While donors and INGOs overtly recognize the importance of the local context in shaping the causes of poverty and relevant responses, nevertheless the conditions placed on funding to NGOs in the two countries are remarkably similar; indeed these conditions and the language of development employed are now universal (Mawdsley et al., 2002).

This chapter presents, albeit briefly, some of the distinctive and common experiences of Uganda and SA: the broad political and socio-economic challenges facing each country and the characteristics of the NGO sector that is trying to work with the international agenda and the needs of the poor.

Uganda

Uganda was in an advanced state of collapse when the National Resistance Movement (NRM) under Museveni took power in 1986, following years of instability, conflict and political isolation. Income levels were very low and there had been a large-scale retreat into subsistence. Social capital was seriously eroded by civil war, and the provision of education and health by the government – essential for building human capital – was almost non-existent; alternative provision, especially by church-based NGOs, was patchy. Uganda was faced with a rising HIV/AIDS pandemic, and the political process and government institutions were deeply damaged; the country faced a huge rehabilitation challenge (Hansen and Twaddle, 1998).

Since 1986 Uganda has undergone rapid change, although war and internal conflicts continue to take their toll up to the present. Structural adjustment programmes were introduced soon after the new government came to power. Aid has accounted for 60 per cent of the national budget until recently, and to access this volume of aid the president, and government, met almost all of the IMF conditions: Uganda was the first country in Africa to receive limited debt relief in recognition of his policies. The country has performed well in macroeconomic stabilization and growth; economic liberalization in a relatively stable political environment contributed to good economic performance, especially during the 1990s, with growth of 3 per cent from 1986 to 1996, while it was only 0.8 per cent for much of the rest of Africa (Wallace, Caputo and Herbert, 1999).

Growth has not, however, translated easily into poverty reduction. Although there have been improvements in the human development indicators (HDI) they remain low, and Uganda was in the bottom 10 per cent of countries worldwide on the HDI index during the research period. Household surveys, based on one poverty indicator, consumption, showed a decrease in poverty from 56 per cent to 46 per cent over a three-year period in the late 1990s, though these figures were not confirmed by the national accounts and are contested by many NGOs in Uganda (Wallace, Caputo and Herbert 1999). The quantitative and qualitative data suggest that poverty for the bottom 20 per cent has worsened. Poverty is predominantly found in the countryside where over 80 per cent of the population still live and is worse in areas affected by conflict. Gender and HIV/AIDS status are two factors closely linked with poverty in a context where women have low status and few rights to assets and where HIV/AIDS is decimating the active working population. Factors such as geography, disability and ethnicity also relate to poverty indicators.

The lack of a clear link between economic growth and effective poverty reduction was a cause of concern to the World Bank and the government in the late 1990s. This led to the adoption of a Ugandan Poverty Eradication Action Plan (PEAP) designed to address poverty, before poverty-focused plans (PRSPs) became the major, compulsory international aid instrument in sub-Saharan Africa for accessing heavily indebted poor countries (HIPC) money (debt relief) and later for receiving direct budget support from donors. At the level of policy it was agreed that there was a weak understanding of the causes of poverty in Uganda and more work was needed to find ways to ensure that economic growth translated into long-term benefits for poor people. One such initiative was the

DFID-funded Uganda Participatory Poverty Assessment Project (UPPAP), which was designed to bring the voices of the poor into the policy arena.

In relation to social provision, the education enrolment figures have improved dramatically since the introduction of free primary education in 1997, when student numbers more than doubled. However, serious continuing problems of educational quality remain at all levels of the education system, which is characterized by a high level of untrained teachers, large classes, and lack of books and other resources. Dropout and illiteracy rates remain high. The poverty of the basic health services and very deficient provision of drugs has been starkly highlighted in Uganda, where HIV/AIDS spread rapidly in 1990s, and where only a tiny number received antiretrovirals (ARVs) in 2005. The focus on addressing the pandemic has been far more rooted in changing behavioural and social norms than relying on a health system that is very weak, especially in rural areas, and where basic drugs for malaria, opportunistic infections and common illnesses are lacking, and where the introduction of cost recovery in the late 1990s deterred poor people from even accessing the little there was (Wallace, Caputo and Herbert, 1999).

Economically, the majority of the population still works in agriculture (56% of women and 53% of rural men). During the 1980s Uganda's agricultural production slumped, cash crops almost disappeared and the agricultural infrastructure collapsed. Even now access to new improved seeds is limited and Uganda had the lowest use of fertilizer in the world in the 1990s. Agricultural technology is basic, still largely relying on hand-held tools. There is limited technological innovation and some observers are deeply concerned that the new poverty plans and direct budget support systems focus more on health and education, and tend to ignore agricultural development (for example Farm Africa is worried by the lack of agricultural focus in most PRSPs). Work on land reform and the modernization of agriculture is well under way, although there are fears that these will not protect the small farmer, the bedrock of the country:

> small farmers have dominated export and food production in Uganda...their position deteriorated sharply in the post-colonial period...from 1972 state control over crop marketing, processing, taxation, and the exchange rate was used to reduce prices to growers to non-sustainable levels...thus small farmers generated most of the government revenue, but were starved of resources for technical change, and continued to use an iron age technology (Brett, 1992: 4).

When the government took power it was committed to promoting democracy in Ugandan society, and the political structure of the original local resistance councils, established after the war from the village to the national levels, evolved into a representative political structure. Decentralization was promoted, with devolved budgets and decision-making increasingly taken at the district or village level. Critical issues now arise around: the evaporation of funds as they move from the centre outwards; the power of centrally controlled policies; and lack of capacity, especially in new districts. However, the commitment to bring planning and implementation closer to the people is evident. This system, based on elected representatives at all levels up to parliament, has been run without political parties, a major issue for the international community. In 2003 the president agreed to move to multiparty democracy, with all the opportunities and dangers inherent in such a process, though there are indications of countervailing trends.

NGOs in Uganda

The NGO sector developed following the end of the war in much of Uganda, largely in response to external donor funding. It has been fast growing ever since, as Dicklich (1998: 4) describes:

Foreign and indigenous NGOs have flooded Uganda since the National Resistance army stormed Kampala in 1986. The invasion of NGOs has impacted on almost every sector of Ugandan life and every region of Uganda, although some districts have higher concentrations of NGOs such as Rakai (badly hit by the AIDS virus), Luwero and Kampala. The flood of NGOs and NGO activities has produced varying degrees of both cynicism and optimism.

NGOs became critical in some areas of service provision; a few went further and entered the arena of awareness-raising and rights for women, and land issues, and lobbying to cancel the debt, for example. The government was cautious about these roles for NGOs:

to a certain extent, years of war have created a culture of suspicion and fear, which has even placed NGO motives and activities under public scrutiny. Consequently many NGOs especially those that can be considered 'political' in any way, are regarded as having ulterior motives and objectives (Dicklich, 1998: 6).

All NGOs have to register with the government, and there have been disagreements over regulation, with NGOs resisting some of the government's more restrictive tendencies laid out in the 2003 NGO bill, which threatened annual registration and increased control of their activities. While NGOs want the freedom to act, they also recognize the problems created by 'briefcase NGOs' set up primarily to access donor money, which change their agendas with every passing phase and bring the sector into disrepute.

Many NGOs, local and international, are based in Kampala; only a minority is in the rural areas where the bulk of the population lives, and there are few working in conflict areas. There is uncertainty about how far NGOs can legitimately claim to reach or represent the poorest in Uganda. The INGOs remain vocal and dominant in Uganda, and while most work closely with local NGOs in partnerships, others remain operational themselves. There is a high degree of competition for funding and dependence on foreign donors for survival; these along with the relative youth and apolitical focus of most NGOs in Uganda suggested the sector in 1990s was not yet a strong vehicle for the development of a democratic civil society capable of pressuring the state and keeping it accountable (Dicklich, 1998).

By 2003, the context had shifted and the advocacy and lobbying agenda became important to NGOs and donors, who wanted NGOs to play different roles (Kanji, 2000). They wanted NGOs, on the one hand, to support local governments at the district level in delivering on their plans for health, education and water; on the other, to contribute to the building of a strong civil society, hold government to account, raise public awareness, form strong organizations and lobby on behalf of the poor. It was in this context of changing agendas that the research took place.

Quantitative analysis of Uganda NGOs

The research into the size and shape of the NGO sector in Uganda was undertaken by Crispin Kintu (Centre for Basic Research) and analysed by Martin Kaleeba and Rashid Sisay. It was the first attempt to describe the sector, although others have since followed (see the World Bank study by Barr, Fafchamps and Owens, 2005) and their work largely supports these original findings. The survey was based on NGO registration data held in the office of the prime minister: a detailed analysis was made of the countries of origin of all the registered NGOs listed, and a random sample of 354 NGOs (one in every 15) was taken to analyse their key activities.

It is important to recognize that these data provide only a snapshot at one point in time. Many local NGOs come and go, although overall the numbers are increasing; 2,655 NGOs were registered in 2000, over 3,000 by 2002 and 4,000 in 2003; some listed in 2000 were defunct by 2002, others were operating but had not yet completed their registration. The number of unregistered community-based organizations (CBOs) was much higher. The situation is fluid; many CBOs and NGOs are transient, responding to an immediate need or short-term available funding. This was highlighted in the World Bank study, which labelled it sector nomadism when NGOs suddenly switch sector or focus in response to the availability of new resources and changes in funding priorities.

There was no attempt to disaggregate the local NGO sector into a neat typology of NGOs. Instead, the key criteria for guiding the analysis emerged during the research: a major difference was identified between INGOs and local ones. They had very different access to resources, communications and networking. For INGOs the important criteria that differentiated them were: size; whether they had local field offices or not; and whether they worked through partners or directly with local communities. For local NGOs the criteria that distinguished them were size, reach, location and sources of funding.

It was hard from the available data to track external funding flows to different NGOs; however, it was possible to distinguish between NGOs that were well established, with stable donor funding, able to access a range of funding through diverse channels (perhaps 50–100 local NGOs plus INGOs), and more fragile

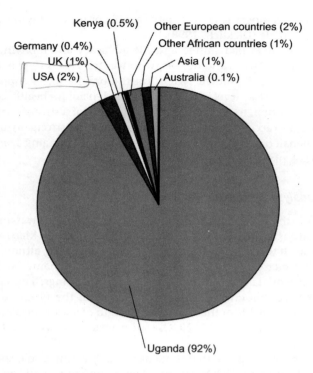

Kenya (0.5%) Other European countries (2%)

Germany (0.4%) Other African countries (1%)

UK (1%) Asia (1%)

USA (2%) Australia (0.1%)

Uganda (92%)

Figure 5.1 Country of origin of NGOs working in Uganda

organizations, mostly small, often new and reliant on only one or two funders. Many of these experience high rates of organizational failure.

Countries of origin of NGOs working in Uganda

The overwhelming majority of NGOs in Uganda are of Ugandan origin (see Figure 5.1). They include church organizations, CBOs, membership groups and associations. A significant number are religious, predominantly Christian.

This research focused only on the international sector and those NGOs they fund locally, which form only a small part of the whole. Relatively few Ugandan NGOs have access to external donor funding, but they are the largest and probably the most significant players, and many have extensive relations with a wide range of smaller NGOs that they, in turn, fund. Funding for local NGOs generated within Uganda is extremely limited and comes from membership and subscription fees, donations and government sources. Organizations relying exclusively on internal funding were excluded from the study and it is recognized that they may behave very differently.

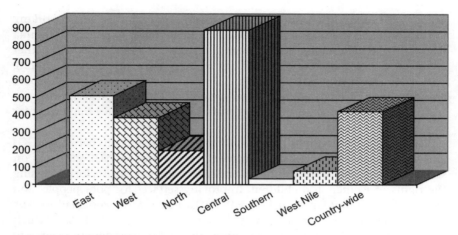

Figure 5.2   Geographical spread of NGOs in Uganda

Geographical spread

While the socio-economic indicators of Uganda indicate that the northern and eastern parts of the country are the poorest, the analysis showed that the majority of NGOs operate in the central region, with Kampala hosting over 550 NGOs, about 18 per cent of registered NGOs (see Figure 5.2). The eastern region hosts the second largest number of NGOs (about 520), again many of which are urban-based; about 14 per cent operate countrywide. The spread of NGOs in Uganda follows patterns noted elsewhere: most NGOs are clustered in areas where security and accessibility are good, and where basic services and communications are in operation.

Sectoral interventions by NGOs in Uganda

The random sample of every 15th NGO taken from the database showed the following sectoral focus for the 354 NGOs analysed. Only the main activity was counted: 15 per cent in evangelism; 12–13 per cent in each of these sectors respectively: agriculture, programmes for women, young people and micro-finance; 9 per cent in environmental protection; 9 per cent in education; 8 per cent in health; 6 per cent in training and capacity-building; 6 per cent in advocacy; and 4 per cent in HIV/AIDS. However, many of these NGOs were engaged in many areas of work and, for example, most tackle HIV/AIDS within their remit. The World Bank study based on 451 NGOs, undertaken in 2002, counted multiple activities for each NGO and found that education, health and micro-finance were the most common sectors, with work in advocacy, agriculture and HIV/AIDS emerging as key intervention areas (Barr, Fafchamps and Owens, 2005). These broadly reflected dominant donor priorities.

The range of NGO activities is diverse and depends partly on the problems and needs of the people in their areas of operation and partly on the different agendas of the funding institutions and government policies. NGOs working in the north and the eastern parts of Uganda are involved in relief, war trauma counselling, rehabilitation, resettlement and recovery work; NGOs in the other areas are involved in development programmes. Many do capacity-building and awareness-raising activities with CBOs and local populations, and some are actively involved in promoting gender and children's rights following the new constitution, which provided an enabling legal and policy framework for such work.

The sector is dynamic and growing. Despite evident tensions between NGOs and the government, and the government's preference for NGOs to work on service delivery only, a constitutional and legal framework exists for addressing the rights of women and children, improving services for poor people, and working on burning issues such as HIV/AIDS, peace and reconciliation. The sector is fluid and can be responsive to local needs such as HIV/AIDS, in which Ugandan NGOs have led the way on innovative and indigenous approaches to prevention and care. The sector continues to grow, largely in response to external funding. The funding sources are diverse and the conditions set by external funders are constantly shifting.

Many local NGOs are engaged in evangelism, something that is often not included in the development agenda at the international level. The lines between evangelism and service are often very porous for faith-based agencies worldwide, and this is especially true in deeply religious Uganda.

Diverse funding channels and changes in donor agendas

The entire sample of local NGOs interviewed depended heavily on donor funding to finance their activities. A few felt they had adequate funding and could competently account for their funds, while others experienced funding gaps and faced problems reporting to their donors. Most had few alternative sources of income other than project funding from donors.

The key donors included DFID, USAID, DANIDA, CIDA, the EU and INGOs. While the donors channelled significant aid through NGOs in 1990s, especially through INGOs, the pattern was changing, with bilateral donors moving to sector-wide or direct budget funding to the government, which was to be forwarded to the districts under decentralization policies: NGOs must now access some of their funding from local government and contribute to district plans on health, education, agriculture, etc.

Competition for declining donor funds was increasing and many NGOs were trying to find new ways to tap into the basket of donor resources and feared tougher times ahead. Donors (including many INGOs) were tightening their funding conditionalities. These shifts were taking place during the research period and had not yet been fully understood by NGOs; the implications of accessing funding locally through district government budgets were under discussion by the time this research ended. There was, however, increasing pressure from the government for INGOs to declare their income and budgets for programmes in a particular district so that they could be included as part of the district budget, and for local NGOs to raise funding in future through district budgets.

During the research period the main channels of funding were: donor grants to INGOs for operational or partnership work with local NGOs; budget support from donors to government, government to local government and then to NGOs; grants directly from donors to local NGOs through new mechanisms of disbursement; and contracts. The preferred channels of funding differed between donors and changed over time. DFID was the largest bilateral funder to Uganda, with the EU (EC and European bilaterals) as the largest multilateral, supplying 51 per cent of Uganda's total aid budget. DFID increased its funding to Uganda during the research period, from £40 million per year in the late 1990s to £55 million by 2000/1, although their funding for NGOs accounted for only 0.1 per cent of the budget in 1998/9. The focus was on the poor; civil society was seen as only one among other legitimate partners for achieving poverty reduction. Over 10 years DFID changed from being a largely responsive funder for NGO-designed projects, to funding projects that fitted into DFID's strategic agenda, to umbrella funding for a few NGOs working strategically at a policy level in Uganda.

There were different routes to DFID funding for NGOs and INGOs working in Uganda. For this reason, and because the funding flows change when the mechanisms change and budgets vary year on year, it was not possible to track how much money was channelled from DFID to NGOs in Uganda (or for that matter, to SA). It was clear, however, that DFID was a critical player in Uganda and that other leading funders, such as the World Bank and the EU, shared DFID's changing agenda for civil society and NGOs; only a tiny percentage of DFID's spending went to NGOs; and most mechanisms were only open to UK-based NGOs, which were also often successful in accessing DFID's local direct funding.

Other funders, such as the Community Fund and Comic Relief, continued to fund through UK NGOs and had no in-country funding. In contrast the EU, which had no previous direct funding to NGOs, was exploring the possibility of establishing new direct funding streams for civil society in 2002; this represented a shift from the past when EU funding in-country was state to state. In 2000/3 there was a lot of donor-funded research examining the changing role of NGOs and how best to fund them, reflecting donors' changing priorities and new approaches to poverty reduction strategies (examples include Lister and Nyamugasira, 2001; Robinson, 2001). In the context of the overall donor shift to directly funding government, Uganda being one of the first countries to receive direct budget support from the late 1990s onwards, donors needed consultants to help them to identify new ways of funding NGOs in redefined roles.

Ugandan NGOs as aid recipients

All the NGOs interviewed were concerned about the increase in funding conditionalities and the shifts in thinking about their roles. Some said that donors had become stricter on accountability, dictating specific planning, reporting and accountability systems because of fraudulent practices and the misappropriation of funds by some Ugandan NGOs. Many local NGOs said there was a tendency for NGOs to develop proposals in response to the interests of the donors in order to get funding, although they might not have the competencies in-house to run certain programmes. This created problems when trying to grapple with implementing activities that they were not well positioned to implement. One senior member of a national NGO noted: 'Sometimes we go out of our way to satisfy the donor. It is because the desire to get funding is high.'

A number of NGOs are funded by different donors: while diversified funding sources make more resources available, they often complicate the working of an NGO by splitting their work into many segments, dictated by the priorities and interests of different funders. This creates problems in the organization and unless an NGO has a strong internal culture it can fail in these circumstances. To deal with many donors, the organization needs to develop special skills for good report writing, computer information systems, auditing (internal and external) and networking with others to understand the language of donors.

Almost all the Ugandan NGOs interviewed said that serious dependency on external donor funding for NGO activities continued: there were few opportunities and little effort made to fundraise locally. The deep dependency of southern NGOs on foreign aid inhibited independent decision-making and mirrored the dependence of the government on external aid, which placed Uganda in a weak negotiating position. Many Ugandan NGOs raised the issues being hotly debated in the media concerning the role of aid and whether it is undermining local democracy and perpetuating a government agenda more responsive to donor demands than local needs. They also highlighted the tendency of many development donors to undervalue indigenous organizations and cultural forms.

Ugandan NGOs did not distinguish between their donors. While INGOs and different donors pride themselves on having very different funding and partnership relationships with local NGOs, this view was not reflected in the interviews. While there were some examples of strong working relationships, these were tied to individual relationships rather than organizational structures, and the claims of many INGOs to fund differently from, for example, the EU, the World Bank or DFID, and from each other, were, by and large, not reflected in the feedback. All donors were definitely experienced as donors and not partners in development, with a few individual exceptions.

Many of the problems of power, externally set agendas and dependency relations were said to be replicated in the funding relations between the larger more powerful NGOs based in Kampala and the smaller local NGOs they supported. These issues were not included in the phase 1 interviews, but were raised in some of the case studies presented later in the report.

South Africa

SA's NGO sector was forged out of its history of struggle against apartheid. Although some NGOs existed from the 1950s onwards, conducting welfare activities predominately linked to urban poverty, a significant number of NGOs emerged in the 1980s to address the needs of blacks in the townships and bantustans. These were organizations that largely defined themselves by their opposition to the apartheid government and that received funding (both openly and covertly) from solidarity organizations based outside the country (Habib and Taylor, 1999). This history and the accompanying radicalization of South Africans have had profound effects on the structure and approaches of many SA NGOs. For instance, NGOs can draw upon staff with international experience and training, who have familiarity with the donors and their constituencies, and who are willing to challenge practices and policies that they question. At the same time, the relentless dismantling of traditional African cultures and structures and the disempowerment of the black population on a massive scale under apartheid left multiple barriers for the new generation to overcome.

There are similarities, however, between the two countries. As in Uganda, only a limited number of the total NGOs and CBOs are linked into international funding streams; the vast majority appears to rely on local and non-grant sources of funding. The 1990s also witnessed similar shifts in the direction of funding, first to NGOs, then government and in SA back to NGOs to a certain extent. Following the installation of Nelson Mandela as president in 1994, donors rapidly changed their funding priorities and many anti-apartheid NGOs were left with limited support as the agenda switched rapidly towards development via the government. A large number of NGO staff drained away from the sector into the government. Initially this permitted close ties between the government and the NGOs, with the latter participating actively in policy debates about land, housing, literacy and gender. However, the NGOs found themselves precariously situated as policy was defined and adopted: the government became increasingly resistant to external critique, some NGOs struggled to find entry points and forms of working with the official departments charged with providing services, and other NGOs were caught between their role as contracted agents to implement programmes and their accountability to their constituents and local beneficiaries. Moreover, many aspiring young black people responded to new opportunities to enter government and the private sector; this led observers and staff in the NGO sector to conclude that there was a crisis of leadership and capacity in many NGOs following the end of apartheid (Smith, 2002).

Until about 1996, NGOs working in development could access international funding with relative ease. Donors were looking for local partners and funds were available to NGOs. This period saw the formation of 'briefcase NGOs' similar to those in Uganda. However, this phenomenon was relatively minor, with the vast majority of NGOs emerging out of community initiatives and becoming well-established; profit seekers often entered the consultancy business instead. After 1996, funders prioritized support to the new government's programmes, ostensibly with a share earmarked for channelling to local NGOs. While there were diverse programmes and donors, in general the conditions placed on funding increased; as in Uganda, highly publicized examples of corruption left donors wary of leniency in oversight and, as already highlighted, back-donors such as DFID tightened constraints on aid disbursement. SA thus provides an example of country in which the past tradition of confrontation and activism is intertwined with potential financial vulnerability and dependency.

Development challenges in South Africa

The country of SA and its people have accomplished much in the last 10 years. The transition from an apartheid state system to a multiracial democracy has been peaceful. Rights and opportunities extend to a wider range of citizens than in the past. Shifts in relationships between the government and residents, community structures and civil society more broadly have occurred, bringing them together around solving common societal problems. A black middle class has emerged, with black professionals in all sectors of the economy. The currency has gained strength over the last few years, and private inward investment has – albeit unevenly – continued. There have been dramatic improvements in the extension of services, such as health care, education and electricity, to rural and township areas. Recent elections were the most peaceful yet, with higher levels of turnout and support for the ANC. All of these constitute signs of the stability of the country.

An emphasis on growth and delivery, in the middle of a fundamental reworking of state structures and policies, has simultaneously meant that some longer-term development objectives have been short-changed: housing development has usually been of poor quality and in peripheral locations (Harrison et al., 2003), job growth has been concentrated in the informal sector (Pieterse, 2003), poverty continues to be concentrated along racial lines, and wider objectives of environmental sustainability, gender equity, immigrant rights and rights more generally have been sidelined, if not in rhetoric then in budget allocations (Budlender, 2002). HIV/AIDS and other health challenges (among them TB, hepatitis, malaria and diarrhoea) strain government and community capacity. Indeed, the gap between the government's rhetoric – of development as empowerment and independence from foreign influence – and the reality of SA's adoption of policies closely in line with those of the World Bank and the IMF has led observers to conclude that president Mbeki 'talks left' and 'walks right' (Bond, 2004).

Although much is written about the developmental challenges facing SA, we highlight only three developmental dilemmas that are particularly crucial for the country: persistent inequality, insufficient employment and HIV/AIDS. The first, persistent inequality is rooted in issues of race and place of residence, critical factors underlying patterns of wealth and poverty; it is a crucial challenge for government and citizens alike. Ten years after the end of apartheid, GINI coefficients, one of the most widely used indices of inequality within a country, remain consistently high. Despite reductions in racial discrimination, three-quarters of the top income decile are white and 90 per cent of those in the bottom six deciles are black (Natrass and Swilling in Pieterse, 2003). Between 40 and 50 per cent of the population is poor, whatever measure is used (May, 1999: 48). Gender inequality is also increasing and conditions for women, especially black rural women, show little if any improvement (Albertyn and Hassim, 2004; Bhorat et al., 2001). The ravages of lack of monetary income, gender-based violence and HIV/AIDS can offset the improved provision of healthcare, housing and water systems.

The second is unemployment and underemployment, which are continuing features of the SA economy. Although the end of apartheid should have signalled an opportunity for previously excluded groups to enter new fields and occupations, formal job growth has not accompanied labour market expansion. Since 1994 an estimated half a million formal jobs have been lost. Unemployment is estimated at 36 per cent, with higher levels experienced by the poorly educated, blacks, women, youth and rural residents.

Industry, in line with recommendations emanating from government and international consultant reports to enhance industrial competitiveness through increased labour market flexibility, is restructuring in ways that have shifted the types of jobs available: from formal to informal, union to non-union, and full-time to part-time or intermittent. The skill mix demanded and the location of work have similarly changed, with rural and unskilled workers most excluded, though trained workers also encounter difficulties in obtaining secure employment. For rural residents, access to land remains a problem, and there are the insufficient opportunities for more than subsistence agriculture (Marais, 2001; Mitchie and Padayachee, 1998; Lester, Nel and Binns, 2000).

The third major problem is HIV/AIDS. By the end of 2001, SA was the country with the highest number of HIV-positive residents in the world, at 4.74 million people; by 2003 the numbers, depending on whose estimates are used, ranged from 5.3 million to a staggering 6.57 million, though the latter figure – from the Department of Health – is acknowledged to be high. One in nine South Africans was HIV-positive; a little over half (56%) were women and most were of working age. Rates of infection have continued to rise, with current estimates of national HIV prevalence at 11 per cent; an estimated 29.7 per cent of women 20–24 years are HIV-positive (Dorrington et al., 2004).

By most accounts, the South African government, with President Mbeki at the lead, has offered contradictory and ineffective leadership in combating the pandemic, questioning the links between HIV and AIDS and refusing to authorize the use of drugs treatment for HIV-positive individuals. Policy debates over HIV/AIDS have galvanized civil-society organizations, of which the most prominent is the Treatment Action Campaign (TAC) (Camay and Gordon, 2001: 9–10; Achmat, 2004). TAC's efforts to highlight the potential of treating AIDS, allowing those with the syndrome to survive longer, has resulted in international campaigns to provide low-cost drugs to poor countries, and national campaigns and court cases to force government hospitals to provide ARVs to pregnant women and newborns. Many other organizations and individuals, including medical staff, have reoriented their work to address the needs of HIV/AIDS-affected people, and in doing so have run counter to government policy and rhetoric. Ironically, several such organizations halted their programmes, including the Children's HIV/AIDS Model Programme and the HIV/AIDS programme of the National Progressive Primary Health Care Network, when international donors started funding the government instead of NGOs (Budlender, 1999). Although the South African government now supports limited access to ARVs and the purchase of low-cost drugs, the debates and the official policies reduced trust in the government and proved a litmus test for government legitimacy.

In addition to these three aspects of poverty and development patterns in SA, there are also institutional changes within and outside the government that affect the way in which these challenges are addressed. The reform of the state following 1994 is designed to 'bring government to the people'. The constitution makes local government the key actor in promoting local development, linking residents' aspirations with the programmes, finance and expertise to bring them to life. The Nonprofit Organizations Act of 1997 gives civil society a privileged position as 'a fourth branch' of the state (Russell and Swilling, 2002: 76). Decentralization, more participatory and developmental approaches in government and greater attention to the potential of linkages to NGOs, the private sector and other governmental divisions are parts of these institutional reforms (Bornstein, 2000). Yet numerous studies suggest that such key elements of new governance approaches fall short of their aims, continuing to feed into patterns of local elite dominance, to neglect alternative views and interest (such as those of women), and to create expectations that the institutions involved cannot meet (Bornstein, 2000; McEwan, 2003).

NGOs in South Africa

For SA NGOs, national efforts to fast-track delivery of essential services, democratize government and galvanize NGOs in support of the ANC's growth and development programmes have generated tensions over possible roles for NGOs. Prior to 1994, many NGOs defined themselves by the struggle for political and social justice and focused their activities on providing vital legal, welfare and developmental services to oppressed communities (Kotzé, 1999: 172). However, in the post-1994 period, established identities and roles as anti-apartheid organizations became less relevant (Habib and Taylor, 1999); NGOs struggled to create new identities, establish a relationship with a democratic government at national and local levels and redefine their relationships with the wider community. As in Uganda, donors may expect NGOs to act as advocates for marginalized peoples, as government watchdogs, as agents of delivery and training, among others. The broader literature – and our research – on NGOs in SA suggest that these potential roles are often incompatible. As a consequence, while some organizations continue to define themselves based on their relationships to beneficiary communities, many are becoming either more commercial in their relations to the government and beneficiaries or more adversarial towards the ANC government. NGO relationships with the government concerning funding, contracts and policy formulation, are all subjects of tension and debate in the NGO sector.

Some South African NGOs find they have advantages in their dealings with donors and the government. The legacies of the struggle, including the experience of returning exiles, the country's relative wealth (which has allowed for excellent schooling for some, access to local resources, etc.) and a national government that is committed publicly to tackling poverty and inequality all contribute to a distinctive environment for development practice. The absence of debt and the lack of explicit conditionalities on official development assistance also play a role. The NGO sector is large and varied, with leaders from a diverse range of racial, ethnic and national backgrounds: some NGO leaders have moved in and out of ANC leadership positions.

There is a range of vibrant institutions focused on the NGO sector and these include coalitions (the SA national NGO Coalition, SANGOCO, and the SA Local Grantmakers Association, SALGA) that have formulated codes of ethics and practice to which non-profits and grant-makers are expected to adhere (Interfund, 1998). There are research and advocacy bodies, both inside and outside universities, which focus on the non-profit sector (e.g., the Institute for Democracy in SA, IDASA, and the Cooperative for Research and Education, CORE). Many funding organizations – national and international – support the exchange of information on NGOs, funders and development practice with publications, seminars, roundtables, conferences and research initiatives (for example, Interfund and *Development Update*). There are numerous SA trainers and support organizations available to work with NGOs located in the country, in addition to initiatives and resources available from abroad. Activist and grassroots initiatives are important arenas for public involvement and debate. Unions are strong, public debate spans a wide (if decreasing) range of political perspectives, and local activism has brought important changes – even in recent years – to government policy and international relations, especially around HIV/AIDS and peace and justice work.

These advantages are counterbalanced by the legacy of apartheid, and the physical, material, ideological and emotional traumas it inflicted on the South African people. The transition terrain is highly contested along every dimension, with some observers worrying:

> that the ideological battle for the imagination of what transition can become is being won by narrow neo-liberal inspired conceptions of the present and the future. In part this is ascribed to the weakness of oppositional voices that may have become vocal but are not necessarily strategic or effective (Pieterse and Meintjies, 2004).

Moreover, patterns of inequality in society are mirrored in civil society itself, and most organizations, including those that are smaller, black-led or unaffiliated with anti-apartheid movements, usually cannot access internationally linked, experienced and broadly informed staff. Personnel instead often lack confidence and experience. In these cases, staff find they have to grapple with alien Western concepts of development and change. They may struggle to cope with Western patterns of thought; they find little is available to them from their own cultures, which have been distorted and sometimes broken:

> Some of those I interviewed questioned why the event could not have talked more with a language and ideas coming from the culture of the region – Southern and Eastern Africa – and from a more locally grounded sense of practise. But in the same breath many have then noted that – particularly in the development sector – they do not see much in ideas or practice that can be said to be authentically locally driven (Harding, 2005).

There are exceptions and the work in peace-building on the ground was one notable exception quoted. As with HIV/AIDS in Uganda, some conflict resolution and peace-building work in SA is rooted in local and appropriate development practice. However, the local training and support that are available for NGOs largely focus on training NGOs in the use of dominant planning and implementation models. In contrast, even the large flagship NGOs in SA, some of which were included in this study, rely on models of analysis and ways of working drawn from Europe: some from the rational management models of development, others from such intellectual traditions as anthroposophy and the work of Austrian philosopher-educator Rudolf Steiner (the founder of the Waldorf schools).

The reliance on imported concepts is as entrenched in SA as it is in Uganda, although the range of external traditions on which NGOs draw is wider and deeper.

NGOs as aid recipients

Continued needs – whether around poverty, health, incomes or rights – have placed SA NGOs in several quandaries. According to some donors, SA is a middle-income country and, as such, should receive limited support. Yet it is also one of the most unequal economies in the world, and one where new opportunities to attack that inequality have only emerged with the end of apartheid. Many organizations and back funders thus opt to provide targeted support. For some of the donors, this situation has meant a focus on policy development, infrastructure and poverty reduction, often via the government. For others, funding is constrained to narrowly defined strategic areas. And for yet others, funding is funnelled to their long-term partners based on relationships forged during the struggle years. As the government moved away from its redistributive focus and towards a neoliberal growth approach in the late 1990s (Bond, 2004; Lester, Nel and Binns, 2000), donors now have to work closely with individual departments, specific places and targeted organizations to ensure that poverty will be alleviated through their funding.

International funds are an important component of the country's efforts to address poverty and inequality. Funds arrive in multiple forms (grants, loans, etc.), from different sources (multilateral agencies such as the United Nations, bilateral sources, private companies and private charities), and with a variety of terms (e.g. prior conditions to be met, timeframe, usage). New organizations and funders have entered the country, many of whom are engaged in donor forums or direct consultation with the government. In all cases, tracing actual quantities of money transferred is surprisingly difficult, whether official development assistance (ODA) or the NGO grants under study here (Sogge, 2002). For aid flowing through NGOs or private charities, there is no central accounting of either committed funds or those spent in country. Yet there are indirect measures that suggest that external funding, whether from official or private sources, fills funding gaps for civil-society organizations. Bond (2001) says that although foreign aid represents less than 2 per cent of the country's national budget, it plays a decisive role in shifting capital towards selected areas and organizations that might otherwise go unfunded. Although 75 per cent of the SA organizations surveyed by IDASA and CORE received no government funding, private foundation funding was an important source of finance in almost 50 per cent of the organizations surveyed (Camay and Gordon, 2001: 28).

Aid tends to fluctuate for any particular donor, with direct implications for the sectors, organizations, and projects they directly support. In addition, from the mid-1990s on, many of the trends identified in the UK and Uganda were also relevant in SA: direct funding for NGOs fell, packaging of funds into larger grants increased, and conditions on programme content, financial management, implementation and reporting expanded.

Conclusion

Although the two African countries in the study differ in many important ways, when examining the expectations of NGOs in the aid chain there are crucial similarities. Prominent among these is the concern apparent in the NGO sector in both countries about their changing roles and the problems of accessing and accounting for external aid. In both countries, donors have changed their focus and expectations of NGOs, albeit in different ways, and NGOs find themselves playing multiple and often conflicting roles. The government in each country does not always support these different roles and tends to prefer NGOs to play a critical part in supporting much needed service delivery in ways that fit with government plans. The tools and training provided to NGOs that are dependent on foreign funding, to help them manage both the new funding environment and the serious challenges of effecting change in complex political environments, have been largely inadequate and the challenges they face are myriad.

departmental spending ceilings and targeted for specific activities [illegible] that poverty [illegible] will be allocated [illegible] their regions.

International funds are an important component of the country's efforts to address poverty and inequality. Funds arrive in multiple forms (e.g. grants, loans, etc.), from different sources (multilateral agencies such as the United Nations, bilateral sources, private companies and private charities), and with a variety of terms and other conditions [illegible]. [illegible] organisations and [illegible] have entered [illegible] engaged in donor funding, or direct consultation with the government. In all cases, tracking actual quantities of foreign funding [illegible] is [illegible] difficult, whether official development assistance (ODA) or private NGO grants [illegible] (Tapscott 2002) [illegible] funding through NGOs [illegible] accounting of external committed funds [illegible]. [illegible] indirect measures that suggest the external funding, whether from official or private sources [illegible] (2001) [illegible] less than 3 per cent of the country's national budget, it plays a decisive role [illegible] and organisations that [illegible]. Although 25 per cent of the 33 organisations surveyed [illegible] received [illegible] foreign funding, private foundation funding was an important source of finance in almost 50 per cent of the organisations surveyed (Camay and Gordon 2001: 25).

All funds [illegible] for any particular donor [illegible] implications for [illegible] organisations and projects they directly support. In addition [illegible] many of the [illegible] identified [illegible] were also [illegible] direct funding for NGOs [illegible] increased, and conditions on programme content, financial management, implementation and reporting expanded.

Conclusion

Although the two African countries in the study differ in many important ways, when examining the expectations of NGOs in the [illegible] there are [illegible] similarities. Prominent among these is the [illegible] in the NGO sector in both countries about their changing roles and the [illegible] and accounting for external aid. In both countries [illegible] and expectations of NGOs [illegible] in different ways, and NGOs find themselves playing multiple and often conflicting roles. The [illegible] in each country [illegible] supports [illegible] different [illegible] and [illegible] plays a critical part in supporting [illegible] needed service delivery [illegible] with government plans. The [illegible] funding provided to NGOs [illegible] to help them [illegible] the new funding environment and the serious challenges [illegible] in complex political environments, have been largely inadequate and the challenges [illegible].

CHAPTER 6
Normative conditions: rational management of the aid chain

From the previous chapters it is clear that donors set conditions for those they fund in a number of different ways, including:

- design and implementation (tools for managing the project cycle);
- funding modalities and accountability systems (the changing nature of grant-giving and accountability/reporting systems);
- content and development purpose (e.g. service delivery, enabling poor people to access their rights, poverty reduction);
- their redefinition of the roles to be played by civil society in poverty reduction and development.

All donors – from Comic Relief to the EU – set a range of conditions, albeit in different ways, to ensure that funds are disbursed in line with their purposes and used effectively (in donor terms) to promote positive, demonstrable changes. Conditions come down the aid chain with the much needed funding for NGOs in UK, SA and Uganda; it is often essential to their survival. All the NGOs interviewed spoke of the significance of these conditions and how they experienced them, sometimes positively, often negatively. While some manage to negotiate and modify conditions on their funding (especially those with multiple sources of funding), many have to accept and work with them as best they can. These conditionalities critically shape the relationships between donors and NGOs and between INGOs and local NGOs.

Among these changing conditions has been a clear trend (in the last decade) towards adopting uniform tools for planning, reporting and accountability. Rational management tools have become the norm, especially in the last five years, and are the dominant disbursement and accountability mechanisms for aid to NGOs. In adopting these approaches donors and INGOs appear to have largely neglected a range of issues of importance in development, including whether evidence and development experience have played any significant role in shaping these tools; how well they support NGO aims to be participatory and responsive to local contexts and needs; what kind of accountability they promote; and whether they promote or inhibit the performance of NGOs on the ground. Standing back a little, it seems at times extraordinary that there is one dominant approach to funding civil-society organizations globally, when the causes of poverty, the political and historical contexts and the role of NGOs in civil society are all so diverse.

Project cycle management tools in the UK

The use of rational management tools, focused largely on project cycle management and the logframe as the key way of doing the planning, implementation, monitoring and reporting/accountability were widely adopted during the 1990s, and became virtually universal (with the exception of some very small and diaspora organizations) by 2003. Before this NGOs had developed their own systems for allocating, tracking and accounting for funding; and very diverse manuals, guidelines and ways of working were used, some light and flexible, others tight and controlled. The spread of project cycle management has accelerated (Wallace, Crowther and Shepherd, 1997), in spite of the existence of critiques of the approach. Indeed some DFID staff, among others, said in response to phase 1 of the research that the flaws of the logframe were well understood and studying it was setting up a 'straw man'; it would, they predicted, disappear by 2000.

However, the reverse has happened and logframes are now ubiquitous, even in countries that were not using them in 1990s such as the Netherlands and Scandinavia. Indeed, many NGO staff new to the development sector do not know there are other ways to undertake project planning, and perceive it to be the central, professional, objective planning tool. All the UK NGOs in the sample used logframes for project cycle management, many placed their programmes and sector-wide approaches in a detailed logframe, and strategic level logframes have been developed by some NGOs, especially those seeking partnership agreements with DFID.

Several critical issues emerged from the UK research into the use of the logframe in practice. While it is presented as a universal objective planning and management tool, there is no one way to complete a logframe. Each agency, and sometimes each individual, defines differently the necessary inputs and outputs required for a logical progression towards achieving expected outcomes. The steps required are sometimes assumed rather than based on field experience, baselines are usually missing, and the factors that will enable or inhibit the project are often poorly known. Yet, there is little discussion about the lack of consistency in the way they are completed, or how they are often revised to meet donors' requirements (sometimes at every level from the field to UK NGOs to back donors). According to a spokesperson from one medium-sized NGO:

> I was in Ethiopia when DFID started inflicting logframes on people. It was done in a very heavy handed/crass manner by people who didn't understand the context. It created massive confusion and bewilderment in local staff. They couldn't see the need or value. Whenever they tried to do one themselves, someone sitting in London would pull it to pieces, but in a very inconsistent way. It was unclear what the correct style/format should be. The residual effects are still felt.

There are myriad ways to package any project or programme and much of the thinking is, in practice, actually quite sloppy and not replicable. As a worker from a large UK NGO said:

the question is whether intelligent rational thinking is aided by a tool like that which has been abandoned by the corporate sector. It has to be said that donors, including DFID, get away with very dodgy logframes. There is very little rigour.

There are evident tensions connected to how to approach the logframe in different departments of UK NGOs, as well as between HQ and field staff. Impact assessment or learning units tend to take a more nuanced approach to the role of the logframe, and try to combine it with more flexible and participatory approaches, while fundraising staff want to fulfil the donors' requirements with clear, unambiguous documents, to secure the funding to ensure the work continues. Similarly, field staff may stress the micro context and complexities, while managers need to present a streamlined plan. In turn, field staff can then feel constrained by the paperwork, for instance a staff member from a large UK NGO reported:

I have a slight concern that logframes are very much a northern tool. There is a real danger that you ask for a logframe, get the money and the person finds themselves in a box. They might not know they are meant to rewrite the thing. I think it is a good tool but it is used really badly – it looks like a box...it can constrain flexible thinking.

The belief that a logframe is a rational account of a project is belied by this constant manipulation to meet different requirements. It is, instead, a written narrative of the work, based largely on assumptions about change, rather than an accurate account of complex realities (Mosse, 2005). The logframe omits much:

in participatory work there is a lot that is intuitive and non-rational. It is what worries me about the logframe...the whole construct of the project has no meaning in people's lives (large UK NGO).

Revisions made to ensure proposals fit NGOs' global or fundraising strategies and current donor requirements often prove hard for staff to implement because they are divorced from what is actually happening and possible.

Further, there is no donor coordination of the use of logframes. Each donor has its own approach, resulting in different logframes being generated for the same project:

DFID want a logframe. Now the EU are taking it up but they are different. You can't necessarily use the same one. The EU logframe is very focused on finance. DFID, the Community Fund and Comic Relief are more development focused (large UK NGO).

While some donors allow a renegotiation of core objectives and activities during the project once experience shows up flaws in the planning, others undertake evaluations against the original logframe whatever modifications have been agreed (Wallace, 2005).

Many NGOs have developed complex guidelines to try to ensure that staff at all levels know how to work professionally with project cycle management.

Some also try to resolve the recognized problems of the logframe by enhancing local involvement in the framework (for example the toolkits of PROMIS and CAMEL developed by large UK NGOs). Some have adopted new ways of understanding and recording impact to complement the quantitative, often rigid focus of logframes, for example, using significant change stories, success ranking and outcome mapping. A few agencies have explored ways of working to promote local ownership and field based learning to counteract the problems of top-down, northern-designed tools (Chapman, David and Mancini, 2004). In practice, the project cycle framework often overshadows the real commitment to people-driven planning and downward accountability and these methods can become add-ons rather than alternative ways of working.

Neither donors nor NGOs were seriously questioning in public how and whether their funding procedures affect the way programming is done, even though conditionality was recognized as a problem for direct government aid and DFID has committed itself to reducing this conditionality, although observers report:

> Britain's controversial new guidelines for providing aid to developing countries are causing widespread confusion around the world, with the government's own officials saying there are 'fundamental concerns' about the way the policy is operating. Campaigners have also criticised the new rules saying the government's pledge to drop unpopular conditions for providing cash and loans is becoming a sham (David Pallister, *Guardian*, 24 September 2005).

Interestingly, the same debates about conditionality appeared absent in relation to NGOs. With a few exceptions, DFID and other donors were not actively relating their aid mechanisms and conditions for funding for NGOs and civil society to whether these were going to help to achieve their (NGO) goals. Indeed it was often unclear how far donors were funding UK NGOs to be implementers of donor strategies (an increasingly dominant trend, see DFID, 2000), or to be independent programmers and advocates. While some donor staff were committed to maintaining NGOs' uniqueness and independence, more were concerned to ensure that NGOs delivered results against overall donor strategies. The belief that NGOs can work effectively for the poor because of their comparative advantages has taken a knock in recent years (Lewis, forthcoming, 2006), and the answer to the problems that have occurred has been for donors to increase control over the conditions of funding. This is in spite of the widespread recognition – or lip service – that conditionality is a blunt instrument for making aid recipients behave as donors wish (Bornstein and Munro, 2003).

Some different trends

Two trends potentially challenge the dominance of the logframe: the emergence of strategic planning as a tool and the introduction of partnership and strategic funding, introduced through PPAs by DFID, and an approach being adopted by other donors (strategic planning is addressed in Chapter 7). Hopes were high that PPAs would forge different ways of working and new relationships between donors and NGOs. However, over time the PPA procedures have become more formalized and regulated by many of the same approaches, and NGOs have reported few changes in their relations with DFID.

PPAs certainly alleviate the pressure on NGOs to account for spending project by project and cut down on paperwork, theoretically allowing time for more strategic reflection. According to one large NGO:

> The PPA seems to relieve us of a lot of bureaucratic reporting. In theory it allows us to insert our own agenda on monitoring, evaluation and learning. In the past we have done evaluations we wouldn't otherwise have done for DFID.

It gives the receiving NGO status, 'DFID PPA funding is only a small percentage of our total funding, but politically it is big. It gives leverage elsewhere' (large UK NGO). However, there is scepticism among NGOs about whether the relationship is a meaningful partnership allowing for mutual learning:

> I see the PPA as a contract for collaboration, not a real partnership. I am not hopeful there will be real learning or support. One problem is that there is a huge turnover of staff at DFID. The text of the PPA was agreed with one person, the Memorandum of Understanding and financial matters with another. Some are in London and some Scotland (large UK NGO).

Despite the wide criticism of logframes for anything but projects (and the concerns around projects are clear) and straightforward event management, DFID now requires PPAs to plan and report against a strategic logframe. As one large UK NGO put it, 'Donors are beginning to take rather rigid project processes and pushing them up to a wider level. Organizations doing a PPA have to do an institutional logframe, which in my opinion is a complete joke.'

Although some of the first NGOs applying for PPAs strongly and successfully resisted many demands to conform to DFID procedures, they are under renewed pressure to do so now. Conditions have tightened and the Performance Assessment Resource Centre (PARC) was funded to help UK NGOs meet DFID's monitoring, evaluation and reporting requirements for PPAs, which are based on a logframe approach.

While many NGO staff are uncritical or have never thought analytically about logframes, someone in every sample NGO said they believe the logframe is: imposed, used inconsistently and without rigour, lacks flexibility and is unresponsive to partners. The use of English is inhibiting and prevents community ownership, and as a project tool it is too complex, often poorly used and inappropriately applied at programme and strategic levels. The discomfort with the approach is evident in the many modifications and additions practitioners and academics have designed to ameliorate some of the problems.

However, overall the logframe was said to be a good tool, which staff and partners must all use.

Project cycle management tools in South Africa

Logframes were also universal in SA. Of 22 case study organizations, only one did not work directly with logframes, though many were adapting them to better meet their needs. Most used logframes because of their donors' expectations; the EU and DFID, either as direct funders or through their intermediaries, expect SA NGOs to use orthodox logframes.

The only NGO that did not use LFA was accountable to an INGO with back funding from an institutional donor in the UK. However, the INGO had to translate its local aid relationship into a logframe to satisfy this back donor and, in order to do this, had to work with the local NGO to ensure that appropriate information was collected and indicators were monitored for reporting. So the logframe logic still guided the project design, information gathering and assessment. One NGO support organization said that although their funded projects were no longer tied to logframes the language of planning matrices has been useful:

> We don't use it ourselves but I think where we do use it is in our thinking. We use that language, where we say we've got this idea for a programme, what are the development goals, what is our immediate objective, who is our target group, what are we trying to get them to do, what could our output be about.

Familiarity with logframes varied greatly. While numerous organizations had participated in special training in logframes during the mid-1990s, during 2000–3 such training had become part of wider management and organizational development training, and/or combined with participatory modifications such as ZOPP (in GTZ), and was focused on select individuals in organizations. Rather than promoting the techniques throughout the organization, designated staff – usually a manager or director – were given responsibility for planning and reporting against logframes. In many cases consultants were hired to draft or fine-tune the planning matrix; in others the INGO partner would assist, often through a specialized division. The research showed that logframe thinking and language have permeated NGOs in SA.

The use of LFA in practice

The majority of NGOs staff indicated that they did not refer to the logframes once funding was secured and implementation began. While time and energy was spent on drafting the frameworks, these were not living, useful documents. The logframe was difficult to translate and communicate to field staff, because of its complexity and because the language was experienced by many as alienating and confusing. In most instances logframes were only referred to again when compiling reports to donors or intermediary INGOs:

> For us, as a development tool, logframes are not carried through to the field level. For our staff it is quite confusing (small NGO).

> [We] find it to be a useful tool, but it fails dismally at the community level and only works with office staff (medium-sized NGO).

For the most part, interviewees expressed ambivalence about project cycle management. They acknowledged the value of the approach in terms of organizing and thinking clearly, but complained about its inflexibility, complexity and tendency to be reductionist. None of the respondents regarded the framework as an indispensable part of their work, and several organizations set up their own simplified systems for staff planning and monitoring activities; thereafter, managers translated this information back into logframes.

Given evident staff ambivalence, and even hostility, to logframes, the research team asked respondents to comment on their ability to negotiate with donors concerning logframe requirements; the findings covered the entire spectrum from outright resistance to unwitting compliance. A very few organizations were able to reject the imposition of LFA and resist pressure from donors:

> We do not use tools. And no, donor requirements don't influence our work at all...We refuse to use logframes. Logframes are an iniquitous, dangerous, reductive trap...[S]ome people don't have a choice (director, training organization).

At the other extreme was an organization extremely dependent on donor funds, which had unknowingly adopted the framework. Donors had pulled this NGO in different directions; the programme documents showed that planning was organized using logframe criteria but this had apparently been done without any training or explanation and the programme manager denied these tools were being used. The logframe was evidently not enhancing capacity or management.

Many organizations in SA were adapting the framework, and some reported that INGOs were becoming more flexible about the formats they would accept for projects, allowing the non-orthodox preparation of project planning documents. They felt that some were recognizing the difficulties of the multiple standards, norms and formats that exist. In turn, several UK NGO representatives interviewed acknowledged their partners' limited capacity for logframe preparation, and others were trying to protect their partners from the demands of project cycle management tools, fearing these would have a negative impact by tying up time and energy better spent on projects themselves. Some accepted the limitations of the logframe itself. However, these UK organizations still needed the logframe for submissions to the donors and the work of completing these became the responsibility of the UK NGOs partnering the local organization. INGO staff in UK and SA invest considerable time translating documentation from donors to local NGOs and back again, often with loss of meaning and distortion of reality.

The experience of one UK organization and its southern partners highlighted this intermediary role. Staff in the UK expressed concern that because of back donors' insistence on logframes and quantifiable indicators they were either forced to pass on rigid programme approaches to their partners in the south, or to do the writing themselves. According to the director of a medium-sized NGO,

> often partners cannot understand the questions and many of them cannot really do logframes, despite training. So [we do] their logframes, which of course undermines participation and partnership. DFID ask for indicators for each NGO in a large project so they have to work out individual NGO indicators, but this undermines the notion of joint work.

The project managers wanted to buffer their southern partners from the rigid planning and reporting requirements and felt that when reworking documents they were becoming aid administrators rather than development workers. Smaller organizations especially tended not to be particularly good at report writing, and UK staff keen to support grassroots NGOs had to augment and tailor their documents for funders. The director said they kept apologizing to partners for making myriad requests for information and documentation and staff felt pressured trying to provide support while making heavy administrative demands. They and the partners felt they had good overall relations, but the time spent querying detail and demanding information caused some tensions and left less time to spend on development.

Other said the logframe is a tool that inhibits partnership. A small NGO said:

> We didn't have the opportunity at the end of funding to tell...[the] donor what the problems were with their requirements. The relationship is just about sending reports and getting money. There is no partnership. Most of our donors only visit once a year anyway.

Many of the problems highlighted by SA NGOs are captured in the following case study, where an NGO tried to combine rational planning with participatory approaches.

Rational planning and participatory practice

This case study (taken from writing and research by Dill, 2005) examines an attempt to systemize a participatory approach to livelihoods around rational project management and planning. The INGO, PEOPLE, had DFID and other non-UK donor funding; the aid chain also involved UK NGOs, other INGOs (some based in SA), SA NGOs and CBOs. The case study involved research with six different organizations.

PEOPLE introduced a new model in the mid-1990s that attempted to marry rational management and planning techniques with a people-centred approach to livelihoods. The adoption of a livelihoods approach as PEOPLE's key programming framework required a reorganization of PEOPLE's headquarters in the north and a heavy push on country offices in the south to incorporate the approach into their programmes. According to staff in PEOPLE's international offices, the new participatory focus had the potential to dramatically reform and improve past development approaches because it was designed as a participatory project management approach focused on rights and livelihoods. It was avowedly people-centred, attempting to involve the community and its stakeholders throughout the cycle of a project. The community was to take an active role in the design process and develop a 'holistic, integrated and flexible framework' to encourage INGOs to respond to the pressing needs of beneficiaries and to avoid focusing only on those sectors where an INGO had the most expertise.

Participation, empowerment and partnership were all principles integral to the approach, along with targeting the poorest. At the same time, the approach used the project cycle and objectives – or result-based – programming. Once a potential project concept was identified it had to be formulated to show direct coherence between inputs and outcomes, with clear stages, milestones, and targets for monitoring and assessment. The resulting logframe was expected to capture community inputs, facilitate structured planning and ensure increased levels of monitoring and evaluation. Indeed, the livelihoods approach was both a participatory methodology and a management strategy using the project cycle tool. The hope was that with this combined participatory managerial approach and by working with partners PEOPLE could better coordinate projects in similar geographic areas, successfully demonstrate results in the field and increase the efficiency of its programs. However, many of these hopes have not been realized and Dill's research suggested that problems lay in pitfalls made in the past within PEOPLE's approach.

Part of the problem was that NGO employees felt that PEOPLE's new approach was imposed top-down. Dill reflected on the dynamics of the approach transfer:

> There are dangers inherent in any major overhaul of management initiated from headquarters, even while such reforms have the potential to greatly improve effectiveness and efficiency. One danger is that, as Goldsmith (1996: 1431) writes, 'the methods can also become ends in themselves, to the disregard of what they are supposed to accomplish'. The difficulties that staff had with the participatory-managerial approach were sidelined; staff were told that you can and should use the approach throughout the project.

There were numerous difficulties. Some PEOPLE employees identified the linear service delivery approach of the project cycle as an impediment to the adoption of the livelihood framework. They found the project cycle rigid and, as such, at odds with its claimed flexibility, community-involvement and a learning-oriented approach. Another problem revolved around the complexity of the participatory project management approach. The field research showed that some SA programme and field staff understood the new programming approach only as a package of participatory techniques and made little distinction between it as a framework for understanding households and their livelihoods, and as a set of tools for collecting information from the community. Although they thought they were using the participatory project management approach to livelihoods, they were engaged simply in participatory rapid appraisal. One reason for this confusion was that while most staff received training, they described it as making it all more perplexing. Many senior staff found it difficult to provide the time and expertise needed to adequately train fieldworkers in the participatory management approach; there were only two or three individuals who could act as trainers and even then the limited time dedicated to training was not accompanied by follow-up. Trained staff found they could use their training for limited purposes only or not at all.

Dill found that, in many programmes, fieldworkers used PEOPLE's approach only for initial field assessment and not later in the cycle of a project. Trainers at PEOPLE's SA country office also found this to be a repeated problem in their work with local partners, a challenge echoed in several internal assessments. While theoretically there should be little difficulty in introducing the approach into an ongoing project – and many senior and field staff advocated such a practice – the research found that this was rarely done. Claims to have improved monitoring and evaluating in the project cycle were similarly not fully supported by the field research; monitoring still did not consistently cover the specified elements of the projects; and problems in the project were not always addressed in a timely manner. The initial assessments of community dynamics using participatory techniques appeared to be the major learning outcome of the training and the only element of the participatory framework used consistently.

In analysing the different interpretations of PEOPLE's approach, a clear tension emerged. The use of competing languages of development – managerial and participatory – sent 'mixed messages to staff…Individuals become confused about [the] purpose and meaning' of the approach and therefore unwilling to commit to it. Dill concluded that the approach 'as designed, fails to achieve all it claims because the ideologies and tools within the framework counteract one another' (Dill, 2005). PEOPLE's experience with using rational management tools in participatory and learning approaches showed that this fused process led to confusion, restricted implementation of the approach in the field and limited, if any, improvements in development practice.

Summary for South Africa

Most NGOs followed the logframe and have incorporated this way of thinking, planning and reporting into their work, even though they knew from experience that this approach did not easily combine with promoting participatory and locally owned ways of working. Many respondents articulated their reservations about logframes, which they found a 'complicated' and 'cumbersome' tool. Training often takes several days, and afterwards trainees may still not be capable of working with it well. Respondents said that the logframe tended to reduce organizations to projects and 'didn't incorporate institutional complexity' or the 'dimension of qualitative progress'. Indeed, the political context for many of these NGOs is quite unstable and respondents said it was not possible to reflect this properly in the logframe, and their work was too complex to translate into basic indicators. They were also critical of the lack of flexibility of the logframe.

Project cycle management in Uganda

Many of the findings were similar in Uganda. During a donor/NGO workshop in Kampala in 2001 local NGO participants listed the major tools required to access external funding:

- written guidelines relating to key issues that have to be addressed by southern NGOs, for example on governance;
- terms and conditions of grant-making, progress reports, etc;
- written agreements between UK NGOs and partners;
- quality frameworks;
- knowledge management;
- logframes;
- monitoring and evaluation frameworks;
- strategic planning, visioning techniques, organizational development, change management;
- participatory research methods;
- toolkits;
- impact assessment;
- branding.

The donors and INGOs that participated in the meeting were not able to tease out the implications of these various tools for the southern NGOs and appeared to use them with little analysis or reflection about their relevance or appropriateness in the local context.

All the UK-based NGOs use logframes in their work in Uganda. They are increasingly required by European NGOs and are central to the way USAID works. Given the predominance of external funding in Uganda because of the lack of locally generated income, it is not surprising that all the local NGOs interviewed tried to use logframes:

the growth of NGOs was so closely associated with the availability of external funding that 'doing well' was synonymous with the ability to attract external funding. Inevitably, NGOs invested their energies in developing their abilities to attract – not engage – donors and sharpening skills to manage their organizations in order to keep funds flowing...donors and their representatives, regardless of however they may have perceived their roles, became task masters, whilst the NGOs saw their roles as implementers whose responsibility it was to continue to churn out results to justify investments and continued funding. Implementing projects and meeting reporting deadlines became demanding tasks that left time for little else (Muyoya, 2005).

The use of the logframe in practice

Many of the Ugandan NGOs interviewed had mastered the skills of developing logframes, or brought in consultants to help them to write them; as in SA, often one or two specialist staff were trained in their use. Although these staff could discuss them with donors, very few NGOs said they could really use them in their development work. The research found that local staff were often ill prepared for the difficulties of working with change in communities and local organizations, and the written project plans were not helpful in guiding their relationships and work practice. Their training had often focused more on project management tools, while the skills of listening, flexibility, inclusiveness, managing conflict and handling change had not been well addressed (Harding, 2004). The logframe was not a relevant tool for helping frontline staff to undertake complex work with poor people and it was usually ignored in practice:

> The use of the logframe in practice often excludes the very people who should play critical roles in the planning, implementation, and management as well as the monitoring and evaluation of the projects (umbrella NGO).

> It is logical, dry and complicated and cannot be understood by ordinary people (small NGO).

Learning how to do the logframe takes a lot of training. Few international donors or NGOs have spent comparable amounts of time or money on training staff in how to build real partnerships and engage with social change at the community level. Indeed many said the logframe actively cuts across this work because staff are required to report progress against predetermined indicators, which have usually been developed without the involvement of grassroots organizations and people. Even when they have been involved in the planning, staff higher up the organization or in the UK have often changed the logframe for donors and the final version may not be known to, or understood by, frontline staff and communities. There was often a gap between the documents held in the field office in town, or by the UK NGO, and those used by implementing staff. Many of the NGO staff interviewed said that, in practice, these tools:

- allow the donors to set the agenda;
- rely on writing rather than face-to-face interactions. Written procedures are seen as more objective and transparent yet they are far less comfortable for, and useful to, many local NGOs which largely operate in an oral culture;
- do not properly reflect or value local knowledge or understanding. They are based on concepts of how to plan drawn from contexts far away;
- value highly the knowledge of the donors with the emphasis on the importance of literacy and use of English over local skills such as knowledge of the local language, cultural sensitivities and the ability to work sensitively with poor people;
- highlight that trust is being lost, and being replaced by written reports seen as mechanisms for control and accountability;

- promote upward accountability to the donors and do little to promote strong bonds between NGOs and the communities they work with;
- squeeze out community voices.

Perspectives from a director who refuses aid if the terms are unacceptable

These extracts from an interview with a reflective practitioner, director of a capacity-building NGO, capture many of the concerns raised by Ugandan NGOs about logframes and the power donors have to require their adoption.

There is, according to him, a need to challenge the existing paradigms and start to experiment and seek out a real Ugandan agenda, not one so closely tied to the dominant World Bank and neoliberal economic agenda. NGOs are currently so easily intimidated by both the Ugandan government and the donors that they find it hard to set their own agenda. NGOs in Uganda need to get clear what they are for, what their agenda is and how they want to address development. Do they have their values and ideology clear and distinct?

It is often hard for many local NGOs to think clearly on these issues, when their focus so much of the time has to be on raising funding for their work. They have to be able to write in English to raise donor funds, and inevitably have to learn the language and requirements of the donors; no donor is working in local languages for funding proposals, or taking time to listen to the discussions and debates on the ground. In this process many NGOs are losing their ability to talk to and listen to the very people they are there to serve, as their time is absorbed meeting these external agendas.

This current system of funding creates a serious dependency and sets agendas for NGO activities, yet most funding is very short-term; chasing funding becomes almost an end in itself and very time-consuming. Donors want to fund programmes that fit their current development agendas, but not the core costs, yet NGOs need equipment, training, materials for their work. This is hard to find, leading them often to inflate budgets to cover core costs, an issue that donors suspect, and so the lack of trust may start.

The structure of aid and the bureaucracy that accompanies it lead many donors, especially for example EU, to set agendas, criteria and parameters. The messiness of reality on the ground is seen as too complex and hard to manage, and the problems and solutions are simplified. A few donors do understand and work with complexity, but when their funding dries up NGOs are passed on to other less understanding donors. The problems of an impersonal bureaucracy, little rapport and no personal relations are major issues preventing the building of good relationships. There are some exceptions.

Lack of flexibility for changes in the use of funding is a major problem for local NGOs, especially when the funding arrives late, as it frequently does. Donors can fail to meet their obligations, yet still demand strict reporting on monies that NGOs have not received in time. They may ask for three months' advance notice for change of use as laid out in the logframe, but external events and unexpected problems can require much more flexibility of response from local NGOs working with communities.

Donors are increasingly setting agendas, and most NGOs feel like beggars in relation to donors, begging for funding and accepting the conditions attached. They often fail to analyse or understand aid and its intricacies, accepting inappropriate conditions and formats. Donors can be questioned, for sure, but most NGOs lack the confidence and negotiating skills to do this. Ugandans should be telling donors how money is to be used in Uganda, the money is aid money and is 'ours'. A few have rejected funding because of unacceptable conditions but it is only the most well-known and strongest NGOs that can risk refusing donor funding because of unacceptable conditions. One or two NGOs have tried to call donors to meetings they convened to discuss critical issues in local terms, but donors do not come to listen. NGOs in Uganda have not yet found a way to demand that donors listen to their needs and perspectives.

Instead NGOs are busy inventing indicators for donors, accepting difficult conditions around budgets, and doing multiple reporting, which all show such a lack of donor trust in the NGOs.

On the whole dependency continues and Uganda has not moved beyond a colonial mindset: people still do not believe that Uganda belongs to us. There is limited independence of thought and the whole aid fabric is set up in a dependent mode of thinking and management. The question remains whether Ugandans have the will to break these existing systems and relationships. Many just want to survive and accept and even promote the status quo: they do not criticize. Many others lack the capacity to take on the donors. A few are raising difficult questions about donors' behaviour and dependency, but they risk jeopardizing funding from some donors in the process.

Summary for Uganda

Almost all the sample NGOs voiced criticism of the application of the logical framework as 'not being ideal in the local situations'. They identified clear reasons for the poor connection between the paperwork and the experiences of development, including the complicated nature of logframes and the fact that they are drawn from a culture very different to their own. They find logframes too rigid and unresponsive to the realities of day-to-day life and its frustrations in Uganda, and because different donors use them in different ways they are very confusing to work with. They are written in English and so removed from the local understanding of the context and the work. However, the majority of Ugandan NGOs are constantly searching for funding and this makes their relationships very dependent; whatever they think of them they struggle to work with logframes to secure income.

Comparative perspectives on the benefits of the logframe

Given the many concerns raised and presented country by country, it is important to note that there were perceived benefits of the logframe and many practitioners, especially in the UK, saw it simply as a neutral tool and therefore not worth too much analysis. In the UK many staff said logframes provide a good shorthand document for busy advisers and assessors because they cut down on narrative and promote a shared project language and analysis. Many staff found logframes easy to learn and use; they focused the work and could be combined with participatory methodologies:

I have found for years that the more sophisticated donor requirements are a way to improve thinking. So many people see the logframe as just boxes. But if you look at a project idea it will have been a logical process. The steps of stakeholder analysis and problem trees are very useful (medium-sized UK NGO).

Logframes are not mandatory but we prefer partners to do them. I think it would be a huge benefit in focusing minds. I think there is a division between those who like logframes and those who don't. I like them...increasingly we are asking programme staff to present a logframe and report against it for institutional donors. There are not many programme staff who don't see the advantage (large UK NGO, not using logframes in 1996).

Others saw the logframe just as a management tool for recording information; they recognized that real life is complex and paper records are inevitably a weak reflection of that. If they are used flexibly they can work, although this does not always happen in practice:

Staff in South Africa who don't necessarily come from a development background think the logframe is it and they just need to apply it. I need to keep telling them it is just a framework. In some cases it means just getting funding. In theory logframes are flexible and they need to be so, and they need to be prepared to change them. In reality the way it is applied and perceived is not always flexible (medium-sized UK NGO).

While most SA NGO respondents were ambivalent about the logframe, the critics all saw some value in the approach. Staff cited them as useful for organizing, structuring and summarizing a project and for being rigorous about objectives:

[LFA] has a lot of useful aspects to it that can assist one to become more rigorous in one's work and be clearer about objectives (SA NGO manager).

[LFAs] are useful monitoring tools. They are useful for clarity on project objectives and are also convenient for reporting to donors as they provide information at a glance (medium-sized SA NGO).

I think it is a great tool for designing and planning. Once you designed and planned though, I think many things can happen. And it can be very difficult to report against that format when things haven't gone according to plan (medium-sized SA training organization).

LFA has been useful in that it promotes a rigorous and disciplined approach to managing projects. However, not everything can go into a framework. While it is useful for structuring and planning, a lot of qualitative stuff has to be captured and reflected differently [in reporting] (small SA partnership organization).

Respondents thought that logframes were particularly useful for donors for project appraisal because they concisely convey selected aspects of a proposed project, permitting rapid initial review, although they are easily manipulated and have not been shown to lead to better selection of projects to fund. Positive aspects were nearly always described in the same breath as negative ones and wholehearted support was rare.

In Uganda about a third of the local NGOs interviewed said that they found aspects of the logframe useful; they helped to be more focused, and identified the real objectives of the project, enabling them to be 'more effective and efficient'. The logical framework was deemed 'to be practical, logical and to give an overview of the whole programme' and helped organizations not meander into activities irrelevant to the realization of the programme's purpose.

All saw logframes as essential for improved accountability to their donors, which can lead to better donor–client relationships. They openly recognize the worry donors have about corruption and the misuse of funds, and the use of a logframe was seen as a transparent way of showing what is to be done and against which actions and achievements can be measured. These benefits were all mentioned at different times, but against a background of strongly expressed concerns about the logframe's use and impact.

Conclusion

Project cycle management tools are the norm and logframes are integral to almost all funding for INGOs and their partners in the south. Although the logframe is recognized as having many positive uses for creating a shared narrative and for management purposes, the research showed that it does not really serve field needs well and its critical importance lies in the way it serves the needs of donors and the aid bureaucracy. Using it enables NGOs to access and account for donor aid.

It has many negative implications, though. The use of these project cycle management tools, however adapted, contributes to creating unequal relationships between INGOs and their partners, because of the external cultural norms they carry, with a heavy reliance on written English and formats for planning and reporting on controlled change. The different cultural approaches and skills of local staff and partners are undervalued or unrecognized, something other researchers have also identified as a critical problem (Mawdsley et al., 2002). The lack of face-to-face interaction, the reliance on written documents and the deeply embedded culturally defined concepts of change embedded in these tools combine to create a difficult climate for building good working relationships between donors and NGOs.

Logframes are changed as they rise through the aid chain; they are rarely used to guide and enhance development practice in communities. What is written is often divorced from reality, both at the planning and reporting stages in the cycle. One NGO director admitted that when staff prepared the logframe they were usually under time pressures, they 'didn't have the luxury of sitting down with stakeholders so they just cooked up assumptions about them'. Some have suggested that logframes are very easy to manipulate: '[you] set targets lower than you can achieve...[this] makes your performance look better and impresses funders.' When the plans do not match the context, reporting becomes based on showing how far the written aims and objectives have been met, rather than grappling with the complexities of what actually happened and why. There is often a real disconnection between the documents and what is taking place, raising serious questions about how far this management system enables honesty and transparency, or rather gets exactly the opposite, as field workers grapple to make their messy experience fit smart matrices.

In spite of the myriad concerns, most organizations continue to adapt themselves to the needs of these tools, sometimes with small modifications; only a tiny minority challenge or reject them. The tools have never been the subject of advocacy and lobbying from NGOs to donors, presumably because the way aid is disbursed has always been largely seen as either non-negotiable or non-contentious. But respondents in all three countries described how they felt bound into a system that was not of their own design and with which they had real problems. The role of project cycle management approaches in promoting or, alternatively, inhibiting local NGOs in their work on projects and programmes, organizational development, learning and accountability are explored in the following chapters.

[illegible] used to guide and enhance [illegible] practice in some markets. What is often [illegible]

[illegible]

In spite of the [illegible] continue to [illegible] themselves to the [illegible] of those [illegible] with [illegible] modification [illegible] because [illegible] But [illegible] and how they [illegible] The [illegible] approach [illegible] to [illegible] explored in the following chapter.

CHAPTER 7
The ties that bind

The challenges of the planning approach of project cycle management were discussed in Chapter 3, and evidence of the benefits and difficulties these pose for development agencies was introduced in Chapter 6. This chapter uses field-level data to explore the ties that bind development work closer to this rational management approach, in spite of the obvious flaws. The chapter also highlights factors that ameliorate the negative impacts or provide alternatives, even though these are often add-ons rather than replacements of the dominant approach.

The forces that bind development workers to the logframe and its many modifications include the accountability systems, the power of the funders and contracting, which is increasingly open to NGOs and can provide sources of significant funding. Some of the countervailing approaches identified through the research include the potential (but not often the reality) of strategic planning, a focus on the power of interpersonal relations to build alternative ways of working and the conscious recognition of the need to address issues of inequality in aid relationships. This research and the wider literature found that while there are many radical alternative approaches being used in practice, for example around participatory and gender methodologies, these all too often become tamed and institutionalized to fit into the current bureaucratic forms of thinking and procedures (Chambers, 2004; Wendoh and Wallace, 2005). Attempts to change the balance of power and work differently encounter high barriers that prove hard to jump.

Questioning the status quo as heresy

The research found that many development staff in the UK and Africa did not question the logframe and associated approaches. Indeed, many did not know there were any other forms of management that could be used. These procedures seem to many to be the way that development is done, and concerns focused largely on how to: improve training and the implementation of these approaches for better results; ensure that participatory methods do contribute to the project cycle at key points; and how to report better. This approach provided a strong management norm that precluded serious discussion of alternative management styles and ways of working, and contributed to limiting choice and channelling thinking into one narrow groove, even where the evidence suggested that this does not necessarily help to 'make the work work' (Seddon, 2005). The experience of the research team was that these approaches have taken on an almost unquestionable status; while modifications to include participation (such as ZOPP, Zielorientierte Projektplanung, or GOPP, goal oriented project planning) or cultural issues (Biggs and Smith, 2002) are welcome. Rejecting the overall approach is almost heresy.

At feedback sessions in Uganda, NGOs identified with the findings of the research and mentioned the colonial and racial dynamics of power relations that made them adopt, by choice or coercion, the dominant approaches to working with poor people that many knew were not very effective or useful on the ground. Reactions to the findings in the UK were sometimes hostile and even aggressive: feedback sessions were held between 2002 and 2004 at the University of Manchester, at ActionAid in London and the Nuffield Foundation, with a wide range of academic and practitioner audiences. Some of the donor and NGO practitioners from large NGOs were the most overtly critical, and many academics, consultants and some NGO staff (especially from smaller NGOs) found the research conclusions relevant. In SA, responses were also mixed: some – especially those from the largest funding agencies – were quite hostile and others, including NGOs and grant-makers, acknowledging the many obstacles associated with the heavy use of logframes. It felt, at times, that asking whether these tools can be participatory, address gender inequalities, create real working partnerships and build strong local autonomous NGOs is offensive. While recognizing the flaws, many NGOs seem to prefer to highlight the many adaptations rather than examine the critical issues at the heart of these approaches, including their embedded cultural and conceptual norms. The ideology of controlled and managed change driven top-down but adopted and owned locally (through often shallow participatory processes) is entrenched and questions are seen by many as a threat or simply dismissed.

Changing these norms feels like a Herculean task; it is a way of thinking and working reinforced by other funders, trustees and increasingly chief executives of UK NGOs, many of whom are drawn from the business and public sectors (Lindenberg and Bryant, 2002). They are an integral part of the political and management culture in the UK; as one commentator observed, 'destroying the working paradigm takes a massive act of conviction from management, admitting that you have been wrong (for years) takes an equally massive act of bravery' (MacLellan, 2005). To date the problems are certainly not generally accepted, so finding that leverage for change is challenging. Indeed, academic observers of one feedback session noted that there was real resistance from UK donors and NGOs to questioning whether the work was working; they resisted accepting the feedback from Uganda and SA that vividly highlighted, in people's own words and based on first-hand experience, the problems caused by the distance between paper-based project cycle management and the reality of making things work for the poor.

The ties that bind

Accounting and accountability

Some of the heavy reliance on the logframe approach appears to lie in a deep-seated anxiety about impact; the response to uncertainty and unclear outcomes is to tighten processes of control through the planning and accountability processes. Once donors tie accountability to planning and reporting documents and require change to be demonstrated in the terms of the initial logframe, the need to use the logframe approach becomes compelling; it is the key to funding.

It was in this area of heavy reporting requirements for monitoring and evaluation (M&E) that NGOs' concerns in SA and Uganda were most apparent; the requirements of upward reporting were heavy, as others have found (Mawdsley et al., 2002 ; Brehm, 2001). Most NGOs interviewed in UK and Africa said reporting requirements were complex and time-consuming and that demands were constantly increasing. Some UK NGOs now demand monthly reporting, financial and narrative, from their project officers or partner NGOs, to ensure that they can meet the requirements of their donors. Reporting for upward accountability binds NGOs to these tools and often squeezes out time for other kinds of accountability; there are in fact no comparable systems in place to establish accountability to partners or participants in the work.

The broad concerns about reporting (including M&E) are summarized in Table 7.1.

The table highlights the worries of donors and NGOs. For NGOs these are especially the heavy demand for reporting, the problems of reporting when field reality is far from the written documentation, the lack of understanding of local realities by many involved in the work, and the problems raised by different donors using different reporting formats and criteria for the same work. While donors say they want to hear the voices from the frontline and learn from the challenges and failures, as well as hearing about successes, and local NGOs want their voices to be heard, it is clear that the current accountability systems squeeze out the problems and complexities in order to ensure demonstration of success against the plans.

The time and energy needed for donor reporting is significant, and often clearly distorts and transforms what is happening into accounts of what NGOs think donors need to hear. The EU was described as a particularly demanding funder, which is important because European bilateral funders increasingly channel their funds to NGOs through the EU:

> What we need to produce for the EU is a huge pain for us as it doesn't fit how people work on the ground (large UK NGO).

> We have found reporting and monitoring to the EU quite difficult. We have been working hard to turn around our performance at the EU. We have difficulties in ensuring programme staff in the field are absolutely aware of

Table 7.1 Broad concerns about reporting, monitoring and evaluation

Donors	NGOs in UK	NGOs in SA and Uganda
Need reports to be accountable to their trustees/parliament	Reporting turns some staff into bureaucrats rather than development workers	Reporting is time-consuming
Reporting from NGOs is poor and often late. Limited time to read them	Reports are not read by donors; often cannot read in detail reports from partners because of lack of time	Reports often not read by partner INGOs
Overwhelmed at times with paper	Little feedback received from donors Too busy to give feedback	Little feedback; feedback often very late, very limited or non-existent
Information is lacking on impact and what has changed	Reporting against the LFA is weak, reports have to be revised for donors to show how the work is meeting the LFA expectations. Need/pressure to demonstrate success	Reporting is against the logframe; not on what is actually happening. Often struggle to do LFA reporting, done by managers not front line staff whose experiences differ too much from logframe plans
Different reporting requirements from different NGOs and different funding streams. Some flexibility of reporting around, e.g. strategic/partnership grants	Some reporting systems are light, e.g. PPAs, others are onerous, e.g. EU. Most are becoming more demanding, except PPAs, including especially Community Fund (detailed tracking forms) and now Comic Relief	Reporting is too frequent, often monthly to INGOs No sense of differential reporting requirements of donors; INGOs make their own guidelines which partners have to follow
Growing concern with showing what has changed. Hard to see what impact NGOs are actually having, what changes they are bringing	Pressure to show success; timeframes often too short for this. Focus on tangibles/deliverables important for donors	Hard to raise problems and complexities, pressure to cover up mistakes or difficulties and claim success. Have to report on change when the time is too short for change to have occurred
Some concern about whose voices they are hearing. Would like qualitative and relationship data as well	Hard to collect the range of data donors say they want. Donors ask for a lot but do not properly fund M&E	Work like significant change, peer review, ALPS is often additional to LFA monitoring and time-consuming. These forms of participatory/ qualitative reporting never replace LFA

Table 7.1   (Contd.)

Donors	NGOs in UK	NGOs in SA and Uganda
New mechanisms for review, e.g. output to purpose reviews (OPR) for contracts for DFID	Very quantitative processes, tied to original logframe. Not participatory, very mechanistic approaches	Reviews are often done very quickly, based largely on paperwork and are judgemental; external consultants often shape the next stages of the project
External evaluations needed for objectivity	Many evaluation policies and guidelines developed, to ensure donor and trustee needs are met. Also try to bring in other participatory approaches alongside LFA reviews	Outside evaluators often lack skills and understanding of local context. Inadequate time to do both LFA and other kinds of review processes; time usually too short for real understanding to develop
Evaluations should focus on results, achievements, impact	Different evaluation approaches are used, but increasing focus on demonstrating impact rather than learning	Many evaluations are externally imposed, far fewer are self-generated and participatory, concerned to learn and understand as well as show results
Different donors have different reporting requirements	Real problems with multiple accountabilities; only a few donors agree to generic reports	Major problems of multiple accounting and writing myriad reports

what the EU want from the outset…the financial reporting requirements are particularly onerous (large UK NGO).

The EU are so concerned about accountability. It is very difficult to be open about things (large UK NGO).

Donors have the power to sanction poor reporting and weak performance by refusing further funding, even though the difficulties for NGOs and communities to fit their diverse, complex realities into the current reporting formats are well known. Many frontline staff find it hard to write well in English and often their INGO partner reworks reports for donors. At each level of the aid chain there is editorial control to ensure the 'right' kind of report reaches the donor, even when NGOs try to encourage partners to write their own reports and present their own voice. Field-level experiences often disappear because of the inherent pressures to demonstrate effectiveness, which result in a focus on neatness of results and success. Although donors say they want reporting on failure, UK NGOs cited many examples where they felt funding was threatened because of openly discussing problems. The current systems are built not on openness or trust but on paperwork tied to funding, which inhibits sharing and learning. Donors, with the exceptions of some foundations, rely on this documentation for accountability and learning, as do chief executives and trustees:

> Trustees have responsibility for all the work and they want detailed management information. They get a summary of the quarterly monitoring report from each country...this could well be over-reporting, it takes a long time and staff want to simplify it. Is it worth the time and effort? The trustees like it and try to balance the financial and monetary issues with what we do more broadly. However, staff find these onerous (large UK NGO).

All the NGOs interviewed in Uganda reported a rise in demands for written reports, partly because of a perceived misuse of funds and a lack of clarity about what local NGOs were doing. They understand that reporting on paper is critical for accountability, especially to distant donors, yet it is onerous and often by its very nature lacking in transparency. Many questioned how useful this heavy reliance on written reporting is for either accountability or learning.

To give one project example, repeated many times during the research, a community project had been developed, providing an essential service that villagers were expected to own and maintain in a village in Uganda. The researchers asked a group of users who owned the resource and who did the maintenance; the users were quite clear that the project belonged to the local NGO, not to them, and they were not anticipating taking over when funding ceased. However, the local NGO felt they had to report that the villagers did own the project, even though their own ways of working with local people had been radically changed when the UK NGO arrived and they had no 'real confidence' in the new approaches to participation and local ownership. They had to work with clear consultation and participation packages designed by the UK NGO, and had to implement the project in externally set timelines and report positive results within a year. Their own understanding was that it would take several years to ensure that the community felt this was work they owned and for which they needed to take responsibility. The NGO itself felt it needed more training and experience to successfully achieve this. The personnel received minimal training support from the UK NGO and the monthly reporting was onerous; what they wrote in reports often differed significantly from what was happening.

Often limited financial support is given to pay for M&E, making it hard to meet the high demands:

> Donors are increasingly asking for monitoring and evaluation (and associated reporting) but in practice are not prepared to support it. For example DFID cut the monitoring officer from the budget for a proposal then later did a review of the project and came up with the verdict that there was weak monitoring (medium-sized Ugandan NGO).

INGO staff in Uganda field offices felt they had little power or influence over the reporting requirements and found themselves writing or editing reports from partners to go to donors of which they had a limited understanding. Many said they did not know if their projects were funded by DFID, Community Fund, Comic Relief or another donor; instead they used standard reporting procedures developed by their own headquarters, designed to meet the needs of the organization, trustees and back-donors. Not one agency with a PPA agreement with DFID had passed this flexible funding and reporting mechanism on to their staff or partners; similarly the flexibility UK NGOs enjoy vis-a-vis Comic Relief or foundations is also not shared with partners. Instead frequent, tight reporting using INGO manuals or guidelines, usually designed to ensure upward accountability, is the norm. While INGOs talk of downward accountability, few have procedures or minimum standards in place for this.

Staff and partners in Uganda said they rarely received feedback on their reports; they seem to disappear into a vacuum. Questions or comments, if they come, may arrive up to a year later, sometimes longer, and the learning and interaction potential of reporting often appear to be missing. There was the perception, and in some cases the admission from donors and INGOs, that six-monthly reports often go unread. Local NGOs were frustrated about the time and effort spent compiling these reports only to have them collect dust on a desk:

Our planning and reporting systems evolved in response to DFID requirements...it is only around reports that DFID and this NGO have much interaction. Staff complain endlessly about the donor requirements and the need of some donors for monthly reports...but is anyone really using the reports? We feel the donors focus on checking not learning from reporting (large UK NGO).

In SA too reporting was seen as a key obligation of NGOs to their funders. Head offices of donor organizations are normally based overseas and project visits are generally few and far between, so reports are the primary means of communication and feedback. It is common practice for reporting guidelines, procedures and timetables to be outlined and agreed upon at the beginning of the funding relationship and for them to form part of the funding contract. Funding is often contingent upon reports being sent out on time and of all the management procedures, the pressure to report comprehensively and on time appears to have the strongest incentive and penalty.

Among SA NGOs, the pressure to report according to donors' expectations was felt at all organizational levels. The process of reporting to and managing donors was found, at management level, to require considerable staff time; it was also tedious and often not internally useful. At the field level, people expressed a lack of confidence about reporting, they were concerned about communicating in English and feared being misjudged or misunderstood. One organization tracked the number of hours spent on donor-related matters (reporting, workshops and meetings) and found that it consumed 230 hours in less than a month. A project manager from another organization observed that reporting to donors now consumed 60 per cent of his time, while in the past he had spent most of his time on programmes.

Many expressed frustration at complying with different reporting requirements from different donors, yet only one organization had managed to take a proactive stance on negotiating a standard reporting format with donors, which worked well for them (one large HIV/AIDS NGO had achieved this in Uganda as well). Some NGO managers explained that the complexity of their work made it very difficult to report against donors' indicators:

> Consultants seem to be the only ones benefiting from complicated reporting and application requirements...There needs to be a middle path between donors' interests and the NGOs' interests...Building relationships and not just systems is key (medium-sized NGO).

When balancing reporting requirements with the actual situation, several NGOs said that there was considerable pressure to demonstrate progress from report to report. Considering that most reporting is done on a six-monthly basis, the type of progress that donors may be looking for is difficult to achieve in such a short space of time:

> the system is not working well, there is no way of aggregating the findings and dissemination is poor. Good information doesn't seem to circulate widely...at present there is a huge amount of reporting, these are often too detailed and overloaded because people want to prove the value of their work to ensure continued funding (umbrella NGO).

There were a few exceptions to this overall rather dismal picture of reporting, and while many NGOs (local and international) do include other kinds of learning and reporting in their guidelines these tend to be additions to the central reporting structure. One exception was an INGO that was working to untie accountability from reports to trustees or donors in order to promote downward accountability to communities through reflection and review processes. These involved staff returning to communities to discuss the progress and relevance of the project or programme and how they were experiencing it. It was a tough experience for many staff, holding up their work for inspection by those they were working with; often the needs of the participants were different from the original design of the projects or programmes, raising difficult challenges. While this INGO is still committed to establishing and deepening mechanisms for downward accountability, the pressures of securing contracts and meeting rigid reporting requirements for donors risk squeezing out the time and new skills needed for deepening this approach (Wallace and Chapman, 2004a).

Another example, from SA, shows a more mixed and complex experience. The Kapa Housing Project (KHP) was researched by Isai Hyman, one of the South African team. She found an organization that attracted multiple funders: the organization was 20 years old, and throughout had been a strong advocate for housing needs for the poor. It had a diverse funding base including the EU,

Oxfam Canada, CIDA, DFID, Interfund, USAID and CAFOD; KHP also raised funds through local donors, hiring out staff services, and the state housing subsidy. It was a highly sustainable and reliable organization with the caveat 'as far as NGO sustainability goes, which is always a relatively insecure situation'.

The founding vision was working for the poor to improve their physical conditions, using employees' valuable professional expertise to make that possible. Staff, many of them trained architects and engineers who could demand higher salaries in the private sector, felt positive about their contributions to social change and equity. Over time both leadership and staff recognized the need for more participatory approaches and a broader approach to the built environment, and KHP experimented with more community-based participatory approaches, and worked more closely with local leadership and decision-making structures.

Gradually donors placed new requirements on KHP. One donor encouraged the formation of an umbrella organization for NGOs nationwide working in the sector, and this was done (the establishment of networks was a common strategy required by donors in SA and one that many complained about). The network became the conduit for proposals and funds, an intermediary between KHP and some of its donors. KHP no longer had direct relationships with donors, although it continued project visits and the specific funding requirements. When the founding director left, the board selected a new director with substantial experience in the private sector, experienced in business plans, productivity and the bottom line and actively seeking out new clients. Logframes, associated M&E, reporting and donor-compatible accounting systems were used extensively, something needed by the umbrella organization: if reports were submitted in alternative formats network staff would request additional information from member NGOs. The benefits of these systems were, however, not apparent to KHP staff.

They observed that the EU's quarterly financial reporting requirements, against specific indicators, were complex and time-consuming; they also required six-monthly narrative reports and timeframes were very strict. All reports on the EU contract went through the intermediary umbrella organization and all members were required to use the same reporting format. They found it challenging to get reports done properly and on time, and the umbrella office would often complain that the quality of members' reports was inadequate. Interestingly, the extensive joint reports did not replace the direct donor oversight of KHP or ease reporting overall for local NGOs. USAID also had very rigorous reporting requirements and sent auditors to KHP to assess their capacity for financial management; they required frequent reports outlining the finances and the successes of the project. Interfund, a local funder, had the strictest reporting requirements of all, requiring six-monthly audited financial reports, perhaps reflecting concern over some high-profile cases of corruption and financial irregularities in SA NGOs in 1998.

Wherever possible, KHP used the formats and indicators of one donor to report to the others. They received little feedback from their funders on the content of the reports, and the umbrella organization's feedback revolved around satisfying requirements of format rather than the quality of work. Staff said that it was difficult and expensive to adapt donor requirements into learning for KHP, and that sometimes reporting did not reflect what actually happened on the ground. The complexity of their work meant it was not always possible for them to encapsulate their activities, achievements and context using donors' formats and indicators. They felt that donors needed more contact with partners to better understand the issues and the work; annual donor visits were not enough. Membership in the umbrella network had made their links to donors even more tenuous and was an additional layer in the process, increasing potential misrepresentation and misunderstanding.

Reporting took skilled staff from their real responsibilities and many were poor at completing the required formats; anyway there were real problems with translating local realities into the formats of the reports. In response the director centralized the responsibility for dealing with donors, assigning a single person to handle proposal writing, reporting and donor relations. That removed the responsibility for representing achievements and difficulties from those intimately involved in implementation, and so limited the learning possibilities. Staff were unhappy with these approaches and felt the new director had been a 'disastrous experiment turning them more into a private-sector delivery agency than a people-centred one'. The experience led them to reflect on the balance between external and internal pressures on NGOs, and one of the main lessons from the experience, according to one manager, was to recognize KHP board's lack of a vision for the organization, which had resulted in choosing a director with a vision that was a drastic departure from the original mandate.

The organization listed numerous constraints they faced that were rooted in donor funding practices and priorities. Managers noted that donors' funding categories did not cover some key community needs, and there was little money for research because donors are sceptical of funding studies. They also found it difficult to access money for pilot projects because most donors find these require too much effort and high administration costs. Another source of frustration is that donors ask KHP to plan years in advance, something that is very difficult in the context of a rapidly changing local policy environment and complex community factors, and yet they rarely give multi-year funding and most donors focus on short-term grants only. While working properly with communities takes time, this is poorly accommodated in some donors' requirements, and like many NGOs KHP faced the dilemma of having to find alternative means of raising funds – often through contracting out to government or the private sector – without compromising their values and identity.

The challenge of attribution

The issues about attribution are well rehearsed. Existing methodologies are weak for tracing direct impact from NGO inputs to community changes:

I have an increasing feeling that all this process planning and monitoring and evaluation are terribly egocentric. They are all organization out. They are arguably trying to set up processes by which we can say if we have done a good job. In many ways this is secondary to how we combine to do a good job. Certainly some of the most interesting monitoring and evaluation we have done is not organisation out but context in (large UK NGO).

There are no methodologies for tracing impact in a causal and attributable way, for one good reason that cause and effect are not linear in development, and the factors contributing to change are many and varied; but the search goes on and absorbs huge amounts of time and money at both donor and NGO levels. While there are interesting methodologies for learning from experience, these require time, painstaking work and analysis by experienced individuals working closely with both written records and a range of stakeholders (Roche, 1999;, Cracknell, 2000). These methods are not seen as high-powered or efficient and cannot easily be standardized and computerized, so are rather devalued as the sector continues to search for ways of measuring and claiming impact.

UK NGOs holding PPAs are striving to measure progress and grapple with attribution against global indicators, while trying to remain participatory and open to learning from the field. The tensions inherent in this approach were evident at a meeting of the large agencies, traditionally funded through core grants from DFID and the British Overseas Aid Group (BOAG) (David, Mancini and Newens, 2003):

(The new monitoring and evaluation system) is a major shift to a standardised process…(there is) a need to focus more on partnership and less on projects and grants, and to report on impact and longer term objectives rather than shorter term objectives and inputs. It will take almost a year before it is rolled out. There is an implicit logframe and in the appendix there are minimum standards (large BOAG agency).

We brought in a corporate planning, monitoring and evaluation system 2–3 years ago. This was developed in conjunction with the field. There is a corporate core to the system…The corporate process of making a strategic plan and the principle guidelines…are the two common strands that all countries operate. Within these frameworks the emphasis is to respond to local needs in the best possible way (large NGO attending BOAG meeting).

There is a big question as to how to monitor and evaluate the global plan (BOAG NGO).

How to do organisational monitoring and evaluation is being discussed at present. It is a challenge to monitor objectives which are very broad and thematic (BOAG NGO).

(I am) increasingly worried about the complexity of the systems NGOs are now developing because what is their effect on working with communities? (large BOAG NGO).

I find ALPS an interesting system trying to promote downward account-ability,...but (where will) the tensions be played out between the needs of trustees and donors and a bottom up approach and accountability to the poor? (large BOAG NGO).

Donor contracts deepening the trends

Pressures on NGOs to adopt logframes and associated procedures are increased when they apply for donor contracts, where they compete with for-profit organizations for lucrative development funds. Contracts require a fluency with planned and controlled management approaches. One very large UK NGO pointed out that NGOs have to learn to work with these new funding mechanisms and fit changing donor priorities; this requires them to understand the specialized demands of tendering and contracts, compete with for-profit agencies and take on the transaction costs that are being shifted away from donors. Contracts are key for accessing large funds but they are highly technical and legally binding. The trend of institutional donors towards increasing contracting and working with fewer larger organizations or consortia is accelerating, making new demands on UK NGOs and possibly threatening their independence. While some agencies have been adept at taking contracts for a long time (e.g., Care and Plan International), several large UK NGOs were only dipping their toes into this world from 2000, seeing contracts as a route to rapidly increasing income and hopefully influence. However, even agencies committed to bottom-up ways of working found contracts were tying them tightly to terms based on initial logframes and preset indicators, and lines of accountability were strictly upward (Wallace, 2005).

The following case study of a sample UK NGO working in Uganda illustrates some of the contradictions and tensions involved in working to tight donor contracts, while trying to work in partnership with local communities and organizations. This case reflects issues faced by other sample INGO taking large contracts, and was undertaken as part of the review of DFID's impact on poverty (Wallace, Caputo and Herbert, 1999).

The Safi health project

The Safi health project is located in one of the poorest districts in Uganda, an area recovering from a vicious civil war, drought and environmental ravages. It was part of a complex project to rehabilitate ruined health centres, increase community involvement, raise demand for and provide efficient and effective reproductive health services, and establish decentralized structures and systems for managing them.

During the life of the project donors shifted the focus from outputs and targets to empowering the district and devolving the project to the district. This shift raised questions for the implementing INGO who wanted (but never got) a tripartite arrangement between the donor, the district and itself; it was unclear to the INGO whether it remained responsible for deliverables in this new context or not.

The project was four years long, a short time horizon for the wide range of purposes, especially for developing a sense of local ownership. The project was slow to get started, as is often the case with complex projects. The legacy of the delay affected relationships at both the village and the district official levels.

The institutional donor was well aware, from past experience, of some of the problems and pitfalls of working with NGOs, including friction about procedures and accounting as well as development approaches. The project was tightly written and the contract contained stringent conditions. The donor and the INGO clashed on the best structure for running the project, but the donor insisted on a structure it had devised. In spite of the delays and the poor start, the INGO team worked hard to build a partnership with the district, which showed a growing sense of ownership.

However, while the NGO worked closely with the district, staff were also responsible for meeting clear contractual targets. They were also trying to implement the project in a way that was participatory with communities; yet the relationship of subcontractor prevented them from implementing in the way they wanted. Some staff talked of the donor handicapping their comparative advantage of getting close to people in the district at all levels, of learning and yet not being able to adapt the project in the light of experience. These concerns came up repeatedly and eventually led to a reworking of the logframe with an external consultant.

Throughout, the donor was clear that the project was theirs, being implemented by a subcontractor. This was marked by small things such as putting the donor's logo and country flag on the offices and vehicles, and requiring the INGO to refer all decisions not covered in the original documents back to the donor; replies often took months to come. The problems of motivating and mobilizing communities, after years of debilitating and divisive war and the trauma of camp life and food aid dependency, were underestimated in the project documents. It was hard to know whether promoting community participation in previously divided communities was a healing process or a process that confirmed old divisions, excluding many.

The NGO was legally contracted to provide a certain number of new clinics each year, yet they were also expected to go at the pace of the community facilitators who were involving a fractured community. This process was inevitably slow, leaving the builders ready but unable to start construction. Friction between different staff was evident and caused stress as they tried to meet tight legal frameworks and work at the community's pace.

The project had many other components including cost recovery, staff training and health education. All caused problems between different staff, who had diverse views on the appropriateness of cost-sharing, the priorities for staff training and the key health messages, which the donor wanted focused on women in spite of the low status and lack of authority these women had in the community. Discussions with local people highlighted that their priority issues were food insecurity, poor water supplies and sanitation; these caused their poverty and poor health, not the lack of clinics. They said if poverty was addressed, their health status would rise. The donor, however, saw improved health rooted in better medical provision and changed health behaviour as the major need.

The project brought to light many critical issues concerning donor contracts:

- the work remains clearly a donor project and the lack of NGO ownership affects the work, learning and lines of accountability;
- the timetables are often too short for developing the sustainable structures and processes expected; they are often not based in local reality;
- often donors require even large, sophisticated INGOs with the financial and managerial capacity to handle contracts to make changes to meet their own management procedures;
- the problems of the community owning this kind of project are many; simplistic equations of people making contributions to the project equalling them feeling ownership are common but unrealistic.
- contracts often focus on interventions not prioritized by the poor; this means they are a low priority for many, raising concerns about sustainability.
- gender issues are often poorly delineated in contracts and target primarily women to make health and other behavioural changes, failing to recognize their lack of control over household and community behaviour.

The issues of insufficient time for project realization, shifting donor procedures and frameworks, lack of local drivers and donor barriers to NGO flexibility embodied in the contracts were all seen in SA as well.

Loosening the ties

The potential of strategic planning to do things differently

Global strategic planning can loosen some of these ties and enable a more creative and open-ended approach to development work. However, as currently practised in NGOs, it has become another tight approach, setting out clear visions, objectives, activities and indicators that must be achieved and measured over between three and five years. Indeed, contrary to its potential to do things differently, much strategic planning has put the power and control of what is to be funded back into the control of NGOs in the UK, where global goals are laid out to which all their funded work must aspire. Strategic planning is done in ways that fit well with the rational model of planning; the aims are global and strategic rather than project-based, but similar processes for setting targets, showing how these are to be achieved, and measuring against those expected achievements, are firmly in place.

While several INGOs do try to make their strategic planning processes consultative and even participatory, the role of feedback from beneficiaries and partners is often unresolved:

We invited stakeholders to take part in planning...In principle it was essential to do the consultation but when involving partners in consultation, there is a danger of raising expectations that they will have a big input into changes when in reality the changes were minimal. Therefore, organisations must be careful not to unrealistically raise expectations about what such consultations will achieve (small UK NGO).

...partners were brought together for a consultative meeting but not told what would happen next with the outcomes from the meeting (large UK NGO).

In the sample of large UK NGOs senior managers usually made the final strategic planning decisions, even after long bottom-up consultation processes. The programme input could, in practice, only be one part of the decision-making process because of the need to take into account the multiple functions of INGOs, including the UK context for advocacy and marketing, and the different strategic options for maximizing their funding base (Fowler, 2000b; Wallace and Burdon, 1993). Once made, senior management appeared to expect strategic plans to be rolled out and staff around the world to be able to change their ways of working, attitudes and skills almost overnight. Little time was allowed for staff and partners to change and adequate support was rarely given to implement major change processes, leaving frontline staff to grapple with new concepts and their implications: shifting from implementation to partnership, projects to programmes, needs to rights, trying to establish new ways of learning. The gap between the aspirations of the strategic plan and what would be needed to enable staff and partners to meet them was often very wide: the language of new strategic ideas is often complex and rooted in debates far from the frontline, hard for staff to grasp or apply (Wallace and Kaplan, 2003).

Some of the medium-sized and smaller UK NGOs had more open-ended strategies, founded more on their values and principles and less on specific outcomes; however, the problem for them lay in the reality that most of their funding comes from project support and they lack the financial resources to realize many of their aspirations within current funding constraints. They strive to access more open forms of funding, such as PPAs, to allow them the flexibility to work in more responsive and less top-down ways. They saw a real value in strategic planning in helping them to focus and clarifying where to work and who to work with, although in practice many remained opportunistic, working in regions and on themes where they could access donor funding. Like the larger INGOs, they teach their partners to undertake strategic planning, although partner NGOs are often even more constrained about where they can find funding and so often have to make pragmatic rather than strategic decisions about where and how to work.

Few of the INGOs questioned the way they do strategic planning, or knew much about the different theories and practices of strategic planning; they follow roughly similar models based on tight approaches, and some (including all those accessing PPAs) even formulate them in logframes. There has been almost no general open debate about how or whether these tight global strategies affect their working relationships with partners in different countries, or how they affect their partner NGOs in their relations with communities. Up to now strategic planning has been perceived as an almost universally positive tool for prioritising, focusing and achieving clarity. However, having a coherent strategy does not necessarily or automatically lead to greater impact, and where strategic planning really does appear to have impact – on partners – has been overlooked.

Strategic plans and the new development thinking they often embody come from the north to NGOs in Africa, and they are expected to find ways to meet the new strategic priorities set from outside. Even where they have been consulted, they say they often fail to see their ideas reflected in the plans that finally emerge. They are experienced by many, according to this research, as another externally imposed set of procedures and ideas that they must learn and use, and where their participation and inputs often seem to have been overshadowed by other global concerns about positioning, fundraising and global advocacy work. The problems of fitting the local into the global in ways that allow bottom-up responsiveness and flexibility largely remain unsolved. The ability to deliver on the plans depends on issues such as their local and national relevance, how well staff and partners understand them, and their skills and willingness to support the strategies in practice. They often find it hard to reconcile strategic global plans with their country-level analysis, and the understanding of corporate strategies by partners and field staff is often tenuous. Significant amounts of time go into developing country plans to fit global strategies, but once these plans have been approved often they are not really referred to again until the strategic reviews take place some years later, by which time priorities have changed again anyway.

Few agencies take time to assess how well their global strategic plans fit with host-government strategies, or local NGOs' plans and aspirations, leaving staff at the field level to struggle to reconcile the global, national and local. Some staff openly said that global strategic plans could inhibit creative thinking and local action:

> The danger is that we will move towards bureaucratisation and lose our research geniuses [and] clever thinkers if we standardise too much. If we become too rigid we will lose our innovative streak (large UK NGO).

This distortion of agendas continues down the aid chain at every level, as this kind of strategic planning becomes the norm and all NGOs who want external funding are expected to be able to carry it out, in contexts where in reality the majority of funding is project funding and not in fact strategic. The following case study shows the kind of struggles that take place locally in trying to communicate the requirements of strategic planning as it is now practised.

Kwikate

Kwikate ('Let's work together') is a non-governmental, Christian interdenominational organization working in eastern Uganda 'to holistically support women, children and people living with HIV/AIDS (PLWHAs) to realize their potential and have control over their lives'. Its key strategies are capacity-building, Christian faith-based work and creating an enabling and supportive environment for its target group. Kwikate includes the economic empowerment of women under difficult circumstances, child advocacy, support to PLWHAs as well as to orphans and needy children through education sponsorship and household Income Generating Activities (IGAs) to improve their quality of life. It strengthens community structures to support and care for needy persons.

Kwikate's main source of income has been a very supportive UK NGO. Other European NGOs have also contributed funds and capacity-building services. Kwikate was a vibrant organization, interested in organizational development and ready to fully engage with the planning, reflection and capacity development provided by Community Development Resource Network (CDRN), funded by an important donor. Kwikate was provided with a strategic planning workshop to help staff to focus their work and sharpen their vision.

CDRN staff encountered many difficulties during the organizational assessment and strategic planning workshops because many of the participants simply did not understand the process, although a wide combination of tools were used and adapted. The overall approach used (which had its origin in the dominant culture that emphasizes efficiency, targets, excellence and quality) did not take root in Kwikate because it was not relevant to their culture, premised on church and extended family system values that emphasize love, concern and harmony as a way of life. These are the values that influence how people are recruited, relate and perform, and they did not fit well with the approach CDRN, a sensitive and local training NGO, introduced.

Participants found it especially difficult to understand and engage with strategic planning; some were quite unaware of current environmental changes (donor trends, development thinking, CSO trends), which are an essential ingredient for proper strategic planning. The model in fact inhibited participation, because people did not understand the concepts, and also reinforced the disempowerment of some members. The facilitators had to adapt the workshop methods greatly, to include group-based methods, diagrams and pictorials in order to suit the non-literate participants. The group discussions were useful in helping the participants to learn about trends they were previously unaware of and participants were supported to develop a broad strategy framework for their organization; there was no attempt to write a fully fledged strategic plan, although this was one of the wishes of the funder.

This experience raised a number of questions and challenges for the facilitators. Was it realistic to involve non-literate community members in the workshop? If they were not involved, how could their legitimate needs and perspectives as members inform Kwikate's activities? Was this model relevant to the context of Kwikate, especially its target group? How could participation be enhanced? A rigorous and difficult strategic planning exercise can be wasteful if the organization does not have the capacity to understand and deliver it, resulting in a well-crafted document that is seen but never put to active use.

After extensive discussions CDRN concluded that small local organizations should be facilitated more slowly to gradually think more strategically and develop a strategy framework rather than be rushed to develop 'fashionable strategic and operational plans', especially where, as in Kwikate, the NGO had a very limited capacity to operationalize new plans.

The importance of personal relationships as a basis for good development interaction

A critical issue that emerged out of the interviews was the role and importance of personal relations in enabling work to be done differently. In the UK NGOs talked of individuals in funding organizations with whom they were able to talk, discuss concerns and share ideas. The value of funding from foundations such as Nuffield and Baring, which was both flexible and provided opportunities for interaction and open discussions with staff, was clear. The loss of face-to-face or telephone contact with funders such as DFID and the EU, which have contracted out their grant management work to consultants or insist on impartial bidding processes, was widely experienced as a negative change. Relationships are overall becoming almost exclusively paper-based with the institutional donors and their contracted agencies, and increasingly paper-based with other funders, a change that NGO staff regret and which will get significantly worse when the Big Lottery Fund contracts out the management of their international grants in 2006. Comic Relief tries to maintain open channels of communication, and convenes partner forums, but over time feedback has shown that some INGOs felt staff were becoming less accessible and open, due to factors such as high workloads and staff turnover. The overall donor trend is to rely increasingly on formal documentation, although several INGOs felt there was great value to be drawn from good interpersonal relations and the sense of working together on shared agendas in diverse and difficult contexts.

The same held true in SA and Uganda. Interviewees called for more face-to-face contact with donors and partners, as Mawdsley et al. (2002) also found. In the majority of NGOs, staff said that their most positive experiences came from developing strong relationships with one or two people in a donor or partner INGO organization. Although we tried to correlate the ability to build good personal relationships with particular agencies – by size, mandate, vision, faith orientation – in fact this was not possible. Instead it became clear that the right person could be located in the World Bank, DFID, a European NGO or any of the UK NGO partners. The personal attributes that created good interactions were not closely associated with any organization or organizational culture (although one or two small agencies were highly praised during the research), but with individuals. Unsurprisingly, the characteristics that were valued by staff and partners included: warmth, respect, an attitude of trust, the ability to listen, responsiveness, an understanding of the context and flexibility. People who had experience in the country or knew the conditions under which agencies were trying to work were valued, as were those who displayed empathy and a willingness to find creative ways of supporting the work. The power of individuals to shape better relationships and create space to work more creatively and participatively in the existing procedures was clear. So too was the loss of these personal relationships where donors have become more remote and less accessible, due to staff turnover and inexperience, heavy workloads, the need to

---

Box 7.1 The UPPAP programme in Uganda

UPPAP (the Uganda Participatory Poverty Assessment Project) is an ongoing initiative of the Ministry of Finance of the Uganda government. Initiated in 1997, UPPAP aimed among other things to enhance knowledge on the nature and causes of poverty (as articulated by the poor), to generate strategies for action and to establish a capacity for participatory policy research in Uganda. It was funded by DFID.

After almost six years of existence, it is generally accepted that UPPAP has been a success story, as evidenced by its contribution to enhancing the centrality of poverty concerns in Uganda (with public resource reallocation towards poverty reduction initiatives) and by its contribution to a widened consensus on poverty reduction strategies. It is also billed as an example of a successful partnership between government, donors and CSOs.

But was this a story of unmitigated success? How participatory was the process? And who benefited from UPPAP? This case study concludes that UPPAP achieved much and many positive lessons can be learned from this. As an example of a partnership between donors, government and CSOs, however, the picture is mixed. On the one hand, UPPAP has provided the various partners involved with an invaluable experience of working together, bringing in different perspectives, as well as a recognition of each other's worth.

On the other hand, for CSOs, the UPPAP partnership has remained substantially devoid of contents: if they learned much from UPPAP, there was a constant contradiction between management style and exclusion from decisions, and the objectives and participatory nature of the project. This reflected the various agendas, cultures and values of the different partners, the lack of skills in establishing and managing partnerships (in spite of the current fashion for such arrangements) and the fact that this was a partnership between very unequal parties: a monolithic government actor, supported by donors, facing fragmented CSOs experiencing considerable skills and vision deficits.

To what extent can a subcontractual arrangement accommodate a genuinely participatory process: are we faced here with an insoluble contradiction between means and ends? Can a participatory process occur in a tightly regulated framework, where participation can all too quickly be reduced to rhetoric: could it be seen as a populist measure giving credence to existing policies (bar a small adjustment here and there) which in the final count may not entail much change in the livelihoods of those UPPAP was meant to listen to?

The study finally argues that the idea of a tripartite partnership was very much owned by one party, the donors, and sold well in international circles. For CSOs (for this is a story from a CSO perspective) who had to live and learn the hard way, the experience of participating in a relationship where power dynamics were skewed meant that important and painful lessons had to be learned.

Source: De Coninck and Vadera, 2003.

cut transaction costs, and the decision to place a growing reliance on documentation as a way of funding and controlling development work. Where donors (institutional, independent or INGO) felt the need to promote their image or brand in relation to the work and successes on the ground, its also cut across good working relationships and made those doing the actual work feel undervalued.

The recognition of power

A different way of potentially opening up new spaces and ways of working, even within the narrow confines of existing procedures, is to work with a clear recognition of where power lies and actively address the power imbalances. One INGO held an internal workshop, organized by field-based staff on the need for and challenges of this way of overtly addressing the problems of power in the aid chain, especially exploring whose voice counts. The findings of that workshop highlighted the entrenched way power is replicated in the aid chain at every level and called for very different and conscious ways of working to change these inequalities (ActionAid, 2001). The workshop challenged the agency in a fundamental way, and perhaps because people held very different views about its value many of the recommendations remain unimplemented.

One innovative programme in Uganda showed the way that the lack of attention to power relations perhaps inhibited the work from reaching its real potential. The case study presented in Box 7.1 was detailed and complex, based on an ambitious vision of the need to include people's voices in developing national poverty plans.

Conclusion

Although the dominant trends are clear, and the systems for planning and reporting on development work are held in place because they fit the current perspectives and needs of those holding the most power in the aid chain, this chapter has highlighted some of the issues that would enable the work to be done differently. These approaches – focusing on building strong interpersonal and respectful relationships, more face-to-face discussions, greater knowledge of the complex realities of poverty, taking more open-ended approaches to strategic thinking and management, and recognizing and addressing the reality of unequal power between different players – provide clues about how to build better partnerships and find more relevant and responsive ways of working to address poverty. The hold of the current systems based so firmly on complex documentation is tight, but perhaps not unbreakable. The case studies from Uganda and SA presented in the next two chapters demonstrate the hold that the current ways of funding and accounting for development have, but also show evidence for the real potential to successfully use different ways of approaching the work.

CHAPTER 8
Relationships: partnerships, power and participation

Introduction

The previous chapters detailed critical dimensions of the way aid is currently disbursed, and the issues these raise for INGOs and NGOs working on poverty issues in SA and Uganda. The emerging picture highlights the power of many donors, and meeting their demands seems to be the compass by which much development work and thinking is set. The paradigm of controlled, measurable change seems to be the norm at every level, even though in reality life is far more complex. Rather than challenging the mismatch between the tools and daily experiences, most NGOs struggle to work with these tensions and in the process relationships can often become distorted, resulting in a lack of transparency and openness between players at each level. Underneath these interactions the work on the ground continues, sometimes but not always in line with the documentation surrounding the work.

The fact that NGOs prefer to try to work within the dominant paradigm rather than confronting the problems it raises in practice is evidenced by the fear shown among NGOs in the sample of being identified as critical of donors. This was universal in all three countries and indeed a condition for participating in the research; only four in the whole sample – apart from the training organizations who were open – said they were happy to be identified. Inevitably, this atmosphere can breed poor practice, especially in the tailoring of plans to fit donors' strategies or priorities, and the distortions of accounting, accountability and reporting endemic in the current M&E and reporting systems. The tight project cycle management procedures, combined with the reality of donors changing agendas and making new demands, create an unhealthy climate for building strong relationships and learning; in this context learning is often a far-off dream for both donors and NGOs. The norms appear so strong that they are rarely challenged directly, although the problems they cause are much discussed behind closed doors. Compliance with these norms is high, in spite of their real and understood shortcomings.

The impact of these tools and agendas are, of course, not uniform and people and organizations have agency within these clear parameters, as already shown in Chapter 7. The parameters in SA are wider for political and historic reasons; they are quite constraining in Uganda, a highly aid-dependent country, as the research showed. This chapter presents some more of the case material from

Uganda in a little more detail, to explore further how relationships are shaped by the congruence of these approaches and the power of those who promote them, how much of what happens in development practice falls outside these normative approaches, and where there are resistance and commitment to alternatives. In each case study (drawn from the Uganda report, Wallace et al., 2004) similar threads were apparent: the importance of meeting donors' requirements in project cycle management and the many problems and failings NGOs face in doing this; the fact that these tools are rarely used at the implementation stages of the work; the many dynamics – including relationships and motivation – that fall outside the current procedures; the evidence of some good interpersonal relationships that do help to overcome some of the power imbalances; and the existence of some autonomy and resistance to externally imposed concepts. The last was well expressed by the Ugandan director who deeply opposed these ways of working, discussed earlier in the book. NGOs in Uganda certainly show creativity and use a range of different approaches to development including PRA, outcome mapping, appreciative enquiry and action learning, but nearly always in addition to, and often subservient to, the project cycle management approach.

The following case studies capture these processes in different ways. In each case the evidence shows that the relationships of power and the procedures used have shaped key aspects of the work, and have sometimes limited the role of participation in shaping the work from the bottom up. Although power is discussed it is rarely put at the heart of the analysis or understanding of what is happening in development (Chambers, 2005); these case studies, along with the UPPAP study from Chapter 7, attempt to remedy this.

Discussions were held with several senior and M&E staff, members of the team and, in some cases, local people involved in projects; their views all contributed to the narratives, all of which were researched and documented by Ugandan members of the research team. Work was also done with the relevant donor/partner INGO in the UK by the UK team. The following, inevitably shortened, case studies try to represent the experiences, important concerns and questions raised as faithfully as possible.

The experiences of a faith-based organization in relating to European donors

This organization is a large faith-based NGO with a reach across Uganda, working at the national right down to the village level, in areas of both peace and conflict. Senior staff felt strongly that the shifts they have been asked to make recently away from service delivery and direct support to the poor have come out of development debates in the north, rather than in Uganda. They feel they are now required to change from the work they did previously, for example, providing a family with a cow and the skills and support to benefit from it, to empowerment projects, which they do not always fully understand or accept. There is an expectation that these changes can be made abruptly, yet the organization works through local, often faith-based staff and structures, and relates directly with local people, who often do not agree with the reasons for ending projects from which they benefited and that they value.

The new agendas of the INGO donors that support them include advocacy, democratization, governance, gender and HIV/AIDS. The senior staff firmly believe that the reason that some of these have been adopted relates more to how INGOs raise their money at home than to needs in Uganda. They well understand that their INGO donors now have to raise money from official and other donors as well as from public-giving in their own countries and need to ensure that they meet the requirements of these funders. Indeed, they suspect that many INGOs are constrained by the agreements they make with their back donors, which they then have to pass on to NGOs in Uganda, who in turn have to adapt quickly to these new agendas because there are few other sources of funding available. While in the past plans and budgets had been set during biannual roundtable discussions between staff and INGO donors from Europe, over time there has been a marked shift in the way negotiations take place. They feel their donors listen less to the local agenda; rather they come with their global strategies and expectations and indicate what they can agree to fund: 'donors have a way of indicating what they want and it sounds like the idea has been initiated locally, but it is dictation.' At the same time their grassroots constituencies, which have expectations based on past experiences, see their roles and responsibilities very differently and this causes many frictions and disagreements for staff trying to implement new international agendas with local people. Sometimes these are agendas local staff do not agree with themselves, making implementation problematic.

This organization senses that there has been an erosion of trust between some of their northern donors and themselves over time. They accept that there have been problems with financial accountability and have been trying to address these with new staff and financial systems. However, the problems of rebuilding trust have been exacerbated by the high turnover of staff from donor INGOs; they often find themselves negotiating new agreements and difficult issues with young people from UK or Europe who lack any experience or understanding of Uganda. There has been a serious lack of staff continuity and on one occasion a new INGO staff member, who was negotiating a difficult issue with them, heard halfway through that his job was being restructured and that he was to cease work in his current post. The drive for the adoption of new externally designed agendas, combined with the inexperience of many INGO programme staff, has cut across the relationships of trust they felt existed between them in the past.

They are now asked to operate in areas donors request and to deliver on new high standards of accounting and reporting. The shift from relating directly with donors they have known for years, on a negotiated agenda, to being asked to help donor INGOs fulfil their back donors' requirements with complex and demanding associated new procedures causes them problems. Their work is based on a set of values and beliefs and not all demands from northern donor

INGOs can easily be met. For example, the common approach to the use of condoms to prevent HIV/AIDS can be understood at the local level as the NGO ignoring their faith and promoting promiscuity. Local people, who feel the loss of concrete help acutely, often resent the withdrawal of direct project support and the introduction of what they see as culturally alien ways. The organization feels it is increasingly trying to adapt to secular development agendas that have been set elsewhere, which causes problems for local people and staff and raises questions about their identity and their role in looking after the welfare of the people.

Another area of concern is the donor focus on mainstreaming gender and the idea of gender as equity. For many this goes against biblical teaching (and Uganda is a deeply religious society, where the teachings of the Koran and the Bible are of critical importance in people's daily lives) and at the local level people can find this gender thinking hard to understand. The organization agreed that the faith-based communities have been slow to move on issues of women's equality and certainly recognize that not all traditional views and practices are good; many do need to be challenged. However, trying to tackle complex and rooted cultural values and behaviour using gender approaches defined by external donors is not easy. While the organization does try to promote the involvement of women to ensure that they benefit from programmes, implementation is slow, especially when working with local partners who hold strong beliefs and are supervised by staff who also share these beliefs. Yet donors are impatient, timetables are short and expectations of measurable change are high.

In recent years this organization has been asked to adopt strategic planning, something they find useful mainly because it has enhanced their dialogue with their donors. They often hire consultants to help them with the process, and employ technical experts to help deliver on the plan. They work to a five-year plan with clear goals and target groups and with improved systems of accounting; there is overall supervision by a management committee. At the grassroots, activities are derived from the overall strategy, although they still try to be responsive to locally developed proposals and encourage participatory ways of developing these, using PRA techniques. However, at the implementation stage there are often misunderstandings and difficulties, and very different understandings emerge about what the organization should be delivering for poor people, and what its priorities are.

This organization is now being asked to undertake advocacy work, which it understands to be the general promotion of development and development solutions. It feels it has always worked on capacity-building, especially building the ability of local staff to run grassroots programmes, but now there is a need to find ways to develop capacities for advocacy. They face difficulties in explaining this role to local people, and one striking image from another NGO in Uganda illustrates why. When waiting to see a local district official the staff member explained to the people attending that this time he would do the talking but in future they were to undertake their own lobbying with district staff, to obtain the education resources that were theirs by right. This had to be explained several times. Slowly the women and men present began to understand and one woman started to smile and then to laugh. She ended by wiping away her tears of laughter and explained her disbelief. Did the staff person not understand or had he forgotten the realities of local politics in the district? The people there came from a minority group in a subcounty largely bypassed by the district; how could they ever expect to be heard by officials who had a political agenda to follow? And the district had inadequate funds for schools, so how would they ever get resources, being last in the pecking order?

The organization has always tried to work in a participatory way, as donors request, but they feel that donor agendas sometimes appear to undermine local needs and voices. They try to mobilize households and communities for local activities and want to see the devolution of power increased down to the local level, yet at times they feel puzzled because some local agendas do not fit well with current donor objectives and poor people effectively have no say in changing predominantly donor-led strategies and plans. Participation appears often to be confined to the community level; it does not seem to reach the organizational levels of planning and accountability: 'However, donors have not stopped prescribing frameworks for the prioritisation or choice of programmes for communities…this makes the whole notion of community choice and the reality that the poor know what they want very superficial.'

The organization grapples with a range of complex issues, including conflicts and rivalries between ethnic groups, tensions between Christians and Muslims in some communities, rivalry between its own groups in some areas, and the local norms of running projects that can conflict with the organizational culture in Kampala, such as involving women and working slowly with them rather than addressing gender inequalities. These issues are difficult to manage and resolve; yet they rarely form part of the discussions with donors.

The organization recognizes the real problems in Uganda of staff 'eating' from grants, a cultural norm involving using project money for other needs, sometimes in illicit ways. Staff work hard to ensure local transparency and accountability but suspicion and distrust remain and partly because of the financial dimension, donors do feel the need for strong control.

Donors encouraging alliances and networking: relationships in practice

(This case study is a summary of the work of Mary Ssonko Nabacwa and was edited by her: Wallace et al., 2004.)

Nabacwa's research explores the relationships between donors and national NGOs that take a gendered approach to development in Uganda, and the networks and alliances created to promote gender advocacy work. She found that both donors and national NGOs subscribe to the need for advocacy to raise the profile of gender and influence policy and practice, but they sometimes have different motivations and their agendas diverge at times. They also diverge from those of their members sometimes. While there are clear lines of domination and control from donors to local NGOs, through various intermediaries, her research shows relations of resistance as well as collaboration and compliance and discusses how these affect the advocacy work undertaken. The tensions caused by matching different agendas, working to multiple constituencies, and managing upward accountability and downward cooperation are clear.

Gender is a key strategic concern in development and the documents on gender and gender mainstreaming are myriad. However, Nabacwa's research showed serious challenges to implementation. Although gender is always present on paper and in the rhetoric, for most donors and NGOs gender was absent in practice unless the organization had a specific focus on gender and women, or there was a motivated individual in an organization. Commitment to gender advocacy and the presence of powerful networks at the national level does not necessarily translate into change at the grassroots.

Nabacwa found that many donors (large and small) have paternalistic relations with the NGOs they fund and she characterized the NGO–donor relationship as a dependency relationship. The relationship between the local NGOs and the INGOS was also frequently that of an inferior and a superior respectively. The donors nurtured and provided for the local NGOs, which they defined as lacking capacity and theoretical frameworks. Local NGOs needed capacities to be built, something they work hard at, and some training inputs were very positive; the INGO donors also provided much needed finance. Many INGOs clearly engaged quite closely in the functioning and programming of the local NGOs they supported and exerted an influence over their areas of operation. They facilitated the formation of national alliances, forums and networks to do gender lobbying at the national level on their behalf. For the INGOs, which who lack direct access to national governments, the issue of linking with southern partners for global advocacy is critical; in spite of the many problems INGOs continue to have in funding it. However, they usually want to be openly recognized for their contribution and ensure that their name is on the local NGO publications and media statements, because recognition in their home countries, for status and financial security, is critical.

The research showed that forming new networking structures had several effects on local NGO relationships. First, the formation of such structures led to an increased number of local NGOs being engaged in advocacy work – actively or inactively – through their membership to the newly formed networks and alliances. Second, relationships to networks and alliances affected the programmes of the membership organizations, and the network could start to act autonomously once the secretariat fundraised for its own funds; assured funding meant that when the members agreed a project would be implemented. Third, the formation of new alternative structures resulted in rifts with existing organizations that felt that they were doing the work including advocacy that the new structures were claiming to be doing. This created quiet and at times overt resistance to the newly formed structures from existing organizations.

The fourth effect was that local structures were sometimes co-opted by big donors to justify their decision-making processes.

Other issues arise during the formation of networks and alliances by donor agencies. Nabacwa learned that INGOs are as vulnerable as their local counterparts to the demand for immediate results for accountability purposes. To try to ensure impact INGOs often build relationships based on trusted or reliable individuals they know. Informal group discussions showed that donors nurture individualism through this approach; they establish personal relationships and then fund the organization based on these individual relationships, 'they lift the veil and see the individual yet this individual is supposed to represent the organization'. Another person said that their organization only led a coalition because one of the staff had been informed by a donor agency that money could be accessed by her for the organization. These personal relationships, used to accessing donor funds, can result in the formation of cliques and rivalries, and momentum can be lost when staff move on.

Local staff in donor and INGO agencies were in a strong position to influence these relationships and agendas. Nabacwa describes it as a buyer/seller situation, where the donors are the buyers and the NGOs the sellers. It is a market where the buyers have particular tastes and the sellers work tirelessly to meet the buyers' demands. However, many local NGOs specialize in the same product, so they work on the catchy (marketable) issues of the day that they brand differently based on the taste of the different buyers (donors) to ensure that it is funded (bought). The buyer asks for bids from various sellers and picks the best seller. In this way donors are forcing NGOs to do advocacy because that is what they want to fund. Such relations nurture and reinforce competition among the NGOs and the bidding process has created a situation of the survival of the fittest.

In addition to buyer/seller relations, the relations between the donors and local NGOs are rooted in accountability. The buyers have control over the sellers' production process and have an interest in the cost-effectiveness of the production process. The sellers thus have to account for the resources received from the buyers. The various donors have varying accountability mechanisms, some more strict and rigid than others, which result in disjointed advocacy initiatives because they buy the products in different packages and at different times. As one NGO staff member said: 'NGOs do not have resources, they cannot go into an issue that is not funded. They have to tailor their activities to what donors want. They also do not have capacity, leading to dissemination of contradictory goals.'

These relations of accountability and buyer/seller result in relations of fear. Nabacwa found the local NGOs fear losing funds because of changes in donors' priorities, or their poor accountability practices, in terms of both activities and funds. The relations of fear may also explain why some, quite dysfunctional, networks continue in spite of resistance they have from their membership. The NGO is 'obliged to sustain and support their donor's baby even though they probably do not like the baby's clothes', as Nabacwa remarked. If these relations did not exist, they could probably have nurtured this baby differently, but NGOs prefer to keep quiet than to expose their feelings in case they affect their access to donors' resources. Relations of overrespect for donors also skew the allegiance of the organizations, resulting in strained relations among the various actors. During a workshop on monitoring the Convention on the Elimination of All Forms of Discrimination against Women (CEDAW), sponsored by one INGO, members were not satisfied by the modalities of work that the local network had agreed upon with the donor INGO. They asked whether the donor would be flexible enough to accommodate the changes in the proposal, taking into account the voices of the workshop. The network, however, was reluctant to renegotiate the Memorandum of Understanding (MOU) and respond to the requests of its members even though the funding INGO gave reassurances that it was happy to make changes.

Another staff member pointed out that because donors fund what fits their agenda, NGOs write very good proposals to meet these priorities to get funding but they often fail to translate the plans into practice. Nabacwa's findings indicated that implementation failure might be due as much to – or even more from – lack of conviction as any lack of capacity, although capacity is the issue donors focus on. Her findings showed that relations of mistrust existed also around macropolicies and poverty reduction agendas. One research subject said that the IMF and the World Bank brought the poverty eradication plan agenda to Uganda, although World Bank policies are in fact not pro-poor but are structural adjustment under another name. While all donor agencies are subscribing to the poverty agenda through PRSPs, in Uganda called the PEAP, many NGOs are very suspicious of this blueprint approach to Uganda's development because gender is very weakly analysed and the big macro-economic issues are ignored (Nyamugasira and Rowden, 2002). Donor agencies often require NGOs to take on reformist approaches to advocacy even though their commitment is to rejecting global policies, as other researchers have also found: According to Panos (2002), for example, the World bank and IMF and many donor governments do not allow debates that question their fundamental economic policies. Participation by civil society in shaping the PRSPs is only allowed within the tight constraints of accepting the dominant economic paradigms of these international agencies.

The competition among the Ugandan NGOs for resources, status and attention is clear and competition is even greater among NGOs with similar interests and characteristics, so many women's organizations find themselves competing for attention in both overt and hidden ways. Much of this competition can only be gleaned through reading organizations' documents and interviewing a cross-section of staff and members of selected NGOs, as Nabacwa did. A study of one network showed clear but hidden competition with its member organizations, which had gone on for a very long time. It was envisaged in the early stages of the network that 'the operations of the network do not and should not weaken the autonomy of its members', and the members agreed to form a 'loose network with a focal point to which the member organizations would convene to review progress on priority issues and the members were to play the lead roll.' One of the founder members said: 'We had an idea of a small advocacy unit, a secretariat not supposed to become an NGO,' rather a strategic rallying point for women's organizations for addressing women's strategic needs. However, to hire staff and hold a bank account, the network needed a constitution and registration as legal requirements, and registration made the network an independent legal entity. This marked the beginning of persistent competition with its members, who wanted a network that depended on them rather than an independent entity with the potential of competing with them. At times, the network and members agreed to collaboration as a better alternative, at other times relations of hostility, passive resistance, lack of involvement and poor communications dominated. These relations have played a critical role in the shaping of its advocacy agenda.

One way in which members resist the network's domination is through provision of limited information. Information is critical for effective advocacy, so limited information puts the network in a precarious situation when they take on advocacy issues but cannot properly back them up:

> It was observed that effective communication between the members and the member organizations was almost non-existent. It was learnt that even where attempts have been made for members of the planning committee to report to their respective organizations, some of the later have continued to isolate themselves from network activities.

One evaluation report analysed by Nabacwa noted that those who participate in the network committees do so as individuals and that there is no systematic mechanism to report back to the members. Communication between the network and members is poor. Committees are poorly attended and the few who attend take decisions on behalf of the many. Fear and suspicion among the members and their network does not allow it to 'reverberate with dynamism', 'the network and the member organizations develop and plan their own programmes in isolation of each other. This hampers the building of synergies between and among the MOs' (evaluation report).

Member organizations compete over constituency (clientele), influence and donors' funding and favours. Recognition issues also contribute to competitive relations and member organizations fear that networks may put their name or logo over their work and claim the credit for it.

> We like to network but at times you network to your disadvantage, you do a lot of work, you fail to have time for your own work that was be accounted against you and in a coalition you would not be recognised, no one will say that you did something.

With limited monitoring mechanisms, one way of measuring one's role in advocacy is the extent to which one is perceived to be advocating. One respondent said competition was mainly about image building, 'to be seen that they are doing something'.

One research subject said that to compensate for lack of members' support and involvement the network's secretariat habitually makes decisions without members' input, creating further dissatisfactions and the quiet withdrawal of members who feel that they have no control over the network. This behaviour is reinforced by the fact that undertaking joint programmes can be problematic because some donors require member organizations to show tangible results; this can lead to conflict over results and recognition, and the fear that individual recognition and identity might be swallowed up by the network. One research subject agreed that donor accountability mechanisms make it difficult to ensure that networks function cooperatively.

The network sharing its proposals and reports with member organizations can greatly improve these relationships; individual relationships can also strengthen networks and build cooperation:

> Resistant non-confrontational means ensure that the members are not seen by the network and donors as sabotaging an important initiative. The network survives and members take from it what they need and reject what they dislike. The secretariat finds ways to manage these relationships and continue to achieve the aims set out in the funding proposals, with or without members' cooperation.

One research subject said that the relationships between individuals in the different organizations were critical in getting members' support and it was important to know the individuals personally:

> The more people you would relate with, the more people you would likely to get them on board to support the network activities. When you look at the organization that really we worked with, I made them to be personal friends, that you know them beyond the organization.

However, individual relationships have their shortcomings, as Nabacwa showed, and one research subject noted that when the mutual trust was among individuals it never trickled into the whole organization, creating discontinuity when they left the organization. In addition the process of building individual buddies resulted in cliques, mainly based on age, old schoolmates or tribe mates, who made some members feel isolated and unimportant.

Overall, however, Nabacwa found that even while the members were often aware of problems and unhappy with the way the network used its identity, they continued being a part of the network. This, according to the informal group discussions, is because the members believe in the issues that the network is working on. The problem is not with the issues but the mechanisms and strategies of handling the issues; one person called the relationship a marriage in which there is some allegiance and where members benefit from the network through profile-raising and capacity development (they learn advocacy, they get ideas, strategies, etc). There is a clear recognition of the power of the network in comparison with the power members have as individual organizations. The network is very popular with donors and these are often the same donors that provide the lifeblood for the continuity of individual NGOs.

The donors also recognized the importance of the web of relations nurtured and maintained by the networks, which enabled them to deal with politically gender-sensitive issues as a collective; members took advantage of numerical superiority to challenge power centres. Providing a platform for sharing common concerns and speaking with one voice was important for them to ensure women's issues became part and parcel of the public debate. A collective voice achieves greater results. In addition many members get emotional and professional satisfaction from belonging to the network. Thus, in spite of relationships that have developed that the members do not like, Nabacwa saw their recognition of the importance of social capital nurtured by the networks and alliances have led to their continued relations with the network and various coalitions such as the Domestic Relations Bill Coalition-(DRB Coalition), Coalition of Politics and Women (COPAW), Coalition Against Violence Against Women (CIVAW), alliances (the Uganda Land Alliance, ULA) and forums (Women Leaders Forum) have been formed. In the process of ensuring that these relations are not endangered, they have at times turned their relations into ones of political convenience. It remains important for members to show the outside world that they belong to a significant network and it is also important for the network to show that it has a very large number of NGOs subscribing to their advocacy agenda.

The level of relations with the grassroots differs among the various NGOs. Some have a direct relationship with the grassroots through their district offices, others relate with the grassroots through their membership organizations; some nurture these relations more than others. The relations between the NGOs and the grassroots are, according to Nabacwa, by and large manipulative relations on the part of the NGOs and the leaders of the grassroots men and women.

One respondent said that through research and consultations with local people local NGOs legitimize their advocacy work, which is actually set at the international level through international conferences like the Nairobi Forward Looking Strategies women's forum in 1985 (and in Beijing in 1995), sponsored by the UN, governments, etc. However, she said that this does not mean the issues are not of importance to people, but that such approaches do obscure listening to what the people have to say. The grassroots, especially the leaders, view the NGOs as having material and non-material resources that they would like to access. Relations and identification with the NGOs provide opportunities for identity, status and recognition enhancement, things that are critical for local politics. The NGOs focus on the leaders as the representatives of the people and this creates a situation in which it is difficult for the NGOs to understand the grassroots level.

In instances where NGOs have related directly with the community it has mainly been in the context of relations of giver and recipient; these forums often take the form of workshops to create an awareness of the policy advocacy initiatives. They may request people at the grassroots to advocate for themselves, so long as they advocate for issues already chosen by the NGO and set out in their strategy papers, giving limited space to the community to exercise power and thus determine the relations they would like to have with the various actors. Nabacwa observed in one of the districts that community men and women, especially in public forums and workshops, – wanted to protect their dignity and thus would keep quiet, say what you want to hear or laugh when issues of gender inequality are discussed. Understanding how communication works at community level is critical for understanding the power relations between the various groups and the NGOs.

Although the relations between the NGOs and the grassroots show NGOs as powerful, the grassroots hold the power because changes in practices have proved to be more influential in changing gender relations at the grassroots level than any law reform. However, the way NGOs have been relating to the grassroots, as seen in the research, has not been appropriate for fostering a good understanding of community needs and perspectives within the NGOs, and has in turn inhibited local people from contributing actively to the advocacy agenda.

Trying to build different, sustainable relations with local NGOs

(This research was carried out by Martin Kaleeba, and was written up in Wallace et al., 2004.)

This third case study is of an INGO trying to work in a new way, to build long-term and sustainable funding relationships with local NGOs, realizing that in the past the work of the INGO was not empowering communities or building sustainable change for poor people. The primary rationale for the local NGOs joining this new partnership agreement was to access reliable and long-term funding and recognition:

> To be associated with such an international development organization like this international NGO gives us a lot of pride. Now the communities we serve take us more seriously when we advise them on development issues, for they hear about the good things the international NGO has done in other areas. Our identity is being promoted through this partnership. We can now develop long-term plans and have time to think about broad development issues (medium-sized Uganda NGO).

While the international NGO emphasized the need to work together to achieve better coverage and a rational use of resources, the two partner NGOs considered security of funding and jobs to be major factors for establishing this long-term relationship. While the INGO's expectations focused on the programme, the partner NGOs had hardware expectations, including finance and physical assets. The communities wanted improvements in their livelihoods as a result of increased funding and other forms of support from all the NGOs.

The envisaged roles and responsibilities of each party in the partnership arrangements were spelt out in the MOU and the INGO's country strategy paper. The INGO saw its role largely in terms of teaching the local NGOs a range of

Table 8.1 Summary of expectations from the partnership

INGO	Local NGOs	Community
Increasing the knowledge base of INGO through sharing and learning with the partner NGOs	Increased and more sustainable funding	More support from NGOs in form of tools, seeds, schools, health units
Reduction in administration and overheads	Learning new skills from INGO	More training from NGOs to gain more skills in
Building long-term funding relations with NGOs	Getting exposed to new development approaches	agriculture, savings and credit management, and HIV/AIDS prevention
Increased coverage of activities countrywide	Establishing links with other development players	Increased support to be able to generate more income to
Creating more networks and alliances of local NGOs for advocacy and policy influencing	Acquiring more facilities and equipment to improve work	meet basic needs like paying school fees and medical bills, buying clothes and
Empowering CBOs	Expanding programme to new areas and activities due to increased funding	assets like radios

Source: Kaleeba's findings, fieldwork, summer 2002, Kampala, quoted in Wallace et al., 2004.

skills currently associated with development aid management, especially management and budgeting, accountability and fundraising, reporting and planning. The development issues stressed were PRA, gender and advocacy. However, the emphasis was more on management and financial issues than on how to enable the two local NGOs to engage fully and appropriately with local communities. Indeed, some of the management requirements may have actively limited the NGOs' close involvement with their local communities, because of the new management and accountability procedures and the need to deliver on the INGO's aims and objectives.

The INGO introduced its own financial policies, procedures and reporting timetables and formats to the partner NGOs. These were tight and did not reflect the loosening of planning and budgeting that the INGO itself was implementing internally, in an attempt to move from top-down to more responsive and flexible ways of working. There was an evident concern to ensure good controls, as financial support was being greatly increased. The relationship appeared rather one-way, with the INGO providing the procedures and training, especially for financial management, but not attending specialized training run by the local NGOs on key HIV/AIDS issues, for example, even though the INGO had much to learn in this field. Indeed, in Uganda, pioneering work has been undertaken by NGOs and PLWHAs on HIV/AIDS and it is one arena where local thinking and innovation have been striking; external players have a great deal to learn from this work. Yet this knowledge and the often unique insights into how to work on prevention, care and mitigation of the pandemic have been largely untapped by the INGO.

Financial training and accountability was seen as the key to managing the partnership relationship, and many other factors, including the recognition that the partner organizations had something to offer the INGO, were marginalized, 'Staff of the international NGO also exhibit superiority complex tendencies and do not exploit the opportunities to learn from the expertise of the partner organizations' (partner NGO). The INGO remained the major provider of the technical, material and institutional support; the local NGOs were seen primarily as recipients. This situation had negative implications for the identity of the local NGOs and undermined their power to make independent decisions; it also meant that learning from local innovations was limited within the INGO.

Kaleeba's study explored the involvement of the partner organizations in decision-making processes and the findings revealed that although responses from the senior management of the INGO indicated that the partner NGOs were at liberty to make independent decisions especially regarding programming, administrative and operational issues, there were certain strategic and policy decisions that the INGO as a partner had to be involved in. Such decisions included changing programme priorities from those written in the proposals and MOU, changing budgetary allocations from one cost centre to another, and major strategic issues like programme expansion or procurement of capital assets.

> Some partners tend to look at decisions made by the international NGO as paramount, especially financial decisions. But we do not blame them, for the financial systems and procedures are all tailored to the international NGO systems...Many times, financial decisions made by partner organizations are turned down by (the INGO) under the guise that the decisions have not been made within the generally acceptable accounting principles. One wonders whether the international NGO takes time to fully explain to the managers of the partner organizations what these principles are (Kaleeba).

The partner organizations felt that having to consult with the international NGO on decisions concerning financing and programming affected their autonomy and identity, and led to delays in programme implementation:

> The international NGO is our funder and this almost predetermines the way we relate in decision-making. As partners in our programmes, the INGO participates in deciding what programmes we should do and not do. This is not bad, however there are situations when we feel that we ought to carry out certain programmes, but if these are not within the five thematic areas of the INGO, we are compelled to drop them. In financial decision-making we are, to a large extent, guided by the INGO in certain cases, we just have to go by what the INGO decides since they hold the purse anyway. For example, in the year 2001, we agreed on our proposed plans and budgets with them at a planning workshop and as required, we got approval from them. A month

later, after we had even started implementing activities and recruited staff to do the work, we were asked to reduce our budget by half! This decision was disastrous and de-motivating on our part...We had to terminate the contracts of the staff we had hired, as well as cutting down on our programme, logistical and administrate activities. This is just one example of how we dance to the tunes of the funding NGO but we cannot do without them (partner NGO).

The study examined the extent to which the partnership relations influenced the identity of the INGO, as well as of the two partner organizations. Most staff in the participating organizations perceived the INGO as a donor rather than a partner. They said that although the INGO provides the funding, not much effort is made by them to explain to the partners, making them feel 'we are not partners of equal footing'. They tend to believe that the INGO works through them but not with them, and it has designed the funding agreement to fit into its own reporting systems and procedures as well as its strategically set programme themes. The partner organizations tried to maintain their identity by retaining their original names and some of the activities they were doing before forming partnerships with the INGO. However, they had to broaden their scope of activities to fit within the five themes of the new programme under the partnership arrangement and in essence, the partner organizations were implementing activities that the INGO would have implemented directly in the past. To the partners, the expansion of the programme activities assures them of continuous funding, which is certainly beneficial, but the expansion of the programmes has to some extent distorted their original identities, which has been disturbing to them. In the eyes of the communities, the two partner NGOs were now seen as a mirror of the INGO.

Staff from the INGO also felt their identity was changing from that of a development organization to one of a donor, as they shifted from direct implementation to working through local partners. One senior officer of the INGO expressed fears that they are increasingly becoming invisible in the partnership programme areas and this may result in their losing their identity as a development NGO. The local NGOs are also changing, to mimic the INGO. The officer remarked that:

Partners are becoming 'small representatives of our organization'. They change their systems and procedures to suit our own ways of doing things. They purchase similar vehicles to those that we have, demand far better office accommodation, some even want to construct their own offices, claim for higher allowances and salaries and are trying to convince us that they need to buy all sorts of sophisticated office equipment, just like ours! The spirit of voluntarism that used to exist in some of these partner organizations is gradually dying out. We seriously need to re-examine our approach.

The two partner NGOs had in the past received funding from various organizations to run their activities. However, when they established long-term partnership relations with this one INGO, they stopped fundraising from other organizations. Although the funding introduced by the INGO assured them of long-term funding, it was risky for them to be complacent about exploring alternative funding sources. There was a sharp rise in funding after the local NGO entered into partnership with the INGO. Although this was good news in terms of having more reliable funds available for programmes, overaccelerated growth in future may have implications on the programmes' capacity to absorb the funds and appropriately account for them. The local NGOs should also learn from the experiences of other partner organizations, whose partnerships with the INGO were abruptly terminated due to lack of a proper accountability of funds that largely resulted from accelerated growth in income. Management was overwhelmed by the big and sudden income, which led to misdirection and/or misappropriation of some funds.

The study revealed that financial resource allocation was highly influenced by the INGO's planning and budgeting guidelines. At the onset of the annual budgeting period partner organizations are issued with planning and budgeting guidelines and embark on a budgeting process based on these. They have had to change their systems and their activities to fit the INGO's priorities and ways of working. It is also worth noting that although one of the key objectives for the INGO forming partnerships with local NGOs is to build their capacity to manage the programmes effectively, only a small percentage (2%) of the budget is allocated to staff development for the partner NGO; over 70 per cent must go to programme activities. Yet if staff capacities are not well developed, their ability to take on new work and procedures is likely to be impaired, adversely affecting the development work as well as its sustainability.

Conclusion

These case studies throw light on many facets of current development practice, and reveal the complexity of the work involved in trying to address deep-rooted problems of, for example, gender inequality and the threats embodied in the HIV/AIDS pandemic. The challenges do include existing cultural attitudes, weak local organizations, competition between NGOs and the motivations of the different actors in the aid chain. The cases show that many of the core challenges are left largely untouched by the current models of financing and accounting for aid disbursement, which remain narrowly focused on planning inputs and documenting outputs and outcomes, bypassing the demands of what implementation means in practice. The difficulty of building cross-cultural relationships often from a distance and of finding good ways to communicate and work alongside small organizations and people at the grassroots, especially, fall outside the scope of the widely used planning tools. So too do the messiness of different interests, conflicting motivations, rivalry and the reality of very different individual and organizational analyses of the causes of poverty and how best to address them in each context.

Much time and effort is put into training local NGOs in project cycle management and accounting for their funding in spite of the fact that so many critical development challenges fall outside their remit. Far less time is spent exploring with CSOs how best they can work with marginalized people, how to engage with and work to change cultural barriers to promote equity, how to ensure that the work both meets the priority needs of poor people and also opens up their thinking to new possibilities. Many experiments with participatory approaches and downward accountability often become packaged in ways that mirror the commitment to frameworks in project cycle management; others are more exciting, especially with HIV/AIDS in Uganda, and yet they usually remain exactly that, experiments.

There are many issues that create obstacles for achieving positive change for the poor; these include personalities, individual relationships and the formation of exclusive cliques within the aid chain. Competition for funding and also for recognition – the need to have your name on each and every event and activity – militates against promoting local ownership and long-term commitment from local people. Trying to tackle harmful local practices that discriminate against vulnerable groups through external frameworks and short timelines appears misguided. High staff turnover, lack of time to listen, lack of real respect, superior attitudes, and feelings of inferiority and dependence all shape what actually happens. The current systems are poorly designed for building strong and open partnerships or developing a responsive, learning practice, and indeed often lead to organizational identities being changed and missions bent to fit changing priorities.

The lack of honesty and transparency and the distortions in communication that now characterize many of the relationships was seen time and time again. So too was the anger and resentment that came from the perceived overvaluing of INGO and donor skills, procedures and resources and the undervaluing of local skills such as language, cultural knowledge, lifelong involvement with the issues and understanding the local concepts of change. The challenges are myriad, the answers are not easy. However, the research in Uganda strongly suggested that the compulsory procedures, which led to a high degree of compliance, with some people feeling coerced by them, did not help to address the critical problems at the heart of development practice, and did not appear to meet Anderson's minimal requirement that development work 'does no harm' (1999).

CHAPTER 9
Chains of influence in South Africa

Chapter 8 explored the effects of changing conditions placed on aid, and the way the procedures of aid are translated down the aid chain, in terms of their impacts on Ugandan NGOs' multiple relationships to donors, other NGOs and the grassroots. The complexity of development work, the centrality of power and relationships, and the ways in which the dominant tools distort these were among the key observations of the last chapter. This chapter picks up on these themes and the power dynamics operative in the aid chain as it extends into and through SA. We do this by critically exploring three aid chains and the way they function. Our concern is to qualify the nature of influence from the north and to explore its effects, again tracing how the strong forces pushing for rational and constrained development approaches shape the relationships of NGOs, and how other local forces may mediate these tendencies. Specifically, this chapter explores the multiple chains of influence, showing how donors' funding strategies and management requirements affects downstream organizations. It also analyses donors' strategies towards diverse components of larger programmes including advocacy, capacity building, partnerships and gender, which all reflect the conceptual frameworks, ideologies and approaches of those upstream in the aid chain. The processes through which they are adopted, understood and negotiated by various individuals along the aid chain also form an integral part of this chapter.

In considering SA NGO's relationships with UK donors, the issue of room for manoeuvre is important. As was shown in Chapter 5, the SA NGOs emerged out of a strikingly different history from those in Uganda. Struggle against the state and apartheid, alliances that spanned the political spectrum from pan-Africanism to Communism, and a potential pool of leaders who had received support from the solidarity movement, or who had trained and worked abroad, all contributed to the formation of an NGO sector with greater capacity to negotiate terms and conditions with donors. This capacity is unevenly spread: some NGOs are quite assertive in their interactions with donors; others are much more akin to those in Uganda, unwilling or unable to challenge requirements, whether due to lack of information on alternatives, fear of losing scarce funding, or other reasons. Differences in the capacity to negotiate appear linked to the strength of the leadership, the support of NGO boards and key stakeholders and (sometimes) the ongoing financial support of independent-thinking donors, rather than the characteristics of the NGO per se (that is, sectoral or geographic focus, size of NGO or location). The existence of organizations and individuals capable of negotiating is important, as their experiences show both the limits of the dominant system and suggest new ways of thinking about and doing development.

The chapter draws on three case studies selected to illustrate the range of donor–recipient relationships encountered in SA. In all three cases, representatives of organizations at all levels of the aid chain are aware of power dynamics and are trying to work towards better partnerships and improved consultation. They do so in very different ways, and with distinct difficulties and successes, as shown below.

South African NGOs as partners: from negotiation to vulnerability

The SA organization linked into the aid chain described here, Faith and Development, typifies the majority of SA organizations receiving international funds: they are capable of negotiating around the margins of funding agreements and requirements but find themselves vulnerable to changes in donor policies, priorities and practices.

Faith and Development, an INGO with operations in many countries, has a strategic approach to funding in which partnerships are a core element. Hyman and Nyar, key members of the SA research team, worked with several of their partners, although only two are presented here. Both of these NGOs were umbrella NGOs operating out of a single province and with a longstanding relationship with Faith and Development. They differed with respect to size (budget and staff) and reputation: the first was a well-established faith-based NGO that used its large budget and staff complement to work with its church membership on economic development, democracy and HIV/AIDS; the second, much smaller, NGO focused its activities on economic development, and had lost much of its staff and budget. A white director headed the first, the second, during the period of research, had two different directors, both black. Both NGOs received funding from Faith and Development, other faith-based entities outside the UK and local sources, though in general the smaller NGO had fewer sources of funding than the larger one; indeed, Faith and Development had ended its funding relationship with the smaller NGO.

According to interviews done in both SA and the UK, the larger NGO enjoyed a supportive and consultative relationship with Faith and Development. As a result, there was room to negotiate on a range of programme elements. Although Faith and Development imposed new systems of impact assessment and evaluation, it was also open to negotiating the format of reports and the composition of evaluation teams. When reporting was found onerous, for example, the director of the SA NGO was able to bring the organization's various donors to an agreement on a common reporting format. When the funding environment became more competitive, senior staff members were invited to attend an exposure visit to learn how to conduct local fundraising.

Particular programme areas, however, were subject to much less negotiation. Respondents at the large NGO felt, for instance, that Faith and Development had 'almost demanded' a gender policy from them. Staff explained that it was not that they were opposed to having a gender policy but that they felt 'held to ransom', that 'either you had a gender policy or you would say goodbye to the funding'. Faith and Development gave the NGO examples of gender indicators to use in the projects. According to the director, 'it wasn't difficult for us actually to establish a gender policy. There was no resistance to it but there was a feeling of perhaps wanting to resist simply because we were being told to do it, made to do it.'

The larger NGO worked closely with a South African organizational development and training institution to examine its own programming, staff development, its board and donor relations. Faith and Development, among other donors, seemingly had considerable respect for both the director of the support organization and used it as a consultant for numerous of their partners, that of the large NGO. Board members, consultants, management and field staff of the organization all describe the donor as responsive, accommodating and committed to the partner's efforts, even while demanding that partners produce extensive reports, use logframes and make changes according to the international organization's programme and strategic shifts.

At the small partner NGO, in contrast, relationships with the donor were strained at the time of the research. Funding had ended because, perhaps among other factors, the small NGO's work did not fit within Faith and Development's new strategic focus on HIV/AIDS. Moreover, Faith and Development had already funded the NGO for many years and, in line with the organization's focus on emerging NGOs, international managers thought the SA partner no longer needed support to build capacity.

Staff members of the organization were 'disappointed' and frustrated by the cut in funding. Similar to the Ugandan case studies, differing expectations of the relationship are central. Managers at this smaller NGO said that while the practice of moving on to other organizations was well-known, they had no warning and there had been no period of transition. In addition, they felt that their work was not well understood or appreciated; donors' discomfort with working with black directors and with a less rule-bound management style may have also played a part (Hyman, 2005). Efforts to bridge cross-cultural, urban–rural and racial divides were minimal. Contact between the INGO and this small partner was limited to project reports and Faith and Development's yearly project visits to the head office. Funders and evaluators did not demonstrate much interest or commitment to going out to the field, with their focus instead on the manner in which funds were being used and reported.

There were also differing expectations of how local NGOs should tackle HIV/AIDS (Nyar, 2005; Hyman, 2005). Faith and Development wanted the SA partner to conduct HIV/AIDS awareness training as a central programme element. Given the ambivalence of government policy during the period, INGOs provided crucial support to SA organizations involved in international campaigns, local activism and community-based care; they also pushed local NGOs actively working in other arenas to think about HIV/AIDS. In some cases encountered in our research, INGO questions about HIV/AIDS programming had led partners in SA to re-orient their activities. In this case, the NGO staff felt that they were addressing HIV/AIDS already and doing so in ways that were effective, using complementary resources available from the public sector and other NGOs. As the NGO staff explained:

> We are involved [with HIV/AIDS] because most of our members are affected... [It] doesn't mean that all organizations must run a workshop or have a project on HIV/AIDS because there are already organizations doing it. We can network...and bring them in to run the workshops. We must have the knowledge but not have it as a project...It doesn't mean that we are not making our members in the community aware of it or that we are not talking about it.

They interpreted their donor's requirements as unfair and uninformed, contrary to what they saw as both locally-driven needs and cost-effective practice. Additionally, staff felt that the lack of field visits by the INGO contributed to the misunderstanding of their work on poverty and HIV/AIDS.

The multiple ways in which INGOs interact with the SA NGO sector merits more attention than can be provided here. The example above suggested two different outcomes from a single INGO's work with two contrasting partner organizations, and defined the relationships as being very different for a range of reasons. These included the confidence of the leadership, the openness of interactions, the degree to which funding was predictable and transparent and how far the NGO felt able to respond to changing donor demands; in this case race was one factor shaping communications. Relations were also shaped by the donors' perception of the competence and willingness of their partners to focus on gender and HIV/AIDS in the way that the INGO wanted. There are, of course, numerous other ways in which INGOs have been involved in the issues of gender and of HIV/AIDS: through legal advice and funding, research, community-based care initiatives and epidemiological work. International support for NGOs to work in HIV/AIDS – or around other contentious policy agendas – has at times led the central ANC leadership to question whether local NGOs were being manipulated by their foreign funders (Bond, 2002). Nonetheless, in the case of HIV/AIDS work, most analysts recognize that local NGOs and activist organizations have often taken the lead in defining civil society's responses to HIV/AIDS in SA, taking on the pharmaceutical companies and challenging international indifference to the plight of HIV/AIDS-affected peoples in poor countries throughout the world.

NGOs and gender mainstreaming: power, tools and meanings

This second case study draws on research by Tallis (2005) to explore the influence of a donor organization operating in SA on understandings of and action around gender inequality and its role in increasing vulnerability to HIV and AIDS. The

HIV/AIDS Gender Link Programme (GLP) aims to support the integration of gender into the work of partner organizations

In the case of GLP and its partners, donors influenced the local development agenda, and that of their partners, through their funding strategy, management requirements, advocacy strategies and, crucially, capacity-building. The GLP began as a joint initiative of several INGOs concerned with reducing the impact of HIV/AIDS and promoting tolerance and respect for those living with and affected by HIV and AIDS through a multisectoral, rights-based approach, attentive to gender integration in all interventions (Tallis, 2005: 94). An initial phase entailed providing the 12 funded organizations with training in programme management and HIV/AIDS mainstreaming, skills identified as lacking in NGOs working in the sector. The second phase entailed funding more organizations in strategic areas, for example the prevention of HIV and other sexually transmitted diseases. Funding was given for three years, with continued funding contingent on the demonstration of good progress and impact.

The emphasis was clearly on training and capacity-building. In the GLP aid chain, Tallis (2005: 95–6) explains, 'lack of capacity has been identified as the key barrier to effectiveness, impact, and development'. She argues that this had two effects: to sideline deeper structural causes of limited impact, and to justify donor involvement in capacity-building and training. Examples are provided below of the implications of such a definition of NGOs' pressing needs in effecting change around gender relations and HIV/AIDS.

Donors often assume that they understand the needs of partner organizations and impose solutions in the guise of capacity-building. For example, in a two-day capacity-building workshop to build skills in (M&E), logframes were used as an example of a possible tool. A year later, the logframe was again presented at a joint GLP–partner forum:

> South African partners began to realize that this was a management requirement...rather than an option as they had assumed. One partner organization argued that: the [logframe] was not the only tool for planning; based on their experience of using it they had problems with its linear nature and rigidity; and they already had plans to use alternative, more qualitative frameworks (Tallis, 2005:103).

GLP representatives said that, in attending the capacity-building workshop, partners had endorsed the plan, and they wanted to prohibit all other approaches to monitoring. Tallis (2005: 103–4) describes the ensuing debate:

> This was challenged by the partner organization, drawing on an earlier discussion about power in the partnership. The organization stated that their understanding of [the] partnership workshop, with the designated time for discussions and debates, gave the impression that GLP was opening up space in which the relationship between donor and partners could be developed through open and honest dialogue; this could include disagreeing with each

other. After a 'cooling-off period' GLP finally agreed to allow the organization to use an alternative planning, monitoring and evaluation framework.

Other organizations present did not question the donor. They were uncomfortable about 'disagreeing with donors for fear of losing support', appearing 'ungrateful' or incurring the wrath of the facilitator; they also were unfamiliar with alternative approaches to M&E, since their training at the capacity-building workshop had been exclusively on logframes and derivative M&E approaches; as above, racial and cultural dynamics may also have played a part.

Tensions between coercion and consent were apparent as well in the overall setting of agendas. Moreover, similar donor requirements can be felt quite differently at different points along the aid chain. Tallis (2005: 104) describes:

> A critical part of the research was to understand the role that both staff (international and local) and partners felt GLP played or should play in influencing gender integration. A staff member at one of the international funding organizations in the GLP aid chain noted that gender mainstreaming, or the integration of gender as a donor driven process, 'cannot be escaped but can be done sensitively'. According to her, GLP's approach is transparent and negotiates power from the outset of the relationship, long before funding is received. Partners know that they are expected to address gender inequality; the donor has a set of guidelines, which are shared with partners. While the organization does not 'do capacity building', it facilitates dialogue between partners by bringing them together to discuss gender.

While this response was typical of respondents from INGOs, further down the aid chain, respondents from SA NGOs saw donor requirements in a different light, as the following passage illustrates:

> in a 'Gender Mainstreaming' workshop an international gender 'expert' facilitated the programme. Local organizations were listed in the programme documents, and a local partner organization was asked to co-facilitate. However, local participation was requested once the programme had already been drafted, and thus seemed, according to one partner NGO respondent, like 'window dressing'. During the workshop two donor-driven themes were identified as critical: 'community resilience' and greater involvement of people living with HIV and AIDS. The assumption was that organizations were not aware of and were not already involving people with HIV. Moreover, partners were not given an opportunity to define for themselves the issues that they thought were critical (Tallis 2005: 104).

As in Uganda, donor-driven practices sidelined local expertise in favour of the knowledge promoted by the international partners, with numerous adverse implications for respect, communication and equality of partnerships.

The material in Box 9.1 further depicts the multiple avenues of influence.

Box 9.1 Common platforms and different views of gender and gender mainstreaming (excerpts from Tallis [2005: 104–6])

The research interviews reflected on GLP's strategies to mainstream gender by asking partners and staff how GLP address the issue of gender. Specifically, respondents were asked about: proposal procedures that included specific gender questions; NGO staff attendance at...workshops addressing gender issues; site visits...for monitoring and support where specific questions around gender are asked; ...use of gender sensitive indicators in monitoring and evaluation; and outcomes of the gender focus that were seen as positive.

Responses... [were] that gender elements had been included at various stages of the grant-making process. Specific questions in the funding proposal process addressed gender, SA NGO staff were expected to attend a two-day training workshop, and site visits by funders – or evaluators – explicitly looked at gender issues. Evaluations...[found that] GLP was a pioneer in linking gender to HIV and AIDS in South Africa, and enabled partners to develop strong sensitivity to the subject...Partners were positive about GLP's strong guidance in relation to gender. The external evaluation found that gender issues were integrated into GLP's monitoring visits and capacity building workshops, and into partners' indicators of success.

The evaluations also identified measures to improve gender mainstreaming, which were subsequently incorporated into strategic plans and programmes. Such measures included: requiring potential partners to include a gender analysis in the problem description of their project proposal; requiring partners to develop gender-sensitive strategies and indicators that reflect a gender analysis for their project; enabling partners to acquire the knowledge, skills and resources that they need in order to mainstream gender into their work; focusing on gender issues, in both partners' projects and organizations, in quarterly monitoring visits and reporting mechanisms, and internal and external evaluations; and monitoring and evaluating GLP's own performance in achieving gender equity.

These objectives demonstrate a clear plan to highlight gender. At the same time, they are mechanistic and focus more on the technical and less on the political. Such an approach requires that partners and GLP have specific gender expertise. The research shows that this expertise largely does not exist. As one example, although partners should have indicators that reflect a gender analysis for their project, GLP have no clear indicators of 'successful' gender mainstreaming. While indicators may not be the best way to measure success, there are clear indicators for all other objectives of the programme; the lack of gendered indicators is thus telling.

Indeed, gendered indicators are also not apparent in most of the partner organizations. Organizations are addressing gender issues often because of the demands of the epidemic and not because the organization uses a gender discourse and lens. Indicators are quantitative not qualitative, poorly adapted to the specifics of programmes and their dimensions, and limited to immediate observable impacts, as opposed to the longer term structural and strategic changes associated with fundamental shifts in power relations. For example, a partner organization has three GLP funded programmes: a peer educator project, home-based care and a youth programme. The peer educator programme targets single, low-income women, many of whom are sex-workers...However, an analysis of the indicators show that gender power relations and the realities of women's lives are not taken into account. In fact, the indicators are the same as those for the youth programme. The organization disaggregates indicators that are used to monitor success by gender, however the indicators include quantifiable measures that in no way address the realities of women's lives.

Mainstreaming gender entails both technical and political processes, and requires shifts in institutional structures, organizational culture, ways of thinking, and resource allocations. For mainstreaming to lead to change, conscientization at a personal level is also required. However, in many instances, 'gender mainstreaming' as a concept has been diminished from its original meaning. This 'watering down' is linked to the emphasis increasingly placed on the technical aspects of gender mainstreaming, using frameworks and tools that can detract from the political dimension of the process and its outcomes. For example, gender audits focus on quantifying the number of women and men in a given position, or reached by a particular programme. Less attention is placed on women's actual meaningful participation...Indeed, we must ask, as do Geisler, Keller and Norman (1999): what is the benefit of gender mainstreaming for target populations? Does mainstreaming actually change the way target groups and stakeholders are dealt with at the project level? The research confirmed observations made by other researchers (Jahan, 1997) that often gender mainstreaming is made into the goal itself, rather than being a means to the goal of gender equity.

Tallis's study examines gender mainstreaming in depth, with several additional observations of particular importance to the issues raised in this chapter. In addition to the watering down of the concept into its more technical elements, donors may have different levels of commitment to and interpretations of what is entailed in integrating or mainstreaming gender. Similar dynamics characterize the SA NGOs. Tallis (2005:110) contends that both GLP and many of its partners understand gender as 'addressing difference and not fundamental power relations'. She speculates that this may be rooted in the focus on gender inequality as a fundamental cause of AIDS that emerges from their work, as opposed to a wider feminist analysis. There were concerns that no one was 'really pushing a gendered agenda'; staff acknowledgement of the link between gender and HIV/AIDS and provision of gender-disaggregated data were all that was required. As a consequence, some respondents suggested that efforts were of limited success, stating, for example, that 'the gender framework of the programme has not always been strongly maintained in practice'. Also apparent is that rather than addressing the complexity and political difficulties of introducing a gender approach into community-based work, training and evaluation focused on project management. Yet such a focus is likely to result in the ritualistic and meaningless inclusion of vague statements of commitment, or numeric targets, rather than real changes in projects and their performance (Geisler, Keller and Norman, 1999; Wallace, 1998).

Beyond negotiation: training and organizational development NGOs in South Africa

The last case study looks at one of several SA NGOs involved in support activities for the NGO sector, and for donors and INGOs (Bornstein et al., 2004). These development practitioners are unusual in that there is tremendous knowledge at many different levels in their organizations, and indeed across the NGO sector more broadly. While many developing countries have local development practitioners whose expertise is based on extensive practice and familiarity with local dynamics and conditions, or alternatively have been trained and are working in dominant frameworks, SA has a particularly deep knowledge base. Many of the distinctive features of the SA environment for development were described in Chapter 5.

A key point is that knowledge generated in this environment is not simply the transmission of expertise constructed in the north. Many practitioners in SA are engaged actively in thinking about contemporary changes to development practice, and the ways it can be improved. Funders also enter into these discussions, and while there are organizations governed by the home office policies, there are also individuals and organizations willing to back less familiar practices and exchanges.

This section examines the ways in which specialist training and organizational development organizations in SA influence the transfer of management knowledge and, ultimately, the practice and impacts of development (Bornstein, 2005b). Specialist organizations vary greatly, from those that are home-grown, to those linked into progressive development networks worldwide, and those that are more dependent on the aid industry itself. All the specialist agencies modify the training information received, filtering and reframing it to meet the local realities as understood by the trainers. Some training organizations develop their own materials, using a range of manuals and examples; other organizations rely heavily on training materials developed and provided by major institutional donors (USAID, GTZ, DFID) or large charities and non-profits (Oxfam-GB, Save the Children, CARE); other specialist trainers sit within the organizational structure of larger donors (e.g., GTZ's gender department and project cycle management divisions). Some trainers clearly frame material and approaches within the norms and values of specific donors, while others actively contest the ways in which aid relationships can dictate more managerial or more subordinate roles for local development NGOs.

Not all countries have specialist training and organizational development institutions. Others have so many that their influence cannot be determined. SA has only a handful of training and organizational development institutions that serve the NGO sector; they are not based in universities, and are acknowledged as dominating the field. Key informants mentioned only a handful of such organizations. Some of these organizations have been conduits for the spread of specific management techniques and all have acted as nodes for the discussion and consolidation of NGO approaches towards development. In SA these organizations have played a crucial role in modifying existing management approaches – those promoted by aid agencies, INGOs and foundations – to include more locally relevant approaches and more local knowledge and expertise. One of the organizations has placed itself at the forefront of management practice globally by defining alternatives to the dominant development management approaches of the aid industry and promoting these alternatives internationally. Other organizations, though acting primarily as vehicles for the transfer of international practice, have participated sufficiently in the SA debates over development management to negotiate and adopt elements radically different from the standard approaches.

Our focus here is on CDRA, one of the four training organizations with which we conducted research. The discussion is confined to an initial introduction followed by a longer piece by Allan Kaplan (see box), the founding director of CDRA, who has since left the organization.

Established in 1987, CDRA has worked to build the capacity of organizations and individuals engaged in development and social transformation work in SA and elsewhere. The focus is on improving learning in the organization and better directing that learning towards improved action. A starting point for CDRA is that 'the more understanding an organization has, the more capacity it has'. CDRA thus works closely with managers, directors, consultants and other development practitioners on organizational and individual development; this is done through research, publications, courses and consultancies. CDRA also works with donors directly on commissioned work.

CDRA does not have a particular methodology or set of techniques that it uses in its organizational development work or its training. There are, however, strong conceptual orientations that guide the work. Key elements include action learning and Steiner-influenced approaches to organizational development. A second related concept is that of a learning organization, which James Taylor, the current director of CDRA, defines as an organization 'which builds and improves its own practice by consciously and continually devising and developing the means to draw learning from its own (and other's) experience'. While all organizations experience learning, in Taylor's view, to be a learning organization there must be intent and commitment to the process, the use of experience as the basis of learning, an ability to put new knowledge and learning into improved practice, and a perpetual spiral of organizational development rooted in a balance of reflection, learning and action.

CDRA has forged a particularly positive relationship with its donors, a relationship summed up as 'remarkable' and described in Allan Kaplan's piece below. Donors currently fund about 75 per cent of CDRA's activities; the remainder is covered by the fees charged for consulting services. CDRA has no UK funders, though CDRA does provide consulting services to UK-based NGOs and works with many NGOs that are part of the aid chain sample in this research. CDRA has moved from an initial position of reliance on a single funder to a diversified set of funders: importantly, it has core funding for its own operations and has also set up a reserve fund that generates annual revenues that are used to cover some of their activities.

There are two specific features about CDRA that are not reflected in the following contribution from Allan Kaplan. First, like some of the other support organizations, CDRA practitioners have taken their own learning and experience and published books, manuals, web-based think pieces and articles on such issues as action learning, development practice, participation, fieldwork and conflict. Second, as part of its training programme, CDRA offers two courses of particular interest. The first is a course in the facilitation of organizational development, directed at NGO staff, in which three six-day modules are combined with back-home projects to allow for learning and translation of that learning into organizational change. The second course is of particular interest to the themes of this chapter: a six-week course for organizational development practitioners, an opportunity to reflect on their personal experience and explore new ways of thinking and understanding their work. The course thus brings together representatives of the NGO training and support organizations from across SA and, with participants from other parts of the world and from other development professions, allows for the sharing of knowledge, learning, ideas and techniques, as well as for the establishment of personal relationships in the sector. The difficulty, of course, is that the types of reflection and learning that take place in these CDRA seminars and workshops are not always easily accommodated in the home organizations of the participants. While CDRA encourages at least two staff members to attend from any organization, this is not always practical. Differing paces, interests and areas of change between individuals, NGO leadership and the organization thus are one risk associated with CDRA's approach.

The problems of dominant NGO approaches and spaces for negotiation for one organization were well captured in a series of interviews with Allan Kaplan carried out by research staff in SA, presented in Box 9.2.

Box 9.2 Allan Kaplan on NGOs and donor relationships at CDRA

The development sector has always taken an engineering approach to the world; it has seen the object of its endeavours as a thing which can be manipulated, a thing which can be controlled. Under this assumption, it seeks to analyse the thing, and then provide inputs which, it presumes to predict, will lead to relevant outputs. In other words, it assumes that the correct inputs will lead, in a more or less linear way, from cause to the predicted effect. It thus seeks to do to, and on behalf of, others, where the other is controllable, and where the effect will be on the other and not on the one who intervenes.

CDRA has always regarded the 'object' of development endeavours as a living being – whether it be an individual, organization, community or social situation – which means that it has its own inherent development process, or movement, in which we intervene. Therefore development work can never assume linearity; we always have to deal with aspects of another being's process which defy any attempts at analysis or prediction, or control. We cannot perform engineering operations on others as if they were things; we can only walk alongside, anticipate, respond, and keep adapting our interventions as the situation changes. This demands that we are at home with ambiguity and uncertainty...

Development work is entirely about relationships. We are a significant part of the relationship. We cannot separate ourselves from the other; while conventional development work presumes to do exactly this. Conventional development work, in recent years, has become far more amenable to concepts of participation and ownership, but still generally as a means to an end; the success of the development project is often assumed to depend on, for example, participation. For CDRA, concepts like participation and ownership are not a means to an end but are the end in themselves; if we can achieve participation and ownership we have done all that we can possibly hope to do.

As well, CDRA has always placed a high premium on the concept of practice. Most development organizations and projects are content to rest with aims and objectives and strategies and indicators for success; they seldom look deeply enough at their methodologies for achieving these, their on-the-ground practice in the field. Too little time is spent interrogating that practice, and improving it.

This takes us to the question of learning. More and more development organizations pay lip-service to the concept of the learning organization, but very few organizations actually engage in rigorous and continuous processes of self-critique, around methodology and practice, in order to improve action. For CDRA, given the ambiguous and uncertain and participatory (with respect to the intervener as well) nature of development, the only real guarantee of good practice is adequate ongoing learning; we have always seen rigorous learning and self-critique as the only true and relevant form of accountability, for a development organization or practitioner. Yet those who fund development, who spend so much energy demanding compliance to their criteria for accountability, seldom are prepared to provide funds for such learning to take place. And even less frequently do they engage in such processes themselves...

Effective development practice demands that we ourselves, as the ones who intervene, are prepared to change and develop. The refusal to fund, and engage with, real processes of learning (not external evaluations, which we all know have only a limited amount to do with learning) is a mark of the cynicism with which many donors and their counterparts approach development work. It is not simply a question of not knowing any better; it's an indication that most of those who engage with development do not themselves see any point or necessity to their own development. And what could be more cynical than that?

CDRA has benefited from core (institutional) funding, from receiving funding for its own learning processes, and from remarkable relationships with many of its donors...It has won these circumstances through struggle, through commitment to a vision of development practice and through a rigorous authenticity. It has never compromised on its vision, not because it has never been forced to, but because when it has been forced it refused to cooperate. For CDRA, compromise has never felt worth it; we have always known that if we're forced to compromise to too great an extent then we would rather throw in the towel and do something else with our lives. What's the point of engaging with development work when you're compromising to such an extent that you're not really doing it anyway? There have been donors who have tried to bend us into the project mode of operation, and we have refused their money, not because we had alternative sources but because then the game would not be worth the candle.

Strategic coherence, for CDRA, has always been paramount; and it has refused project funding except on grounds when it would not compromise this stance. The vehemence of CDRA's argument, and its inherent rationality, has often forced donors' hands simply because it has refused the conventional wisdom which has it that NGO's, as beggars, cannot be choosers. We have demanded an intelligent relationship with our donors, and we have been rewarded by having intelligent donors, who are often even prepared to go against the dictates of their agencies, and who have sometimes, as a result, had an instructive influence on the funding policies of their agencies. This is the way things work; it is the approach CDRA has always taken, also with those whom it serves. You have the ability to influence your world; don't think of yourself as a pawn in the game of others. This is a deep underlying message contained within CDRA's approach to development and organizational work, and it plays itself out as much with our donor relationships as it does in our work with clients.

Development, for CDRA, is essentially about people; it is work performed in the realm of relationships. It has everything to do with authenticity; anything less is technique, which brings us back to the engineering approach. CDRA has carried that approach, that way of being, perhaps, into its relationships with its donors. It has always tried to relate from a place of authenticity – transparency, honesty, equality, rigour – and it has been rewarded through having authentic relationships with donors. Where this has failed, it has simply failed, and we have fallen out of relationship, and we have moved on. But it's very dangerous for NGOs to think that they are subservient, unable to influence. The truth is, I believe, that it is that very thinking which creates the subservience. I find it remarkable that the higher you go in the donor hierarchy, the more the donors themselves will complain that their hands are tied. The closer to the centre, the closer to the source of power, it seems, the more powerless people become. This is a dynamic which CDRA has been obliged to explore in some depth. In the development world, it sometimes feels as though everyone thinks of themselves as a pawn. The only way to move beyond this dynamic is to move beyond it...and not sit around waiting for circumstances to change.

CDRA has always assumed that it has something to contribute. This is another reason for the different dynamic with donors. CDRA has had funding for its learning processes partly because it has engaged seriously with those processes and has tried to share its learning – unadulterated, transparent and honest – with the outside world. Thus it has proved the value of the funding, not by ticking off quantitative indicators in a logical framework but by making sense. It's surprising (or not) how much sense it makes, to make sense!

Conclusions

The case studies presented in this chapter illustrate the range of relationships in funding that are emerging in SA. NGOs vary in their dependency on external funding. Some SA NGOs experience their relationships with donors – and intermediaries – as the recipients of directives and conditions, with the corollary imposition of tools designed to control and depoliticize development processes; these relationships are similar to those that characterize many NGOs and donors in Uganda. There are also alternatives. Some of these alternatives emerged out of the explicit and informed resistance of key actors in SA organizations, and sometimes out of equal intent on the part of international representatives. These alternatives bring questions of learning, reflecting and creating space for dialogue and for action to the fore. In all cases they are moving against powerful tendencies, and there remains a strong reluctance to look critically at the tools and conditions used widely in the largest and most powerful funding agencies.

A number of key themes became apparent. Foreign funding organizations have the potential to affect the identity and operational focus of SA NGOs, either directly – through the availability of funding for certain programmes or explicit requests for programme or organizational developments – or indirectly. This can be seen as coercion to conform to the dominant norms. The extent to which such changes are welcomed or anticipated by local organizations is crucial to the success of the relationship, and ultimately to the developmental impact of the organization.

The capacity of NGOs in SA to negotiate the terms of funding, including the programme approach and the tools used to manage it, are affected by the leadership of the organization, and also by the commitment of other stakeholders to that leadership. The commitment of staff and other stakeholders – board members, a key donor, a government division, or beneficiaries – to a vision and set of principles that can help guide an organization's work and relationships are crucial. The commitment of parties to a relationship of funding may take radically different forms, with expectations and the sense of partnership varying accordingly. It can be defined primarily by a funding relationship, a concern to maximize capacity for delivery or political influence, by a model of organizational empowerment and capacity building, or by a mutual learning approach. The quality of communication, mutual governance, a willingness to support the partner and an engagement with learning – perhaps in unanticipated ways – are elements that appear fundamental to improving development practice and its ultimate outcomes.

CHAPTER 10
Listening to the past and building a new future

Other research supports our findings, which are relevant globally

The questions raised by this research took the team and the authors into so many different issues and challenges. The scale of the development project is vast and any research can only lift the veil and shine a light on to part of the story; this research focused primarily on the aid policies and procedures of disbursement and accountability. The research led to findings that have a lot in common with other researchers thinking about these issues, and the voices heard were strikingly similar in the different countries that have been the subject of this kind of research (Mawdsley et al., 2002; Brehm, 2001). The similarity of the findings across Africa, Asia and Latin America, based on listening to key players in the aid chains of development funding, reveals how critical the issues are, and yet these findings appear largely ignored, and even resisted, by both academics and practitioners. Any problems identified are usually assumed to be ones that can be rectified through tweaking the existing policies and procedures, for example by revising the guidelines, promoting alternative approaches alongside the dominant procedures, and adding training or workshops or consultations on to the existing forms and logistics of aid. Yet the research showed, beyond doubt, that the current rules governing funding for civil society have a profound effect on the way the majority of NGOs go about their business, and they do not address some of the fundamental challenges at the heart of development practice for achieving justice and poverty reduction.

The research highlighted the range of dominant approaches to development being employed by the major donors in the UK and largely adopted by UK NGOs and staff, and their partner organizations they work with in the south. Comparative research and our own findings show that the patterns of behaviour identified apply well beyond UK and are commonly found in many donor–recipient development aid chains round the world. The issues are global, not only of relevance to UK-generated aid relationships.

The key findings concerning the policies and procedures of the aid chain

The constantly evolving nature of aid and the changing volumes of funding spent through civil society in the north and the south were clear, as were the current characteristics of that aid: strategic focus, rigorous control of and accounting for aid, and identifying a quantifiable measurable impact. Meeting global targets is paramount, and increasingly funding for NGOs is closely tied to the MDGs and the agendas of the donors and governments trying to meet them. However, when tracing the progress of this aid through the aid chain the importance of history, politics and culture were highlighted and the concept of globally relevant and applicable goals became problematic. The need for a careful attention to context and the role of human agency in these global systems, which question their relevance and approach, came through the survey interviews, the literature review and the deeper case studies.

In spite of the underlying the variations and differences, the evidence showed that donor and internationally led approaches were strong and powerful, having a significant and at times overwhelming influence on what NGOs (north and south) did and the way they did it, almost regardless of country, the mission and the mandate of the NGO itself. The systems developed to address donor concerns about how to understand and have some control over what is happening often thousands of miles away, in contexts where corruption is often a fact of life, and where past development expectations have not been met, have a profound effect on the work of the UK NGO sector and the NGOs they partner overseas. These partners encounter major tensions and contradictions in trying to meet the needs of those at the top of the funding stream, who control the access to funding, while also trying to respond to those they are supposed to work closely with, to find locally appropriate ways to address poverty. These systems create major difficulties for staff at all levels of the aid chain who are involved in trying to turn these policies and procedures into good development practice. Yet they are now virtually universal and set the conditions that few NGOs feel able to challenge: many comply with them, accepting them as the global norm, and rarely question them at all, while others see their deep flaws but feel compelled to comply in order to continue to access funding and exist. In all three contexts a small number of agencies or individuals did stand up to be counted and openly voiced their opposition to the dominant ways of funding and accounting for development aid.

Indeed, challenging these dominant systems is increasingly hard for practitioners, as the policies and procedures become firmly entrenched. It is now almost heresy to ask whether logframes actually do what is expected of them, whether upward accountability is as critical as accountability to the poor, whether the endless frameworks, guidelines and training delivered from the top to the bottom of the aid chain are what is really needed. There is an almost invisible and little analysed bias towards valuing and favouring the systems, documentation and approaches that are developed in the north and are only really accessible to top-level staff in the south. The accompanying detailed explanations, models and practices privilege these approaches over the local knowledge, concepts, language ability and understanding of civil society of staff and local organizations in the south which are often verbally communicated and hard to capture in a system that relies so heavily on documentation.

Certainly there are many weaknesses and challenges at all levels of the aid chain, from the bottom to the top, and knowledge is not the exclusive domain of any level or any organization, but local NGOs have to learn the new aid paradigms if they want to be included and funded. It is interesting that there are no similar requirements for donors and international agencies to learn the local language, political economy or cultural norms as an integral part of their work, to enable them to be sure that their paradigms are appropriate and will support positive change.

The research showed the extent of the compliance with these dominant norms, however hard they were to use in practice. The concepts of coercion and compliance were useful in highlighting how these approaches set the scene and why they are adopted in spite of the evidence of the problems they can create for practitioners. There was of course also evidence of resistance and opposition, and individuals and some agencies did adapt aspects of the current aid procedures to better fit their aims. The commitment of many NGOs and individuals in them to high ideals of solidarity, poverty reduction, inclusion and justice remain, but the way that aid has over the past 10–15 years become big business, with clear rules of engagement, competition and success, threatens at times to undermine the very purposes of these organizations. Some critics have accused the researchers of believing in a golden age of NGOs and harking back to memories of a past that never in fact existed. That is not the case; the faults and flaws in NGO practice over the years have been clear and well documented and many of the current attempts are designed to rectify past failures. What has changed beyond doubt, though, is the shifting commitment of NGOs, especially in UK. There has been a major shift away from raising funds independently from the giving public, towards a drive for major growth, which requires accessing institutional and donor funds globally. This in turn involves raising the profile of the NGO, often through marketing (and this is also a by-product of advocacy work), seeking contracts and working much more with governments, donors and multilateral agencies to change the global policy context rather than focusing on meeting the needs of poor people more directly or through supporting those who work with them. The most recent moves have been to work with and accept funding from the private sector, something some INGOs pursue aggressively now with joint marketing ventures.

NGOs have undergone major changes, especially the large and very large ones. Some have shifted out of direct operational work into partnership, others have moved away from development work as their primary purposes into emergency and global advocacy work. There is evidence of huge competition between them for media coverage, funding and being included in international debates and conferences. Many have opened offices across the north, others have formed alliances of all their branches, and there is evidence of a constant search for new sources of funding. Many smaller and medium-sized NGOs started in response to donor funding during the boom time of funding for civil society, and were allowed a relatively free rein in where and how they worked. Over time they have found their autonomy increasingly squeezed as donors have taken over more of the development agenda in an effort to meet their strategic targets. Some are finding it impossible to survive in the new aid context, with increasing funding going to fewer larger consortia and NGOs, more being spent directly in Africa, the rise of contracting and the need to increasingly conform to the MDG agenda.

So while no golden age is posited, there is certainly a recognition by the authors that these massive shifts in the aid architecture have had huge implications for UK NGOs, and the terrain is totally different from when the research first started in the mid-1990s. INGOs have responded differently to these changes according to their size, the driving focus of their leadership and their understanding of what will best facilitate sustainable changes for the poor. These responses, especially to the changing funding agendas, have had a major impact on where they find their legitimacy, their lines of accountability and their autonomy, which have been altering significantly in recent years. So too have their roles and their relationships to official aid. Whether or not these changes do enable them to have a greater impact on addressing poverty remains an open question and one which exercises both donors and INGOs greatly now, perhaps because greater impact would vindicate their decisions and the changes they have made to adapt to the global aid structures. What is already clear, however, is that these changes mean INGOs have become an integral part of the global aid business in new ways, and this has had major implications for the way most INGOs work with the aid requirements, both in UK and with their partners in the south.

Tracing these changes and their effects on behaviour through the aid chain inevitably brought the researchers up against the issue of power. Power is acknowledged to be an issue in international development in donor and INGO circles, but usually quickly glossed over (with some exceptions, e.g. the work of Groves and Hinton, 2004); such an approach proved impossible in this research, where the power of individuals and agencies to make demands and give or withhold funding, recognition and inclusion in policy circles was so clear. At every level, from the top down, demands are made that affect – both positively and negatively – what is done at the next level down. There are real sanctions for refusing to play by the current rules that come down the aid chain: reputations can be tarnished, money withdrawn, places at the top table of development debates refused. Those at the bottom of the chain rarely have similar power to exert, and the great pressure for upward accountability that was so clearly seen held sway largely we believe because of where power lay, not because those at the top necessarily had better answers to the deep and challenging problems of development work.

The current systems are changing and evolving, but interestingly were seen to have been built firmly on foundations that have been questioned for a long time, inside and outside development, and which some key donor staff believed would disappear at the end of the 1990s, because of their well-known flaws. Instead, the reality of a universal core set of tools is undeniable. The experience of developing the logframe and later reporting against it is acknowledged as the critical way of accessing and accounting for funding, although many complained and said these systems are becoming increasingly burdensome.

The research showed that many staff in both the north and south complained that they felt more like bureaucratic aid administrators than development workers and that more time was spent on paperwork than development. Indeed, staff on the frontline, staff with extensive field experience, staff engaging with these procedures while trying to work with local realities all said that the tools do not work once implementation starts. There were no exceptions; this was a really striking finding. The disjuncture between the paper-based plans, objectives, activities and indicators and the day-to-day realities that poor people and NGO staff try to grapple with in a wide range of different contexts and cultures is too great to be bridged. The paper-based plans and timetables are left in the office, while NGO staff try to find ways – many innovative, others very inappropriate – to work with poor communities, marginalized groups and the neglected. They then revert to the written tools again when it comes to reporting and accounting for donor aid money; often one set of people do the frontline development activities, while others complete the required paperwork. More time, training and focus are given in most aid chains to ensuring that managers and finance staff can complete the documentation to a satisfactory level, than is given to training frontline staff. Yet the evidence shows their deep need for support and training on issues as diverse as understanding the meaning and shape of gender inequality in different cultures, listening to the most disadvantaged, finding ways to give excluded people the confidence to join in development activities, and how best to develop trust and good communication with groups, individuals and communities that have so long been bypassed by development.

The research showed that aid chain presented at the start of the book looks, in practice, more like Figure 10.1.

There is a fracture between the documented targets, plans, timelines and indicators of how to work to ensure the expected outcomes, and the work that is actually undertaken. The plans and guidelines often prove irrelevant at best, distorting at worst, and do little to support or enhance the development work being undertaken. The tools dominate and often mean that, in fact, development staff report on and account for aid funding against the paperwork, rather than analysing the challenges and reporting on their learning from the rough-and-tumble of the implementation phase. Such learning does take place among communities, frontline staff and sometimes their managers and visitors to the project, but the complex relationships, cultural subtleties, discoveries and insights developed through the work often fall outside the original plans and so are not usually included in the reporting up the aid chain. While donors and INGOs insist they want to learn from reality and constantly ask NGOs to report on failures and problems and what they have learned on the ground, as well as try to prove they have met the expectations of the logframe, in fact the way the systems are structured and embedded mean that staff feel more confident about reporting against the logframe and are afraid to venture out into the contradictions, tensions or ups-and-downs of experience. As those doing the

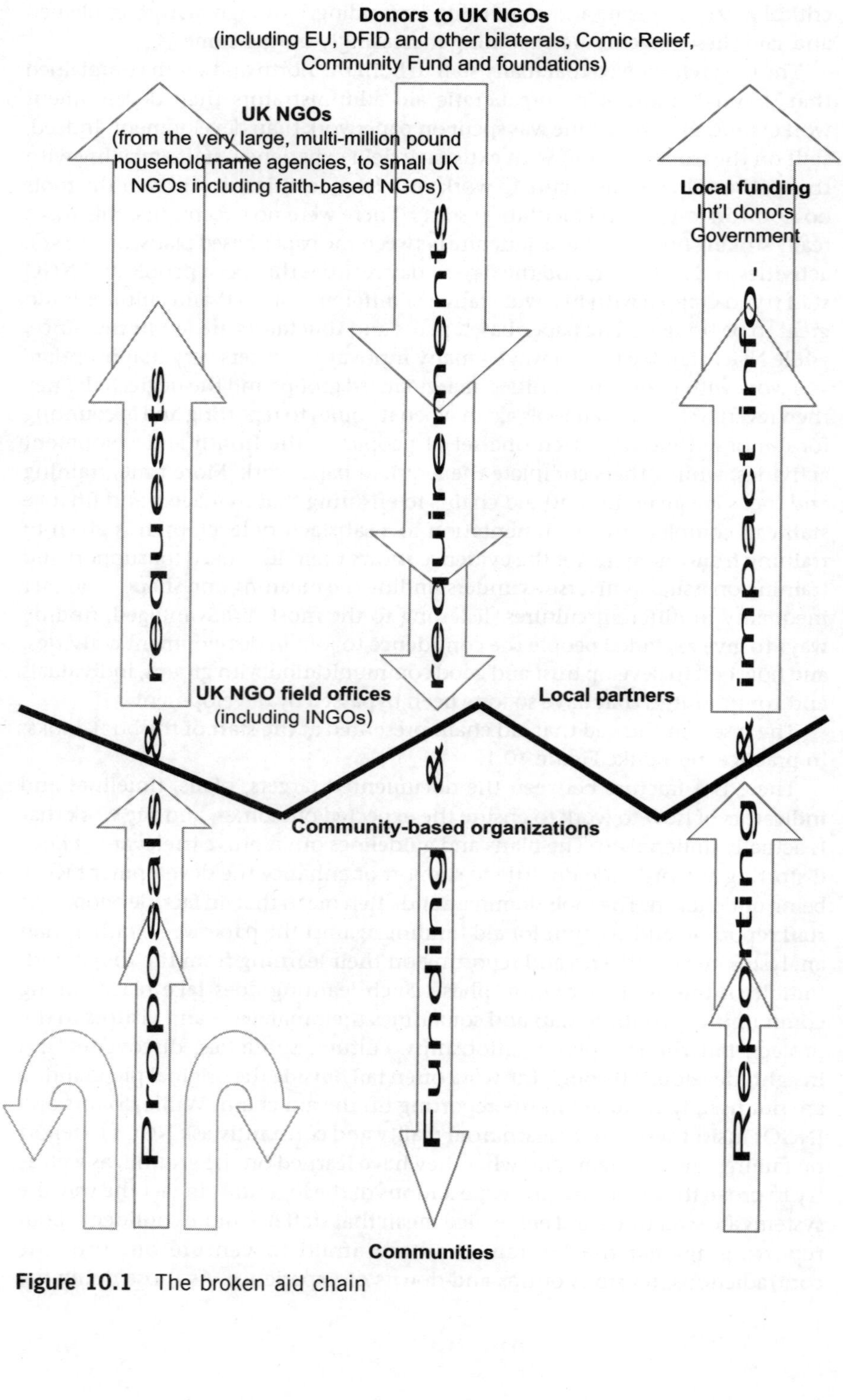

Donors to UK NGOs
(including EU, DFID and other bilaterals, Comic Relief,
Community Fund and foundations)

UK NGOs
(from the very large, multi-million pound
household-name agencies, to small UK
NGOs including faith-based NGOs)

Local funding
Int'l donors
Government

requests

requirements

impact info.

UK NGO field offices
(including INGOs)

Local partners

Community-based organizations

Proposals &

& Funding

Reporting &

Communities

Figure 10.1   The broken aid chain

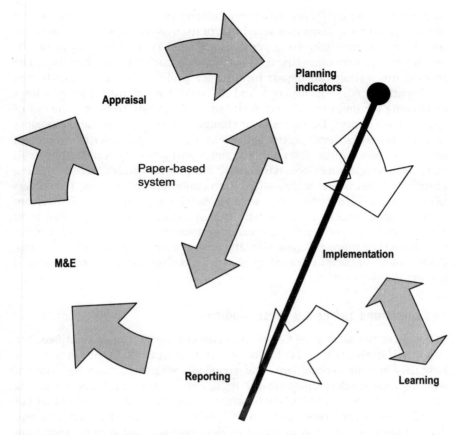

Figure 10.2 The project management cycle in reality

work are often not those writing the reports and reports get doctored up the chain to ensure future donor confidence and funding, the chances of reporting becoming more honest seem unlikely in the near future. The systems and reward structures for NGO staff usually prevent the voices of those on the frontline reaching the distant funders.

Although some of the small and medium-sized donors really do want to hear more directly from the field and learn about the real challenges, successes and failures of the work on the ground, the dominant systems means that few, except the smallest and most inexperienced – often diaspora organizations – find they can break out of the patterns of planning and reporting that have become so familiar and widely accepted.

The conditions for accessing and reporting on donor funding, especially bilateral and multilateral, set norms that have become dominant and do not allow for local flexibility, even though NGOs are working in the most difficult contexts, in diverse cultures facing very different problems. Within this way of disbursing aid most donors are searching for innovative work, something new, something exciting, forgetting perhaps that what is familiar to them can be new for villagers encountering the ideas and approaches for the first time. The rush to innovation can bypass funding for projects developed slowly and participatively, where local people and NGO staff have identified the best ways of working for them in their context; but these happen to have gone out of fashion with donors. Donor fashions change continuously, as they reconsider what works best for development, with the swings through gender, environment, scaling up, innovation, sustainability, rights and advocacy well known to all working in development. NGOs that fail to meet the new and constantly shifting criteria find themselves marginalized from major funding sources. The drivers of change in understanding what works in development are rarely drawn from the evidence or experience of the field, that of communities and frontline staff; they are more often driven by the changing bureaucratic needs of donor agencies and those they fund, and new thinking emerging from think-tanks and large development agencies engaged in global discussions on how to define and achieve development.

The questions raised by these findings

Many questions were raised for the researchers by the key trends identified. The first was, if the tools do not enhance or enable better work on the ground, why have they become so dominant? The second was what impact did these ways of working have on development work itself, and the possibilities of enhancing the development expertise of civil-society organizations. A third major area of concern was heard repeatedly: isn't this research rather depressing and demoralizing for those committed to development and poverty reduction through civil-society organizations? Don't these findings promote cynicism and despondency, and so – by implication – shouldn't they be ditched? The book closes with a reminder about the different practices that do exist, and highlights what can be drawn from these and the research findings to guide development work in new ways in the future.

Understanding the dominance of these tools

In some ways it was hard for the researchers to understand why a set of tools, based on approaches to planning, development and change that have been so questioned and discredited over decades, has come to dominate aid funding processes. While it was possible to locate the rational management approach to change and the concept of change as being a controlled process where inputs lead causally to the expected outputs and then to the desired targets and outcomes within the wider political context of the UK, it was not really possible to go further to understand why this is the dominant paradigm in the UK and elsewhere in Europe and the US at the start of the 21st century.

The thinking clearly has been shaped by the concepts of rational economic man and behaviour, whereby people are understood to behave in rational and predictable ways to meet their best interests. There is a wide literature and public management practice to support this view, although the concept of the rational man has been widely questioned by many economists, and some are very aware of the irrational aspects of human behaviour and patterns of behaviour. Other influences include the broad effects of Newtonian science on thinking in general and social and organizational thinking in particular, where things tend to be understood by trying to break them down into their component parts. The focus on the working of the parts can make it difficult to see the whole and work with complex issues such as interrelationships. The research looked at a range of other theories and approaches that support the rational management approach to controlled change to try to situate this thinking within the wider context.

Without going too deeply into the history of thought concerning change and human behaviour, the research was able to trace the relationship between the current development tools and the dominant political and managerial paradigms in the UK. These focus on centralized targets, performance standards and measurement, and tight documentation, in preference to support for professionals to work in ways that appear to them the most appropriate in any specific context. Trust in the judgement of those doing the work and local decision-making and responsibility are replaced by structures of command and control. While heavily critiqued by some important commentators, and deeply resisted and disliked by public and voluntary sector workers, the rational management paradigm does currently shape UK public and NGO work cultures, and development thinking broadly reflects and promotes these approaches in quite uniform ways in diverse cultures across the globe.

The way the tools shape the work

A number of the major findings that emerged from the research have implications for the way development work, funded by external aid, is currently undertaken by civil society in the north and the south. The use of these dominant frameworks has certainly had direct effects on the relationships built between northern and southern NGOs, their priorities and the work they undertake; this was the case in spite of the room for manoeuvre available to individuals and organizations in different contexts, with different values and levels of confidence. The inequalities inherent in the funding relationships between agencies in the north and in the south have not been ameliorated by the use of these tools; rather these tools seem to exacerbate the hierarchy of power in many ways. They ensure the tools are adopted because those with power require them, they privilege the concepts and procedures carried in these tools over local ideas of how to plan and work, and they are used even when local realities show they do not and cannot help to improve the development work being undertaken.

The range of implications is discussed briefly here, drawing from the evidence of the fieldwork. First, southern NGOs have to learn these tools, which are complex and time-consuming. A great deal of training is given and even then the tools are not always easy to use. The tools favour external concepts and approaches to planning change over local concepts and ways of thinking, and the inbuilt bias towards the control and power of the donors is evident. Certain aspects of the frameworks especially disadvantage southern players: the fact that they have to be written and submitted in English, the detailed reporting requirements and the tight timetables which rarely match the stop-start nature of development which is, in reality, so deeply affected by political instability, climate, resource availability, staff turnover, and illness (especially HIV/AIDS). Staff and communities find themselves working to timetables that do not fit their own experience, translating local concepts into English for reporting, or worse, using English terms that they do not well understand and which cannot be translated but are required by the documentation. All across Africa conversations in the vernacular are dotted with English words, which are possibly, by now, universally known to rural communities that have contact with development agencies – gender, strategic planning, rights, advocacy – but which often have little meaning to those using them.

In these ways the balance of power is tilted further in favour of the donors, who already hold the inevitable advantage of having the financial and other resources, including knowledge of the global development agenda, comparative perspectives on work in each country, communications and access to key development players, all largely denied to all but a handful of NGOs in the south. Donor and international knowledge, perspectives, language and demands are privileged over those of NGO staff and communities living and working in Africa. Far from following the exhortation of Chambers in 1997 to put the last first and to ensure that the voices of those most affected shape the development agendas, the rational management approaches ensure that these voices are often excluded and the thinking and understanding of those with more power fill the space.

Second, the time spent on these tools takes time away from training and attention to how to do development work, including, for example, exploring methodologies for better engaging with local people, enabling staff to work to develop their skills and confidence so local people can better address their own problems, learning to listen, understanding the complex and hierarchical nature of communities as well as the wider national context, and learning how to be responsive and flexible and ensure good communication between NGOs and beneficiaries. While gender training and training in PRA and other methodologies for development are undertaken, the research showed that the time spent on these is usually much less than the time spent ensuring southern NGOs can meet the bureaucratic demands of the planning and reporting cycle of project management.

Third, the focus on logframes and working to preset indicators undoubtedly biases the reporting towards showing how the indicators have been met, rather than learning from experience. The realities of fieldwork and the learning that takes place among frontline staff are often not easy to fit into the planning and reporting formats. This is, perhaps, one reason why the hoary chestnut of learning still evades so many NGOs: the skills, attitudes and knowledge needed for learning from experience are different from those needed to report against expected changes, which seem to carry within them the inevitable pressure to prove success wherever possible to ensure future donor funding and confidence. Learning may – or may not – be taking place on the ground, but often that learning is tangential or unexpected and there is no requirement, or even space, to talk about it in most of the reporting formats.

Some southern NGOs can work within these constraints and still find innovative ways of working, some northern-based INGOs work hard to do much of the aid bureaucracy themselves, freeing up their partners' time for more important work in service delivery, networking, advocacy and finding ways to empower people who are poor and marginalized. But many find the demands of the project cycle management system heavy; they take time away from the development work that NGO staff, especially local people, are supposed to be doing.

It would seem that while the commitment of most NGOs is, according to their missions and mandates, to address poverty, often through building strong autonomous and vibrant civil societies, able to express the interests of the poor, challenge inequalities, call governments to account and provide services which otherwise are unavailable, the tools being used at best do not enhance their ability to fulfil these commitments well, and at worst may make their fulfilment less likely. The time taken to meet the documentation requirements of development aid requires that southern NGOs become more skilled in writing and bureaucratic activities, and staff feel that they are judged more on their paperwork than on what they actually do and how well they relate and work on the ground. These top-down requirements and the pressure for upward compliance and accountability undermine many aspects of the partnerships that INGOs seek out and crave to develop with southern agencies. They also affect the ability of southern NGOs to relate well to their communities as they struggle to understand and meet the externally driven demands: the time taken to ensure donor conditions are met takes time away from local discussions and negotiations over whether the best approaches are being used and what the priorities are for local NGOs and communities, and developing alternative ways of thinking about and accounting for the work. Although many NGOs in Africa are involved in initial consultations before project planning, they all too often find that the final logframe that has been funded has changed and no longer properly reflects their perceptions and priorities, or those of the people they are trying to work with. Some, indeed, find it easier to simply respond to changing international agendas and spend little time listening to or working with their intended beneficiaries or participants. Subsequently, they find that implementing plans that have been negotiated far from them or developed in response to new aid agendas is challenging, and the process can seriously undermine their sense of ownership of the work, of being a real partner and their legitimacy if the plans are too far away from the expectations and priorities of those they work with and seek to represent.

The disconnect between the work that development requires – often slow, building trust over time, in complex contexts of entrenched and deep poverty and inequality – and the paper trail that is self-reinforcing was evident in many interviews. The mismatch between the core tools of aid disbursement and the stated purposes of that aid perhaps explains why NGOs are still agonizing over issues of legitimacy, effectiveness, learning, participation, the nature and meaning of partnerships and the value of aid to civil-society organizations years after these issues were first raised as major challenges. Their aspirations and commitments are poorly served by the terms and conditions under which they access much of their funding.

While there is increasing work by INGOs and donors on standards and strategies for development, and everyone repeats their commitment to partnership, the need for local ownership and control, the importance of participation as an end as well as a means to democratic working (these values and approaches are evident in almost every INGO strategic plan and, for example, in the Sphere standards for humanitarian aid), in fact the core tools that govern aid disbursement do not support these. Instead their bias is towards promoting upward accountability, favouring the skills and knowledge of the north over the south; they are written in a language most of those affected cannot understand, and use concepts of change, time, efficiency and effectiveness which are culturally alien and rarely well explained. Indeed, some commentators, like Apthorpe (2003), have said that the written tools currently in use have created a fantasy 'aidland' or 'lala land', a developing country which has no history, geography or culture, where standard inputs can be turned into predicted and desired outcomes in a causally linked and apparently unproblematic way. The external players who have the power know best what will work and how development should be undertaken to achieve the desired ends.

The new DFID logframe governing direct budget support to governments certainly fits this description well, where the expected goals of poverty reduction, accountable government and a vibrant civil society are causally linked to direct budgetary inputs by arrows showing a linear progress of several steps of what this support can reasonably be expected to deliver in all contexts; local differences, political and economic as well as social and cultural, are only seen as elements that might affect the process achieving the laid-out goals (Lawson and Booth, 2004). However, and unsurprisingly, the early evaluations of direct budget support have shown that, in fact, the desired ends do not emerge automatically following its application, and the context matters greatly in affecting what actually happens. Local people may resist or misunderstand the process; they may do things differently; their responses and different perspectives may mean that the expected outcomes do not, in fact, ever occur. The logframe largely ignores the role of civil society but assumes that a vibrant civil society, along with strengthened local institutions and systems, will emerge once governments feel themselves to be in charge of national poverty agendas and decentralized planning structures (all requirements for receiving direct budget support) are in place. In fact the roles assigned implicitly to NGOs in the direct budget support paradigm are contradictory and inherently likely to weaken the independence of NGOs, and it is hard to see where or how a new vibrant civil society will be supported. It potentially offers a further threat to the NGO sectors in the countries where it is implemented.

In spite of the evidence that assumptions and causal links are so often not valid in practice, this way of thinking and planning persists, and the research showed that it undermines the building of strong relationships and partnerships, real participation, learning and openness to new experiences. In Uganda the rigours of the logframe and the associated procedures weighed heavily on many NGOs and cut across their communication, trust and relationships with their donors. In SA this was also the case for many NGOs, but perhaps as much or even more worrying was the multiple conditionality of donors, especially their demands for working in networks and addressing HIV/AIDS. Both were being imposed with little understanding of the context, the constraints, the different agendas and aims of the NGOs there, causing some real problems in implementing these issues in practice.

But isn't this all very depressing?

The research has been widely presented in the UK and Uganda especially, with some seminars held also in SA. Interestingly, the participants from the south, especially in Uganda, found the research reflected their experiences, and they found it energizing to have open discussions about things that they are usually grappling with behind closed doors. For them, learning about the wider changes in the aid architecture and the changing UK context was important and opened their eyes to many issues they knew little about, especially the pressures on donors and INGOs, the changing global context and the evolving development agendas of the most powerful development agencies. These they are largely unaware of, and are rarely involved in; the lack of knowledge, even among staff of INGOs, about the wider aid context was in some ways shocking and highlighted the lack of information from their UK offices. They saw themselves in the case studies and the broad findings presented here. They also understood that donors and INGOs are grappling with complex problems of distance, corruption and a lack of evidence of positive change, and had some sympathy with their attempts to maintain control over the funds and how they are used.

They also acknowledged that they have a set of strategies to deal with the constantly changing demands connected to external aid funding. These range from willing compliance and buy-in, in order to get a place at the table and access as much funding as possible, to silent resistance, late reports or poor accounting for example. Some of this is due to lack of skills and capacity, but sometimes it reflects hostility and a lack of willingness to accept all the rules of the funding game. In Uganda the colonial image of 'black faces, white masks' was used several times to describe the negative aspects of the relationships that were being created around aid funding. Yet always there were exceptions, organizations or individuals who break through the current norms and ways of interacting and relating to build good friendships and relations of trust and mutuality, where listening, respect and negotiation allow for more flexible and appropriate ways of working in difficult contexts. In SA there was a greater sense that some INGOs and donors were trying to find ways to lift the heavy burden of these tools to allow different and more productive ways of working to develop, but lack of time and long distances often prevented these coming to fruition. Some NGOs in SA had the confidence and competence to challenge and even reject some of the terms and conditions of funding and found spaces for exploring and developing very different concepts and tools. A few in Uganda were also taking this path, although the constraints of accessing funding in Uganda and the more limited contact with international debates made that a hard choice. Some raised their awareness about the issues through this research and were planning to rethink their tools and approaches in future.

So, from our experiences of presenting the findings in the south, the research was in no way depressing. It has been described as informative, enlightening, even empowering, enabling NGOs to understand better the aid context and where they might be able to negotiate harder and challenge some of the rules further. They said that their many and diverse experiences were captured, and that within their diversity they recognized the dominant trends being presented, which do impact heavily on them. They learned a lot from the research, as did the researchers, and it is hoped that debates started can continue, especially exploring where Ugandan NGOs can find more room for manoeuvre within the aid chain.

It is donors and NGOs in the UK and other European countries where the research has been discussed that say the findings are depressing. They feel undermined by the feedback from southern NGOs, and do not see themselves in the research; it does not represent their perception of their role in the aid chain, or at least the role they discuss in public. The responses have been far more mixed in private discussions, as happened in phase 1, where the researchers learned that in respecting confidentiality they had to listen to public challenges about their findings from the very individuals who had in fact provided the information being presented. In public fora UK NGOs talk of their partnerships as much more equal than they appear in the research findings, of the rational management tools they use being much more useful in focusing and sharpening thinking, and of the possibility of doing logframes in responsive and participatory ways. They detail the many and diverse methodologies and modifications they have developed to supplement and support the project cycle management approach. They have poured time, energy and commitment into finding ways to meet donors' and trustees' requirements for control and evidence of change, while ensuring that there is real participation, local accountability and learning on the ground. The feedback that these are not really working well in many cases was not welcomed. The challenges of trying to ensure upward and downward accountability, of trying to work with the necessary tensions between participatory approaches and logframes, of managing the inherent conflicts between offices based in London and staff and partners in the field were in fact experienced by many staff in the UK, especially those closer to the programme work. But they believed that it was possible to work well with these contradictions and tensions, and in public they are usually put to one side rather than put squarely on the table.

The language of partnership is widely used in the UK NGO sector, but much more rarely in the south. The way it is used covers the full spectrum of relationships, from those of contractor to subcontractor and donor to client through to those that really do build on mutual respect, listening and learning together. Being challenged openly to look at what is happening in practice around participation, partnership, representation, power and control is not comfortable or welcomed, although the evidence showed that they are all freely discussed internally in NGOs of all sizes and mandates in UK. The lack of transparency about these problems and the concerns of many INGOs are clear from the demands for confidentiality in the research. The issues are known and often analysed in depth internally, but agencies that discussed their disquiet about what they saw happening in the aid chain in private did not want to be named in open workshops or in the written research. This problem is hard to tackle without breaking the promised confidentiality.

Of course this research did not cover every angle, every relationship, every exception – far from it. It is only one step in the process of trying to understand the impact and influence of the way NGOs access and use their funding from institutional and other donors on development. It raised new questions and echoed those raised by others in recent years, who also find themselves largely ignored. However, the research certainly showed the need for far more openness, discussion and research about the relationships and realities in the aid chain. To us what was depressing was this denial in public of many of the problems that certainly do exist in the current aid paradigm and are shared in private. It is hard to see how there can be any shifts or positive changes unless the situation that exists is analysed and discussed, rather than denied. The cynicism that is certainly rife in development circles comes less from a critical analysis of what is going on in many though not all aid chains and more, in our view, from the denial that there are any real problems. The evidence is there, not only from the voices and experiences of development workers in the south, but also from the reality that INGOs are still grappling with core concerns about their role, their relationships with donors and governments, where their legitimacy should derive from, the meaning of participation and partnership and how to promote real learning in contexts of strict accountability regimes.

There were of course examples of good and better practice, which certainly offer pointers for the future. But two of the issues arising from the research experience gave cause for special concern. The first was the fact that the perspectives of northern and southern NGOs were very often far apart, revealing huge gaps in communication. These gaps were also seen in INGOs' relationships with their back donors. While some argued that the southern NGOs took the researchers for a ride and enjoyed portraying themselves as victims, and some donors said the same of the INGOs, the substance of the findings went far beyond that kind of manipulation. Some INGOs did recognize the feedback and had much closer and more responsive relations with their southern partners, but many flatly denied the findings. The second was the desire to keep these issues away from the public gaze and discuss things privately; fear of reprisals from trustees, chief executives and donors was apparent, and people felt unable to be disloyal to what they saw as the public image of their organization and its achievements. Yet unless there is more openness and willingness to explore these findings, whatever their limitations, the depressing reality is that the problems are unlikely to be addressed or changed.

Alternative ways of working

The book is not calling for the end of aid or the end of NGOs, far from it, and most of the researchers are still deeply involved in working in the NGO sector in these three case study countries. Rather it has tried to hold up a mirror to the dominant trends that are there, but are perhaps often unquestioned or unacknowledged, to ask whether NGOs should continue to follow the paths deeply established over the past 10 years, or whether the sector as a whole should start to think and act differently. There are many other possible models and ways of thinking and working out there; the research revealed diverse styles of positive leadership and the importance of the role of charismatic and well-informed individuals in questioning the norms. It also found interesting participatory methodologies, and witnessed the radical potential of some of the work, for example in gender, and innovative and creative responses, including those to HIV/AIDS, that were locally rather than externally driven. There were some good examples of local knowledge and international perspectives coming together to create new ways of thinking and working, even where relationships remained uneven.

The finding that individuals can build good working relations in the current system provides interesting food for thought. If partnerships can be built on relations of respect, trust, openness and listening, the question posed is how these skills can best be prioritized in staff selection and training. When local organizations find new and innovative ways of responding to crises and poverty, the challenge is to see how these can be properly built into the responses of the wider international organization. Where partners have insights into local priorities and ways of thinking, it is important to learn about the best ways for INGOs to listen, learn and respond to agencies that are dong this. When INGOs have methods and skills for sharing international knowledge with their partners, enabling them to speak for themselves on the global stage, this is a good approach for others to follow. There were examples of NGOs and individuals doing these things, and there was no lack of good ideas and experiences to build on.

The models and ideas for working with partners, for enabling participation, for ensuring respect, for addressing the complexities of working in culturally appropriate ways to overcome negative traditions, for promoting downward accountability and enabling those most affected to have a say in shaping poverty policies and practices are all to be found across the three NGO sectors, which were rich and diverse. The problem was not one of lack of ideas, experience or innovation, but these remained one-offs or often isolated from the mainstream and were not coming to the fore to replace current aid paradigms. Rather they were struggling to exist alongside the project cycle management requirements, which eat up time and demand different skills. Perhaps this situation will continue until the depth of the problems raised by current ways of disbursing and accounting for aid is recognized and the need for change is accepted.

Recognizing the issues is one step, and one that many individuals and organizations, especially in the south, have taken. Challenging the norms and refusing continuing compliance will be a huge challenge for all NGOs, which work in highly competitive environments where survival and growth – and the increasing need for funding from external donors for this – appear paramount. The context may get harder as donors increasingly focus their aid on governments and expect NGOs, north and south, to fit in with donor targets and national government plans; special funding lines for NGOs are likely to decrease and more of the aid available will probably be tied more tightly to meeting donor strategies. This provides a difficult context for the conclusions emerging for this research, which are that aid systems for supporting NGOs need to change. The dominant aid policies and procedures should be replaced with very different approaches if NGOs are to be enabled to fulfil their commitments to meeting the needs of the world's poor and promoting their rights through building strong, independent and empowered local civil-society organizations. For sustainable change they must be enabled to set and work to agendas appropriate and relevant to their context, and to join the social movements to challenge the wider global, political and economic realities that are so detrimental to combating poverty.

The [illegible] for working with partners. The aim [illegible] for ensuring [illegible] recognising the complexities of working in culturally appropriate ways [illegible], the primarily downward accountability [illegible] practices [illegible] to be found [illegible]. The three NGOs [illegible] which were [illegible] and diverse. The problem was not one of lack of ideas [illegible] but these [illegible] and were [illegible] current aid paradigms. Rather they were struggling to [illegible] the project [illegible] management requirements, which [illegible] time and demand different skills [illegible]. This situation will continue until the [illegible] of the problems [illegible] current ways of disbursing and accounting for aid is recognised and the need for change is accepted.

Recognizing the issues is one step, and one that many individuals and organizations, especially in the South, have taken. Challenging the norms and [illegible] will be a huge challenge for all NGOs, which work in highly competitive environments, where survival and growth – and the increasing need for funding from [illegible] – appear paramount. [illegible] donors increasingly focus their [illegible] and expert NGOs, north and south, to align with [illegible] national government plans, overall funding [illegible] is likely to decrease, and more of the aid available will probably be [illegible] tightly to [illegible]. This provides a difficult context for the conclusions emerging for this research [illegible] and systems [illegible] supporting NGOs need to change. The dominant aid policies and procedures should be replaced with very different approaches, if NGOs are to be enabled to fulfil their commitments to tackling the roots of [illegible] and promoting their rights through building strong, independent and empowered local civil society organizations. For sustainable change they must be enabled to set and work to agendas appropriate and relevant to their context, and to join the social movements to challenge the wider global political and economic realities that are so antithetical to combating poverty.

Appendix

Organizations interviewed for the mid-level survey of NGO-donor relations in South Africa and Uganda (see Figure 1.2 in chapter 1) that were not in the original aid chain sample established in the UK (see Table 1.1 in chapter 1).

A small number of agencies from this sample did form part of the in-depth case study work, because it proved important to include agencies selected in Uganda and SA, as well as agencies that were in the sample based on the UK end of the aid chain, in the deeper study.

In the text none of these agencies are identified, to honour the commitment made to ensure their confidentiality.

AGENCY	Interviewed in SA	Interviewed in UGANDA
Aids Info Centre (AIC)		Yes
AFRA	Yes	
ANCRA	Yes	
Appropriate technology Uganda (AT)		Yes
BESG	Yes	
CDRA		
CDRN		Yes
Charities Aid Foundation	Yes	
Charles Stewart Mott	Yes	
Deniva		Yes
Diakonia Council of Curches	Yes	
Diakonia Sweden	Yes	
Habitat for Humanity International	Yes	
Hurinet (Human Rights Network)		Yes
Living Earth Uganda		Yes
Molteno Project	Yes	
National Union of Disabled Persons in Uganda (NUDIPU)		Yes
NGO Forum		Yes
Non-Profit Partnership	Yes	
Olive (training org)	Yes	
Planact	Yes	
Planned Parenthood Assoc of SA	Yes	
Sedibeng (training org)	Yes	

Straight Talk		Yes
TASO		Yes
Uganda debt network		Yes
Uganda Land Alliance		Yes
Uganda Women's Finance Trust		Yes
Ugandan Women Network (Uwonet)		Yes
UPPAP		Yes
Urban Sector Network	Yes	
USDC		Yes

References

Achmat, Z. (2004) 'HIV/AIDS and human rights: a new South African struggle', John Foster lecture, pp. 1–39, available online at: http://www.nu.ac.za/ccs/default.asp?3,28,10,1434

ActionAid (2001) 'Transforming Power, Participatory Methodologies Forum' papers, ActionAid, London (February).

Albertyn, C. and Hassim, S. (2004) 'The boundaries of democracy: gender, HIV/AIDs and culture', *Development Update*, 4 (4), pp. 137–64.

Altshuler, A. (1965) *The City Planning Process: A political analysis*, Cornell University Press, Ithaca, NY.

Anderson, M. B. (1999) *Do No Harm: How aid can support peace – or war*, Lynne Rienner Publishers, Boulder, CO.

Apthorpe, R. (2003) 'The disorder of development', paper presented at Order and Disjuncture conference at SOAS, London University, London (September).

Barr, A., Fafchamps, M. and Owens, T. (2005) 'The governance of non-governmental organisations in Uganda', *World Development*, 33 (4), pp. 657–79.

Bhorat, H., Leibbrandt, M., Maziya, M., van der Berg, S. and Woolard, I. (2001) *Fighting Poverty, Labour Markets and Inequality in South Africa*, University of Cape Town Press, Cape Town.

Biggs, S. and Smith, S. (2002) 'A paradox of learning in project cycle management and the role of organisational culture', unpublished, University of East Anglia.

Bond, P. (2001) *Against Global Apartheid: South Africa meets the World Bank, IMF and international finance*, University of Cape Town Press, Cape Town.

Bond, P. (2004) *Talk Left Walk Right: South Africa's frustrated global reforms*, University of KwaZulu Natal Press, Durban.

Bornstein, L. (2000) 'The institutional context for poverty alleviation in South Africa', in J. May (ed.), *Poverty and Inequality in South Africa: Meeting the challenge*, pp. 173–206, David Philip and Zed Press, Cape Town.

Bornstein, L. (2003) 'Management standards and development practice in the South African aid chain', *Public Administration and Development*, 23, pp. 393–404.

Bornstein, L. (2005) 'Negotiation, learning and differentiation in SA NGOs', in L. Bornstein (ed.), 'Negotiating aid: UK funders, NGOs and South African development', research monograph, School of Development Studies, University of Natal, Durban.

Bornstein, L. and Fungulane, B. (2000) 'Community-level tensions and conflicts: a study of Gorongosa and Cheringoma', research report, Universidade Catolica, Beira, Mozambique (October).

Bornstein, L., Hyman, I., Nyar, A. and Smith, T. (2004) 'South African NGOs (SA NGOs) and foreign funding: following streams of development finance, influence and impact; South Africa report for the research project on negotiating aid', School of Development Studies, University of Natal, Durban, June.

Bornstein, L. and Munro, W. (2003) 'Agency, space and power: the geometries of post-conflict development', in M.S. Smith (ed.), *Globalizing Africa*, Africa World Press, Lawrenceville, NJ.

Braden, S. (2004) *Participation – A promise unfulfilled?*, ActionAid, London.

Brehm, V.M. (2001) *Promoting Effective North–South Partnerships*, Intrac, Oxford.

Brett, E.A. (1992) *Colonialism and Underdevelopment in East Africa: The politics of economic change*, Ashgate, Aldershot.

Brinkerhoff, D. and Tuthill, J. (1987) *La Gestion Efficace des Projets de Développement*, Kumarian Press, West Hartford, CT.

Brown, G. (2004) Speech to the National Council for Voluntary Organizations (London).

Budlender, D. (1999) 'Human development', in J. May (ed.) *The Poverty Agenda in South Africa: Meeting the challenge*, David Philip and Zed Press, Cape Town, pp. 97–139.

Budlender, D. (2002) *The Third Women's Budget*, Institute for Democracy in South Africa (IDASA), Cape Town.

Camay, P and Gordon, A. (2001) 'Two commas and a full stop: CIVICUS index of civil society South Africa country report', SANGOCO for CORE/IDASA, Braamfontein.

Cernea, M., ed. (1991) *Putting People First: Sociological variables in rural development*, published for the World Bank by Oxford University Press, New York.

Chambers, R. (1997) *Whose Reality Counts? Putting the first last*, Intermediate Technology Publications, London.

Chambers, R. (2004) 'Ideas for development: reflecting forwards', IDS *Working Paper* No. 238, IDS, University of Sussex.

Chambers, R. (2005) *Ideas for Development*, Earthscan, London.

Chapman, J., David, R. and Mancini, A. (2004) 'Transforming practice in ActionAid: experiences and challenges in rethinking learning, monitoring and accountability systems', in L. Earle (ed.), *Creativity and Constraint: Grassroots monitoring and evaluation and the international aid arena*, pp. 137–54, INTRAC, Oxford.

Chapman, J., Pereira Jr, A., Prasad Uprety, L., Okwaare, S., Azumah, V. and Miller V. (2005) 'Action research on planning, assessing and learning in people-centred advocacy: summary of learning', *Advocacy Action Research Working Paper* No. 1, ActionAid International, Johannesburg.

Cornwall, A. (2000) 'Making a difference? Gender and participatory development', IDS *Discussion Paper* No. 378, IDS, University of Sussex.

Cornwall, A. and Welbourn, A. (2002) *Realizing Rights: Transforming approaches to sexual and reproductive well-being*, Zed Books, London.

Cox, A. and Chapman, J. (1999) *The European Community External Cooperation Programmes: Policies, management and distribution*, European Commission, Brussels.

Cracknell, B. (2000) *Evaluating Development Aid: Issues, problems and solutions*, Sage, London.

Crewe, E. and Harrison, E. (1998) *Whose development? An ethnography of aid*, Zed Books, London.

Development Assistance Committee of EU (DAC) (1999) *DAC scoping study of donor poverty reduction policies and practices*, ODI, London.

David, R., Mancini, A. and Newens, M. (2003) 'Report on BOAG meeting on monitoring and evaluation', ActionAid, London

De Coninck, J. and Vadera, M. (2003) 'The untold story: competing cultures in development partnerships. The UPPAP partnerships, "a new way of working in development"?', CDRN and ActionAid Uganda.

Demos (2003) 'Inside out: rethinking inclusive communities', Demos report, Barrow Cadbury Trust, Birmingham (February), available online at: http://www.demos.co.uk/uploadstore/docs/INCO_ft.pdf.

Department for International Development (DFID) (2000) Papers from 'Civil society and national policy, donor policy workshop in Glasgow', DFID, London.

DFID (2002) 'Development Effectiveness Review', draft, DFID, London.

DFID (2003) 'National Audit Office report, 2000–2003', HC 1227, DFID, London.

Dicklich, S. (1998) *The Elusive Promise of NGOs in Africa: Lessons from Uganda*, Macmillan Press, London.

Development Initiatives (2000) 'White paper on globalisation: background note for section 4.1. Roles of NGOs and other charity flows', Development Initiatives, Somerset (July).

Dill, S. (2005) 'PEOPLE, participation and management techniques', in L. Bornstein, (ed.), 'Negotiating aid: UK funders, NGOs and South African development', research monograph, pp. 81–6, School of Development Studies, University of Natal, Durban.

Dorrington, R. Bradshaw, D., Johnson, L. and Budlender, D. (2004) 'The demographic impact of HIV/AIDS in South Africa: national indicators for 2004', Centre for Actuarial Research, South African Medical Research Council and Actuarial Society of South Africa, Cape Town, available online at: http://www.mrc.ac.za/bod/demographic.pdf.

Earle, L. (2003) 'Lost in the matrix: the logframe and the local picture', paper presented at INTRAC Evaluation Conference, The Netherlands.

Earle, L., ed. (2004) *Creativity and Constraint: Grassroots monitoring and evaluation and the international aid arena*, INTRAC, Oxford.

Escobar, A. (1995). *Encountering Development: The making and unmaking of the third world*, Pluto, London.

Esteva, G. (1992) 'Development', in W. Sachs (ed.), *The Development Dictionary: A guide to knowledge as power*, Zed Books, London.

Eyben, R. (2002) 'Patterns of donor behaviour with recipient governments', paper presented at IDS workshop on power and partnerships, IDS, University of Sussex (May).

Fanon, F. (1967, 1991) *Black Skin, White Masks*, Grove, New York.

Ferguson, J. (1990) *The Anti-Politics Machine: Development, depoliticization and bureaucratic power in Lesotho*, Cambridge University Press, Cambridge.

Forester, J. (1999) *The Deliberative Practitioner: Encouraging participatory planning processes*, MIT Press, Cambridge, MA.

Foroohar, R. (2005) 'Where the money is: the $1.6 trillion non-profit sector behaves (or misbehaves) more and more like big business', *New Statesman* (5 September).

Fowler, A. (2000a) 'Beyond partnership: getting real about NGO relationships in the aid system', *IDS Bulletin*, **313**, pp. 1–11.

Fowler, A. (2000b) *The Virtuous Spiral: A guide to sustainability for NGOs in international development*, Earthscan, London.

Fowler, A. and Biekart, K. (1996) 'Do private aid agencies really make a difference?', in D. Sogge (ed.), *Compassion and Calculation*, pp. 107–28, Pluto Press, London.

Fraser, N. (1989) *Unruly Practices: Power, discourse, and gender in contemporary social theory*, Polity Press, Cambridge.

Freire, P. (1972) *The Pedagogy of the Oppressed*, Penguin, London.

Gasper, D. (2000) 'Logical frameworks: problems and potentials', Institute of Social Studies, The Hague (5 September).

Gaventa, J. (1980) *Power and Powerlessness*, University of Illinois Press, Urbana, IL.

Geisler, G., Keller, B. and Norman, A.L. (1999) 'WID/gender units and the experience of gender mainstreaming in multilateral organisations. Knights on white horses?', report submitted to the Norwegian Ministry of Foreign Affairs by Lawyers for Human Rights (LHR) and Chr. Michelsen Institute, available online at: http://odin.dep.no/ud/engelsk/bn.html.

Goldsmith, A. (1996) 'Strategic thinking in international development: using management tools to see the big picture', *World Development*, **24** (9), pp. 1431–9.

Goudge, P. (2003) *The Whiteness of Power: Racism in third world development and aid*, Lawrence & Wishart, London.

Groves, L and Hinton, R., eds (2004) *Inclusive Aid: Changing power and relationships in international development*, Earthscan, London.

Gujit, I. and Shah, M.K., eds (1998) *The Myth of Community*, ITDG Publishing, London.

Habib, A. and Taylor, R. (1999) 'South African anti-apartheid NGOs in transition', *Voluntas*, **10** (1), pp. 73–82.

Hailey, J. (2003) 'Measuring success, issues in performance management', paper presented at the INTRAC Evaluation Conference, The Netherlands (April).

Hansen, H.B. and Twaddle, M., eds (1998) *Developing Uganda*, Fountain Publishers, Kampala, Uganda.

Harding, D. (2002) 'A discourse on strategy and all things strategic', unpublished.

Harding, D. (2004) 'Working effectively with the challenge of organisational change', People in Aid, London.

Harding, D. (2005) 'Organizational development event review for CDRA', unpublished paper, CDRA, South Africa.

Harrison, P., Huchzermeyer, M. and Mayekiso, M., eds (2003) *Confronting Fragmentation: Housing and urban development in a democratizing society*, University of Cape Town Press, Cape Town.

Harrison, R. (1995) 'Steps towards the learning organisation', in R. Harrison, *Collected Papers of Roger Harrison*, McGraw-Hill, London.

Hirsh, J. (2003) 'The state's new clothes: NGOs and the internationalisation of states', *Rethinking Marxism, a Journal of Economics, Culture and Society*, **15** (2), pp. 237–62.

Hofstede, G. (1984) *Culture's Consequences: International differences in work-related values*, Sage, London.

Howes, M. (1992) '*Linking paradigms and practice: key issues in the appraisal, monitoring and evaluation of British NGO projects*', Journal of International Development, **4**, pp. 375–96.

Hulme, D. and Edwards, M. (1997) *NGOs, States and Donors, Too Close for Comfort?*, Macmillan, London.

Hyman, I. (2005) 'Faith and Development and partners', in L. Bornstein (ed.), 'Negotiating aid: UK funders, NGOs and South African development', research monograph, School of Development Studies, University of Natal, Durban.

Interfund (1998) 'Guidelines for good practice for Northern NGOs working in South Africa', *Development Update*, **2** (1), pp. 69–79.

Jahan, R. (1997) *The Elusive Agenda. Mainstreaming women in development*, Zed Books, London.

Kanji, N. (2000) 'An assessment of DFID's engagement with civil society in Uganda: past work and current shifts', working paper, DFID, Uganda.

Kaplan, A. (2000) 'Understanding development as a living process', in D. Lewis and T. Wallace (eds), *New Roles and Relevance: Development NGOs and the challenge of change*, Kumarian Press, West Hartford, CT, pp. 29–38.

Kaplan, A. (2002) *Development Practitioners and Social Process Artists of the Invisible*, Pluto, London.

Kapoor, I. (2002) 'The devil's in the theory: a critical assessment of Robert Chambers' work on participatory development', *Third World Quarterly*, **23** (1), pp. 101–17.

Killick, T. (2004) 'Politics, evidence and the new aid agenda', *Development Policy Review*, **22** (1), pp. 5–29.

Kotzé, H. (1999) 'Swimming in a wild sea: new challenges facing civil society', in G. Maharaj (ed.), *Between Unity and Diversity: Essays on nation-building in post-apartheid South Africa*, Idasa and David Philip, Cape Town, pp. 171–98.

Lawson, A. and Booth, D. (2004) 'Evaluation framework for general budget support', report to management group for the joint evaluation of general budget support, ODI, London.

Lester, A., Nel, E. and Binns, T. (2000) *South Africa: Past, present and future*, Prentice Hall, London.

Lewis, D. (2001) *The Management of Non-Government Development Organisations: An introduction*, Routledge, London.

Lewis, D. (2003a) 'Practice, power and meaning: frameworks for studying organisational culture in multi-agency rural development projects', *Journal of International Development*, **15**, pp. 541–57.

Lewis, D. (2003b) 'Christian Aid external review', report, Christian Aid, London, (September).

Lewis, D. (forthcoming, 2006) *Journal of International Development*, special issue.

Lindblom, C. (1959) 'The science of muddling through', *Public Administration Review*, **19**, pp. 79–88.

Lindenberg, M. and Bryant, C. (2002) *Going Global: Transforming relief and development NGOs*, Kumarian Press, West Hartford, CT.

Lister, S. (2004) 'The future of international NGOs: new challenges in a changing world order', BOND, London (April).

Lister, S. and Nyamugasira, W. (2001) 'A study on the involvement of civil society in policy dialogue and advocacy', DFID, East Africa.

Lockwood, M. (2005) *The State They're In: An agenda for international action on poverty in Africa*, ITDG Publishing, Rugby.

Long, C. (2001) *Participation of the Poor in Development Initiatives: Taking their rightful place*, Earthscan, London.

Long, N. and Long, A. (1992) *Battlefields of Knowledge*, Longmans, London.

Loquai, C. (1998) 'The European Community's approach towards poverty reduction in developing countries', ODI Working Paper, ODI, London.

McEwan, C. (2003) '"Bringing government to the people": women, local governance, and community participation in South Africa', *Geoforum*, **34**, pp. 469–81.

MacIntyre, A. (2002) *After Virtue: A study in moral theory*, Gerald Duckworth, London.

MacLellan, B. (2005) 'Review of J. Seddon, *Freedom from Command and Control*', available online at: www.lean-service.com/5-5.asp.

Maina, W. (1998) 'Kenya: the state, donors and the politics of democratisation', in A. van Rooy (ed.), *Civil Society and the Aid Industry*, Earthscan, London, pp. 133–65.

Marais, H. (2001) *South Africa: Limits to change. The political economy of transition*, Zed Books, London.

Marsden, D. (2003) 'Rights, culture and contested modernities', paper presented at INTRAC Evaluation conference, The Netherlands (April).

Martens, K. (forthcoming, 2006) 'NGOs in the United Nations system: evaluating theoretical approaches', *Journal of International Development.*

Matthews, S. (2003) 'Investigating NEPAD's development assumptions', paper presented at ROAPE conference, University of Birmingham (September).

Mawdsley, E., Townsend, J., Porter, G. and Oakley, P. (2002) *Knowledge, Power and Development Agendas: NGOs north and south*, INTRAC, Oxford.

May, J. ed. (1999) *The Poverty Agenda in South Africa: Meeting the challenge*, David Philip and Zed Press, Cape Town.

Mintzberg, H. (1998) *Readings in the Strategy Process*, Prentice Hall, Englewood Cliffs, NJ.

Mitchie, J. and Padayachee, V. (eds) (1998) *The Political Economy of South Africa's Transition*, Dryden, London.

Mosse, D. (1997) 'The ideology and politics of community participation', in R.D. Grillo and R.L. Stirrat (eds), *Discourses of development: anthropological perspectives*, Berg, Oxford.

Mosse, D. (2005) *Cultivating Development: An ethnography of aid policy and practice*, Pluto, London.

Mosse, D. (n.d.) 'The making and marketing of participatory development', working paper, Department of Anthropology, SOAS, London University.

Muyoya, T. S. (2005) 'Is commitment enough?', Resource Alliance, available online at: http://www.resourcealliance.org/page.php?sectionid=6&subsectionid=28&pageid=17

Nelson, N and Wright, S. (1995) *Power and Participatory Development: Theory and practice*, Intermediate Technology, London.

Nyamugasira, W. and Rowden, R. (2002) 'Do the World Bank PRSC and the IMF's PRSP actually support the poverty reduction goals outlined in Uganda's PEAP?', paper presented at the Uganda NGO forum, Kampala (January).

Nyar, A. (2005) 'HIV/AIDs case study', in L. Bornstein (ed.), 'Negotiating aid: UK funders, NGOs and South African development', research monograph, School of Development Studies, University of Natal, Durban.

O'Neill, O. (2002) Lecture 1 'Spreading suspicion', Lecture 2 'Trust and terror', Lecture 3 'Called to account', Lecture 4 'Trust and transparency', BBC Reith Lectures (March), available online at: www.bbc.co.uk/radio4.

Parfitt, T. (2002) *The End of Development: Modernity, post-modernity and development*, Pluto Press, London.

Paton, R. (2003) *Managing and Measuring Social Enterprises*, Sage, London.

Petras, J. and Veltmeyer, H. (2001) *Globalisation Unmasked: Imperialism in the 21st century*, Zed Books, London.

Pieterse, E. (2003) 'Rhythms, patterning and articulations of social formations in South Africa', *Development Update*, **4** (4), pp. 107–36.

Pieterse, E. and Meintjies, F. (2004) *Voices of the Transition: The politics, poetics and practices of social change in South Africa*, Heinemann, Johannesburg.

PLA Notes (1988) 'Participatory learning and action notes', International Institute for Environment and Development, London.

Pomerantz, P. (2004) *Aid Effectiveness in Africa: Developing trust between donors and governments*, Lexington Books, Oxford.

Quinn, E. R. (1988) *Beyond Rational Management. Mastering the paradoxes and competing demands of high performance,* Jossey-Bass Publications, San Francisco, CA.

Rahnema, M. (1992) 'Participation', in W. Sachs (ed.), *The Development Dictionary: A guide to knowledge as power,* Zed Books, London, pp. 116–31.

Reality of Aid (2002) *The Reality of Aid Report: An independent review of poverty reduction and development assistance,* J. Randel, T. German and D. Ewing (eds), Earthscan, London, available online at: http://www.realityofaid.org.

Richmond, J. (2003) 'Are our voices being heard? Civil society participation in African poverty reduction strategy processes', MPhil for CWAS, Birmingham, and paper presented at ROAPE conference, University of Birmingham (September).

Robinson, M. (2001) 'Aiding civil society? Democracy assistance and public policy in Africa' DFID funded project for IDS, University of Sussex. (There are many IDS working papers available on this research project.)

Roche, C. (1999) *Impact Assessment for Development Agencies: Learning to value change,* Oxfam, Oxford.

Rodney, W. (1973) *How Europe Underdeveloped Africa,* Bogle L'Ouverture, London.

Rondanelli, D. (1993) *Development Projects as Policy Experiments: An adaptive approach to development administration,* Routledge, London.

Rostow, W. (1953) *The Process of Economic Growth,* Oxford University Press, Oxford.

Russell, B. and Swilling, M. (2002) 'The size and scope of the non-profit sector of South Africa' working paper, School of Public and Development Management and the Centre for Civil Society, Johannesburg and Durban, available online at: http://www.nu.ac.za/ccs/files/jhu%20study.pdf.

Sachs, J. (2005) *The End of Poverty,* Penguin Press, New York.

Sachs, W. ed. (1992) *The Development Dictionary: A guide to knowledge as power,* Zed Books, London.

Said, E. (2003) *Orientalism: Western conceptions of the Orient,* Penguin, London.

Sandercock, L. (1998) *Making the Invisible Visible: A multicultural planning history,* University of California Press, Berkeley, CA.

Schein, E. (1999) *Process Consultancy Revisited: Building the helping relationship,* Addison Wesley, Reading, MA.

Schön, D. (1983) *The Reflective Practitioner: How professionals think in action,* Avebury Press, Hampshire, UK.

School of Public Policy (2000) 'Evaluation of DFID support to poverty reduction', Birmingham University and DFID, London.

Scott, J. C. (1998) *Seeing Like a State: How certain schemes to improve the human condition have failed,* Yale University Press, New Haven, CT.

Seckinelgin, H. (forthcoming, 2006) 'The multiple worlds of NGOs and HIV/AIDS: rethinking NGOs and their agency', *Journal of International Development.*

Seddon, J. (2005) *Freedom from Command and Control: A better way to make work work,* Vanguard Books, Buckingham.

Senge, P.M. (1990) *The Fifth Discipline: The art and practice of the learning organization,* Century, London.

Simbi, M. and Thom, G. (2000) 'Implementation by proxy', in D. Lewis and T. Wallace (eds), *New Roles and Relevance: Development NGOs and the challenge of change,* Kumarian Press, West Hartford, CT, pp. 213–22.

Smith, T. (2002) 'Questioning the crisis: international donors and the reconfiguration of the South African NGO sector', research paper, School of Development Studies, University of Natal, Durban.

Soal, S. (2002) 'NGOs on the line: an essay about purpose, rigour, rhetoric and commidification', *CDRA Annual Report 2001 to 2002*, CDRA, Cape Town.

Sogge, D. (2002) *Give and Take. What's the matter with foreign aid*, Zed Books, London.

Stiglitz, J. (2002) *Globalization and its Discontents*, Penguin Books, London.

Tallis, V. (2005) 'Gender and aid: power and negotiation in gender mainstreaming', in L. Bornstein (ed.), 'Negotiating aid: UK funders, NGOs and South African development', research monograph, School of Development Studies, University of Natal, Durban, pp. 94–109.

Taylor, J. (2002) 'So now they are going to measure empowerment?', CDRA, Cape Town.

Teveodjre, A. (2002) 'Winning the war against humiliation: report of the Independent Commission on Africa and the challenges of the third millennium', UNDP, New York.

United Nations Conference on Trade and Development (UNCTAD) (2000) 'The least developed countries 2000 report: aid, private capital flows and external debt: the challenge of financing development in LDCs', United Nations, New York.

Uphoff, N. (1986) *Local Institutional Development*, Kumarian Press, West Hartford, CT.

Uphoff, N. (1996) *Learning from Gal Oya – Possibilities for participatory development and post-Newtonian social science*, Intermediate Technology Publications, London.

Van Rooy, A. (1998) *Civil Society and the Aid Industry*, Earthscan, London.

Wallace, T. (1998) 'Institutionalising gender in UK NGOs', *Development in Practice*, **8** (2), pp. 159–72.

Wallace, T. (2004) 'NGO dilemmas: Trojan horses for neoliberalism?', in L. Panitch and C. Leys (eds), *Socialist Register, the New Imperial Challenge*, Merlin, London, pp. 202–19.

Wallace, T. (2005) 'Participatory review of the Support to the International Partnership Against AIDS in Africa', ActionAid Regional Office, Nairobi. Summary available online at: www.actionaid.org.

Wallace, T. and Burdon, T. (1993) 'Strategic planning review', unpublished, Oxfam, Oxford.

Wallace, T., Caputo, E. and Herbert, A. (1999) 'Evaluation of DFID support to poverty reduction: Uganda report', DFID, London.

Wallace, T. and Chapman, J. (2004a) 'An investigation into the reality behind NGO rhetoric of downward accountability.' in L. Earle (ed.) *Creativity and Constraint: Grassroots monitoring and evaluation and the international aid arena*, INTRAC, Oxford, pp. 23–46.

Wallace, T. and Chapman, J. (2004b) 'The current landscape of UK NGO development management: what shapes it, how is it done and what are the implications of dominant practice?', research report, DFID, London.

Wallace, T., Crowther, C. and Shepherd, A. (1997) *Standardising Development: Influences on UK NGOs' policies and procedures*, Worldview Press, Oxford.

Wallace, T. , Kaleeba, M., Vadera, M., Adong, R., De Coninck, J., Ssonko, M., Mulindwa, P. et al. (2004) 'The current procedures and policies dominating the disbursement of aid: are they building strong relationships and enabling NGOs to meet their stated aims?', research report, DFID and Nuffield Foundation, London.

Wallace, T. and Kaplan, A. (2003) 'The taking of the horizon: lessons from ActionAid Uganda's experience of changes in development practice', with foreword by Meenu Vadera, ActionAid, London.

Webber, M. and Rittel, H. (1973) 'Dilemmas in a general theory of planning', *Policy Sciences*, **4**, pp. 155–69.

Welbourn, A. (1995) *Stepping Stones; A training package*, Strategies for Hope, ActionAid, London.

Welbourn, A. (1999) Talk to DSA study group on learning, written up by T. Wallace and available from Oxfam.

Wendoh, S. and Wallace, T. (2005) 'Rethinking gender mainstreaming in African NGOs and communities', *Focus on Development, Mainstreaming Gender: A Critical review*, Oxfam, Oxford.

White, S. (1996) 'Depoliticising development: the uses and abuses of participation', *Development in Practice*, **6** (1), pp. 6–15.

Whitehead, A. (2003) 'Failing women: a report on PRSPs for GAD network', Womankind, London.

Websites

ActionAid International: www.actionaid.org

Bretton Woods: www.brettonwoodsproject.org/article.shtml?cmd[126]=x-126-315555

Development Initiatives: www.devinit.org

DFID: www.dfid.gov.uk

DFID statistics: www.dfid.gov/statistics

Europa: http://europa.eu.int

Farm Africa: www.farmafrica.org.news.uk/news.cfm?id=40

Financing for Development: http://www.un.org/esa/ffd

IDS website on participation: www.ids.ac.uk/participation

M & E website: www.mande.co.uk

Reality of Aid: www.realityofaid.org

Index

access issues
  DFID funding 53–6
  research methodology 9–10, 11
accountability 2, 111–18
  languages 8, 31
  logframe analysis 39–40
  new aid architecture 24–5
  rational management tools 91
  relationships 135
  research findings 174–5
  strategic planning 44
  Ugandan NGOs 82
accounting 111–18, 131–2
ACORD *see* Agency for Cooperation
  and Research in Development
ActionAid International 28
advocacy work
  faith-based organizations 132–3
  gender 133–40
  Ugandan NGOs 77
  UK NGOs 71
Africa
  cross-cultural dynamics 46–7
  development practice 19–21, 23, 27–8
  NGO context 73–89
  rational management 48
  research 9
  strategic planning 124
  UK NGO relocation 69–70
  volume of aid 1–2
  see also South Africa...; Uganda...
African National Congress (ANC) 84,
  86–7
agency
  commitment 5–6
  definition 6
  development languages 31
Agency for Cooperation and Research
  in Development (ACORD) 28

agriculture 75
aid architecture 23–6
aid chain/stream/flow
  broken 166
  definition 12
  diverse funding channels 80–2, 89
  influence 147–60
  mapping 13
  through NGO sector 49–72
  policies/procedures 161–8
AIDS *see* HIV/AIDS
alliances 133–40
alternative approaches 176–7
ANC *see* African National Congress
apartheid system 83, 84, 87
application forms, Community Fund
  65
Apthorpe, R. 38–9, 172
assessors
  Comic Relief 66
  Community Fund 65
attribution 118–20
autonomy 130

back donors 11, 84, 131
Barings 68–9
  funding flows 1997–2003 51, 52
  personal relationships 126
Big Lottery Fund 66, 126
  see also Community Fund
black South Africans 83, 84–5
BOAG *see* British Overseas Aid Group
Bretton Woods institutions 19, 20, 28
'briefcase NGOs' 76, 83
British Overseas Aid Group (BOAG)
  119–20
broad research 12–13, 14
Brown, Gordon 41
budget lines, EU 61–2, 63

bureaucratic management 2, 37, 103
buyer/seller relations 135

capacity-building
  gender mainstreaming 151–2
  negotiation 147–8
capitalism 26
case studies 16
CBOs *see* community-based
  organizations
CDRA *see* Community Development
  Resource Association
CDRN *see* Community Development
  Resource Network
CEDAW *see* Convention on the
  Elimination of All Forms of
  Discrimination against Women
Chambers, R. 46
change concepts 31
  emergent change 45
  logframe analysis 106–7
  MDGs 35
  participatory planning 43
  rational management 35–6, 168–9
  strategic planning 44
civil society
  development practice 20, 22–3
  DFID funding 54, 56
  logframe analysis 172–3
  South Africa 73, 88
  Uganda 73
Civil Society Challenge Fund (CSCF)
  56, 57–9, 60
civil society organizations (CSOs) 127
Civil Society Unit (CSU) 53, 60
co-financing scheme, EU 61–3
coalitions 87, 139
coercion 4–5, 163
Comic Relief 63–4, 66–8
  funding flows 1997–2003 51, 52
  impact assessment 40
  personal relationships 126
commitment 5–7, 171
communication
  development management 46–7
  gaps 175–6
communities
  forums 139–40
  research 17

sustainable relationships 141
community-based organizations
  (CBOs) 77
Community Development Resource
  Association (CDRA) 156–9
Community Development Resource
  Network (CDRN) 125–6
Community Fund 63–6
  funding flows 1997–2003 51, 52
comparative studies 12, 104–6
competition 72, 76, 80–1, 136–7
compliance 4–5, 163
Comprehensive Development
  Frameworks 21
conditions/conditionalities
  changes 56–60
  coercion/compliance 4–5
  definition 12
  new aid architecture 24
  new funding mechanisms 21
  rational management norms 91–107
  research findings 173
condoms 132
confidentiality in research 9, 16, 174, 175
contracts
  DFID funding 60–1
  donors 109, 120–2
  EU funding 61–2
control 24–5, 32, 34, 37
  see also power
Convention on the Elimination of All
  Forms of Discrimination against
  Women (CEDAW) 136
countries of origin, NGOs in Uganda 78
country-specific research 12–17
cross-cultural dynamics 46–7
CSCF *see* Civil Society Challenge Fund
CSOs *see* civil society organizations
CSU *see* Civil Society Unit

debt relief 20, 74
decentralization 22–3, 62–3, 75–6, 80
decentralized cooperation concept 62–3
deep research 12, 14, 16–17
democracy 75–6
Department for International
  Development (DFID) 10, 22, 52–6
  accountability 40
  changes 56, 57–9, 60

contracts 60–1
funding flows 1997–2003 51, 52
local funding 60
logframe analysis 172–3
personal relationships 126
rational management tools 92–5
reporting requirements 115
Ugandan NGOs 80–1
dependency *see* power
development
changing context 19–29
definitions 26–8
DFID funding 53, 54
donor/NGO relationships 50
EU co-financing scheme 61
gender 133–40
management of 31–48
NGO/donor relationships 50
PEOPLE 100
personal relationships 126–8
practice 2, 7–8, 19–29
relationships 50, 126–8, 130–2, 144–5
research 7–8, 161, 168, 170
SA NGOs 155–9
South Africa 84–9
ties that bind 109–28
Development Initiatives 24
DFID *see* Department for International
Development
diverse funding flows 80–2, 89
donors
accountability 39, 111–18
accounting 111–18
alliances/networking 133–40
changing priorities 32–3
coercion/compliance 4
communication gaps 176
contracts 109, 120–2
definition 11
development practice 20
effectiveness of aid 1–2
faith-based organizations 130–3
funding flows 1997–2003 51–2
gender mainstreaming 151–2
influence chains 147–60
legitimacy of aid 1–2
networking 133–40
new funding mechanisms 21–3
NGO relations 179–80

NGOs as donors 73
normative conditions 91, 94, 97,
101–4, 106
participatory planning 42–3
personal relationships 126–8
power in development 38
relationships 126–40
relative sizes 52
research findings 162–4, 167–8, 173–5
research methodology 10
South African NGOs 83–4, 86–7,
88–9
Ugandan NGOs 77–8, 80–2
UK donors 49–73
see also institutional donors
drivers of funding mechanisms 22–3

economic growth 9, 19–20, 23, 74
see also development
economic model of development 26–8
education 75
effectiveness of aid 1–2
emergent change 45
empowerment approach 43
ethnicity 17–18
European Union (EU) 61–3
faith-based organizations 130–3
logframe analysis 93
personal relationships 126
reporting requirements 111, 113, 117
Ugandan funding 81
evangelism 80
external funding *see* donors

Fair Trade movement 25
Faith and Development INGO 148–50
faith-based organizations 130–3
fear, relations of 135–6
feedback sessions 110
field offices, UK NGOs 69–71, 93
financial control 24–5
financial data, UK 49
financial flows *see* funding flows
flow of aid *see* aid chain/stream/flow
forums 139–40
foundations 68–9
funding flows 1997–2003 51, 52
personal relationships 126
funders *see* donors

funding flows
1997–2003 51–2
diversity 80–2, 89
through NGO sector 49–72
see also aid chain/stream/flow
funding mechanisms
new 21–3
UK NGOs 59
see also donors
future-building 161–77

gender 17
mainstreaming 150–4
NGO partnerships 149
platforms/views 153–4
PRSPs 25
South Africa 85, 149
Uganda 132, 133–40
Gender Link Programme (GLP) 151–4
geographical spread, Ugandan NGOs
79
global relevance of research 161–2
global strategic plans *see* strategic
planning
GLP *see* Gender Link Programme
governments
development practice 19–22, 24–5
South African NGOs 83–4, 86–7, 89
Ugandan NGOs 76, 80–1
grant models 50
changes 56–60
medium-sized UK donors 65–8
small UK donors 68–9
Ugandan NGOs 81
grassroots... *see* local...
growth *see* economic growth

Harding, D. 44
HDI *see* human development indicators
health services 75, 120–2
Highly Indebted Poor Countries (HIPC)
20
historical issues
development definitions 26–7
research 9, 10–11
see also past lessons
HIV/AIDS
donor conditions 173
Faith and Development INGO 149–50

gender mainstreaming 150–1, 154
South Africa 85–6
Uganda 74–5, 79–80, 125, 132, 141
housing 116–18
human development 40–3
human development indicators
(HDI) 74
humanitarian aid 54
Hyman, Isai 116

identity
INGOs 143
local NGOs 142–3
IMF *see* International Monetary Fund
impact assessments 40, 118–19
implementation alternatives 44–5
income estimates, UK NGOs 51
individual practice 7, 176
individual relationships *see* personal
relationships
inequality 84–5, 88
influence chains 147–60
information provision 137
INGOs *see* international NGOs
innovation 168
institutional donors 3
contracts 120–1
new aid architecture 23–6
relationships 49, 51
research interviews 15
UK NGO funding 70
see also donors
institutional reforms, SA 86, 87
Interfund 117
internal funding 78
International Development Act
(2002) 52
International Monetary Fund (IMF)
development definitions 27–8
relationships 136
see also World Bank
international NGOs (INGOs)
accounting/accountability 115
coercion/compliance 4–5
communication gaps 175–6
definition 12
donor contracts 120–1
Faith and Development 148–50
personal relationships 126, 135

rational management 91, 96–9, 101
relationships 126, 131–2, 134–6, 140–4
research findings 164, 171–3, 176
South Africa 89
strategic planning 122–3
sustainable relationships 140–4
theories/paradigms 2–3
Uganda 76, 77, 80–1, 82
interpersonal relationships 45–6
see also personal relationships
interview format 16

Joint Funding Scheme (JFS) 53–5, 56, 57–9

Kaleeba, Martin 77, 140–4
Kampala, Uganda 76, 79
Kapa Housing Project (KHP) 116–18
Kaplan, Allan 156, 157–9
Kenya 23
KHP *see* Kapa Housing Project
Killick, T. 23
Kintu, Crispin 77
Kwikate (Uganda) 124–6

languages
development 31, 43, 47, 50, 100
logframe analysis 96–7
partnerships 38, 175
power 103–4
rational management 34–6, 38
research findings 170, 172
UK NGOs 8
learning
relationships 129
reporting usefulness 114, 116, 118
research findings 165, 171
see also training...
learning organizations 156
legitimacy of aid 1–2
LFA *see* logframe analysis
livelihoods approach 98–100
lobbying work
Ugandan NGOs 77
UK NGOs 71
local funding, DFID 60
local knowledge 41–3, 139–40

local NGOs 140–4
see also South African NGOs; Ugandan NGOs
logframe analysis (LFA) 34, 36, 39–40
change concepts 106–7
comparative studies 104–6
DFID 172–3
donor contracts 120–1
research findings 164–5, 170–1, 174
SA NGOs 96–101
strategic planning 44
ties that bind 109–12
trends 94–6
Ugandan NGOs 101–4
UK NGOs 92–4
see also project cycle management
lottery funding *see* Community Fund

M&E *see* monitoring and evaluation
MacIntyre, Alisdair 7, 37
Maina, W. 23
mainstreaming gender 150–4
Make Poverty History campaign 25
management models 2
development 31–48
local NGOs 141
SA NGOs 155–6
see also project cycle management; rational management
Mandela, Nelson 83
market-led approaches 19, 20
Marxian analysis 26
Mbeki, President 84, 85
MDGs *see* Millennium Development Goals
medium-sized UK donors 63–8
mid-level research 12, 13–14, 179–80
Millennium Development Goals (MDGs) 1, 20
change management 35
DFID 52
monitoring and evaluation (M&E)
accountability 111–13, 114
gender mainstreaming 151–2

Nabacwa, Mary Ssonko 133–40
national contexts, research 9
national lotteries *see* Community Fund
National Resistance Movement (NRM), Uganda 73–4

negotiation
    capacity building 147–8
    SA NGO partnerships 148–50
neoliberalism 19–20, 26–7
NEPAD *see* New Partnership for Africa's
    Development
networking 133–40
New Partnership for Africa's
    Development (NEPAD) 27
non-governmental organizations
    (NGOs)
    African context 73–89
    changing context 19–29
    effectiveness of aid 1–2
    flow of aid through 49–72
    legitimacy of aid 1–2
    medium-sized donors 64
    packaging aid 32–4
    research 3–4, 9–11
    small donors 68, 69
    see also international NGOs; South
        African NGOs; southern NGOs;
        Ugandan NGOs; UK NGOs
Nonprofit Organizations Act (1997) 86
norms
    challenging 177
    coercion/compliance 4
    rational management 91–107
    relationships 129–30
    status quo 109–10
northern NGOs *see* UK NGOs
not-for-profit organizations 3
NRM *see* National Resistance
    Movement
Nuffield Foundation 10, 68–9
    funding flows 1997–2003 51, 52
    personal relationships 126

OD *see* organizational development
O'Neill, O. 40
operating costs, UK NGOs 70
organizational development (OD) 14,
    155–9
organizational relationships 6
overrespect, relations of 136
Oxfam 49

packaging of aid 32–4
paper-based plans 165

paradigms
    development 26, 27–8
    norms 129
    research findings 163
    tensions 2–3
PARC *see* Performance Assessment
    Resource Centre
participation/participatory approaches
    coercion/compliance 4
    development 31–2, 34, 40–3
    Kapa Housing Project 117
    language of 8
    power 109–10, 127
    rational planning combination 98–
        100
    relationships 129–45
    strategic planning 125
partnerships
    language of 38, 175
    relationships 129–45
    SA NGOs 148–50
    see also Programme Partnership
        Agreements
past lessons 161–77
    see also *historical issues*
peace-building work, SA NGOs 88
PEAP *see* Poverty Eradication Action Plan
PEOPLE 98–100
people living with HIV/AIDS (PLWHAs)
    125
    see also HIV/AIDS
Performance Assessment Resource
    Centre (PARC) 95
personal relationships
    commitment 6
    development 45–6, 126–8
    INGOs 135
    networks 138
personnel changes 50, 131
planning
    development 32, 34–8, 40–5
    loosening ties 122–6
    rational/participatory 98–100
    research findings 165, 167
    trends 94
PLWHAs *see* people living with HIV/AIDS
policies 17
    alternative approaches 177
    research findings 161–8

political role of NGOs 19–20
Poverty Eradication Action Plan
  (PEAP) 74
poverty reduction 1
  debt relief 20
  growth relationship 9, 19–20, 23, 74
  South Africa 84–6
  Uganda 74, 136
Poverty Reduction and Growth Facility
  (PRGF) 26
Poverty Reduction Strategy Plans
  (PRSPs) 21–2, 25–6, 35
power 17
  coercion/compliance 4–5
  development management 31, 38–9
  gender mainstreaming 150–4
  influence chains 147–60
  languages 103–4
  recognition 127, 128
  relationships 129–45
  research findings 164, 169–70
  ties that bind 109–28
  Ugandan NGOs as aid recipients 82
see also relationships
PPAs see Programme Partnership
  Agreements
practitioners, development
  management 45
PRGF see Poverty Reduction and Growth
  Facility
privatization 19
procedures 17, 161–8
professional practice 7
Programme Partnership Agreements
  (PPAs) 56, 57–9
  attribution 119
  strategic planning 123
  trends 94–5
project cycle management
  relationships 129–30
  research findings 167, 177
  SA NGOs 96–101
  Ugandan NGOs 101–4
  UK NGOs 8, 92–4, 97–8
see also logframe analysis
projects
  definitions 26–8
  new funding mechanisms 22
'promise inflation' 70

PRSPs see Poverty Reduction Strategy
  Plans
public donations 51

quantitative analysis 77–8

race 17–18, 83, 84–5
rational management 31–2, 37–8, 48
  conceptual basis 35–6
  language/practice 34–6
  norms 91–107
  practice/language 34–6
  research findings 168–9, 174
  strategic planning 44
  ties that bind 109–28
recipients of aid
  South African NGOs 88–9
  Ugandan NGOs 82
  UK NGOs 69–72
recognition
  networks 137–8
  power 127, 128
reflective practitioners 45
relationships
  alliances/networking 133–40
  coercion/compliance 4–5
  development management 45–7
  donors/NGOs 49–51, 179–80
  influence chains 147–60
  languages 38
  networking 133–40
  NGOs/donors 49–51, 179–80
  partnerships/participation 129–45
  policies/procedures 17
  research 8–9, 175, 176
  UK donors/NGOs 49–51
see also personal relationships; power
reporting
  accountability 111–18
  Comic Relief 67
  logframe analysis 34
  research findings 167
  SA NGOs 98
  Ugandan NGOs 131–2
research 7–9
  alternative approaches 176–7
  country-specific processes 12–17
  DFID funding 53, 54
  key findings 161–76

methodology 9–11
NGO data 3–4
questions 11–12, 168–73
South Africa 87
supporting research 161
Ugandan NGOs 77–8

SA *see* South Africa
SA NGOs *see* South African NGOs
Safi health project 120–2
Sector Wide Approaches (SWAPs) 21
sectoral interventions, Uganda 79–80
Seddon, J. 37
selectivity concept 1–2, 21, 24
Sisay, Rashid 77
small UK donors 68–9
SNGOs *see* southern NGOs
Soal, Su 6–7
social movements 27, 28
South Africa (SA) 83–4
  development challenges 84–9
  EU co-financing scheme 63
  influence chains 147–60
  language of development 38
  research 9, 10
South African NGOs (SA NGOs) 73, 83–
    4, 86–8
  accountability 111–13, 115–18
  accounting 111–13, 115–18
  definition 12
  donor relations 179–80
  gender mainstreaming 150–4
  human development 41
  influence chains 159–60
  logframe analysis 105–6, 173
  organizational development 155–9
  partnerships 148–50
  personal relationships 126
  power relations 110
  project cycle management 96–101
  recipients of aid 88–9
  relationships 129
  research 8, 13–14, 15–16, 174
  training 155–9
  UK donor relationships 147
southern NGOs (SNGOs)
  communication gaps 175–6
  definition 12
  development practice 28

research 8, 162, 169–72
theories/paradigms 3
see also South African NGOs;
    Ugandan NGOs
staff *see* personnel changes; volunteers
status quo, questioning 109–10
strategic planning 44–5, 94, 109, 122–6,
    132
subjectivity 45–6
sustainable relationships 140–4
SWAPs *see* Sector Wide Approaches

TAC *see* Treatment Action Campaign
Tallis, V. 153–4
Taylor, James 156
theories, debates 2–3
tools *see* logframe analysis; rational
    management
tracking financial control 24
trade/poverty relationship 25
training
  gender mainstreaming 151
  local NGOs 141–2
  logframe analysis 96, 102
  participatory approaches 100
  research findings 165, 170
training organizations 14–16, 87, 155–9
transaction costs
  medium-sized UK donors 68
  new funding mechanisms 22
Treatment Action Campaign (TAC)
    85–6
trust
  commitment 5–6
  relationships 131, 133, 138
trusts 51, 52, 68–9

Uganda 73–6
  development languages 38
  new aid architecture 24
  research 9, 10
Uganda Participatory Poverty
    Assessment Project (UPPAP) 75, 127,
    128
Ugandan NGOs 73–4, 76–82
  accounting/accountability 111–15
  countries of origin 78
  definition 12
  donors 80–1, 179–80

geographical spread 79
Kwikate 124–6
logframe analysis 106, 173
personal relationships 126
power 110, 127, 128
project cycle management 101–4
quantitative analysis 77–8
recipients of aid 82
relationships 126, 129–45, 179–80
research 8, 13–14, 15–16, 173–4
Safi health project 120–2
sectoral interventions 79–80
UK donors 49–72, 147
UK NGOs
accounting/accountability 111–15
aid chain diagram 12, 13
changing priorities 32–3
definition 11–12
development practice 22, 28
DFID funding 53, 55
donors 49–51, 120–2
funding mechanisms 59
local funding 60
logframe analysis 40, 105
medium-sized donors 63, 65, 66–7
personal relationships 126
power in development 38

PPAs 56, 95, 119, 123
project cycle management 92–4, 97–8
recipients of aid 69–72
relative donor sizes 52
research 8, 10, 14–16, 162–4, 173–5
SA funding 73
status quo 110
strategic planning 122–3
Uganda/SA funding 73
umbrella organizations 117–18
unemployment/underemployment 85
universities 11
UPPAP *see* Uganda Participatory Poverty
    Assessment Project

voluntary organizations 3
volunteers 5
VSO funding 56
vulnerability 148–50

'wicked problems' 35–6
women *see* gender
World Bank 20–1
    development definitions 27–8
    PRSPs 25
    rational management 38
    relationships 136